To Rab
with best wishes
from Mair
December 6th 2005.

WHITAKER'S

WORLD

OF FACTS

WHITAKER'S
WORLD
OF FACTS

RUSSELL ASH

A&C BLACK • LONDON

First published in 2005 by
A&C Black Publishers Ltd
37 Soho Square
London W1D 3QZ
www.acblack.com

www.whitakersworld.com

Designer Ralph Pitchford
Editors Jinny Johnson and
Mary-Jane Wilkins
Assistant editor Katie Jennings
Editorial assistants Aylla Macphail
and Louise Reip
Picture research Su Alexander

Design manager Terry Woodley
Editorial director Sarah Fecher

Illustrators Alan Baker (Illustration),
Julian Baker, KJA-artists

Heraldry consultant Henry Bedingfeld,
College of Arms
Religions consultant Martin Palmer,
ICOREC
Sports consultant Ian Morrison

A CIP catalogue record for this book
is available from the British Library.

ISBN 0-7136-6879-2

Printed in Italy by Rotolito Lombarda SpA

A&C Black uses paper produced with
elemental chlorine-free pulp, harvested
from managed sustainable forests

CONTENTS

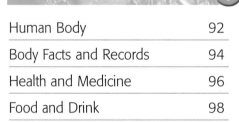

Contents

Back in 1868, *Whitaker's Almanack* set out to record events that change every year, such as the phases of the Moon, the tides and holidays, as well as facts about countries and other useful information. Over its long history it has expanded to become Britain's leading single-volume reference book.

 Whitaker's World of Facts is its latest descendant, a brand new version specially designed for children and families. This exciting new compendium of general knowledge contains facts and figures on everything from space travel and science to rock music and sport. It is the perfect reference book to dip into for fun, as a starting point for school projects, or to settle arguments – and perhaps start a few!

Everything you want to know

Whitaker's World of Facts is divided into 20 sections – Space, Planet Earth, Human Body, World History, People, Music and Performance to name but a few. It includes information on a huge range of subjects, from the Solar System to the most successful films, with data from authoritative sources and specialists on every subject under the Sun.

 A section on countries gives essential facts such as population, capital city and currency for every country in the world, as well as the flag of each one.

Timelines on subjects such as telecommunications, astronomy, medicine and inventions give a useful overview and pinpoint major milestones.

 If you've ever wondered when telescopes were invented, which are the hottest and coldest places in the world or how much a baby blue whale weighs, our fast fact boxes provide the answers. And there is a fascinating selection of lists on all kinds of subjects, including the fastest animals, types of insect, all the US presidents, the world's reigning monarchs, all geological ages, child inventors and every astronaut who has been to the Moon. Find out which is the most poisonous frog, who had the longest beard, how many times a mouse's heart beats in a second, and much, much more…

 Useful tables and formulae include conversions and scales, from Beaufort (weather) to Richter (earthquakes). A series of *One and Only* boxes let you into some special secrets, such as the one and only English Pope and the only train ever powered by fish.

Other features

Web link boxes suggest useful websites to explore subjects further. *See also* boxes guide you to information on a particular subject elsewhere in the book. There is an extensive index at the back of the book, as well as a list of sources.

Whitaker's World Website

You can write to me with comments, suggestions and corrections at the publisher's address on page four or via the *Whitaker's World of Facts* website www.whitakersworld.com

Russell Ash

ABOUT THIS BOOK

Coloured bars identify each section of the book

Lists give you the latest facts and figures, dates and top tens for all kinds of subjects

Fast fact boxes provide information about record-breakers and other extraordinary facts

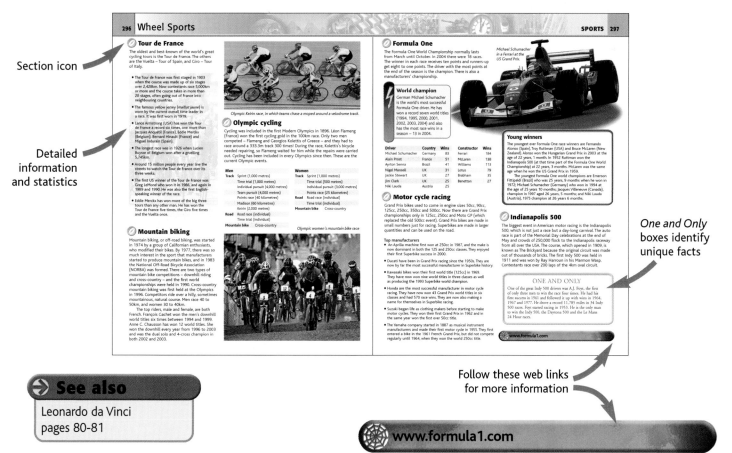

Section icon

Detailed information and statistics

One and Only boxes identify unique facts

Follow these web links for more information

See also

Leonardo da Vinci
pages 80-81

Find cross-references throughout the book in these boxes

www.formula1.com

All living things have some sense of time and people have always attempted to measure time by observing natural events such as the movements of the Sun and Moon. Through the centuries different societies have developed many ways of dividing the year and telling the time.

TIME

The universe in a year!

The American astronomer Carl Sagan (1934–96) first suggested a "cosmic calendar" as a way of helping people understand the history of the Universe. He put everything into the scale of a calendar year: the galaxies are formed over nine months and the Earth appears in September. All human history is crowded into the last five minutes of the last day of the year. Recent time has to be divided into seconds and fractions of a second. So everything that happened over the last 475 years takes place in less than the last second of the last minute of the year.

Date/time		Event
1	Jan (midnight)	Big Bang – Universe forms
15	Mar	First stars and galaxies form
1	May	Milky Way galaxy forms
8	Sep	Sun forms
9	Sep	Solar system forms
12	Sep	Earth forms
13	Sep	Moon forms
20	Sep	Earth's atmosphere forms
1	Oct	Earliest known life on Earth
7	Oct	Earliest known fossils
18	Dec	First many-celled life forms
19	Dec	First fish
21	Dec	First land plants; first insects
23	Dec	First reptiles
24	Dec	First dinosaurs
26	Dec	First mammals
27	Dec	First birds
28	Dec	First flowering plants
28	Dec	Dinosaurs extinct
31	Dec (11:55 pm)	*Homo sapiens* (modern human) appears

hour:minute:second/fractions of second

11:59.50.487 pm	Great Pyramid is built (2520 BC)
11:59.55.333 pm	Great Wall of China is built (215 BC)
11:59.56.785 pm	Roman Empire falls (AD 476)
11:59.58.026 pm	Battle of Hastings (1066)
11:59.58.921 pm	Columbus lands in America (1492)
11:59.59.128 pm	Shakespeare writes his first plays (1588–90)
11:59.59.874 pm	World War II ends (1945)
11:59.59.891 pm	Mount Everest is climbed (1953)
11:59.59.924 pm	Man lands on the Moon (1969)
Midnight	Today

Time zones

The Earth is constantly turning on its axis. If people everywhere set their clocks to the same time, midnight would be in the middle of the night on one side of the globe, but the middle of the day on the opposite side. To avoid this problem the Earth is divided into artificial time zones. These generally follow lines of longitude – imaginary lines running from the North to the South Pole. Some large countries, such as the USA, cover several time zones. Mainland USA is divided into Atlantic, Eastern, Central, Mountain, Pacific and Alaska zones, with Hawaii and other islands falling into further zones.

Since the Greenwich Prime Meridian (0°) was established in 1884, there have been 24 time zones, each of 15° longitude and an hour apart. Those to the east are ahead of Greenwich by one hour per zone. Those to the west are behind by one hour each. Some countries, such as India, have chosen zones halfway between those on either side, so that the whole country can use the same time.

The International Date Line

The Earth makes one complete turn in every 24 hours. In that time, each of the 360 degrees of longitude passes the Sun. This means that time progresses eastwards by four minutes for every degree of longitude.

The International Date Line is an imaginary line running between the North and South Poles which marks the end of one day and the beginning of another. Countries to the east of the Date Line are always a day ahead of those to the west. Travellers who cross the line either gain or lose a day, depending on which direction they are going.

Most of the Date Line follows the 180° Meridian (on the opposite side of the globe from 0°, the Greenwich Meridian). The line generally passes through sea, but where it would pass through or near certain land areas, it is adjusted. It zigzags around islands, putting them either into the west or the east, and avoids dividing Siberia into two time zones.

Royal Observatory, Greenwich – site of the Greenwich Meridian

The world in a single day

In one day (24 hours or 3,600 minutes or 216,000 seconds) the world turns once on its axis. During that time, on average:

- 352,764 people are born
- 152,078 people die
- 200,686 are added to the world's population.

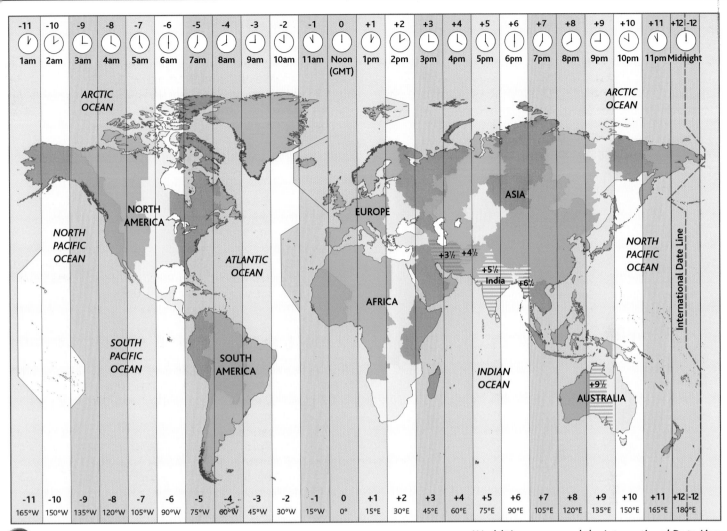

World time zones and the International Date Line

Time tellers

The following are some landmarks in the history of telling the time.

1500–1300 BC
Sundials are used in Egypt: as the Earth rotates, the gnomon – the upright part of the sundial – casts a shadow which moves to indicate the time.

c 400 BC
Water clocks are used in Greece: as water drains from a container, each level it reaches represents a period of time.

c 890
In England people use candles marked with time intervals.

12th century
The hourglass, familiar to us as an eggtimer, is used by monks to show times of prayer.

1325
The first clock with a dial is installed in Norwich Cathedral, England.

1335
The first clock to strike the hours is made in Milan, Italy.

1350
The oldest known surviving alarm clock is made in Würzburg, Germany.

1364
Clocks are first used in people's homes.

1386
Salisbury Cathedral's clock is installed. This is the world's oldest clock in working order.

1462
The earliest description of a watch is written in Italy.

1641
The idea of the pendulum clock is proposed by Vincenzio Galilei, son of astronomer Galileo.

1657
The first pendulum clocks are made in Holland.

c 1665
The first watches with minute and second hands are made.

1759
John Harrison's marine chronometer is made. Accurate timekeeping at sea is important for calculating position, but previously the rolling of a ship had made it impossible.

1833
A "time ball" is installed on the roof of the Royal Observatory, Greenwich: it falls daily at 1.00 pm.

1880
Greenwich Mean Time becomes the standard from which time around the world is set.

1880
The first practical wristwatches are made for the German navy.

1928
The first quartz crystal clock is made.

1949
The first atomic clock is built.

1957
The first battery watches are marketed in the USA.

1969
Quartz wristwatches are first sold in Japan.

1970
Digital watches and displays become widely used and can be made and sold cheaply.

See also

Leonardo da Vinci: pages 80–81

Names of months

The names of the months in English (as well as in many other languages) come from Latin words.

January
Januarius – this month was dedicated to Janus, the Roman god of doors. Janus had two faces, one looking back at the old year and the other looking forward to the new year.

February
Februarius – Februa was the Roman purification festival, which took place at this time of year.

March
Martius – from Mars, the Roman god of war.

April
Aprilis – from *aperire*, Latin for open, because plants begin to open during this month.

May
Maius – probably comes from Maia, the Roman goddess of growth and increase.

June
Junius – either from a Roman family name Junius, which means young, or perhaps after the goddess Juno.

July
Julius – after Julius Caesar. This month was named in Caesar's honour by Mark Antony in 44 BC. Previously this month was called Quintilis from the word *quintus*, five, as it was the fifth month in the Roman calendar.

August
Augustus – named in 8 BC in honour of Emperor Augustus.

September
September – from *septem*, seven, because it was the seventh month in the Roman calendar.

October
October – from *octo*, eight (as in octopus, which has eight legs), the eighth month in the Roman calendar.

November
November – from *novem*, nine, the ninth month in the Roman calendar.

December
December – from *decem*, ten, the tenth month in the Roman calendar.

Thor was the Scandinavian god of thunder and war. He is often shown brandishing a hammer. Thursday, or Thor's day, is named after him.

Just a second

A second does not sound very long, but by the time you have read this sentence, almost five of them will have gone by. Watch an average-length film and more than 5,000 seconds will tick away. In a lifetime of 80 years, there are more than 2.5 billion seconds – but you will spend more than 800 million of them asleep!

Period	Seconds
1 minute	60
1 hour	3,600
1 day	86,400
1 week	604,800
1 year	31,536,000

Naming the days of the week

The ancient Babylonians, then the Romans, named the days of the week after planets and other bodies they saw in the sky.

Monday
Moon's day.

Tuesday
Tiu's-day: Mars, the Roman god of war, was adopted in Scandinavian mythology as the warrior Tiu or Tiw.

Wednesday
Woden's day: the Roman god Mercury became the Scandinavian god Woden.

Thursday
Thor's day: like the Roman god Jupiter, Thor was a thunder god.

Friday
Freyja's day: like Venus, Freyja or Frigg was the goddess of love.

Saturday
Saturn's day.

Sunday
Sun's day.

www.physics.nist.gov/GenInt/Time

Time words

Here are some of the words used to describe units of time.

chronon
One-billionth of a trillionth of a second (the time a photon would take to cross the width of one electron at the speed of light)

picosecond
0.000000000001 (one-trillionth) of a second

nanosecond
0.000000001 (one-billionth) of a second

microsecond
0.000001 (one-millionth) of a second

millisecond
0.001 (one-thousandth) of a second

second
1/60 of a minute

minute
60 seconds

hour
60 minutes

day
Sunrise to sunrise, or sunset to sunset, or midnight to midnight; 24 hours

circadian
Every 24 hours

week
Seven days; in Shakespearean times, it was also called a sennight, or seven nights

fortnight
Two weeks (from the Old English for 14 nights)

month
Originally the period from full Moon to full Moon; 1/12 of a year; 4 weeks, or 28, 29, 30 or 31 days, depending on which month

bimester
Two months

trimester
A period of three months

year
365¼ days, 52 weeks, or 12 months

solar day
The time it takes for a place on the Earth directly facing the Sun to make one revolution and return to the same position (approximately 23 hours 56 minutes)

solar year
The time taken for the Earth to make a complete revolution around the Sun, equal to 365.24219 solar days or 365 days 5 hours 48 minutes 45.51 seconds; also called a tropical year or astronomical year

leap year
366 days

quadrennium or Olympiad
Four years (from one Olympic Games to the next)

decade
10 years; also called a decennium

century
100 years

millennium
1,000 years; also called a chiliad

bimillennium
2,000 years

era
A period of time measured from some important event

aeon or eon
A long period of time, usually thousands of years; in geology and astronomy it is one billion years

epoch
A geological era or very long period of time

Watches at sea

At sea, the 24-hour day is traditionally divided into seven watches.

First Watch	8 pm to midnight	2000 to 0000
Middle Watch	midnight to 4 am	0000 to 0400
Morning Watch	4 am to 8 am	0400 to 0800
Forenoon Watch	8 am to noon	0800 to 1200
Afternoon Watch	noon to 4 pm	1200 to 1600
First Dog Watch	4 pm to 6 pm	1600 to 1800
Last Dog Watch	6 pm to 8 pm	1800 to 2000

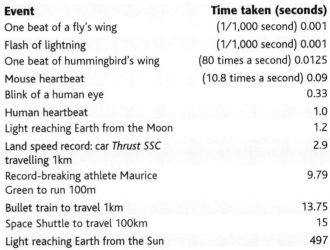

Members of the crew of a liner on their watch

How long does it take?

Event	Time taken (seconds)
One beat of a fly's wing	(1/1,000 second) 0.001
Flash of lightning	(1/1,000 second) 0.001
One beat of hummingbird's wing	(80 times a second) 0.0125
Mouse heartbeat	(10.8 times a second) 0.09
Blink of a human eye	0.33
Human heartbeat	1.0
Light reaching Earth from the Moon	1.2
Land speed record: car *Thrust SSC* travelling 1km	2.9
Record-breaking athlete Maurice Green to run 100m	9.79
Bullet train to travel 1km	13.75
Space Shuttle to travel 100km	15
Light reaching Earth from the Sun	497

A hummingbird hovers on fast-beating wings.

➔ See also

Geological time chart: page 34

⧖ Calendar timeline

Most of the world's countries and cultures use the Gregorian calendar, but some base their calendars on more ancient systems. Other countries have adopted an alternative calendar at some point in their history.

3761 BC	Jewish calendar starts
2637 BC	Original Chinese calendar starts
45 BC	Julian calendar adopted by Roman Empire
0	Christian calendar starts
79	Hindu calendar starts
597	Julian calendar adopted in Britain
622	Islamic calendar starts
1582	Gregorian calendar introduced in Catholic countries
1752	Julian calendar abandoned, Gregorian calendar adopted in Britain and its colonies, including America
1873	Japan adopts the Gregorian calendar
1949	China adopts the Gregorian calendar

⧖ Mayan calendar

The Mayan people lived in the Yucatan area of present-day Mexico and the neighbouring region. They built amazing pyramids and temples, and had an astonishing knowledge of astronomy. Their culture had declined by the time Spanish invaders occupied their territory in the 16th century, but we know something about it from the remains found. The Haab or civil calendar of the Maya had 18 months made up of 20 days each. Five extra days – considered particularly unlucky – were added at the year's end, known as Uayeb, giving a year of 365 days.

Months		Months		Months	
1	Pop	7	Yaxkin	13	Mac
2	Uo	8	Mol	14	Kankin
3	Zip	9	Chen	15	Muan
4	Zotz	10	Yax	16	Pax
5	Tzec	11	Zac	17	Kayab
6	Xul	12	Ceh	18	Cumku

Time pyramid

The Mayan pyramid at Chichen Itza, Mexico, built around 1050, has four staircases, each with 91 steps, and one platform. This made 365, the number of days in a year.

⧖ Gregorian calendar

The Gregorian calendar is the one most used nowadays. It is named after Pope Gregory XIII who introduced it in 1582. There is a leap year every four years (or more precisely, 97 leap years every 400 years). This means that the year corresponds closely with the astronomical year (365.24219 days) so that it is just one day out in every 3,300 years.

	Month	Days		Month	Days
1	January	31	7	July	31
2	February	28*	8	August	31
3	March	31	9	September	30
4	April	30	10	October	31
5	May	31	11	November	30
6	June	30	12	December	31

* In a leap year, February has 29 days

Calendar problems

Some non-Catholic countries such as Britain refused to adopt the Gregorian calendar at first. The Julian calendar previously used in Britain was based on a solar year, the time taken for the Earth to rotate around the Sun. This is 365.25 days, which is fractionally too long (it is actually 365.24219 days), so the calendar steadily fell out of line with the seasons. In 1752 Britain decided to correct this by abandoning the Julian calendar in favour of the Gregorian. By doing so, 3 September instantly became 14 September – and, as a result, nothing whatsoever happened in British history between 3 and 13 September 1752. Many people believed their lives would be shortened. They protested in the streets, demanding, "Give us back our 11 days!"

Chichen Itza, Mexico

Chinese calendar

Present-day China uses the Gregorian calendar for most purposes, but traditional festivals such as Chinese New Year take place according to the ancient Chinese calendar. Legend has it that this was started during the reign of Emperor Huangdi in 2637 BC, and relates to the positions of the Moon and Sun. It follows a 60-year cycle which combines a heavenly stem and earthly branch, represented by a zodiac animal. The first year of the cycle is jia-zi, the second yi-chou, and so on; the 11th year is jia-xu, 12th yi-hai and 13th bing-zi. This continues until the 60th year (gui-hai) and then starts again. Each earthly branch is believed to be linked with certain qualities. Children born in the year of the dragon, for instance, are thought to be especially lucky.

Chinese calendar and Gregorian equivalents

Heavenly stems		Earthly branches		Zodiac animal	Gregorian calendar year beginning
1	jia	1	zi (rat)	Dog	10 Feb 1994
2	yi	2	chou (ox)	Pig	31 Jan 1995
3	bing	3	yin (tiger)	Rat	19 Feb 1996
4	ding	4	mao (hare or rabbit)	Ox	7 Feb 1997
5	wu	5	chen (dragon)	Tiger	28 Jan 1998
6	ji	6	si (snake)	Hare	16 Feb 1999
7	geng	7	wu (horse)	Dragon	5 Feb 2000
8	xin	8	wei (sheep or ram)	Snake	24 Jan 2001
9	ren	9	shen (monkey)	Horse	12 Feb 2002
10	gui	10	you (rooster)	Sheep	1 Feb 2003
		11	xu (dog)	Monkey	22 Jan 2004
		12	hai (pig or boar)	Rooster	9 Feb 2005

Chinese dragon

Calendars meet

The Islamic year is about 11 days shorter than a year in the Gregorian calendar. Although the Islamic calendar started 622 years later, it is gaining on the Gregorian. The two will eventually coincide – but not until the year 20874.

Hebrew and Islamic calendars

The Hebrew (Jewish) and Islamic (Muslim) calendars are based on the lunar (Moon) cycle. Every month starts approximately on the day of a new Moon, or when a crescent is first seen after a new Moon. But because the visibility of the Moon varies according to the weather, the start date cannot be determined in advance, so printed calendars may vary by a few days. Tishri/Muharram corresponds approximately with September/October in the Gregorian calendar, Heshvan/Safar with October/November, and so on.

Hebrew months		Days	Islamic months
1	Tishri	30	Muharram *
2	Heshvan	29	Safar
3	Kislev	30	Rabi'a I
4	Tevet	29	Rabi'a II
5	Shevat	30	Jumada I
6	Adar	29	Jumada II
7	Nisan	30	Rajab *
8	Iyar	29	Sha'ban
9	Sivan	30	Ramadan †
10	Tammuz	29	Shawwal
11	Av	30	Dhu al-Q'adah *
12	Elul	29	Dhu al-Hijjah

* Holy months   † Month of fasting

Indian calendar

The Indian calendar is based on the motions of the Sun and Moon and is dated from the so-called Saka Era, equivalent to AD 79. It is used for dating religious and other festivals, but the Gregorian calendar is used for official dates.

Months		Days	Gregorian date which coincides with first day
1	Caitra	30*	22 March
2	Vaisakha	31	21 April
3	Jyaistha	31	22 May
4	Asadha	31	22 June
5	Sravana	31	23 July
6	Bhadra	31	23 August
7	Asvina	30	23 September
8	Kartika	30	23 October
9	Agrahayana	30	22 November
10	Pausa	30	22 December
11	Magha	30	21 January
12	Phalguna	30	20 February

* In a leap year, Caitra has 31 days, and 1 Caitra coincides with 21 March

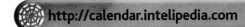

http://calendar.intelipedia.com

Humans have always been fascinated by the mysteries of space, and during the last 50 years there have been amazing advances in space exploration. Men have walked on the Moon and scientists have succeeded in sending a spacecraft to distant Titan, one of the moons of Saturn.

SPACE

Twinkle twinkle little star...

Stars seem to twinkle because we see them through the layers of the Earth's atmosphere. As light passes through these layers, it is distorted so that the amount we actually see changes constantly. The stars nearest the horizon appear to twinkle the most because the light is passing through a greater depth of atmosphere. Stars do not twinkle when viewed from space, which is why telescopes in space, such as the Hubble, give the best possible view of distant stars and galaxies.

Star facts

A star is a luminous body of gas, mostly hydrogen and helium. Stars generate light, which makes it possible for us to see them with a telescope or the naked eye. They also release energy from nuclear fission reactions in their core.

Spiral galaxy

Brightest
Not counting the Sun, the brightest star as seen from Earth is Sirius, known as the dog star, in the constellation of Canis Major. It has a diameter of 149,598,020km and is more than 24 times brighter than the Sun. The star Cygnus OB2 No 12, discovered in 1992, is so far away that it cannot been seen from Earth. It may be the brightest star in the galaxy – up to six million times as bright as our Sun.

Heaviest
HDE 269810 is a star in the Large Magellanic Cloud – 170,000 light years from Earth (a light year is the distance light travels in a year). It has been discovered by the Hopkins Ultraviolet Telescope to be 190 times as heavy as our Sun.

Largest
The largest star is the M-class supergiant Betelgeuse, or Alpha Orionis. It is the top left star in the constellation of Orion, which is 310 light years away. It has a diameter of 700 million km, which is about 500 times greater than that of the Sun.

Nearest
Proxima Centauri, discovered in 1915, is 4.22 light years (39,953,525,879,212km) from Earth. A spaceship moving at 40,000km/h – which is faster than any human has yet travelled in space – would take more than 114,000 years to reach it.

Supernovae
These are vast explosions in which a whole star is blown up. They are extremely bright, rivalling for a few days the combined light output of all the stars in the galaxy. Supernovae are rare – the last one in our galaxy was seen in 1604 by the German astronomer Johannes Kepler.

Quasars
Quasars are extremely distant radio galaxies – galaxies giving out large amounts of radio energy – and the brightest objects in the Universe. Even those near the most distant edge of the observable Universe are easily detected by small radio telescopes. Their radio emission is typically 1,000,000 to 100,000,000 times greater than that of a normal galaxy, and they are as bright as or brighter than the brightest radio galaxies.

Black holes
A black hole is a star that has collapsed into itself. It has a surface gravity so powerful that nothing can escape from within it.

Galaxy facts

Galaxies are groups of billions of stars that are held together by the force of gravity. Most galaxies are either spiral or elliptical, but some are irregular in shape.

The Milky Way
The best known galaxy is the Milky Way. The word galaxy itself comes from the Greek word for milk. This is because before telescopes were powerful enough to prove that they were made up of individual stars, galaxies looked like milky or cloudy areas in the sky. Our relatively small Solar System is only one of 100–200 billion stars in the Milky Way galaxy, which is 100,000 light years in diameter. The Sun and all the planets take about 200,000,000 years to complete one orbit around its centre.

Brightest galaxy
The Large Magellanic Cloud, which is visible only in the southern hemisphere, is 170,000 light years from Earth and 39,000 light years in diameter.

Largest galaxy
The central galaxy of the Abell 2029 galaxy cluster was discovered in 1990. It is 1,070 million light years distant and has a diameter of 5.6 million light years, 80 times the diameter of our own galaxy. It has a total light output equivalent to 2 trillion times that of the Sun.

Nearest galaxy
The Sagittarius Dwarf, discovered in 1994, is 78,000 light years from Earth, and is being torn apart.

Remotest visible object
The most distant thing in the Universe that can be seen with the naked eye is the Andromeda Galaxy, which is 2,309,000 light years from Earth. This galaxy has 300 billion stars and a diameter of 180,000 light years. The light we see now from Andromeda left there just after the first humans appeared on Earth.

Most distant galaxy
In 2003, the Subaru Deep Field space telescope in Hawaii discovered a galaxy 12.8 billion light years away. It doesn't yet have a name.

Travelling at the speed of light

In space, light travels at a speed of 299,792.46km a second, or 1,079,252,956km an hour. When we look at even the nearest star, what we are seeing is light that left it more than four years ago. Many stars are so far away that if someone could stand on one 65 million light years away and look at Earth, they would see light that left at the time the dinosaurs became extinct. And from a distance of 4.7 billion light years they could watch the Earth and Sun being formed!

Light years

A light year measures distance, not time. Distances in space are often described as light years, the distance light travels in a year.

Body	Light reaches Earth in
Moon	1.26 seconds
Sun	8 minutes 17 seconds
Furthest planet (Pluto)	5 hours 20 minutes
Nearest star	4.22 years
Distance at which the Sun would no longer be visible to the naked eye	60 years
Most distant star in our galaxy	62,700 years
From nearest body outside our galaxy	174,000 years
Furthest visible star	2,309,000 years
Most distant known quasar	14,000,000,000 years

Constellation of Orion

Constellations

Groups of stars form patterns in the night sky called constellations. There are 88 constellations known, and the Sumerians, a Middle Eastern civilization, probably named them about 5,000 years ago. They called them after the shapes, objects or animals that they thought they looked like, or after mythological characters.

The largest constellation is Hydra, the sea serpent, and the smallest is Crux Australis, the Southern Cross. Centaurus, the Centaur, has the most stars that can be seen with the naked eye (a total of 94). Others include Aquila, the Eagle; Draco, the Dragon; Canis Major, the Great Dog; and Orion, the Hunter (a mythological character).

A view of distant space, more than 2.2 billion light years away, from the Hubble Space Telescope.

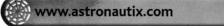
www.astronautix.com

 Solar System

The Solar System was formed about 4,560 million years ago. It is made up of the nine planets – Mercury, Venus, Earth, Mars, Jupiter, Saturn, Uranus, Neptune and Pluto – as well as their moons, comets and other bodies. These all orbit around our Sun, to which they are attracted by gravity.

 Mercury

Date of discovery:	Ancient (visible with naked eye)
Origin of name:	Roman messenger of the gods, son of Jupiter
Diameter:	4,880km
Mass:	3,302,000,000,000 tonnes
Average distance from Sun:	57,909,175km
Rotation:	58.6462 days
Orbit:	87.969 days
Average temperature:	+166.86°C
Moons:	0

Mercury was named after the speedy messenger of the gods because it seemed to move more quickly than the other known planets.

 Venus

Date of discovery:	Ancient
Origin of name:	Roman goddess of love
Diameter:	12,103.6km
Mass:	48,690,000,000,000 tonnes
Average distance from Sun:	108,208,930km
Rotation:	243.0187 days
Orbit:	224.701 days
Average temperature:	+456.85°C
Moons:	0

In size, mass, density and volume Venus is the planet most similar to Earth. Venus rotates backwards, from east to west, so the Sun would appear to rise in the east and set in the west.

Earth

Origin of name:	Land
Diameter:	12,756.3km
Mass:	59,720,000,000,000 tonnes
Average distance from Sun:	149,600,000km
Rotation:	0.99727 days
Orbit:	365.256 days
Average temperature:	+15°C
Moons:	1

Earth is a watery planet – 70 per cent of its surface appears blue – and the only one capable of supporting life. It's not true that the Great Wall of China is the only manmade object that can be seen from space: astronauts have observed cities, lights, forest fires, roads, airports, dams and other large structures such as the Great Pyramid.

Mars

Date of discovery:	Ancient
Origin of name:	Roman god of war, son of Jupiter
Diameter:	6,794km
Mass:	6,421,900,000,000 tonnes
Average distance from Sun:	227,940,000km
Rotation:	1.025957 days
Orbit:	686.98 days
Average temperature:	-63°C
Moons:	2

Space probes such as *Mars Pathfinder* and *Mars Global Surveyor* have sent back information about the planet's atmosphere and surface features. The Martian volcano Olympus Mons is the tallest mountain on any planet in the solar system. At 27km, it is over three times as high as Mount Everest.

 Jupiter

Date of discovery:	Ancient
Origin of name:	Roman god, son of Saturn
Diameter:	142,984km
Mass:	18,986,000,000,000,000 tonnes
Average distance from Sun:	778,412,010km
Rotation:	9 hours 50 minutes
Orbit:	11 years 314 days
Average temperature:	+14.85°C to +19.85°C (30,000°C at core)
Moons:	63

Jupiter

Jupiter is the largest planet in the Solar System and is big enough to contain more than a thousand Earths. Four of its many moons were among the first ever astronomical discoveries made with a telescope, by Galileo in 1610. More were identified by later astronomers and in 1979 by the space probe Voyager 2.

Saturn

Date of discovery:	Ancient
Origin of name:	Roman god, father of Jupiter
Diameter:	120,536km
Mass:	5,684,600,000,000,000 tonnes
Average distance from Sun:	1,426,725,400km
Rotation:	10 hours 34 minutes
Orbit:	29 years 168 days
Average temperature:	-139.5°C
Moons:	34

Saturn is the second largest planet but the least dense. Its distinctive rings are made of pieces of ice and rock which were probably parts of comets and asteroids. These rings are being examined by the joint NASA/European Space Agency project *Cassini/Huygens*. Launched in 1997, *Cassini* began a four-year orbit of the ringed planet in July 2004.

Uranus

Date of discovery:	13 March 1781, William Herschel (Britain)
Origin of name:	Greek god
Diameter:	51,118km
Mass:	868,320,000,000,000 tonnes
Average distance from Sun:	2,870,972,200km
Rotation:	17 hours 17 minutes
Orbit:	84 years 4 days
Average temperature:	-197.15°C
Moons:	27

All the named satellites of Uranus are called after characters from either William Shakespeare's plays or Alexander Pope's poem *The Rape of the Lock*. Some have only recently been discovered and as yet do not have names. Uranus has rings like those of Saturn, but they are visible only with a powerful telescope.

Neptune

Date of discovery:	23 September 1846, Johann Galle (Germany), Urbain Le Verrier (France)
Origin of name:	Roman god of the waters, son of Saturn
Diameter:	49,522km
Mass:	1,024,700,000,000,000 tonnes
Average distance from Sun:	4,498,252,900km
Rotation:	16 hours 7 minutes
Orbit:	164 years 298 days
Average temperature:	-200.15°C
Moons:	13

The orbits of Neptune and Pluto cross each other. Neptune is the furthest of the nine planets currently, and for 20 years of every 248. Surface winds are the strongest of any planet at up to 2,000km/h. Neptune's year is so long that it has not completed an orbit round the Sun since its discovery and will not until 2011.

Pluto

Date of discovery:	18 February 1930, Clyde Tombaugh (USA)
Origin of name:	Roman god of the underworld, son of Saturn
Diameter:	2,390km
Mass:	129,000,000,000 tonnes
Average distance from Sun:	5,913,520,000km
Rotation:	6 days 9 hours 18 minutes
Orbit:	247 years 256 days
Average temperature:	-215.35°C
Moons:	1 (Charon)

Though discovered by an American, Pluto's name was suggested by an 11-year-old British schoolgirl, Venetia Burney. Pluto is the only planet that has not yet been visited by a spacecraft.

Sun facts

The Sun is 149,597,893km from Earth and has a diameter of 1,391,940km. This is more than 100 times larger than Earth. Its mass is equivalent to 99.98 per cent of the mass of the entire Solar System.

Elements
The Sun is mostly made up of two light gases, 75 per cent hydrogen and 23 per cent helium, with relatively small quantities of other elements – including metals such as gold. Helium was discovered in the Sun before it was detected on Earth. Its name comes from *helios*, the Greek word for sun.

Temperature
The Sun has a surface temperature of 5,880K (see box below), but it can be 5,600,000K at its core. There, nuclear fusion constantly changes hydrogen into helium, and the energy and heat released from this process rise to the surface. The yellow surface we see is called the photosphere.

The corona
The outermost layer of the Sun extends millions of kilometres into space but is visible only during eclipses. At a height of 75,000km in the corona, the temperature may reach 2,000,000K.

Rotation
The Sun rotates once every 25.4 days, but because it is not solid like a planet or moon, the poles spin at a different rate, taking as much as 36 days to complete a single revolution.

Solar eclipses
When the Moon lies between the Earth and the Sun, it blocks out the light causing either a partial or total eclipse. At this time, astronomers are able to observe the corona in detail.

A solar eclipse

Kelvin temperature

Astronomical temperatures, such as those on the Sun, are measured by the Kelvin scale, named after British physicist Lord Kelvin (1824–1907) who developed it. Absolute zero (the lowest possible temperature) is 0 Kelvin (when they are written, Kelvin temperatures do not use the degree symbol or word). A Kelvin temperature can be converted to Celsius (Centigrade) by subtracting 273.16.

Moon facts

Earth's Moon is the most familiar and also the largest satellite in relation to its planet in the entire Solar System. It is the first body in the Solar System on which vehicles from Earth landed, and the only one to be explored by humans.

Diameter:	3,475.6km
Distance from Earth:	406,711km (furthest, 1912) to 356,375km (closest, 1984), 384,403km (average)
Mass:	734,556,000,000 tonnes; a person weighing 65kg on Earth would weigh 10.79kg on the Moon
Rotation:	27 days 7 hours 43 minutes 11.5 seconds
Surface temperature:	-163°C to +117°C
Largest crater:	South-Pole Aitken (far side) 2,100km diameter, 12km deep (largest in the Solar System)

ONE AND ONLY

The only human remains on the Moon are those of geologist Eugene Shoemaker who was an expert on planetary collisions. His ashes were carried aboard NASA's *Lunar Prospector* spacecraft, which was crashed into a crater on 31 July 1999.

Moon's near side

Our Moon's far side

The far side of our Moon always faces away from Earth, so it was unknown until October 1959, when the Soviet *Luna 3* probe sent pictures back to Earth.

Titanic moon

Titan is the largest of Saturn's 34 moons. It is 5,150km in diameter – larger than the planets Mercury and Pluto. Dutch astronomer Christiaan Huygens discovered Titan in 1655. We still have no idea what its surface looks like because Titan has a dense atmosphere containing nitrogen, ethane and other gases which shroud its surface – not unlike that of Earth four billion years ago.

Information sent back by the space probe *Voyager 1* during 1980 and recent radio telescope observations suggest that Titan may have ethane "oceans" and "continents" of ice or other solid matter. *Cassini*, a space probe launched by NASA and the European Space Agency, arrived in Saturn's orbit on 1 July 2004. On 14 January 2005 it launched the *Huygens* probe on to the surface of Titan and sent back scientific data.

Titan, moon of Saturn

Neptune's moon

Triton, discovered in 1846, is the only known large moon in the Solar System with a retrograde orbit. It revolves around its planet (Neptune) in the opposite direction to the planet's rotation.

Halley's comet

British astronomer Edmond Halley (1656–1742) was the first to prove that comets travel in orbits, making it possible to calculate when they will next be seen from Earth. He predicted that that the comet he saw in 1682 would return in 1759. It did and was named in his honour. The regular 76-year orbit of Halley's comet means that we can find historical accounts of its appearances going back more than 2000 years. They were often believed to foretell important events such as these examples.

Date closest to Sun	Observations
25 May 240 BC	Seen in China
10 October 12 BC	Believed to mark the death of Roman general Agrippa
AD 28 June 451	Believed to mark the defeat of Attila the Hun
20 March 1066	William (later known as William the Conqueror) took the appearance of the comet as sign of his imminent victory over King Harold at the Battle of Hastings. The comet and the battle feature in the Bayeux Tapestry, made in the 11th or 12th century
9 June 1456	The defeat of the Turkish army by Papal forces was thought to be linked to the comet
15 September 1682	Observed by Edmund Halley, who predicted its return
13 March 1759	The comet's first return, as predicted by Halley, proving his calculations correct
16 November 1835	The American author Mark Twain was born this year. He always believed that his fate was linked to that of the comet, and soon after it reappeared in 1910, he died
10 April 1910	There was panic as many believed the world would come to an end
9 February 1986	The Japanese *Suisei* probe, Soviet *Vega 1* and *Vega 2* and the European Space Agency's *Giotto* space probes passed close to Halley's comet. They were battered by dust particles, and astronomers concluded that the comet is made of dust held together by water and carbon dioxide ice
28 July 2061	Next due to appear

Since Halley's discoveries, many other periodic comets have been discovered. More than 20 comets return more regularly than Halley. The most frequent visitor is Encke's comet, named after the German astronomer Johann Franz Encke (1791–1865). In 1818 he calculated the 3.3 year period of its orbit.

The closest a comet has ever come to Earth was more than 500 years ago. On 20 February 1491, the so-called comet of 1491 came within 1,406,220km of Earth.

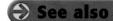

See also

Kings and queens of Britain: page 109

Part of the Bayeux Tapestry, showing the comet top left

Asteroid facts

Asteroids are sometimes called minor planets. They are lumps of rock orbiting the Sun, mostly in the asteroid belt between the orbits of Mars and Jupiter.

● The first and largest asteroid, Ceres, is 936km in diameter and was found on New Year's Day 1801. Since then thousands have been found. Twelve of them are more than 250km wide and 26 are larger than 200km in diameter. As telescopes have improved, more and more small asteroids have been detected. There are probably about 100,000 asteroids larger than 1km in diameter. Some experts think there may be as many as 1.2 million.

● Vesta, the fourth asteroid to be discovered (in 1807), is the only one bright enough to be seen without a telescope.

● Astronomers believe that, on average, one asteroid larger than 0.4km strikes Earth every 50,000 years. Some 65 million years ago a 10-km diameter asteroid crashing to Earth may have been responsible for wiping out the dinosaurs. It would have caused a catastrophic explosion, affecting the climate and chemical composition of the atmosphere and destroying the plants and animals on which the dinosaurs fed. As recently as 1991 a small asteroid came within 170,600km of Earth, the closest recorded near-miss. On 30 Jan 2052 an asteroid is predicted to pass as close as 119,678km.

● Toutatis (asteroid 4,179) was discovered in 1989. It is named after the Celtic god Toutatis, whose name is used as an oath by the comic strip character Astérix the Gaul. Toutatis measures 4.6 by 2.4 by 1.9km. It passes Earth every four years and is one of the largest space objects to come so close to us. On 29 September 2004 Toutatis came within 1,555,818km of Earth. Its next visit will be on 9 November 2008, when it will come within 7,524,773km.

Astronomy

Astronomy milestones

Astronomy is the scientific study of the Universe and the bodies it contains (excluding Earth). Astronomers are the scientists who study astronomy.

Year	Milestone
585 BC	First prediction of eclipse of the Sun
130 BC	Hipparchus calculates distance and size of Moon
AD 1543	Copernicus shows that the Sun is at the centre of the Solar System
1609	Johannes Kepler describes laws of planetary motion
1610	Galileo Galilei discovers moons of Jupiter
1655	Christiaan Huygens discovers Titan, moon of Saturn
1668	Isaac Newton builds first reflecting telescope
1687	Isaac Newton publishes theories of motions of planets, etc
1705	Edmond Halley predicts return of comet
1671–84	Giovanni Cassini discovers four moons of Saturn
1774	Charles Messier compiles star catalogue
1781	William Herschel discovers 7th planet, Uranus
1801	First asteroid, Ceres, discovered by Giuseppe Piazzi
1846	Johann Galle and Urbain Le Verrier discover 8th planet Neptune
1787–89	Herschel finds two moons of Uranus and two of Saturn
1839–40	First photographs of the Moon
1894	Flagstaff Observatory, Arizona, founded
1905	Einstein's Special Theory of Relativity first proposed
1908	Giant and dwarf stars described
1923	Galaxies beyond the Milky Way proved
1927	Big Bang theory first proposed
1930	Pluto, the 9th planet, discovered by Clyde Tombaugh
1959	First photographs of the far side of the Moon by Soviet satellite *Luna 3*
1961	First quasars discovered
1967	First pulsars identified
1971	Black hole first detected
1973	*Skylab* space laboratory launched
1976	Rings of Uranus are discovered
1977	*Voyager* deep space probes are launched
1971	*Mariner 9* spacecraft maps Mars
1980	*Voyager 1* explores Saturn
1978	Space probes *Pioneer 1* and *2* reach Venus
1985–89	*Voyager 2* discovers moons of Uranus and Neptune
1994	Comet Shoemaker-Levy observed crashing into Jupiter
1995	*Galileo* probe reaches Jupiter
1997	*Mars Pathfinder* lands
1997	*Cassini* probe launched to Saturn
1998	International Space Station construction starts
1999	Chandra X-Ray Observatory launched
2003	*Galileo* probe deliberately crash-landed on Jupiter

Telescopes and observatories

The following are some of the world's most famous telescopes and observatories.

Royal Observatory, Greenwich, London
Founded by King Charles II in 1675, but atmospheric and light pollution in London reduced its efficiency. In 1884 the Prime or Greenwich Meridian, 0°, which passes through the Observatory, was adopted as the basis for all mapping and measurements. Longitude measurements refer to west or east of the meridian.

Herschel's "Forty-foot" reflector, Slough
A giant telescope built in 1788 with a 1.2m mirror.

Birr Castle, Co Offaly, Ireland
The Earl of Rosse's 1.8m reflecting telescope, built in 1845, was used to discover the spiral form of galaxies. It was the world's largest until the opening of Mount Wilson and it was recently restored and opened to the public.

Yerkes Observatory, Williams Bay, Wisconsin, USA
This 1m telescope is the biggest refracting instrument made up to this time. It was completed in 1897.

Mount Wilson Observatory, California, USA
The telescope was installed in 1917 with a mirror size of 2.5m. It was the world's largest until the Hale.

Hale Telescope, Palomar Observatory, California, USA
The Hale's 5m telescope was first used in 1949.

Jodrell Bank, Cheshire
Britain's first and once the world's largest radio telescope, with a 76m dish, began operating in 1957.

Yerkes Observatory, Wisconsin, USA

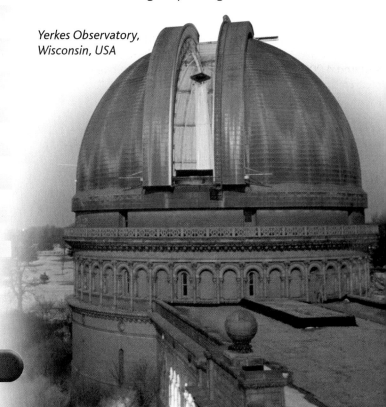

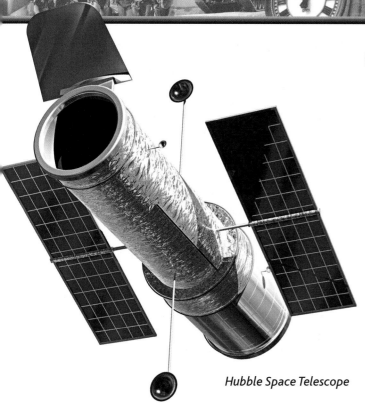

Hubble Space Telescope

Famous astronomers

John Couch Adams (Britain, 1819–92) studied the Leonid meteor shower and predicted the existence of Neptune, which was discovered in 1846.

Edward Emerson Barnard (USA, 1857–1923) discovered Barnard's Star and Amalthea, a moon of Jupiter.

Nicolaus Copernicus (Poland, 1473–1543) showed that the Sun was at the centre of the Solar System.

Galileo Galilei (Italy, 1564–1642) was a mathematician who made important discoveries concerning gravity and motion. He built some of the first telescopes used in astronomy and used them to discover many previously unknown space objects.

George Ellery Hale (USA, 1868–1938) pioneered the astronomical study of the Sun and founded observatories, one with a major telescope named after him.

Edmond Halley (Britain, 1656–1742) predicted the orbits of comets, including the one that bears his name.

William Herschel (Germany/Britain, 1738–1822) built huge telescopes, compiled catalogues of stars and discovered moons of Saturn and Uranus.

Edwin Hubble (USA, 1889–1953) made important discoveries about galaxies. The Hubble Space Telescope was named in his honour.

Christiaan Huygens (Holland, 1629–95) discovered Saturn's rings and devised the wave theory of light.

Percival Lowell (USA, 1855–1916) was founder of the Lowell Observatory, Arizona. He predicted that a planet would be found in the region where Pluto was later discovered.

Charles Messier (France, 1730–1817) studied comets and eclipses, but he is best known for his catalogue of stars.

Isaac Newton (Britain, 1643–1727) is considered one of the greatest of all astronomers. His theories of gravity and the motions of planets revolutionized the subject.

Heinrich Olbers (Germany, 1758–1840) discovered asteroids and comets, one of which was named after him.

Giuseppe Piazza (Italy, 1746–1826) compiled star catalogues and discovered the first asteroid, Ceres, in 1801.

Isaac Newton

Arecibo Observatory, Puerto Rico
Completed in 1963, this is the world's most powerful radio telescope. Its uses include searching for pulsars and quasars and the search for alien life forms under the SETI (Search for Extra-Terrestrial Intelligence) programme. Its giant 305m dish features in the final scenes of the James Bond film *GoldenEye* (1995).

Hubble Space Telescope
The HST was launched in 1990 and orbits 600km above Earth's atmosphere. It can photograph distant objects with ten times the detail possible with ground-based telescopes.

Keck I & II Telescopes, Mauna Kea Observatory, Hawaii, USA
The two Keck telescopes were opened in 1992–96. They are situated 4,000m up a Hawaiian mountain, so above 40 per cent of the Earth's atmosphere. They are the world's most powerful ground-based instruments, with a 10.82m total aperture made up of 36 hexagonal mirrors.

Hobby-Eberly Telescope, McDonald Observatory, Texas, USA
This telescope is designed to collect light for spectrum analysis rather than for visual exploration. In operation since 1999, it has an overall diameter of 11m, making it one of the largest optical telescopes ever built.

First telescopes
The first telescopes were made in 1608 by Dutch optician Hans Lippershey. Italian astronomer Galileo built his own soon afterwards and used it to discover Jupiter's moons. The earliest type of telescope, known as a refracting telescope, produced a slight distortion of images (called aberration). Since about 1670, astronomers have preferred to use reflecting telescopes, which use mirrors that compensate for the distortion.

Animal space pioneers

Before humans went into space animals were used to test equipment. The first animal to be sent up in a rocket – but not into space – was Albert 1, a male rhesus monkey. He was launched in a US Air Force converted German V2 rocket in 1948. He and his successor, Albert 2, died during the tests, as did another monkey and some mice in 1951 tests. However, on 20 September 1951 a monkey and 11 mice were recovered after a launch in a US *Aerobee* rocket. Many further animal experiments were carried out before the first manned space flight to test the effects of radiation and weightlessness on living bodies.

Space dogs, and a cat
Laika, a female Samoyed husky, became the first animal in orbit after being launched by the USSR in *Sputnik 2* on 3 November 1957. There was no way to bring her down and she died after ten days in space. More dogs were launched in tests before human cosmonauts went into orbit. Two female Samoyed huskies, Belka and Strelka, orbited successfully on 19 August 1960. Strelka later gave birth to six puppies, one of which was given to US President John F. Kennedy. On 18 October 1963, a French *Veronique AGI* rocket launched a cat called Félix into space and returned him safely to Earth by parachute.

Monkey business
Able, a female rhesus monkey, and Baker, a female squirrel monkey, were launched by the USA on 28 May 1959. They did not orbit and successfully returned to Earth. On 29 November 1961 Enos, a male chimpanzee, completed two orbits and survived. Many other chimpanzees and monkeys have since orbited. The USSR's first space primates were monkeys Abrek and Bion, who orbited on 14 December 1983 in one of a series of Bion satellite experiments, which also carried tortoises, rats, insects, fish, newts and frogs.

Flying frogs
On 9 November 1970, the USA's Orbiting Frog Otolith satellite (OFO-A) launched two bullfrogs into orbit for a week. Between 2 and 10 December 1990, Toyohiro Akiyama, a Japanese journalist, took six green tree frogs to the Soviet *Mir* space station to conduct weightlessness experiments.

Worldwide web
Arabella, an orb-weaving garden spider, arrived at the US *Skylab-3* on 28 July 1973. She spent almost 60 days in orbit in an experiment to test the effect of weightlessness on her web-weaving skills.

A space menagerie
The *STS-90* mission of space shuttle *Columbia* (17 April to 3 May 1998) contained the *Neurolab* – a space menagerie with 170 baby rats, 18 mice, 229 swordtail fish, 135 snails, four oyster toad fish and 1,514 cricket eggs and larvae.

Can of worms
On 1 February 2003, space shuttle *Columbia STS-107* broke up on re-entry and its crew of seven astronauts were killed. On-board animal experiments involving silkworms, spiders, carpenter bees, harvester ants and Japanese killfish were destroyed, but, amazingly, canisters of worms were recovered alive.

 ## Planets visited by spacecraft

No human has yet set foot on any space body other than Earth and the Moon. But unmanned spacecraft, such as *Galileo* (below) or robot explorers have either flown past and photographed and made scientific readings or actually landed and sent back data from eight of the nine planets in the Solar System. Pluto is scheduled for its first visit in 2007.

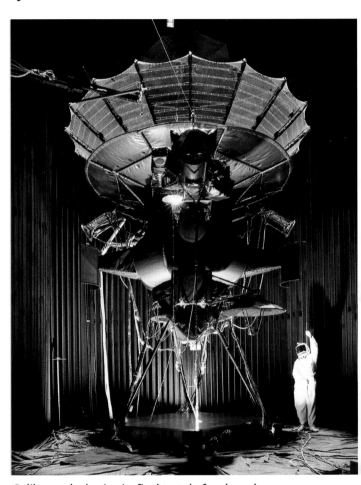

Galileo probe having its final tests before launch

Body	Spacecraft/country	Year
Venus	*Mariner 2* (USA)	flyby 1962
	Venera 4 (USSR)	landed 1967
Mars	*Mariner 4* (USA)	flyby 1965
	Mars Pathfinder (USA)	landed 1997
Jupiter	*Pioneer 10* (USA)	flyby 1973
	Galileo (USA)	landed* 2003
Mercury	*Mariner 10* (USA)	flyby 1974
	Messenger (USA)	scheduled to enter orbit 2009
Saturn	*Pioneer 11* (USA)	flyby 1979
	Cassini/Huygens (USA/ESA)	orbiter/lander 2004/2005
Uranus	*Voyager 2* (USA)	flyby 1986
Neptune	*Voyager 2* (USA)	flyby 1989
Pluto	*New Horizons* (USA)	scheduled flyby 2007

* Deliberately destroyed entering Jupiter's atmosphere, rather than risk contaminating moon Europa with bacteria from Earth.

Space rockets

Thrust is the force required to lift a vehicle such as an aircraft or rocket off the ground. Rockets often have several stages. Each one provides a proportion of the thrust required to carry a satellite, space shuttle or other vehicle into orbit or into space, dropping away as their propellant has been used so that their weight no longer needs to be carried.

Rocket/country/dates	Length (m)	Weight (tonnes)	Thrust (tonnes)
Saturn V (USA) 1967–75 Launched *Apollo* spacecraft	102	3,039	3,440
STS (space shuttle, USA) 1981–	56	2,040	2,630
Titan 4 (USA) 1989–98	54	906	1,448
Ariane (France) 1996– Carries satellites up to 16 tonnes into orbit	54	746	1,162
Delta IV (USA) 2001–	70.7	733	884
Long March (Chang Zheng) CZ 2-C (China) 1975–93	35	192	302
Atlas Centaur SLV-3D (USA) 1973–83	38	149	148

The first artificial satellites

The best-known use of satellites is for communications (radio, television and telephone). They are also used to provide information on weather conditions and environmental changes on Earth, and for navigation, military reconnaissance and astronomy.

Artificial satellites for use as radio relay stations were first suggested by the British science fiction writer Arthur C. Clarke in 1945. Twelve years later they became a reality with the launch of the USSR's *Sputnik 1*, the first ever artificial satellite to enter Earth's orbit. This 83.6kg metal sphere transmitted signals back to Earth for three weeks before its batteries failed. It fell back to Earth and burned up on 4 January 1958.

Vanguard 1, a 1.47kg satellite launched on 17 March 1958, has remained in space the longest, because it is in high orbit. Although it is no longer functioning, it is likely to continue to orbit for a further 200 years.

Satellite	Country	Launch date
Sputnik 1	USSR	4 Oct 1957
Sputnik 2	USSR	3 Nov 1957
Explorer 1	USA	1 Feb 1958
Vanguard 1	USA	17 Mar 1958
Explorer 3	USA	26 Mar 1958
Sputnik 3	USSR	15 May 1958
Explorer 4	USA	26 Jul 1958
SCORE	USA	18 Dec 1958

Space junk

When satellites reach the end of their useful life, they may be deliberately directed back in such a way that they burn up as they re-enter the Earth's atmosphere or come down in the oceans or away from places where they could cause damage. So far, no one has been killed or seriously injured by space debris. The 69-tonne *Skylab* re-entered in 1979, scattering large chunks in the Australian desert, and Russia's *Mir* space station, which weighed 120 tonnes, came down in the Pacific.

About 100–200 objects each larger than a football re-enter every year, but there are still many pieces of space junk in orbit. A survey carried out in June 2000 calculated that there are 90 space probes and 2,671 satellites still in space. There are also 6,096 other pieces of space debris, including parts of rockets: an *Ariane* rocket booster exploded in 1986 scattering 400 fragments large enough to be tracked. In 1991 space shuttle *Discovery STS-48* narrowly avoided a discarded Soviet rocket.

All kinds of tools and equipment have been lost during spacewalks, including the Hasselblad camera dropped in 1966 by *Gemini 10* astronaut Michael Collins. Other items include thousands of "dead" satellites and fragments that have not re-entered the Earth's atmosphere and burned up. These survive as orbiting hazards to spacecraft such as the space shuttle – its windows are bombarded and have to be replaced before the shuttle can fly again. Even tiny objects can be a danger in space. Flecks of paint from spacecraft travelling at 40,000km/h could puncture a spacesuit during a spacewalk.

Space shuttle Atlantis *blasts off*

Astronauts and cosmonauts

In 1880 a science novel was published called *Across the Zodiac*, by British writer Percy Greg. It told a story of interplanetary travel in a space ship named *Astronaut* (the Greek for star sailor). By the late 1920s, the word came to mean a space voyager rather than his ship, and by the 1950s, when the era of human travel looked as though it was becoming a reality, it was this sense that became widely used. The Russian equivalent is cosmonaut (universe + sailor).

Apollo 11 *astronauts: Neil Armstrong, Michael Collins and Buzz Aldrin*

12 April 1961 First person in space
Soviet cosmonaut Yuri Gagarin made a single orbit of Earth in *Vostok 1*, a flight that lasted 1 hour 48 minutes.

5 May 1961 First American astronaut
America's first astronaut, Alan B. Shepard Jr, entered space aboard *Mercury 3*, but did not orbit during his 15 minute 22 second mission.

6 August 1961 First flight of over 24 hours
Gherman S. Titov (USSR) in *Vostok 2* made the first flight of more than 24 hours and was also the youngest ever astronaut at 25 years 10 months 25 days.

20 February 1962 First US orbit
John H. Glenn Jr in the *Friendship 7* capsule made the first US orbit, completing three orbits in 4 hours 55 mins.

16 June 1963 First woman in space
Valentina V. Tereshkova (USSR) in *Vostok 6* was the first woman in space. She spent 2 days 22 hours 50 minutes 8 seconds in space. She was also the youngest (26 years 3 months 10 days) woman in space and the first to be married to another space traveller, *Vostok 3/ Soyuz 9* cosmonaut Andrian Nikolayev. Their daughter Elena, born 1964, was the first child of two parents who had been into space.

18 March 1965 First space walk
Aleskei Leonov (USSR) made the first space walk, from *Voskhod 2*. It took 24 minutes and it almost ended in disaster when his spacesuit ballooned. He was unable to return through the airlock until he reduced the pressure in his suit to a dangerously low level.

23 March 1965 First two-man US mission
John Young and Virgil "Gus" Grissom made the first two-man US mission in *Gemini 3*. Grissom was the first astronaut to make a second flight.

3 June 1965 First US spacewalk
Edward H. White II made a 36 minute spacewalk from *Gemini 4*.

24 April 1967 First space death
After 18 orbits in *Soyuz 1*, cosmonaut Vladimir M. Komarov died when his parachute became tangled and his capsule crash-landed.

24 December 1968 First manned spacecraft to orbit the Moon
Apollo 8 (followed in 1969 by *Apollo* missions *9* and *10*) orbited the Moon but did not land.

20 July 1969 First Moon landing
Neil Armstrong and Edwin E. "Buzz" Aldrin become the first men on the Moon. The capsule in which they returned to Earth can be seen at the Smithsonian Air & Space Museum, Washington DC, USA.

18 June 1983 First US woman in space
Sally Ride was launched in space shuttle *Challenger STS-7*, the first reusable space vehicle.

18 May 1991 First British astronaut
Helen Sharman travelled to the *Mir* space station and spent a week in space.

29 June 1995 First space shuttle/ space station docking
Space shuttle *Atlantis STS-71* docked with Soviet space station *Mir*.

26 September 1996 US endurance record
On her 5th mission, US astronaut Shannon Lucid completed 188 days aboard the Russian *Mir* station, setting a world record for women. Lucid was born in China. She flew more missions than any woman and at 53 was the oldest female in space.

4 December 1998 International Space Station
First stage was established.

2 November 2000 First crew on ISS
An American and Russian crew began living aboard the International Space Station.

28 April–6 May 2001 First space tourist
US millionaire Dennis Tito became the first space tourist, paying $20 million for his Russian *Soyuz TM-32* flight to the International Space Station.

Naming the space shuttles

Unlike space rockets, NASA's space shuttles, or orbiter vehicles, were designed to be re-used. Each has a name, but every mission on which it goes is given a unique number. The acronym *STS* (Space Transportation System) has been used throughout the shuttle programme. The first nine flights were simply numbered *STS-1* (12–14 April 1981) to *STS-9*. A more complicated system was then used, but the original system of *STS* + number has been revived. They do not always follow precise numerical order, as missions may be delayed and a later-numbered mission may have to take place before a previous one can be rescheduled.

Five space shuttles were built. Of these, *Discovery* (first launch 1984), *Atlantis* (1985) and *Endeavour* (1992) remain in service. *Challenger* was destroyed during its 10th mission (*STS-51-L*) on 28 January 1986 and *Columbia* was lost on re-entry from its 28th mission (*STS-107*) on 1 February 2003.

Endeavour was named after a competition among American schoolchildren. Its name commemorates that of 18th-century British explorer Captain James Cook's ship, which sank in Newport Harbor, Rhode Island, in 1778.

Manned space missions

During the 1950s, there was a "space race" between the USA and Soviet Union for the honour of being the first country to send a human into space. NASA's *Mercury* missions were originally unmanned, or carried only animals, and the USSR gained a lead by launching the first man into orbit in 1961. Each country's subsequent space missions had different aims. The USA focused on Moon landings with their *Apollo* programme and later the re-usable space shuttle. The Soviets and later Russia concentrated on long-duration missions, with the *Mir* space station. The latest manned mission is the International Space Station, which is four times larger than *Mir*. The USA, Russia and 14 other countries are cooperating in this amazing space programme.

Mir *space station*

Mission	Country	Years
Mercury	USA	1959–63
Vostok	USSR	1961–63
Voskhod	USSR	1964–65
Gemini	USA	1965–66
Apollo	USA	1967–72
Soyuz	USSR	1967–76
Salyut	USSR	1971–82
Skylab	USA	1973
Apollo Soyuz	USA/USSR	1975
Space shuttle	USA	1981
Mir space station	USSR/Russia	1986–2001
International Space Station	USA, Canada, Japan, European Space Agency, Russia, Brazil	1998–

All the men on the Moon

The human exploration of the Moon lasted just over three years and involved a total of six missions. In each, a pair of US astronauts went down to the surface in a LEM (lunar excursion module) while a third orbited in a CSM (command service module). The missions provided scientists with a huge amount of information about the Moon. The *Apollo 17* duo spent the longest on the Moon. They remained on the surface for 75 hours, part of that time in a lunar roving vehicle.

	Astronaut	Spacecraft	Total EVA* hr:min	Mission dates
1	Neil A. Armstrong	*Apollo 11*	2:32	16–24 Jul 1969
2	Edwin E. "Buzz" Aldrin	*Apollo 11*	2:15	16–24 Jul 1969
3	Charles Conrad Jr	*Apollo 12*	7:45	14–24 Nov 1969
4	Alan L. Bean	*Apollo 12*	7:45	14–24 Nov 1969
5	Alan B. Shepard	*Apollo 14*	9:23	31 Jan–9 Feb1971
6	Edgar D. Mitchell	*Apollo 14*	9:23	31 Jan–9 Feb 1971
7	David R. Scott	*Apollo 15*	19:08	26 Jul–7 Aug 1971
8	James B. Irwin	*Apollo 15*	18:35	26 Jul–7 Aug 1971
9	John W. Young	*Apollo 16*	20:14	16–27 Apr 1972
10	Charles M. Duke Jr	*Apollo 16*	20:14	16–27 Apr 1972
11	Eugene A. Cernan	*Apollo 17*	22:04	7–19 Dec 1972
12	Harrison H. Schmitt	*Apollo 17*	22:04	7–19 Dec 1972

* Extra vehicular activity: time spent out of the lunar module on the Moon's surface

The six US Apollo missions above resulted in successful Moon landings. *Apollo 13*, 11–17 April 1970, was aborted and returned to Earth after an oxygen tank exploded.

Lunar roving vehicle

Longest space walk

The record for the longest-ever spacewalk was broken from 10–11 March 2001, when mission specialists James Voss and Susan Helms stepped outside space shuttle *Discovery STS-102* to do construction work on the space station. Their EVA (extra vehicular activity) lasted 8 hours 56 minutes.

Nearly three-quarters of the surface of our planet is covered by ocean, which plays a vital role in controlling our weather and climate. Earth's land has been shaped into varied landscapes over millions of years, ranging from deep canyons to soaring mountains.

PLANET EARTH

Layers of the Earth

The Earth is made up of a number of layers. At the top is the crust – the thinnest layer. Next is the mantle, then the outer and inner cores. The outer core is probably liquid and the inner core solid.

Layer	Average depth (km)
1. Inner core	5,125–6,371
2. Outer core	2,865–5,125
3. Mantle	21–2,865
4. Crust	21
5. Ocean	3

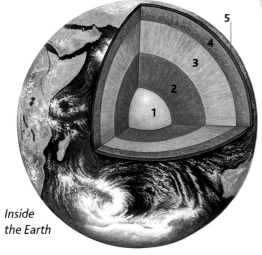

Inside the Earth

Giant meteorites

About 500 meteorites reach Earth every year. Many fall in the sea and in unpopulated areas and are never seen. The Hoba meteorite, the largest in the world, was found in Namibia in 1920. It measures 2.73 x 2.43m and is 82 per cent iron and 16 per cent nickel. It weighs more than 60 tonnes. Second largest is the "Tent", found in Greenland in 1894 and now known by its original Eskimo name, Ahnighito. This meteorite weighs about 57.3 tonnes and is on display in the New York Museum of Natural History.

Geological time

Era	Period	Epoch	Years ago	Life
Cenozoic	Quaternary	Recent/Holocene	11,000–present	Modern humans
		Pleistocene	1,800,000–11,000	First humans
	Tertiary	Pliocene	5,000,000–1,800,000	Ape-like human ancestors
		Miocene	23,000,000–5,000,000	Apes and whales appear
		Oligocene	38,000,000–23,000,000	Cats and dogs appear
		Eocene	54,000,000–37,000,000	Grasslands appear
		Palaeocene	65,000,000–54,000,000	First large mammals
Mesozoic	Cretaceous		146,000,000–65,000,000	Dinosaurs extinct, first flowering plants
	Jurassic		208,000,000–146,000,000	First birds and mammals
	Triassic		245,000,000–208,000,000	First dinosaurs and flying reptiles
Palaeozoic	Permian		286,000,000–245,000,000	Deciduous plants
	Carboniferous			
	Pennsylvanian		325,000,000–286,000,000	First reptiles
	Mississippian		360,000,000–325,000,000	First winged insects
	Devonian		410,000,000–360,000,000	First amphibians
	Silurian		440,000,000–410,000,000	First land plants and insects
	Ordovician		500,000,000–440,000,000	First corals and molluscs
	Cambrian		544,000,000–500,000,000	First fish and shelled creatures
Precambrian	Proterozoic		2,500,000,000–544,000,000	Earliest fossils, first jellyfish
	Archaic		3,800,000,000–2,500,000,000	First living cells
	Hadean		4,500,000,000–3,800,000,000	Environment unable to support life
			4,500,000,000 or earlier	Formation of Earth

A meteorite crater in Arizona

The largest meteorite craters

Many astroblemes or collision sites on Earth have been altered by weather over millions of years. Scientists are not always certain whether crater-like structures were caused by meteorites or are the craters of extinct volcanoes. Those listed below are all agreed to be meteorite craters, but new evidence based on photographs from space may reveal other even larger ones.

Crater/location	Diameter (km)
1 Vredefort, South Africa	300
2 Sudbury, Ontario, Canada	250
3 Chicxulub, Yucatan, Mexico	170
4 Manicougan, Canada	100
5 Popigai, Russia	100

The 10 degrees of hardness

The Mohs scale, named after German mineralogist Friedrich Mohs (1773–1839), is used for comparing the relative hardness of minerals. Each mineral on the scale can be scratched by the harder ones below it.

Mohs scale No. Substance		Mohs scale No. Substance	
1	Talc	6	Orthoclase
2	Gypsum	7	Quartz
3	Calcite	8	Topaz
4	Fluorite	9	Corundum
5	Apatite	10	Diamond

Rock or mineral?

Rock
There are three categories of rock – igneous, sedimentary and metamorphic.

• **Igneous rocks** originate deep in the Earth. They erupt from volcanoes as magma and cool or solidify as they rise to the upper layers. Basalt is an igneous rock and so is granite, a very hard rock often used in building. Pumice stone is a soft igneous rock that is ejected from volcanoes. As it cools, it often fills with so many air bubbles that it floats in water.

• **Sedimentary rocks** can be formed by deposits in water (and occasionally by wind). Sandstone is a common example – Uluru (Ayers Rock), Australia, is the largest known rock (see box). Organic sedimentary rocks are formed by living plants and animals – coal comes from plant matter and limestone from the calcium from billions of plants and animals. Chemical sedimentary rocks occur when chemical processes take place and minerals are deposited.

• **Metamorphic rocks** are igneous or sedimentary rocks that have changed as a result of high temperatures or pressures. Slate used on roofs is a familiar example.

Minerals
Minerals are naturally occurring substances with a definite chemical composition. Most mineral names end in "ite". Many have a practical use or contain a chemical compound or element that can be extracted and used commercially. Bauxite, for instance, is the main source of aluminium. Gems are minerals that are highly prized for their rarity or appearance, eg diamonds, sapphires, emeralds and rubies.

Uluru

The rock formerly known as Ayers Rock, Northern Territory, Australia, is believed to be the world's largest free-standing rock. It is made of sandstone and measures 335m high, 3.6km long and 2km wide. It was originally called after South Australian premier Sir Henry Ayers, but it is now known by the name given to it by local Aborigines, to whom it is sacred.

Largest deserts

Deserts cover about a quarter of the world's land area. They range from extremely arid and barren sandy deserts (about four per cent of the total land surface of the globe), through arid (15 per cent) to semi-arid. Most deserts have features of all these, with one zone merging into the next, so the start and finish of any desert is not exact. Many of the world's largest deserts are broken down by geographers into smaller desert regions – the Australian Desert includes the Gibson, Great Sandy, Great Victoria and Simpson, for example.

Desert	Location	Approx area (sq km)
1 Sahara (below)	Northern Africa	9,100,000
2 Australian	Australia*	3,400,000
3 Arabian Peninsula	Southwest Asia#	2,600,000
4 Turkestan	Central Asia†	1,900,000
5 Gobi	Central Asia	1,300,000
6 North American Desert	US/Mexico√	1,300,000

* Includes Gibson, Great Sandy, Great Victoria and Simpson
\# Includes an-Nafud and Rub al Khali † Includes Kara-Kum and Kyzylkum
√ Includes Great Basin, Mojave, Sonorah and Chihuahuan

Sahara Desert

Longest mountain ranges

A mountain range is a continuous chain of mountains – a mountain is land that rises 300m or more above its surroundings.

Range	Location	Approx length (km)
1 Andes	South America	7,242
2 Rocky Mountains	North America	6,035
3 Himalayas/Karakoram/Hindu Kush	Asia	3,862
4 Great Dividing Range	Australia	3,621
5 Trans-Antarctic Mountains	Antarctica	3,541

Highest mountains

People used to think that Kangchenjunga was the world's highest mountain. Then in 1852 the Great Trigonometrical Survey of India was completed, which measured all the country's land features. The survey showed that Everest (then called Peak XV) was the world's highest mountain. Its height was then reckoned to be 8,840m, which has since been adjusted as improved measuring methods have been used. The mountain's name was suggested in 1865 as a tribute to Sir George Everest, the Surveyor General of India who had led the survey.

Everest

Mountain	Location	Height* (m)
1 Everest	Nepal/China	8,850
2 K2 (Chogori)	Pakistan/China	8,607
3 Kangchenjunga	Nepal/India	8,598
4 Lhotse	Nepal/China	8,511
5 Makalu I	Nepal/China	8,481

* Height of principal peak; lower peaks of the same mountain are excluded

Geysers

Geysers are jets of boiling water and steam that erupt from beneath the ground where water is heated by volcanic activity. The name geyser comes from a hot spring called Geysir at Haukadalur, Iceland. Yellowstone National Park in Wyoming, USA has more geysers than anywhere else. There are 500 active ones. including Steamboat geyser, which erupts to a height of 120m, and Old Faithful geyser, which erupts every 75 minutes.

Largest island

An island is a piece of land surrounded by water. Australia is so large it is a continent, not an island; otherwise it would rank first. The largest US island is Hawaii, which measures 10,456sq km, and the largest off mainland USA is Kodiak, Alaska, at 9,510sq km. The smallest island with country status is Pitcairn, at just 4.53sq km.

	Island	Approx area* (sq km)
1	Greenland (Kalaatdlit Nunaat)	2,175,600
2	New Guinea	789,900
3	Borneo	751,000
4	Madagascar (Malagasy Republic)	587,041
5	Baffin Island, Canada	507,451
6	Sumatra, Indonesia	422,200
7	Honshu, Japan	230,092
8	Great Britain	218,041
9	Victoria Island, Canada	217,290
10	Ellesmere Island, Canada	196,236
11	Celebes, Indonesia	179,000
12	South Island, New Zealand	151,971
13	Java, Indonesia	126,900
14	North Island, New Zealand	114,489
15	Newfoundland, Canada	108,860
16	Cuba	104,945
17	Luzon, Philippines	104,688
18	Iceland	102,819
19	Mindanao, Philippines	94,630
20	Ireland	84,406

* Mainlands, including areas of inland water, but excluding offshore islands

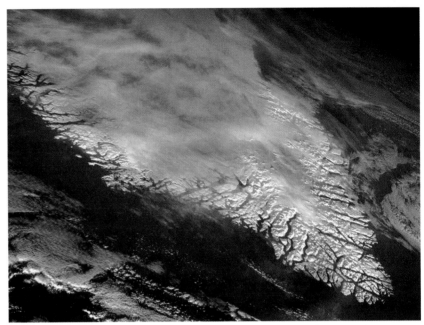

Greenland seen from space

Lowest places

Sea level is the average height of the sea at a point midway between high and low tides. The shore of the Dead Sea is the lowest exposed ground below sea level, but the sea bed is lower still – 728m below sea level. The deepest point of Lake Baikal in Russia is 1,741m. Some land in Antarctica is 2,538m below sea level, but is covered by a 2,100m-deep ice cap.

	Depression	Location	Maximum depth below sea level (m)
1	Dead Sea	Israel/Jordan	400
2	Lake Assa	Djibouti	156
3	Turfan Depression	China	154
4	Qattâra Depression	Egypt	133
5	Mangyshlak Peninsula	Kazakhstan	132

The seven continents

The Americas are named after Amerigo Vespucci (1451–1512), explorer with Christopher Columbus. Africa was perhaps originally a Berber tribal name. It was adopted by the Romans as the name of their province, and later spread to the whole continent. Europe is of uncertain origin, it may simply mean mainland. Asia is probably from the Assyrian, *asu*, sunrise, or east, the name given to the eastern province of the Roman Empire. Australis is Latin for southern; Australia, with New Zealand and other islands, is also considered as part of Oceania, a name invented by the geographer Conrad Malte-Brun (1775–1826). Antarctica is Greek for opposite the Arctic. Arctic comes from the Greek word for bear, as the region lies under the stars of the Great Bear constellation.

Europe
Land area: 10,498,000sq km
% of world total: 7.1

North America
Land area: 24,349,000sq km
% of world total: 16.4

Asia
Land area: 43,608,000sq km
% of world total: 27.3

Africa
Land area: 30,335,000sq km
% of world total: 20.4

South America
Land area: 7,611,000sq km
% of world total: 11.8

Antarctica
Land area: 13,340,000sq km
% of world total: 9.0

Australasia
Land area: 8,923,000sq km
% of world total: 6.0

Longest river

The source of the Nile was discovered by Europeans in 1858 when British explorer John Hanning Speke reached Lake Victoria Nyanza, in what is now Burundi. Almost a hundred years later, in 1953, the source of the Amazon was identified as a stream called Huarco flowing from the Misuie glacier in the Peruvian Andes mountains. After following a series of feeders, it joins the Amazon's main tributary at Ucayali, Peru, giving a total length of 6,448km. By following the Amazon from its source and up the Rio Pará it is possible to sail for 6,750km, which is slightly more than the length of the Nile. But geographers do not consider the entire route to be part of the Amazon basin, so the Nile, with an overall length of 6,695km, is considered the world's longest river.

River	Flows through	Length (km)
1 Nile	Burundi, Dem. Rep. of Congo, Egypt, Eritrea, Ethiopia, Kenya, Rwanda, Sudan, Tanzania, Uganda	6,695
2 Amazon	Peru, Brazil	6,448
3 Chang Jiang (Yangtze)	China	6,378
4 Huang He (Yellow)	China	5,464
5 Amur	China, Russia	4,415

Greatest waterfalls*

The flow of many waterfalls varies according to the season, and some have been reduced by building dams to harness their power for hydroelectric plants. The flow of the Boyoma waterfall is equivalent to 17 million litres a second – enough to fill more than 140,000 baths per second, or enough for every person on Earth to have two baths a day!

Waterfall	Country	Average flow (m³/sec)
1 Boyoma (Stanley)	Dem. Rep. of Congo	17,000
2 Khône†	Laos	11,330
3 Niagara (Horseshoe)	Canada	5,830
4 Grande	Uruguay	4,500
5 Paulo Afonso	Brazil	2,800

* Based on volume of water
† Also the world's widest waterfall at 10.8km

Greatest rivers*

The volume of water flowing from the mouth of a river varies according to the season. The figures given are highest averages. The outflow of the Amazon would be enough to fill almost two million baths every second.

River	Outflow/sea	Average flow (m³/sec)
1 Amazon	Brazil/South Atlantic	219,000
2 Ganges	Bangladesh/Bay of Bengal	43,900
3 Zaïre (Congo)	Angola–Congo/South Atlantic	41,800
4 Chang Jiang	China/Yellow Sea	31,900
5 Orinoco	Venezuela/South Atlantic	31,900
6 Plata-Paraná-Grande	Uruguay/South Atlantic	25,700

* Based on rate of discharge at mouth

Highest waterfalls

Waterfalls form when a river or stream passes over a drop from one level to another, often where softer rocks are eroded faster than harder ones. The drop is the distance from the top to bottom of the waterfall.

Waterfall	River	Location	Total drop (m)
1 Angel	Carrao	Venezuela	979*
2 Tugela	Tugela	South Africa	850
3 Utigård	Jostedal Glacier	Nesdale, Norway	800
4 Mongefossen	Monge	Mongebekk, Norway	774
5 Mutarazi	Mutarazi River	Zimbabwe	762
6 Yosemite	Yosemite Creek	California, USA	739
7 Østre Mardøla Foss	Mardals	Eikisdal, Norway	656
8 Tyssestrengane	Tysso	Hardanger, Norway	646
9 Cuquenán	Arabopo	Venezuela	610

* Longest single drop 807m

Niagara Falls

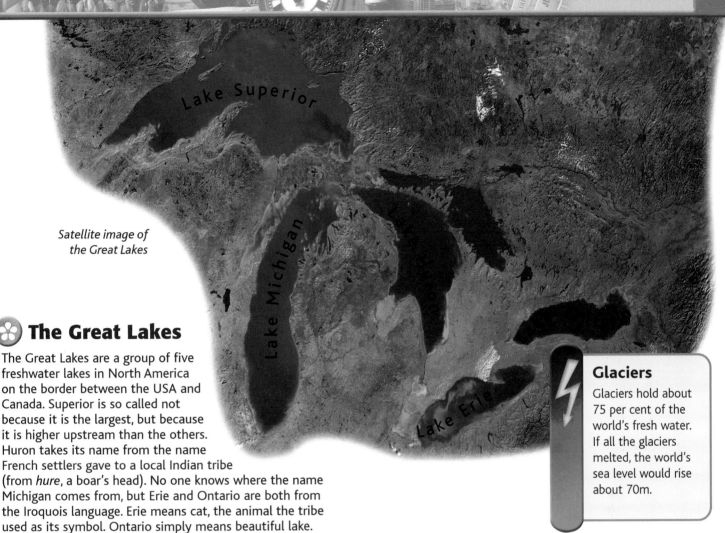

Satellite image of the Great Lakes

The Great Lakes

The Great Lakes are a group of five freshwater lakes in North America on the border between the USA and Canada. Superior is so called not because it is the largest, but because it is higher upstream than the others. Huron takes its name from the name French settlers gave to a local Indian tribe (from *hure*, a boar's head). No one knows where the name Michigan comes from, but Erie and Ontario are both from the Iroquois language. Erie means cat, the animal the tribe used as its symbol. Ontario simply means beautiful lake.

Lake	Location	Area (sq km)
1 Superior	Canada/USA	82,414
2 Huron	Canada/USA	59,596
3 Michigan	USA	58,016
4 Erie	Canada/USA	25,719
5 Ontario	Canada/USA	19,477

Longest glaciers

During the last Ice Age, more than 30 per cent of the Earth's surface was covered by glaciers – frozen rivers of ice that move very slowly. Even today, as much as 10 per cent is covered with glaciers. The Lambert-Fisher Glacier is the longest in the world and was only discovered (from the air) in 1956. The longest glacier in North America is the Hubbard Glacier, Alaska, which measures 146km. The longest in Europe is the Aletsch Glacier, Switzerland, at 35km.

Name	Location	Length (km)
1 Lambert-Fisher	Antarctica	515
2 Novaya Zemlya	Russia	418
3 Arctic Institute	Antarctica	362
4 Nimrod-Lennox-King	Antarctica	290
5 Denman	Antarctica	241

Glaciers

Glaciers hold about 75 per cent of the world's fresh water. If all the glaciers melted, the world's sea level would rise about 70m.

Lake fact file

Largest lake by volume and area
The Caspian Sea (Russia, Kazakhstan, Turkmenistan, Azerbaijan and Iran) has a volume of 78,200 cubic km and an area of 374,000sq km, making it the world's largest body of inland water. It would take 400 years for the entire contents of the Caspian to flow over Niagara Falls!

Largest freshwater lake by area
Some people think that Lake Michigan and Lake Huron (US and Canada) are one lake. Together they have a combined area of 117,612sq km and have a larger area than half the world's countries.

Largest freshwater lake by volume and deepest lake
Lake Baikal, Russia, contains 22,995 cubic km of water. It has an average depth of 730m and is 1,741m at its deepest point – deep enough to cover more than four Empire State Buildings piled on top of one another.

Fastest-shrinking lake
In 1960 the Aral Sea (Kazakhstan and Uzbekistan) was 64,501sq km. Since then feeder rivers have been diverted for irrigation and the lake has shrunk to about 28,000sq km. It is now in danger of disappearing altogether.

Coastline of southern California, USA

Longest coastlines

The coastline of Canada, including all its islands, is more than six times as long as the distance round the Earth at the Equator (40,076km). Greenland (Kalaalit Nunaat) is not in this list as it is part of Denmark, not a separate country, but its coastline measures 44,087km.

Country	Coastline length (km)
1 Canada	265,523
2 USA	133,312
3 Russia	110,310
4 Indonesia	95,181
5 Chile	78,563
6 Australia	66,530
7 Norway	53,199
8 Philippines	33,900
9 Brazil	33,379
10 Finland	31,119
11 China	30,017
12 Japan	29,020
13 Sweden	26,384
14 Mexico	23,761
15 Papua New Guinea	20,197
16 UK	19,717
17 New Zealand	17,209
18 India	17,181
19 Greece	15,147
20 Myanmar	14,708
World total	**1,634,701**

Wave height scale

The wave height scale describes the sort of waves that sailors might meet at sea. Wave height varies according to wind speed. High waves can be very dangerous, especially to small boats.

Code	description	Height range (m)
0	Glassy	0
1	Calm	0–0.30
2	Rippled	0.30–0.60
3	Choppy	0.60–1.2
4	Very choppy	1.2–2.4
5	Rough	2.4–4
6	Very rough	4–6
7	High	6–9
8	Very high	9–14
9	Ultra high	14+

A huge wave breaks near the shore in the Pacific Ocean.

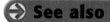 **See also**

2004 Tsunami: page 105

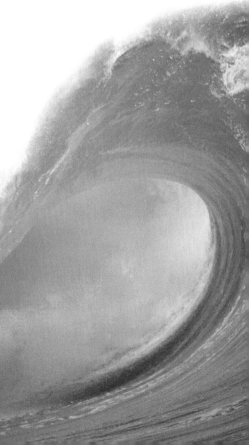

Oceans and seas

Ocean is a geographical term for the world's sea water, except for landlocked seas such as the Caspian. More than 70 per cent of the planet's surface is occupied by oceans – the Pacific Ocean alone is more than 25 per cent larger than the planet's entire land area. Smaller divisions of some oceans are separately named as seas.

Name	Approximate area (sq km)	Name	Approximate area (sq km)
Pacific Ocean	166,240,000	Andaman Sea	797,700
Atlantic Ocean	86,560,000	Hudson Bay	730,380
Indian Ocean	73,430,000	North Sea	575,300
Arctic Ocean	13,230,000	Red Sea	437,700
South China Sea	2,974,600	Black Sea	436,400
Caribbean Sea	2,753,000	Baltic Sea	414,400
Mediterranean Sea	2,510,000	Caspian Sea	371,800
Bering Sea	2,261,000	Yellow Sea	294,000
Gulf of Mexico	1,542,985	Persian Gulf	238,790
Sea of Okhotsk	1,527,570	Gulf of California	162,000
East China Sea	1,249,150	Irish Sea	103,600
Sea of Japan	1,012,945	English Channel	89,900

Deepest oceans and seas

Ocean/sea	Greatest depth (m)	Average depth (m)
Pacific Ocean	10,924	4,028
Indian Ocean	7,455	3,963
Atlantic Ocean	9,219	3,926
Caribbean Sea	6,946	2,647

Deep-sea trenches

There are about 20 deep trenches in the world's oceans. The eight deepest of these would be deep enough to submerge Mount Everest, which is 8,850m high. The Marianas Trench is the deepest point in the deepest ocean, the Pacific. It was discovered in 1951 and explored on 7 January 1960 when Jacques Piccard (Switzerland) and Donald Walsh (USA) descended in their bathyscaphe *Trieste 2* to a depth that has since been calculated as 10,911m. This is almost 11km down, or almost 29 times the height of the Empire State Building.

The highest mountain?

The height of mountains is usually measured from sea level. Hawaii's tallest, Mauna Kea, is only 4,245m above sea level, but it rises a total of 10,203m from the floor of the Pacific Ocean, making its overall height 1,353m greater than Mount Everest!

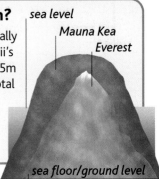

sea level
Mauna Kea
Everest

sea floor/ground level

Iceberg fact file

An iceberg (below) is a large piece of ice that has broken away from a glacier. Icebergs in the North Atlantic mostly come from glaciers on Greenland, and those in the South Atlantic from the Antarctic.

- The word iceberg probably comes from the Dutch *ijsberg*, or ice hill.

- Icebergs float because they are made of fresh water which is less dense than sea water.

- Seven-eighths of an iceberg is below the surface of the sea, hence the expression "the tip of the iceberg", which means that more is concealed than can be seen.

- One of the biggest icebergs of recent times, known as B-15, broke away from the Ross Ice Shelf, Antarctica, in March 2000. It had an average length of 295km and width of 37km, giving it a total area about the size of Jamaica!

- Small icebergs (those less than 1m high and 5m wide) are known as growlers, because of the noise they make.

- The air trapped in iceberg ice – which is "harvested" and sold for use in drinks – may be as much as 3,000 years old.

- At least 500 incidents have been recorded of ships striking icebergs. In 1875, the 82 crew members of the schooner *Caledonia* were rescued after their ship sank and they spent a night sitting on an iceberg. The worst-ever disaster involving an iceberg happened when the *Titanic* struck an iceberg on 14 April 1912 and 1,503 lives were lost.

- During World War II, Lord Mountbatten, the British Chief of Combined Operations, led a programme to build artificial icebergs to use as aircraft carriers, but the project, codenamed Habbakuk, was abandoned.

ARCTIC
OCEAN

Beaufort
Sea

Greenland

Baffin
Bay

Bering
Sea

Gulf of
Alaska

Rocky Mountains

Hudson
Bay

Labrador
Sea

NORTH
AMERICA

Great
Basin

Mojave
Desert

Sierra Madre

Gulf of
Mexico

Caribbean
Sea

ATLANTIC
OCEAN

PACIFIC
OCEAN

SOUTH
AMERICA

Andes

Atacama Desert

Patagonian Desert

Climate

Weather and climate are not the same. Weather is how hot, cold or wet a place is at a particular time. Climate is the average weather of an area over time. Several things decide the climate of an area, including how far it is from the Equator, how far from the sea, its height above sea level and its wind systems. The position of a place on an area of land and the size of that land area also affects the climate. Scientists divide the world into different climate regions: polar and tundra, temperate, tropical, desert and mountain.

The sea affects the climate of coastal regions, keeing them warmer than inland areas in winter and cooler in summer.

Biomes

Both the climate of an area (especially the temperature and the amount of rain) and the type of soil decides which plants can grow there. Zones with similar features are called biomes. The biomes are what the world would be like without human interference. Humans have changed the landscape by cutting down forests, growing crops, rearing animals and building roads and cities. So there are unchanged biomes only in places where no one lives.

Warm temperate
These areas have mild winters and warm to hot summers. There is rain all year round, but there are plenty of sunny days. This is an ideal climate for growing crops such as citrus fruits, grapes and olives.

Mountain
The climates of mountain areas vary according to altitude. The higher the mountain, the colder it is. At a certain point, called the tree line, trees can no longer grow. The climate in mountain areas is usually wetter than in the lowlands around them.

Key

Polar and Tundra

Cool temperate

Desert

Warm temperate

Tropical

Mountains

ARCTIC OCEAN

Barents
Sea

Kara
Sea

Arctic Circle

Kölen

Baltic Sea

Cool temperate
These areas have warm summers and cool
winters. In the northern areas the winters can
be very cold. Rain falls all year round. Much of
this area was once covered with forest.

Sea of
Okhotsk

Polar and tundra
The area around the
North Pole is called
the Arctic and the area
around the South Pole is the
Antarctic. Both are bitterly cold,
with an average temperature of
0° to 10°C in summer and as
little as −50°C or so in winter.
Few plants can grow. The tundra
is the land surrounding the Arctic.
In summer small plants grow here.

EUROPE

Alps

Black Sea

Caucasus

Caspian Sea

Kirghiz Steppe

Altai Mts

ASIA

Mediterranean Sea

Kara Kum

Hindu Kush

Tien Shan

Takla Makan

Kunlun Mts

Plateau of Tibet

Himalayas

Gobi
Desert

Sea of
Japan

Zagros Mts

The Gulf

Thar Desert

Tropic of Cancer

Sahara
Desert

Red Sea

Arabian
Peninsula

Arabian
Sea

Bay of
Bengal

South
China
Sea

Philippine
Sea

PACIFIC
OCEAN

Ethiopian
Highlands

AFRICA

Equator

INDIAN
OCEAN

Java Sea

Arafura
Sea

Coral
Sea

Namib Desert

Kalahari
Desert

Great Sandy
Desert

Gibson
Desert

Simpson Desert

AUSTRALIA

Great Victoria
Desert

Tropic of Capricorn

Tropical
These areas are hot all the year
round. In some parts there is heavy
rain all year round, too, and that is
where rainforests grow. Rainforest
plants fruit and flower all year.
In other tropical areas, such as
savannas and scrubland, there
are dry seasons and rainy seasons,
when most of the year's rain falls.

Desert
True deserts are very hot –
40°C or more – during the day,
but cold at night. They are very
dry and what little rain there is falls
in short sudden bursts and evaporates
quickly. Few plants can grow in deserts
but some animals manage to survive.

Tasman
Sea

Southern Alps

SOUTHERN OCEAN

Antarctic Circle

ANTARCTICA

View of a hurricane from space

Cloud layers

There are ten types of clouds. Each has a characteristic shape and appears at certain levels in the sky. All types would not appear together as in this diagram.

Cloud type	Altitude (m)	Cloud type	Altitude (m)
Stratus	below 450	Altostratus	2,000–7,000
Cumulus	450–2,000	Altocumulus	2,000–7,000
Stratocumulus	450–2,000	Cirrus	5,000–13,500
Cumulonimbus	450–2,000	Cirrostratus	5,000–13,500
Nimbostratus	900–3,000	Cirrocumulus	5,000–13,500

The Beaufort scale

The Beaufort scale was introduced in 1806 by British Admiral Sir Francis Beaufort (1774–1857) to describe wind effects on a fully rigged man-of-war ship. It was later extended to describe how winds affect land features such as trees. The Beaufort scale is divided into a series of values, from 0 for calm winds to 12 and above for hurricanes. Weather forecasters often describe winds by their force number – for example, a force 10 gale. Wind speed can also be measured in knots: 1 knot = 1.85km/h.

Force	Description	Speed km/h	Effects on land and sea
0	Calm	0–2	Smoke rises vertically; sea is mirror smooth
1	Light air	3–6	Smoke indicates the direction of the wind
2	Slight breeze	7–11	Wind felt on the face and leaves rustle in trees
3	Gentle breeze	12–19	Wind extends a light flag
4	Moderate breeze	20–28	Loose paper blows around; frequent whitecaps at sea
5	Fresh breeze	29–38	Small trees sway
6	Strong breeze	39–49	Wind whistles in telephone wires; some spray on sea surface
7	High wind	50–61	Large trees sway
8	Gale	62–74	Twigs break from trees; long streaks of foam on the sea
9	Strong gale	75–88	Branches break from trees
10	Whole gale	89–102	Trees uprooted; sea takes on a white appearance
11	Storm	103–117	Widespread damage
12	Hurricane	118+	Structural damage on land; storm waves at sea

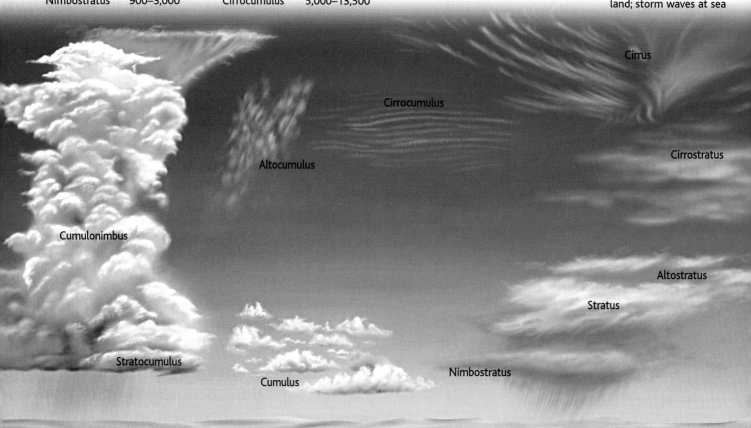

Cirrus

Cirrocumulus

Cirrostratus

Altocumulus

Cumulonimbus

Altostratus

Stratus

Stratocumulus

Nimbostratus

Cumulus

World extremes

Windiest place on Earth
Commonwealth Bay, Antarctica, has recorded some of the most consistently high wind speeds, occasionally reaching 320km/h. The highest individual gust of wind measured was 371km/h at Mount Washington, New Hampshire, USA, on 12 April 1934.

Hurricane wind speed
The fastest sustained winds in a hurricane in the USA measured 322km/h, with 338km/h gusts, on 17–18 August 1969, when Hurricane Camille hit the Mississippi/Alabama coast.

Tornado wind speed
Fastest 450km/h at Wichita Falls, Texas, USA, on 2 April 1958.

Hottest place on Earth
Dallol in Ethiopia had an average temperature of 34.4°C during 1960–66.

Highest shade temperature recorded
Al'Aziziyah, Libyan desert, 57.8°C on 13 September 1922. A temperature of 56.6°C was recorded at Greenland Ranch, Death Valley, California, USA, on 10 July 1913.

Driest place
Atacama Desert, Chile, where average annual rainfall is officially nil (also longest drought – 400 years up to 1971). The average rainfall on the Pacific coast of Chile between Arica and Antofagasta is less than 1mm.

Least sunshine
At the South Pole there is no sunshine for 182 days every year, and at the North Pole the same applies for 176 days.

Coldest place
Pole of Cold, or Polus Nedostupnosti, Antarctica, -57.8°C.

Greatest snowfall in 12 months
31,102mm at Mt Rainier, Washington, USA, from 19 February 1971 to 18 February 1972 (this is an incredible 31m, equivalent to 17 people standing on each other's heads!).

Greatest depth of snow
11.46m at Tamarac, California, USA, in March 1911.

Freak snow storm
In the Sahara Desert, Algeria, 18 February 1979.

Greatest annual rainfall (annual average)
Mawsynram, India, with 11,870mm a year; and Tutunendo, Colombia, 11,770mm.

Greatest annual rainfall (extreme example)
Cherrapunji, Assam, 26,461mm between 1 August 1860 and 31 July 1861 – which is close to the length of a tennis court! Also, at the same place, the greatest in one calendar month – 9,300mm fell in July 1861. That's about the same as five people standing on each other's heads.

Most rainfall in 24 hours
Cilaos, La Réunion, Indian Ocean, 1,870mm, 15–16 March, 1952.

Most rainy days in a year
Mt Waialeale, Kauai, Hawaii, USA, up to 350 days a year. The total rainfall is about 11,684mm, which approaches the annual record.

Heaviest hailstones
750g, 19cm diameter, 44.45cm circumference, Coffeyville, Kansas, USA, 3 September 1970 – almost the size of a tenpin ball, 21.6cm.

Extreme weather – UK

Highest temperature
Brogdale near Faversham (Kent), 10 August 2003: 38.5°C

Lowest temperature
Braemar, Grampian, 10 January 1982 and 11 February 1895: -27.2°C; Altnaharra, Highland, 30 December 1995: -27.2°C

Highest 24-hour rainfall
Martinstown, near Dorchester, Dorset, 18 July 1955: 279mm

Highest 60-minute rainfall
Maidenhead, Berkshire, 12 July 1901: 92mm

Highest 5-minute rainfall
Preston, Lancashire, 10 August 1893: 32mm

Most monthly sunshine
Eastbourne and Hastings, Sussex, July 1911: 384 hours

Highest gust of wind (low-level site)
Fraserburgh, Aberdeenshire, 13 February 1989: 228km/h

Highest gust of wind (high-level site)
Cairngorm (1,245 m above sea level), 20 March 1986: 278km/h

Tools of the trade

Weather forecasters use a range of instruments. Some of these have been around for hundreds of years while some are modern electronic versions of earlier mechanical instruments. In recent times, balloons, radar stations and orbiting satellites provide increasingly accurate weather information, and computer programs are able to make detailed forecasts that earlier meteorologists could not imagine.

Anemometer
Wind speed is measured by a cup anemometer. This device has three or four hollow cups that rotate round a vertical rod. The speed at which the wind spins the cups round is recorded by a counter. A wind vane shows the direction of wind, and an anemograph records the speed of the wind on a chart.

Rain gauge
Rain gauges – containers designed to measure the amount of rain that has fallen – date from ancient China and India. In 1662, British architect Sir Christopher Wren invented a tipping bucket rain gauge, which emptied itself when it was full.

Thermometer
Galileo invented the thermsocope, an early form of thermometer. Later developments led to sealed thermometers using mercury, which expands in a narrow tube as the temperature rises. Gabriel Fahrenheit's scale dates from 1714, and that of Anders Celsius from 1742. The maximum and minimum thermometer, which records the highest and lowest temperatures reached over a period of time, was invented by James Six at Cambridge in 1780.

Hottest and coldest

The hottest place in the world where people live is Djibouti, in the Republic of Djibouti, Africa. The average temperature is 30.0°C. Next hottest are Timbuktu in Mali and Tirunelevi in India, both 29.3°C. The coldest place where people live is Norilsk, Russia, with an average temperature of –10.9°C. Next coldest is Yakutsk in Russia, at –10.1°C.

Volcanic eruptions

Santorini
The eruption of the Greek island of Santorini in c1450 BC is believed to have been one of the most powerful ever.

Vesuvius, Italy
On 24 August AD 79 Vesuvius erupted with little warning, engulfing the Roman city of Herculaneum in a mud flow. Nearby Pompeii was buried under a vast layer of pumice and volcanic ash. This preserved the city, including the bodies of many of its inhabitants, until it was excavated by archaeologists in the 19th and 20th centuries. As many as 20,000 people died. Vesuvius erupted again in 1631, killing up to 18,000 people.

Laki, Iceland
Iceland is one of the most volcanically active places on earth, but the population is small so eruptions seldom cause many deaths. On 11 June 1783 the largest lava flow ever recorded engulfed many villages in a river of lava up to 80km long and 30m deep. It released poisonous gases that killed those who managed to escape the lava flow, up to 20,000 people.

Unsen, Japan
On 1 April 1793 the volcanic island of Unsen or Unzen completely disappeared, killing all 53,000 inhabitants.

Tambora, Indonesia
On the island of Sumbawa the eruption of Tambora between 5 and 12 April 1815 killed about 10,000 islanders immediately. A further 82,000 died later from disease and famine. This made it the worst ever eruption for loss of human life.

Krakatoa, Sumatra/Java
The uninhabited island of Krakatoa exploded on 27 August 1883 with what may have been the biggest bang ever heard by humans. People heard it up to 4,800km away!

Lava pouring from an erupting volcano

Mont Pelée, Martinique
Mont Pelée began to erupt in April 1902, after lying dormant for centuries. The 30,000 residents of the main city, St Pierre, were told that they were not in danger, so stayed in their homes. They were there on 8 May when the volcano burst apart and showered the port with molten lava, ash and gas, destroying all buildings and killing as many as 40,000 people.

Nevado del Ruiz, Colombia
In 1985 this Andean volcano gave warning signs that it was about to erupt, but the local people were not evacuated soon enough. On 13 November the hot steam, rocks and ash ejected from Nevado del Ruiz melted its icecap, causing a mudslide. This completely engulfed the town of Armero, killing 22,940 people.

Mount St Helens in Washington, USA, erupting

Avalanche!
An avalanche caused by the eruption of the Mount St Helens volcano, Washington, USA, on 18 May 1980 was reckoned to have travelled at 400km/h.

Earthquake

Earthquakes are movements of the Earth's surface, often as a result of a fault or fracture deep in the crust. They are more common in some parts of the world than others. When they happen in heavily populated areas, such as Japan, they cause great damage to buildings and loss of life.

Worst ever
An earthquake affecting the Middle East and North Africa on 20 May 1202 may have been the worst in human history. As many as 1,000,000 people were killed, 110,000 in Cairo, Egypt alone. In Baalbek, rockfalls caused by the earthquake killed 200 rhubarb pickers. A quake in Shenshi, China, on 2 February 1556 is said to have killed 820,000 people, and one in Calcutta, India, on 11 October 1737 left 300,000 dead.

Worst modern earthquakes
In Kansu Province, China, on 16 December 1920, an earthquake and the landslides it caused left 180,000 dead. A Muslim leader known as Ma the Benevolent declared a holy war, but moments later, he and 300 of his followers were buried by a landslide. An earthquake in Tang-shan, China, on 28 July 1976 killed 242,419.

Longest-lasting
Most earthquakes last only a minute or two, but the Alaska quake of 27 March 1964 continued for at least five minutes and registered 8.6 on the Richter scale. It killed only 131 people but caused more than $450 million worth of damage.

Most powerful
Although offshore earthquakes of 8.9 on the Richter scale have been recorded, the worst affecting an inhabited area was the earthquake of 12 June 1897 in Assam, India, which is reckoned to have reached 8.7, killing about 1,500. The Colombia/Ecuador earthquake of 31 January 1906 was 8.9 on the Richter scale. Fortunately, it was 300km off the coast, and so resulted in fewer than 1,000 deaths on land.

Worst natural disasters

Drought
Serious heatwaves and droughts kill both people and livestock and destroy crops. The drought in Australia during 1982 cost £3.5 billion, and one in Spain in 1995 cost £3 billion.

Flood
Floods caused by China's Huang He, or Yellow River, were first recorded in 2297 BC. Since then, the river has flooded at least 1,500 times. In spring 1887 floods killed at least 1.5 million people and perhaps as many as 7 million, making it the worst flood of all time.

Tsunami
On 26 December 2004 a tsunami created by an undersea earthquake caused catastrophic floods in Indonesia, Sri Lanka, Myanmar, the Maldives, Malaysia, India and parts of Africa. More than 289,000 people died.

Tornado
At Shaturia, Bangladesh, on 26 April 1989 about 1,300 people were killed and 50,000 left homeless when a tornado swept through the area.

Hailstones
On 20 April 1888 in Moradabad, India, 246 people (along with more than 1,600 sheep and goats) were killed by hailstones, some as big as cricket balls.

The Richter scale

Seismic waves are the vibrations from earthquakes that travel through the Earth and can be recorded on very sensitive instruments called seismographs. These can measure earthquakes even at great distances and calculate their strength and location. The Richter scale was invented in 1935 by American seismologist (earthquake expert) Charles F. Richter (1900–85) and Beno Gutenberg. It indicates the magnitude or strength of an earthquake based on the size of the seismic waves (the distance the ground moves). The biggest earthquake (9 on the Richter scale) is a billion times greater than the smallest.

0	Detected by sensitive seismographs (very sensitive ones can even detect magnitudes of less than zero!)
1	Detected by instruments
2	Lowest felt by humans
3	Slight vibration; more than 100,000 a year around the world
4	Up to 15,000 a year; at 4.5, would be detected by seismographs worldwide, but cause little damage.
5	3000 a year; the 1960 earthquake in Agadir, Morocco was 5.6
6	100 a year worldwide
7	20 a year; the 1995 earthquake in Kobe, Japan was 7.2
8	Major destructive earthquakes; average two a year; the 1904 San Francisco earthquake was probably 8.25
9	No quake higher than 8.9 has been recorded, but 9.0 or even higher is theoretically possible

Earthquake detector
Chinese astronomer Chan Heng (AD 78–139) invented an earthquake detector made of a vase adorned with dragons' heads and surrounded by metal frogs. In each of the dragons' jaws was a carefully balanced ball. When the first tremors of an earthquake made the device vibrate, the balls fell into the frogs' mouths making a noise to warn of the coming danger.

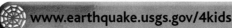
www.earthquake.usgs.gov/4kids

The world contains an astonishing range of living things, from microscopic plants and bacteria to towering trees and blue whales, the largest creatures that have ever lived. Without plants and other animals, humans could not survive, so we need to protect the natural world for the future.

LIFE SCIENCES

Top food plants

Every year the people of the world eat two billion tonnes of cereals, more than 850 million tonnes of vegetables and nearly 500 million tonnes of fruit. These figures come from the Food and Agriculture Organization of the United Nations, or FAO, which is based in Rome. The aim of the FAO is to help people around the world grow more food and eat a better diet.

Crop	Yearly production (tonnes)
Sugar cane	1,318,178,070
Maize	705,293,226
Wheat	624,093,306
Rice	608,496,284
Potatoes	328,865,936
Sugar beet	237,857,862
Soya beans	206,409,525
Cassava	195,574,112
Barley	155,114,564
Sweet potatoes	127,535,008
Tomatoes	115,950,851
Watermelons	93,481,266
Bananas	70,629,047
Cabbages	68,389,593
Grapes	65,486,235
Oranges	63,039,736
Pulses (beans, peas, etc)	61,310,171
Sorghum	60,224,964
Apples	59,059,142
Coconuts	53,473,584

Rice drying after harvest

Carved pineapple on a gatepost at Ham House in England

American plants

As many as 30 per cent of the world's most useful plants originally came from North, Central and South America. Early European explorers discovered the plants while on their travels and took them back home to grow. This was not always easy. Pineapples were so difficult and expensive to cultivate in Europe that they became a symbol of wealth – pineapple carvings can be seen on the gates of many grand houses.

Here are some of the plants that originally came from the Americas:

avocado	chilli pepper	peanut	quinine	tomato
beans (kidney,	cocoa	pecan	rubber	vanilla
French, etc)	corn	pineapple	squash/gourd	
cashew nut	cranberry	potato	sunflower	
cassava	loganberry	pumpkin	tobacco	

Important crops

These are the most important crops grown for uses other than food.

Crop	Uses	Yearly production (tonnes)
Cotton	Clothing, household items	67,375,042
Rubber	Tyres, shoes, balls, erasers	8,338,768
Tobacco	Cigarettes, cigars	6,587,677
Jute	Sacks, rope	2,773,642

Dangerous plants

Not all plants are safe to eat or even touch. Nettles sting and other plants, such as euphorbia and poison ivy, may blister your skin. Many quite common plants, including buttercups, are poisonous if eaten because they contain chemicals called phytotoxins. Strangely, some plant poisons (such as curare, digitalis and strychnine), are used in minute quantities to cure illnesses.

- Potatoes are safe to eat when cooked, but the stems and leaves of the plants contain a poison called solanine. If potatoes turn green, they may also contain solanine.

- Ricin is extracted from the seeds of the castor oil plant and is more poisonous than cyanide or snake venom. Even minute doses of ricin can be fatal.

- Opium is extracted from the juice of a poppy and contains morphine. Small quantities of both are used legally as pain-relieving medicines and illegally as drugs. Both can easily cause death.

- The death cap is a highly poisonous mushroom. It is responsible for almost 90 per cent of deaths from eating fungi. The poison causes severe diarrhoea and vomiting.

- Curare is extracted from the bark of certain trees and is used by South American Indian tribes to tip their poison arrows when they go hunting.

- Deadly nightshade is also known as belladonna. It contains a poison called atropine. Less than ten milligrams could kill a child.

- Nicotine is a yellow oily liquid found in tobacco. About 50 milligrams of nicotine would kill an adult within minutes.

- The leaves of the purple foxglove contain digitalis and eating just a few can be fatal. Digitalis is used in tiny doses to treat people suffering from heart disease.

- Strychnine comes from the koochla tree, which grows in Myanmar and India. It is one of the most deadly poisons known.

World forests

Forests cover 29.6 per cent of the Earth's land area and almost a quarter of these are in Russia. There are three main types of forest which grow in particular climates in different parts of the world.

- Tropical forests or rainforests grow near the Equator where it is always hot and wet. Here, temperatures are about 20–25°C and there is more than 200cm of rain a year.

- Temperate forests grow in places that have hot summers and cold winters. The summers can be as hot as 30°C and winters as cold as –30°C. Average rainfall is about 75–150cm a year. Many of the trees are deciduous – they lose their leaves in autumn and grow new ones in spring.

- Boreal or taiga forests grow in Russia, Canada and elsewhere in the far north. Winters are long and very cold. There is rainfall of 40–100cm a year, but most falls as snow. Most trees are evergreen conifers. These are cone-producing trees with needle-like leaves.

Record-breaking plants

Tallest tree
The world's tallest tree is called the Stratosphere Giant. It grows in the Rockefeller Forest, Humboldt Redwoods State Park, California. At 112.32m, this redwood is almost three times the height of the Statue of Liberty in New York. Most of Britain's tallest trees are in Scotland: a Douglas fir growing in Tayside, Scotland, is the record-holder at 64.5m.

Biggest living thing
The General Sherman giant sequoia in Sequoia National Park, California, USA, is the world's largest living thing. It is 83.8m tall and measures 2.53m round its mighty trunk. Including its huge root system, the tree weighs about 2,000 tonnes. It contains enough timber to make shelves for almost a million books. If all this timber was made into pencils and they were laid end to end, they would more than reach round the Equator.

Oldest trees
The bristlecone pines in California and Nevada, USA are almost 5,000 years old and were long believed to be the oldest trees. Latest research suggests that creosote bushes in the USA's Mojave Desert may be even older – some of these plants began life nearly 12,000 years ago. Other long-lived trees include:

Giant sequoia tree

Tree	Age in years
Japanese cedar	7,200
Baobab	5,150
Yew	5,000
Sequoia	3,000–4,000
Olive	2,000–4,000
Oak	500–600

Smallest flowering plant
Wolffia, a kind of duckweed, is just 0.6mm long and weighs about as much as two grains of salt. Its seeds are also the tiniest known – they weigh only 70 micrograms, as much as a single grain of salt.

Largest seed
The seeds of the coco-de-mer palm are up to 30cm long and weigh an amazing 20kg.

Largest and smelliest flower
The flower of the rafflesia, or stinking corpse lily measures almost 1m across and weighs 11kg. It is also one of the world's smelliest flowers, with an odour like rotting flesh. The smell attracts flies, which pollinate the plant.

Fast growers

Bamboo plants can grow 90cm in a day and reach 3m tall in three months. Another fast grower is the Malaysian tree called *Albizzia falcata*. One measured in 1974 grew 10.75m in just over a year.

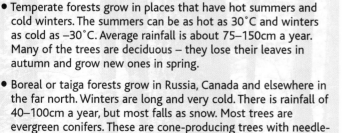

Life on Earth

The first simple life forms began to appear on Earth almost four billion years ago. More familiar animals appeared about 500 million years ago, and humans only within the past two million. We know a little about extinct creatures and early humans from fossil remains found in rocks from each period.

Millions of years ago	Period	Life forms
3,900–2,500	Archaean	Earliest marine life (blue-green algae)
2,500–540	Proterozoic	First many-celled organisms evolve
540–490	Cambrian	First fossils of animals with shells and skeletons
490–443	Ordovician	Molluscs, some corals, fishlike vertebrates
443–417	Silurian	Fish develop jaws, first sharks
417–354	Devonian	Fish dominant, amphibians (first land animals) evolve
354–290	Carboniferous	Insects, first reptiles
290–248	Permian	Insects evolve into modern types, reptiles evolve
248–206	Triassic	Early dinosaurs, marine reptiles
206–144	Jurassic	Reptiles dominate land, sea and air, *Archaeopteryx* (first bird) appears, first mammals
144–65	Cretaceous	Dinosaurs become extinct, snakes and lizards appear
65–55	Palaeocene	First large land mammals
55–34	Eocene	Modern land mammals and whales appear
34–24	Oligocene	Modern mammals dominant
24–5	Miocene	Modern mammals including primates, birds
5–1.8	Pliocene	Manlike apes appear
1.8–10,000	Pleistocene	Humans appear
10,000–present	Holocene	Human civilization

Grouping living things

Living things are organized by scientists into five groups called kingdoms, of which the animal kingdom is one. The common and scientific names of these are: Animals (Animalia); Algae and protozoans (Protoctista); Bacteria (Prokaryotae); Mushrooms, moulds and lichens (Fungi); Plants (Plantae).

The animal kingdom alone has thousands of different species. A species is a type of animal, and animals of the same species can breed successfully with each other. Similar species are grouped in a genus. Genera are grouped into families, families into orders, right up to the level of phylum. The phylum chordata contains all vertebrate animals – animals with a backbone. Here's how a human and a giant panda are classified.

	Human	Giant panda
Phylum	Chordata	Chordata
Class	Mammalia	Mammalia
Order	Primates	Carnivores
Family	Hominidae	Ursidae
Genus	*Homo*	*Ailuropoda*
Species	*sapiens*	*melanoleuca*

Animal species

Below is a list of the animals we know about. No one knows exactly how many species there may be altogether. New species are always being found and there may be tens of millions not yet discovered. Some experts think there may be millions of species of insects and at least a million species of deep-sea fish that no one has ever seen. About half of all known creatures and plants live in tropical rainforests. In one study of just 19 trees in a tropical rainforest 1,200 beetle species were found. About 80 per cent of these had never been seen before.

Class	Approx no of known species
Insects	1,000,000+
Molluscs (snails, clams, etc)	70,000
Arachnids (spiders, scorpions, etc)	75,500
Crustaceans (shrimps, crabs, etc)	40,000
Fish	28,100
Nematodes (unsegmented worms)	20,000
Flatworms	17,500
Segmented worms	12,000
Sponges	10,000
Birds	9,932
Jellyfish, coral, etc	9,000
Reptiles	8,240
Starfish	6,000
Amphibians	5,578
Mammals	4,814

Zoo shopping list

Shopping to feed 650 different species of animals is hard work, but that is the task of keepers at one of the world's most famous zoos. London Zoo, founded in 1828, was the first zoo to be established as a scientific centre and was opened to the public in 1847. Below is the zoo's basic shopping list for a year.

Food	Tonnes	Food	Tonnes	Food	Number
Hay	47	Carrots	13	Eggs	38,000
Bananas	29	Meat	9	Lettuces	15,860
Apples	29	Oranges	4.5	Cabbages	8,320
Straw	28	Grapes	4	Milk (litres)	975
Clover	26	Potatoes	3.1		
Fish	19	Tomatoes	2.78		*Food for*
Food pellets	18	Honey	0.25		*zoo animals*

Cheetah

 # How fast?

Most of the creatures in this list can only keep up these speeds for a short time – not as long as an hour. The peregrine falcon achieves its record-breaking speed as it dives through the air to catch prey – not in level flight.

Animal	Average speed (km/h)
Peregrine falcon (diving speed)	298
Spine-tailed swift	171
Eider duck	113
Sailfish (fastest fish)	110
Cheetah (fastest on land)	105
Pronghorn antelope	89
Racing pigeon	80
Lion (charging)	80
Brown hare	72
Ostrich (fastest flightless bird)	72
Blue shark	69
Horse	69
Greyhound	68
Killer whale	56
Death's head hawkmoth (fastest-flying insect)	53
Guano bat (fastest-flying mammal)	51
Butterfly	48
California sea lion	40
Dolphin	40
Fastest man over 100m	37
Gentoo penguin	35
Cnemidophorus lizard (fastest reptile)	30
Blue whale	24
Black mamba snake	19
Bumblebee	18
Rat	9.5
Tegenaria atrica spider	1.8
Common garden snail	0.05
Army ant	0.032

 # How long do they live?

Who would have thought that a sea anemone could live for 80 years? All these figures are the longest ever recorded. Most of these animals will have much shorter lives.

Animal	Longest life-span (years)
Quahog (marine clam)	200
Giant tortoise	150
Human	122
Killer whale	90
Sea anemone	80
Asiatic elephant	78
American alligator	66
Blue macaw	64
Horse	62
Chimpanzee	56
Hippopotamus	54
Slow-worm	54
Beaver	50
Bactrian camel	50
Grizzly bear	50
Blue whale	45
Boa constrictor	40
Domestic cat	34
Lion	30
Pig	27
Common rabbit	18
Queen ant	18
Giant centipede	10
Millipede	7
House mouse	6
Bedbug	6 months
Common housefly (male)	2 weeks

How many legs?

Some animals have as few as two legs, others as many as 750. Some, such as snakes and worms, have none at all! Most people think that centipedes have 100 legs and millipedes 1,000. But centipedes, depending on their species, have anything from 28 to 354 legs and millipedes up to 750.

Creature	No of legs
Birds	2
Mammals	4
Reptiles with legs	4
Insects	6
Spiders	8
Crabs, shrimps	10
Woodlice	14
Most caterpillars	16
Most millipedes	30
Centipede with most legs	354
Millipede with most legs	750

A giant millipede

http://animaldiversity.ummz.umich.edu

Types of mammal

A mammal is a warm-blooded vertebrate (animal with a backbone) with some hair on its body. Female mammals feed their young on milk from their mammary glands. Most mammals give birth to live young which develop inside the mother's body, but echidnas and the platypus lay eggs. Marsupial mammals such as kangaroos give birth to live young, but they are very small and weak. They finish their development in a pouch on the mother's body. There are 21 main groups, or orders, of mammals.

Listed below are the names of the main mammal groups, examples of the animals and the approximate number of known species. Common names are given where possible.

Rodents
Beavers, squirrels, mice, rats, porcupines, voles, guinea pigs, chinchillas 2,052

Chiroptera
Bats 977

Insectivores
Shrews, moles, hedgehogs, tenrecs 440

Primates
Lemurs, lorises, tarsiers, marmosets, monkeys, gibbons, apes, humans 270

Marsupials
Opossums, koalas, bandicoots, kangaroos, wallabies, numbat 292

Carnivores
Dogs, foxes, wolves, cats, bears, hyenas, raccoons, civets, mongooses, weasels, pandas 249

Even-toed ungulates
Pigs, peccaries, giraffe, okapi, hippopotamuses, deer, camels, llamas, antelopes, cattle 225

Cetacea
Whales, dolphins, porpoises 83

Lagomorphia
Rabbits, hares, pikas 80

Pinnipedia
Seals, sea-lions, walruses 34

Edentates
Anteaters, sloths, armadillos 29

Odd-toed ungulates
Horses, asses, zebras, rhinos, tapirs 19

Scandentia
Tree shrews 19

Macroscelidea
Elephant-shrews 15

Monotremes
Duck-billed platypus, echidnas 5

Hyracoidea
Hyraxes 8

Pholidota
Pangolins 7

Sirenia
Manatees, dugong 4

Proboscidea
Elephants 3

Dermoptera
Flying lemurs 2

Tubulidentata
Aardvark 1

Male gorilla

Biggest and smallest

The following are the biggest land mammals according to their weight.

Mammal	Weight (kg)
African elephant	7,000
White rhinoceros	3,600
Hippopotamus	2,500
Giraffe	1,600
American bison	1,000
Arabian camel (dromedary)	690
Polar bear	600
Moose	550
Siberian tiger	300
Gorilla	220

The following are the smallest land mammals, according to length. Kitti's hog-nosed bat is smaller than a bumblebee. It was discovered in caves in northern Thailand in 1973 and has not been seen anywhere else.

Mammal	Length (cm)
Kitti's hog-nosed bat	2.9
Pygmy shrew	3.6
Pipistrelle bat	4.0
Little brown bat	4.0
Masked shrew	4.5
Southern blossom bat	5.0
Harvest mouse	5.8
Pygmy glider	6.0
House mouse	6.4
Common shrew	6.5
Water shrew	7.0
Bank vole	8.0
Pygmy possum	8.5

Who's the cleverest?

This list of the most intelligent mammals is based on research carried out by Edward O. Wilson, Professor of Zoology at Harvard. He defined intelligence on the basis of how fast and how well an animal can learn a wide range of tasks. He also takes into account the size of the animal's brain compared with its body.

1 Human
2 Chimpanzee
3 Gorilla
4 Orang-utan
5 Baboon
6 Gibbon
7 Monkey
8 Small toothed whale
9 Dolphin
10 Elephant
11 Pig

Polar bear

Bears of the world

Scientists have long argued about whether the giant panda should be grouped with the raccoon family or the bears. DNA tests have now proved that it belongs with the bears. The koala, often called koala bear, is actually a marsupial not a bear.

Bear	Length (cm)	Weight (kg)
Polar bear (Arctic)	up to 257	200–800
Brown (grizzly) bear (North America, Europe, Asia)	up to 290	136–390
American black bear (North America)	127–191	60–300
Asiatic black bear (Southern Asia)	127–188	100–200
Sloth bear (Asia)	152–191	80–140
Giant panda (China)	122–152	up to 125
Spectacled bear (South America)	152–183	70–113
Sun bear (Asia)	122–152	27–65

Male lion

Monkeys and apes

Monkeys and apes (and humans) belong to the group of mammals called primates. There are 256 known species of primate. The smallest primate is the pygmy mouse lemur, which weighs only 30g.

Largest primates	Average weight (kg)
Gorilla	220
Human	77
Orang-utan	75
Chimpanzee	50
Baboon	45
Mandrill	45

Champion divers

Lots of mammals can dive underwater, including humans, but whales are the champions. All have to hold their breath.

Mammal	Average dive (mins)
Northern bottlenose whale	120
Sperm whale	112
Greenland whale	60
Seal	22
Beaver	20
Dugong	16
Hippopotamus	15
Porpoise	15
Muskrat	12
Duck-billed platypus	10
Sea otter	5
Human pearl diver	2.5
Human	1

Big babies

The African elephant has the longest pregnancy of any mammal. She carries her baby for an average of 660 days. When the baby is born it weighs 90–120kg. A baby blue whale is even bigger. It weighs 2,000kg and is 7m long. It puts on weight at the astonishing rate of 90kg a day.

Big cats

Big cats such as lions are perhaps the most powerful of all mammal predators. These measurements are from the nose to the tip of the tail. The length of tail varies – a leopard's tail can be as long as 110cm and a jaguar's tail as short as 45cm.

Species	Max length (cm)
Tiger (Asia)	330
Leopard (Asia, Africa)	320
Lion (Africa, Asia)	280
Jaguar (North, Central and South America)	271
Mountain lion (North, Central and South America)	245
Snow leopard (Asia)	240
Cheetah (Africa, Asia)	220
Clouded leopard (Asia)	197

Danger in the water

Most creatures living in the world's oceans and rivers are harmless to people, but there are a few that can be very dangerous if you are unlucky enough to encounter or provoke them.

- The tiny candiru fish lives in South American rivers. It can enter your body and kill you unless it is surgically removed.

- Cone-shells, found in the South Pacific and Indian Oceans, have poisonous barbs that cause paralysis and occasionally death if you touch them. The geographer cone is probably the most dangerous of all.

- Freshwater electric eels live in South America and are the most powerful of all the electric eels. They can release up to 650 volts, which is enough to kill a person. Fortunately, this rarely happens.

- Certain parts of the Japanese puffer fish, also known as the maki-maki or deadly death puffer fish, contain a powerful nerve poison that can kill you if you eat it. There is no known antidote. Despite the danger, puffer fish are eaten in Japan, where they are a very expensive delicacy. People are specially trained to prepare them because eating the wrong part causes death in about 60 per cent of cases. About 50 people a year in Japan die after eating incorrectly prepared puffers.

- Several species of octopus are dangerous. The sting of the blue-ringed octopus, which lives in the Australian seas, can cause paralysis and even death.

- Piranha are small but incredibly ferocious fish which live in rivers in parts of South America. They hunt in groups, attacking any creatures in the water – including humans unlucky enough to encounter them. They strip their prey to the bone in minutes.

- Sea wasps, also known as box jellyfish, live off the coast of Australia. They have tentacles up to 9m long and venom as powerful as that of a cobra. Australian lifeguards often wear nylon tights to protect them against stings, which can cause death within three minutes.

- Most sharks are harmless but a few species have been known to attack people. The great white and the bull shark are the most dangerous. In 2003 there were 55 shark attacks on humans. Four of these were fatal. On the other hand, people kill more than 100 million sharks every year.

- Stonefish lie on the seabed where they resemble rocks encrusted with seaweed. Unsuspecting swimmers who tread on the fish receive a very painful sting from their spines. In severe cases, victims may die.

Great white shark

Marine mammals

The biggest creatures in the sea are whales, which are mammals not fish. The blue whale is the largest creature that has ever lived. Whales spend all their lives in the sea, but there are other mammals that spend most of their time in water and some time on land. These include seals, sea lions and otters.

Biggest marine mammals

Mammal	Length (m)	Weight (tonnes)
Blue whale	33.5	130.0
Fin whale	25.0	45.0
Right whale	17.5	40.0
Sperm whale	18.0	36.0
Grey whale	14.0	32.7
Humpback whale	15.0	26.5
Sei whale	13.7	20.0
Baird's whale	5.5	11.0

Blue whale

A blue whale can be as long as three buses.

Smallest marine mammals

- The marine otter, which lives off the western coast of South America, is the smallest marine mammal. It weighs up to 4.5kg and measures about 1.15m. The sea otter of North American coasts is slightly larger.

- The smallest sea lion is the Galapagos fur seal, which weighs up to 64kg and is 1.5m long. The smallest seal is the Baikal which lives in Lake Baikal, Russia. It is 1.4m long and weighs 63.5kg.

- Smallest dolphins include Hector's dolphin, which lives in the waters off New Zealand. It is rarely more than 1.5m long and weighs less than 57.2kg.

- The pygmy right whale is the smallest whale. Most are less than 6.4m long and 3.2 tonnes in weight – less than a fifth of the length of a blue whale.

Big fish

The whale shark is probably the biggest fish in the world. Whale sharks are usually up to 12m long – though one caught off Thailand in 1919 was reckoned to be 18m long. Despite being enormous, these giant fish eat only plankton – tiny animals and plants that float in water. Basking sharks also eat plankton, but most other big fish are hunters.

Whale shark

Fish	Weight (kg)
Whale shark	21,000
Basking shark	14,515
Great white shark	3,314
Giant manta	3,000
Beluga	2,072
Sharptail mola	2,000
Ocean sunfish	2,000
Greenland shark	1,020
Tiger shark	939
Great hammerhead shark	844
White sturgeon	816

Top food fish

Fish and shellfish are popular foods for people all around the world. These are the top catches.

Type of fish	Total catch in 2002 (tonnes)
Herrings, sardines, anchovies	22,472,563
Carps, barbels, cyprinid	17,285,109
Cod, hake, haddock	8,393,924
Tunas, bonitos, billfish	6,097,782
Oysters	4,504,079
Shrimps, prawns	4,271,812
Clams, cockles, arkshell	4,256,471
Squid, cuttlefish, octopus	3,173,286
Salmon, trouts, smelts	2,606,381
Tilapias, cichlids	2,188,443
World total caught for food	**132,989,226**

Amazing sea creatures

Most eggs
The black marlin fish lays as many as 226 million eggs.

Largest crustacean
The giant spider crab's body measures up to 30.5–35.6cm across and it has a claw span of 2.4–2.7m.

Smallest crustacean
Pea crabs measure only about 64mm across the shell.

Heaviest crustacean
An Atlantic lobster weighing 19.25kg was caught off Virginia, USA in 1934. It was nicknamed Mike.

Heaviest mollusc
A giant squid caught in 1878 had tentacles 10.7m long and weighed about 1,814kg.

Largest clam
A clam known as *Tridacna derasa* measures up to 124cm across and weighs 263kg. *Tridacna gigas* is usually smaller, but a 115-cm specimen was found that weighed 333kg.

Largest gastropod
The gastropod group includes snails. Largest is the trumpet or baler conch. It lives off Australian coasts and weighs up to 18kg. Its shell measures 77cm long and 101cm round.

Largest jellyfish
The lion's mane jellyfish (*Cyanea arctica*) is up to 2.3m long, with tentacles that add an extra 37m.

Largest sponge
The barrel sponge of the Caribbean is up to 1.8–2.4m tall.

Deep sea divers

- Emperor penguins sometimes dive to depths of 265m.

- In 1987 a leatherback turtle fitted with a depth-gauge reached a depth of 1,200m.

- Sperm whales regularly dive to 1,200m and experts think they may sometimes go down to twice this depth.

- Fish called brotulids are the deepest-living vertebrate animals. They have been found in deep-sea trenches, such as the Puerto Rico Trench, at 8,300m – that is almost as deep as Mount Everest is high.

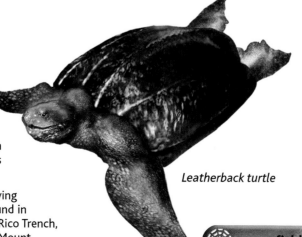

Leatherback turtle

Smallest fish

The smallest fish are also the smallest of all vertebrate animals. The pygmy goby is only 7.5–9.9mm long and the stout infantfish, discovered in 2004, is only 7mm long.

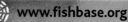

www.fishbase.org

Bird fact file

Birds are vertebrate animals with two legs and front limbs that have become adapted to form wings. All birds have feathers and most, but not all, can fly. Birds reproduce by laying eggs from which their young hatch.

Largest flying birds

Bird	Wingspan (m)	Weight (kg)
Great bustard	2.7	20.9
Trumpeter swan	3.4	16.8
Mute swan	3.1	16.3
Albatross	3.7	15.8
Whooper swan	3.1	15.8
Manchurian crane	2.1	14.9
Kori bustard	2.7	13.6

Largest flightless birds

Bird	Height (m)	Weight (kg)
Ostrich	2.74	156.5
Emu	1.52	40.0
Cassowary	1.52	33.5
Rhea	1.37	25.0
Emperor penguin	1.14	29.4

Smallest bird
The smallest bird is the bee hummingbird, which is 5.7cm long and weighs 1.6g.

Longest beak
The bird with the longest beak in relation to its body length is the sword-billed hummingbird – its beak measures 10.5cm and the bird's body is only 13.5cm long. The bird with the longest beak of all is the Australian pelican. Its beak measures 47cm.

Highest flyer
Ruppell's griffon is the highest-flying bird. In 1973 one was recorded at 11,278m above sea level – 2,427m higher than Mount Everest – after colliding with an airliner.

Longest migration
The Arctic tern migrates further than any other bird. Every year it flies from the Arctic to Antarctica and back again – a round trip of at least 40,000km.

Arctic tern

All about feathers

Feathers are made of keratin, the same material as our hair and nails. The body of a feather is called its vane, the shaft is known as the rachis and the individual tufts are known as barbs. The barbs have hooks called barbules that cling to the others like Velcro.

- Birds shed their feathers at intervals and grow new ones. This process is called moulting. Feathers fall in a set pattern and in pairs, one from each side, so that the bird's flight is not unbalanced. Birds that do not fly, such as penguins, moult all over.

- A songbird such as a sparrow has about 3,000 feathers in the summer but as many as 3,500 in the winter to keep it warm. A chicken has about 9,000 feathers and a swan may have 25,216 or more – up to 20,000 of them on its head and neck. The bird with the fewest feathers is the ruby-throated hummingbird with only 940.

- Native American Indians used feathers from hawks and other birds of prey in their head-dresses. They believed that they would gain the birds' strength and powerful eyesight.

- Traditionally, a white feather was a sign of cowardice. This may have come from the old sport of cockfighting – inferior birds were often crossbreeds with a white feather in their tails.

- Grebes eat their own feathers. They are thought to form pellets that help the birds regurgitate (bring up) the bones and scales of the fish they eat.

- The Japanese phoenix fowl is a domestic bird. It is bred with tail feathers measuring up to 10.6m, the longest of any bird. Various types of pheasant have tail feathers of 2m long or more and a peacock's tail feathers (left) can be 1.5cm long.

- Pens for writing were once made from the quills or feathers of geese, turkeys and other birds. The word pen comes from the Latin *penna*, a feather. Quills were sharpened with a penknife (hence the origin of that word) and dipped in ink.

- Each feather weighs very little, but together they make up a large part of the weight of a bird, especially as flying birds have very light skeletons. The skeleton of the frigate bird, a large bird with a 2.1m wingspan, weighs just 113g, less than the weight of all its feathers.

Peacock feather

ONE AND ONLY

The poor-will of North America is the only bird that hibernates. In autumn the bird dozes off in a rock crevice or an old nest and sleeps through the winter months. Its heart rate and breathing slow down and its body temperature drops from its normal 41°C down to 13°C so it uses as little energy as possible.

Birds' eggs

The biggest ostrich eggs weigh as much as 2.35kg, but they are not the largest eggs of all time. The extinct elephant bird, *Aepyornis maximus*, of Madagascar laid eggs that were up to 33cm long and contained 8.88 litres of liquid. This is larger than the eggs of any dinosaur, seven times bigger than an ostrich egg, 180 times bigger than a chicken egg and over 20,000 times the size of a hummingbird's egg!

Bird	Average weight of egg (g)
Ostrich	1,600
Albatross	595
Kiwi	450
Emperor penguin	450
Mute swan	340
Little spotted kiwi	310
Eagle	145
Snowy owl	83
Domestic hen	65
Mallard	54
Peregrine falcon	52
Sparrow	3.0
Wren	1.3
Goldcrest (smallest UK)	0.6
Vervain hummingbird	0.375

Flying mammals

Bats are the only mammals capable of true flight. They belong to the order Chiroptera, which means hand-wing. Instead of front legs, bats have wings made of skin which are supported by the bones of the arms and hand.

There are about 977 species of bat. Flying foxes are among the largest. These bats are 45cm long, have wings that span 1.7m and weigh up to 1.6kg. The Kitti's hog-nosed bat, which lives in Thailand, is the smallest. It weighs 2g (less than a table tennis ball) and is only 2.9cm long, making it the smallest of all mammals.

Bats sleep during the day and wake up at night when they go in search of food. Most bats are insect-eaters – a little brown bat can catch 1,200 insects an hour – but others eat fruit or nectar from plants. Some larger species catch frogs, birds and fish.

Many bats live in large groups called colonies. Bracken Cave in Texas contains the world's largest bat colony, about 20 million animals. This is one of the densest populations of any mammal and there can be as many as 5,000 newborn babies per square metre. These bats eat 1,000 tonnes of insects every night.

Bat bombs!

During World War II American scientists devised a plan to attach tiny fire bombs to bats and release them in Japanese cities. The bat bomb project, codenamed Project X-Ray, was tested in caves in Texas, New Mexico and California but never carried out.

Flying fox

www.bsc-eoc.org/avibase/avibase.jsp

Types of insect

The body of most insects is made up of three parts – head, thorax and abdomen. Insects have three pairs of legs and many have two pairs of wings. Listed here are all the main groups, or orders, of insects. Numbers include only the species that we know about and have been named. There may be many thousands more still to be discovered. Total numbers of insects are colossal. Together, all the insects in the world would weigh at least 12 times as much as all the people in the world and at least three times more than all other living animals put together.

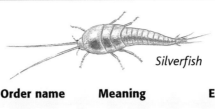

True fly

Silverfish

Earwig

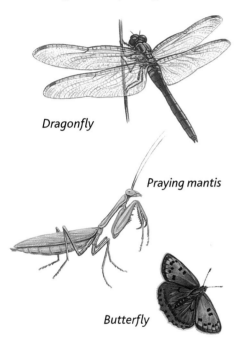

Dragonfly

Praying mantis

Butterfly

Order name	Meaning	Examples	Approx number of known species
Coleoptera	Hard wings	beetles	370,000
Hymenoptera	Membrane wings	ants, bees, wasps	198,000
Lepidoptera	Scaly wings	butterflies, moths	165,000
Diptera	Two-wings	midges, mosquitoes, true flies	122,000
Hemiptera	Half wings	aphids, cicadas	82,000
Orthoptera	Straight wings	crickets, locusts, grasshoppers	20,000
Trichoptera	Hairy wings	caddisflies	8,000
Collembola	Sticky peg	springtails	6,500
Phthiraptera	Louse wings	biting and sucking lice	6,000
Odonata	Toothed flies	dragonflies	5,500
Thysanoptera	Fringed wings	thrips	5,000
Neuroptera	Net-veined wings	ant-lions, lacewings	4,000
Blattodea	Insect avoiding light	cockroaches	4,000
Pscoptera	Milled wings	hook and bark lice	3,500
Isoptera	Equal wings	termites	2,750
Ephemeroptera	Living for a day	mayflies	2,500
Phasmatodea	Like a ghost	leaf insects, stick insects	2,500
Mantodea	Like a prophet	mantids	2,000
Plecoptera	Wickerwork wing	stoneflies	2,000
Siphonaptera	Tube without wings	fleas	2,000
Dermaptera	Leathery wings	earwigs	1,900
Mecoptera	Long wings	hanging flies, scorpion flies	550
Thysanura	Fringed tail	silverfish	370
Archaeognatha	Ancient jaw	bristletails	350
Embioptera	Lively wings	web-spinners	300
Megaloptera	Large wings	alderflies, Dobson flies	250
Raphidioptera	Embroidered wings	snakeflies	150
Zoraptera	Pure + wingless	angel insects	30
Grylloblattodea	Cricket cockroach	rock crawlers	25

Funnel-web spider

 ## Spiders

Spiders are not insects. They belong to a separate group called arachnids, which also includes scorpions. A spider's body is divided into two parts linked by a narrow waist. It has four pairs of legs tipped with claws, but no spiders have wings. All spiders can make silk but not all spin webs.

There are at least 35,000 species of spider. Most are harmless but a few can be deadly. The banana spider of Central and South America produces 6mg of venom, enough to kill six adults. Other deadly spiders are the funnel-web, which lives in Australia, and the wolf spider of Central and South America. The black widow and various tarantulas are also very dangerous and can kill.

Biggest spider
The goliath bird-eating spider, which lives in South American rainforests, has legs up to 25cm long.

Smallest spider
A species called *Patu marplesi* from Western Samoa is the smallest known spider. It measures only 0.46mm long.

Amazing insects

Most abundant

- Insects called springtails live in topsoil all over the world. There are probably as many as 600 million per hectare. Together they weigh more than the entire human race.

- There can be up to five billion aphids per hectare in a swarm.

- A swarm of desert locusts may contain 50 billion insects. One seen in 1889 was reckoned to have 250 billion locusts weighing a total of half a million tonnes.

Longest
Stick insects have the longest bodies. Some measure up to 51cm long, including their legs.

Heaviest
Goliath beetles (below) can be 11cm long and weigh 100g.

Largest wingspan
The wings of the female Queen Alexandra birdwing butterfly of Papua New Guinea measure 28cm across.

Smallest
The wings of battledore wing fairy flies, a kind of parasitic wasp, measure only 0.21mm.

Longest-lived
Jewel beetle larvae, or young, may live inside timber for 30 years or more before becoming adult insects.

Shortest-lived
Male houseflies live about 17 days and females about 29 days. Mayflies may live for a single day as adults, but for two or three years as larvae.

Noisiest
Colonies of hundreds of male cicadas make loud noises to attract females. These sounds are as noisy as heavy traffic.

Long-distance fliers
Butterflies have been tracked travelling 4,828km.

Fastest
Dragonflies can fly at speeds of 28.7–32km/h.

Bee facts

There are about 20,000 different types of bee. The best known is probably the honeybee, but not all bees live in colonies like the honeybee. Many live alone and build their own nests.

Honeybee

- Wallace's giant bees are the world's largest at up to 4cm long. They were first found in Indonesia in1858 but were then thought to have become extinct. In 1981 the bees were rediscovered.

- The smallest bee is the Brazilian *Trigona duckei* at 2–5mm long.

- Honeybees are the only insects that make food which humans eat. Bees make honey to feed the inhabitants of their hives during winter. The honey they do not eat is harvested by beekeepers. Bees also make beeswax which is used for making candles and furniture polish.

- One beehive may contain 50,000 worker bees – these are the bees which collect nectar from flowers to make honey.

- Honeybees visit up to five million flowers to make one kilo of honey. They fly a total distance equal to flying four times round the Earth.

- Queen bees can lay two or three thousand eggs a day – as many as 200,000 eggs a year. They may live as long as five years, so can produce a million eggs.

- Honeybees' wings beat 11,400 times a minute. These wing movements make the bees' familiar buzz.

- 1.3 million tonnes of honey are produced worldwide every year. China is the main producer with 276,000 tonnes, followed by the USA with 82,000.

- Some people are allergic to bee stings, which can even be fatal. In 1962 in Rhodesia, Johanne Relleke was stung 2,243 times by wild bees, but survived!

Eating insects

In many countries insects are a popular food. Insect dishes include omelette made from silkworms and fried honeybees in China, fried locusts in Thailand and red ant chutney in India. Many of us may eat insects without realizing it – the red food colouring called cochineal is made from the dried bodies of a Mexican cactus-eating scale insect.

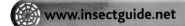 www.insectguide.net

Reptiles

A reptile is a vertebrate animal with a body covered in tough scales. Most reptiles live on land, but turtles and some kinds of snake live in water. Crocodiles and their relatives spend time on land and in water. There are more than 8,000 species of reptiles divided into the following groups.

Order	Approx number of species
Lizards	4,765
Snakes	2,978
Turtles and tortoises	307
Amphisbaenians (worm lizards)	165
Crocodiles, alligators, caimans	23
Tuataras	2

Snake facts

Largest snakes
Many people believe that the South American anaconda is the longest snake. There are reports of anacondas up to 36.5m long, but this has never been proved. US President Theodore Roosevelt once offered $5,000 to anyone who could produce the skin or vertebrae of an anaconda of more than 9m long. The US Wildlife Conservation Society increased this offer to $50,000, but the prize has never been claimed. The reticulated or royal python is probably the longest snake at up to 10.7m, but the anaconda may be the heaviest at up to 230kg.

Smallest snake
The thread snake is rarely longer than 108mm. The spotted dwarf adder is the smallest venomous snake at 22.8cm long.

Deadliest snakes
The coastal taipan of Australia injects the most venom per bite with 120mg. Since just 1mg is enough to kill a person, the venom from a single bite could kill 120 people. The common krait's venom is even more dangerous – only 0.5mg can be fatal.

The fast-moving black mamba of central and southern Africa kills 90 to 100 per cent of the people it bites. Up to 3,000 people a year die from snakebites in India and 1,000 in Sri Lanka, where Russell's viper is the most likely cause. This snake once killed as many as 50,000 people a year, but there have been fewer deaths since antivenin (the antidote to snake venom) became more widely available.

Reticulated python

Alligators and crocodiles

There are 23 species in the crocodile family, including alligators, caimans and gavials. All are large reptiles with long bodies and short legs. Most alligators and caimans have wide U-shaped snouts, but crocodiles have narrower V-shaped snouts. The gavial has very long slender jaws – just right for catching fish.

In alligators and caimans the teeth of the lower jaw fit into pits in the upper jaw and cannot be seen when the mouth is closed. In crocodiles the fourth tooth on each side of the lower jaw fits into a notch on the upper jaw, so they are always visible. Crocodiles are generally bigger and more aggressive than alligators.

Name	Average length (m)
Alligators	
American alligator (southern USA)	4–4.5
Chinese alligator (China)	2
Spectacled caiman (South America)	2–2.5
Broad-snouted caiman (South America)	2
Yacaré caiman (South America)	2.5–3
Black caiman (South America)	4–6
Cuvier's dwarf caiman (South America)	1.5–1.6
Schneider's or Smooth-fronted caiman (South America)	1.7–2.3
Crocodiles	
American crocodile (southern USA, Mexico, Central and South America)	5
Slender-snouted crocodile (West Africa)	2.5
Orinoco crocodile (northern South America)	6
Australian freshwater crocodile (Australia)	2.5–3
Philippine crocodile (Philippines)	3
Morelet's crocodile (Central America)	3
Nile crocodile (Africa)	5
New Guinea crocodile (New Guinea)	3.5
Mugger or Marsh crocodile (India, Sri Lanka)	4–5
Estuarine or Saltwater crocodile (Southeast Asia, Australia)	6–7
Cuban crocodile (Cuba)	3.5
Siamese crocodile (Southeast Asia, very rare)	3–4
African dwarf crocodile (Central and West Africa)	1.9
False gharial or gavial (Southeast Asia)	5
Gavials	
Indian gavial or gharial (India, Pakistan, Bangladesh, Nepal)	5–6

ONE AND ONLY
The flowerpot blindsnake is the only snake to reproduce without being fertilized by a male's sperm – a process called parthenogenesis. The snake lays up to seven eggs and produces only females. There are no males of this species. The flowerpot blindsnake is also one of the most common snakes. Its habit of hiding in flowerpots has led to it being spread all around the world in the soil of potted plants.

Fisherman holding a goliath frog

Turtles and tortoises

These reptiles all have a hard shell that protects the body. There are about 250 species, some of which live in the sea, others in freshwater and the rest on land.

Biggest
- Fossils of the extinct turtle *Stupendemys geographicus* have been found with shells up to 3m long. They would probably have weighed more than 2,040kg.

- The largest living turtle is the leatherback. A male washed up on the coast of Wales in 1988 holds the record – he was 291cm long and weighed 916kg. The turtle probably died from swallowing a piece of plastic.

- The Aldabra giant tortoise, which lives on an island in the Seychelles, weighs up to 304kg and is the largest land-living tortoise. It is also one of the longest-lived land creatures, at more than 150 years, and one of the slowest tortoises. It moves at an average speed of 0.27km/h.

Smallest
The smallest turtle or tortoise is the common musk turtle which is 7.62cm long and weighs 227g.

Amphibians

An amphibian is a vertebrate animal that spends at least some of its life in water. Its skin is not scaly. There are about 5,578 species of amphibian, divided into the following groups.

Order	Approx number of species
Frogs and toads	4,896
Newts and salamanders	517
Caecilians (legless amphibians)	165

Salamander

Caecilian

Fantastic frogs and toads

Largest frogs and toads
- The world's largest known frog is the goliath frog, which lives in central Africa. It measures up to 87.63cm long and weighs as much as 3.66kg.

- The largest tree frog is *Hyla vasta*, which lives only on the island of Hispaniola. It is more than 12cm long and has huge round finger and toe disks which grip like superglue.

- The world's largest toad is the South American marine toad. Giants with a body length of over 23cm and weighing 1.2kg have been found. This toad has been introduced to all the places in the world where sugar is grown in order to eat crop-destroying sugar beetles. Unfortunately the toads also kill the local amphibians.

Smallest frog
The smallest frog and the world's smallest amphibian is the Cuban arrow-poison frog, which measures only 8.5–13mm.

Egg laying
The marine toad lays 35,000 eggs a year, but the Cuban arrow-poison frog lays only one egg.

Highest and lowest homes
The green toad has been seen at 8,000m in the Himalayas and toads have been discovered more than 3,048m down a coal mine.

Most poisonous
The arrow-poison frogs of Central and South America are the most deadly. The world's most poisonous amphibian is the golden arrow-poison frog of Western Colombia. One adult contains enough highly toxic poison in its skin to kill 1,000 people.

Smelliest
The smelliest frog is the Venezuela skunk frog, which was discovered in 1991. It warns off its enemies by releasing a bad-smelling chemical identical to the one produced by skunks.

Longest jumps
- On 21 May 1977, a female sharp-nosed frog leaped 10.2m in three consecutive jumps at a frog derby at Larula Natal Spa, Paulpietersburg in South Africa.

- The cricket frog is only 3.5cm and can jump 36 times its own length. If an adult human jumped 36 times his own length, the long-jump record could stand at 65.8m!

Life on man

As many as 100 trillion viruses and bacteria live on each of us. However much we wash, there are always ten million or so bacteria on every square centimetre of our skin.

There are also many tiny creatures called parasites, which can live inside or on the human body, feeding on our blood. Parasites such as roundworms, hookworms, flukes and tapeworms – which can grow as long as 9.75m – can live inside our bodies. They may cause such diseases as elephantiasis, in which the patient's limbs swell to gigantic sizes. Head lice live on human heads and feed on blood. The lice lay little white eggs, called nits, which cling to individual hairs.

Follicle mites are in everyone's hair, even among our eyelashes. They were first described by 19th-century scientist Richard Owen (the man who first named dinosaurs), but are so tiny that few people have ever seen them or are even aware that they are there.

Some of the tiny creatures that feed on us may also transmit diseases. Tsetse flies carry African sleeping sickness. Mosquitoes can infect humans with diseases such as malaria, dengue fever and yellow fever when they bite. Malaria has killed more people in human history than any other disease.

Ticks can carry diseases such as encephalitis and Lyme disease. Mites and chiggers (baby mites) cause skin diseases and may transmit typhus. Fleas are perhaps the most dangerous creatures of all – they were the carriers of the deadly bubonic plague that killed millions of people in medieval times.

The first teddy bear

Teddy bears are named after US President Theodore (Teddy) Roosevelt. The story began when the president refused to shoot a young bear while on a hunting trip. This incident appeared in a cartoon by Clifford K. Berryman, published in the *Washington Post* on 16 November 1902. Soon after, Morris Michtom, a New York shopkeeper, started making stuffed bears and advertising them as "Teddy's Bears" with Roosevelt's permission.

At about the same time, Margarete Steiff, a German toymaker, started making her first toy bears and exported them to the USA to meet the demand created by Teddy's Bears. In 1903 Steiff's factory produced 12,000 bears. By 1907, the figure had risen to 974,000. Steiff teddy bears, with a distinctive tag on their ear, are still made and are sold internationally. Early examples are prized by collectors.

 ## Top farm animals

These are the most popular farm animals worldwide. They are kept for their meat, eggs and milk. The total number of these types of animal alone is three times that of the world's human population.

Animal	World stocks (2004)
Chickens	16,194,925,000
Cattle	1,334,501,290
Sheep	1,038,765,370
Ducks	1,019,479,000
Pigs	951,771,892
Goats	780,099,948

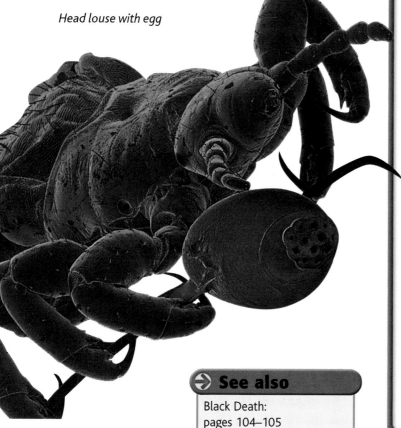

Head louse with egg

Counting sheep

There are about 1,034,007,820 sheep in the world – an average of one sheep for every six people. In some countries there are twice as many sheep as humans.

Country	No of sheep	No of people	Sheep per person
Falkland Islands	690,000	2,379	290
New Zealand	40,065,000	4,076,140	9
Australia	94,500,000	20,264,082	4
Mongolia	12,000,000	2,832,224	4
Uruguay	9,780,000	3,431,932	2
Mauritania	8,700,000	3,177,388	2

➔ See also

Black Death:
pages 104–105

Humans and animals

Since ancient times humans have used many types of animals for a vast range of purposes.

Meat, milk and honey
Humans have always hunted and eaten wild animals. Milk from such animals as cows, goats, sheep, camels, buffalo, reindeer, llamas and yaks is drunk, used in cooking and made into butter and cheese. The eggs from birds such as hens, ducks, geese and quail are another important food. Honey has long been taken from the hives of wild bees, and now from domesticated bees kept in artificial hives.

Wool, fur and skin
Wool is shorn from live sheep, which then regrow their coats. The fur and leather of many other animals can be taken only after the animal has been killed. Cattle, goats, rabbits, mink, seals, wolves, foxes, kangaroos, big cats such as leopards, and alligators and snakes are among the many animals that have been used in this way. There are some very special uses for animal skin: for example, medieval manuscripts were written on vellum, made from calfskin.

Silk
Silk comes from the silkworm, the caterpillar of the silkmoth. Silkworms eat a tonne of mulberry leaves to make 5kg of silk.

Beasts of burden and transport
Strong animals such as horses, donkeys, camels, reindeer and buffalo are used to pull agricultural equipment and carts, and to carry people. Elephants drag heavy logs, pit ponies once drew trucks in coal mines, and dogs – usually huskies – pull sledges.

Performers
Animals such as horses, dogs, elephants, lions, tigers, bears, seals, chimpanzees and monkeys have traditionally been trained to perform in circuses. They have not always been treated well and many countries have now banned animal circus acts. Snakes are used by snake charmers; dolphins, killer whales and other marine mammals perform in dolphinariums; and many different animal actors appear in films and advertisements.

Security
Guard dogs (and even guard geese), police dogs and sniffer dogs (to detect drugs) are widely used. Search and rescue dogs help to find missing people, lost walkers and climbers, and earthquake victims.

Helpers
Sheepdogs, hunting hounds, retrievers and guide dogs for the blind are among the best known, but other animals, such as monkeys, can be trained to aid the disabled. Less well-known human helpers include pigs used to find truffles (edible fungi) and cats kept by the British Post Office to prevent mice from eating the mail! Animals kept as pets also provide millions of people with companionship.

Military
The warhorse is one of the most familiar of all military animals, but elephants have also been successfully used in battles. Many military organizations use dogs, goats and other animals as regimental mascots. Message-carrying dogs and carrier pigeons have been used by armies. During the Iraq war in 2004 dolphins were trained to find mines.

Indian elephant carrying a log at a logging camp.

Science
Dogs, monkeys and other animals were used in the early tests on space vehicles. Some drugs and other products are tested on animals before they are used on humans, although some people are opposed to this practice.

Sport
Racing animals include horses, camels, sled dogs, greyhounds, ostriches and pigeons. Bullfighting, rodeos and polo are other sports that involve animals.

 ### Maneater
A tigress known as the Champawat maneater, after the part of India in which she lived, killed a record 436 people over five years. She was shot in 1907 by British big-game hunter Colonel Jim Corbett (1875–1955).

Countries with most pets

These totals include cats, dogs, birds, fish, small mammals (hamsters, guinea pigs, etc) and reptiles.

Country	Pets	Country	Pets	Country	Pets
USA	366,370,000	Italy	63,100,000	Canada	22,558,000
China	271,774,000	France	56,000,000	Turkey	22,547,000
Japan	75,372,000	Russia	50,790,000	Poland	21,315,000
Germany	72,600,000	UK	46,590,000	Spain	20,519,000
Brazil	67,005,000	Australia	26,625,000	Ukraine	17,635,000

Top UK pets

Almost 45 per cent of households in the UK own a pet, ranging from dogs, cats and rabbits to more exotic snakes and spiders.

Pet	Number owned
Goldfish	14,700,000
Tropical fish	9,300,000
Cat	7,700,000
Dog	5,800,000
Reptile	1,890,000
Rabbit	1,100,000
Bird*	1,060,000
Hamster	860,000
Budgerigar	750,000
Guinea pig	730,000
Canary	260,000

* other than budgerigars and canaries

Ancient Egyptian statue of a cat

Cat-alogue

First known named cat
The first cat recorded as having a name was called Nedjem, meaning star. It lived in the reign of Egyptian Pharaoh Thutmose III (1479–1425 BC).

Heaviest
Himmy, owned by Thomas Vyse of Queensland, Australia, weighed 21.3kg. He had a 38.1cm neck and an 84cm waist – similar to that of an adult human! He died in 1986 at the age of ten.

Smallest
Tinker Toy, a male Blue Point Himalayan owned by Katrina and Scott Forbes of Illinois, USA, is 7cm tall, 19cm long and weighs 625g.

Biggest breed
Maine Coons are a North American breed of muscular, big-boned cats. Males often reach 6–8kg in weight.

Oldest
There are several contenders for this title. Most reliable is French-born Grandpa Rex's Allen, a Sphynx cat owned by Jake Perry of Austin, Texas, USA. The cat died in 1998 at the age of 34.

Largest litter
In 1970 Tarawood Antigone, a female Burmese owned by Valerie Gane of Kingham, Oxfordshire, gave birth to 19 kittens. Fifteen survived.

Best mouser
Towser, a female tortoiseshell owned by Glenturret Distillery, Tayside, caught an estimated total of 28,899 mice during her time there. She died in 1987, aged 24.

Famous cat-lovers

Winston Churchill and Margate
A black kitten turned up at 10 Downing Street on 10 October 1953 and was adopted by Churchill. It was named Margate to commemorate an important speech Churchill was to make in the town that day. Later cat occupants of Number 10 have included Harold Wilson's Siamese cat Nemo and Margaret Thatcher's Wilberforce. Humphrey, a stray cat, moved in during Mrs Thatcher's residence and stayed on with John Major and then Tony Blair.

Charles Dickens and Williamina
Williamina was called William until she gave birth to a litter of kittens. One of these, known as The Master's Cat, used to put out Dickens' candle with its paw.

Domenico Scarlatti and Pulcinella
The Italian composer's cat used to jump on to his harpsichord keyboard and stroll along the keys. This inspired Scarlatti to compose *The Cat's Fugue*.

Abraham Lincoln and Tabby
Tabby was one of the first White House cats. More recent examples include J.F. Kennedy's Tom Kitten, Ronald Reagan's Cleo and Sara, and Bill Clinton's Socks.

Edward Lear and Foss
Foss was the subject of a number of Lear's nonsense poems and comic drawings (below). When Foss died in 1887, Lear said he was 31 years old.

One of Edward Lear's cat cartoons

Most cats

Country	Cats
USA	76,430,000
China	53,100,000
Russia	12,700,000
Brazil	12,466,000
France	9,600,000
Italy	9,400,000
UK	7,700,000
Ukraine	7,350,000
Japan	7,300,000
Germany	7,000,000
Canada	6,811,000
Poland	5,465,000
Vietnam	4,331,000
India	3,193,000
Spain	3,191,000

Racing greyhounds

Dog-alogue

Largest dog
In 1989 Aicama Zorba of La-Susa, an Old English mastiff owned by Chris Eraclides of London, weighed 155.58kg and measured 2.5m from nose to tail.

Smallest dog
A Yorkshire terrier owned by Arthur Marples of Blackburn in the 1940s was just 6.3cm tall and weighed 113g.

The fastest dogs

Breed	Maximum recorded speed km/h
Greyhound	67.14
Saluki	64+
Ibizan hound	60.8–64
Whippet	54.42
Sloughi	57.6

Oldest dog
Bluey, an Australian cattle-dog owned by Les Hall of Victoria, Australia, died in 1938 at the age of 29 years 5 months.

Largest litter
In 1944, Lena, an American foxhound, produced 23 puppies, all of which survived. Other dogs have equalled this record, but not all the pups have survived.

Longest jump
Bang, a greyhound, jumped 9.14m while chasing a hare at Brecon Lodge in Gloucestershire.

Greatest climber
Tschingel, a female beagle, climbed more than 50 mountains in the Alps, including the 4,165m Jungfrau and the 3,974m Eiger.

Most dogs

Country	Dogs
USA	61,080,000
Brazil	30,051,000
China	22,908,000
Japan	9,650,000
Russia	9,600,000
South Africa	9,100,000
France	8,150,000
Italy	7,600,000
Poland	7,520,000
Thailand	6,900,000
Mexico	6,855,000
Vietnam	6,579,000
UK	5,800,000
Ukraine	5,425,000
India	5,260,000

Famous dog-lovers

Francis Barraud and Nipper
British artist Francis Barraud sold a painting called *His Master's Voice* to the Gramophone Company. It showed his dog Nipper listening to a gramophone. The company adopted it as its trademark and later changed its company name to His Master's Voice or HMV.

J.M. Barrie and Luath
Luath, a Newfoundland dog, was the model for Nana in Barrie's book *Peter Pan*.

Elizabeth Barrett Browning and Flush
The English poet's cocker spaniel became famous from Virginia Woolf's book *Flush: A Biography* (1933), which looks at the world from the dog's point of view.

George Bush and Millie
The US President's springer spaniel Millie had a bestselling "autobiography" *Millie's Book*, written by First Lady Barbara Bush.

John Gray and Greyfriars Bobby
Bobby was a Skye terrier who faithfully guarded his master's grave at Greyfriars, Edinburgh, for 14 years from 1858. The true story of the devoted dog has been the subject of books and films.

Charles Schulz and Spike
American cartoonist Charles Schulz based his comic character Snoopy on his family's Basset hound Spike. In later strips a dog called Spike appears as Snoopy's brother.

Most intelligent dogs

American psychology professor and pet trainer Stanley Coren ranked 133 breeds of dogs for intelligence. He studied their responses to a range of IQ tests, as well as the opinions of judges in dog obedience tests. The five top breeds were the border collie (below), poodle, German shepherd (Alsatian), golden retriever and Doberman pinscher.

Homeward bound
There are amazing stories of cats and dogs that travel great distances home after getting separated from their owners. Bobbie, a collie dog, made one of the longest journeys. He was lost on a family holiday in Indiana, USA on 15 August 1923. Six months later, he arrived home in Silverton, Oregon, 4,828km away. He became known as Silverton Bobbie, The Wonder Dog of Oregon.

Dinosaur fact file

Dinosaurs first appeared about 230 million years ago during the Triassic period. These amazing reptiles then dominated life on Earth until they became extinct 65 million years ago. The first dinosaurs to be described were *Megalosaurus* (great lizard) by William Buckland in 1824 and *Iguanodon* (iguana tooth) by Gideon Mantell in 1825. They were named before the word "dinosaur" had been invented. The name *dinosauria* (terrible lizards) was suggested by British scientist Richard Owen in July 1841. Since then 700 different species have been identified. Not all dinosaurs were enormous – some measured less than 60cm long, about the size of a chicken.

Biggest dinosaurs

Dinosaur	Weight (kg)	Length (m)
Seismosaurus	99,792	45.7
Argentinasaurus	90,720	36.6
Supersaurus	54,432	36.6
Ultrasaurus	63,504	30.5
Brachiosaurus	54,432	30.5

Sizes of dinosaurs are mostly estimates worked out from the sizes of leg and other bones. The largest known complete skeleton is of a *Brachiosaurus* dinosaur and is 22.3m long. The skeleton is in the Humboldt Museum, Berlin, Germany.

- The dinosaurs listed above were all herbivores. *Tyrannosaurus rex*, one of the largest carnivorous dinosaurs, measured up to 15m long and weighed 60,000kg or more. Its huge jaws were packed with 60 teeth, the biggest of which were a terrifying 23cm long!

- The longest single dinosaur bone yet discovered is the 2.45m shoulder blade of *Ultrasaurus*.

- The largest flying prehistoric creatures were pterosaurs. The wings of the biggest pterosaur, *Quetzalcoatlus*, measured 10.96m from tip to tip.

- The largest known dinosaur egg belonged to *Hypselosaurus*. The 100 million-year-old egg measures 30cm by 25.5cm and is about three times the volume of an ostrich egg.

- The fastest dinosaur, *Ornithomimus*, could probably run at a speed of up to 70km/h. The ostrich runs at a similar speed today.

- Dinosaurs have been in space! Fragments of bone and an eggshell of *Maiasaura peeblesorum* were taken into space by astronaut Loren Acton in 1985. A *Coelophysis* skull was taken into space by astronaut Bonnie Dunbar in 1998.

Tyrannosaurus rex

Coelacanth: a living fossil

Palaeontologists discovered a large fish known as the coelacanth from fossil remains. They thought it had become extinct, along with the dinosaurs, about 65 million years ago. But on 22 December 1938 one was caught alive in the fishing net of a trawler off East London in South Africa.

This strange-looking creature, about 1.7m long, snapped at the hand of Captain Henrik Goosen, but died soon afterwards. Captain Goosen realized that he had found something unusual so took the fish to a local museum where scientists identified it as a "living fossil". Since then, more than 200 coelacanths, some measuring up to 1.9m long, have been caught, mostly off the Comoros islands. They live in deep sea conditions, and none have survived after capture, although they have been seen alive by scientists in mini-submarines.

Animals in danger

In the past 500 years, hundreds of species of animals have become extinct – they have disappeared from Earth for ever. In many cases this is because the animals have been hunted by humans, or the areas where they lived have been destroyed. Some creatures become extinct in the wild but have survived in artificial settings, such as zoos. If they can be successfully bred, they may be taken back to the wild. Przewalski's horse, for example, became extinct in the wild but has since been bred in captivity. Now there are herds of these wild horses in their old home around the Gobi Desert. Other species are defined as "threatened", or in danger of becoming extinct. According to the degree of threat they may be considered "critically endangered", "endangered" or "vulnerable".

Species	Total known	Total threatened
Birds	9,932	1,192
Mammals	4,814	1,137
Molluscs	70,000	939
Fish	28,100	742
Insects	1,000,000	557
Crustaceans	40,000	409
Reptiles	8,240	293
Amphibians	5,578	157
Others	130,200	27

The end of the tiger?

Some very familiar animals are under threat of extinction. They include the gorilla, African and Asian elephants, the black rhino, the giant panda, and many species of whale, such as the blue, right and fin whale.

Tigers are also in serious danger. A century ago there were more than 100,000 tigers in the wild. Of the eight known subspecies of tiger, three – the Bali, Caspian and Javan – are already extinct. There are now fewer than 7,500 tigers left in the wild because their habitats have been destroyed and they have been illegally hunted for their bones and other parts used in traditional Chinese medicines. Numbers of the Amur or Siberian, the largest tiger, have fallen to 360–406 in the wild, with fewer than 490 in wildlife parks and zoos. The Sumatran tiger is down to about 400, with 210 in captivity. The Bengal, including the rare white tiger, numbers 3,159–4,715, with 333 in zoos, and there are only 1,227–1,785 of the Indochinese, with 60 in zoos. Rarest of all is the South China tiger. Its population is down to only 20–30 in the wild and 47 in zoos.

Last seen alive

Sabre-toothed tiger	12,000 years ago
Woolly mammoth	10,000 years ago
Moa	1,000 years ago
Aurochs (giant wild ox)	1627
Aepyornis (elephant bird)	1649
Dodo	1681
Steller's sea cow	1768
Great auk	1844
Tarpan (wild horse)	1851
Labrador duck	1875
Quagga (zebra-like creature)	1883
Pilori muskrat	1902
Badlands bighorn sheep	1905
Japanese grey wolf	1905
Passenger pigeon	1914
Carolina parakeet	1918
California grizzly bear	1922
Schomburgk's deer	1938
Arabian ostrich	1941
Euler's flycatcher	1955
Eskimo curlew	1963
Guam flying fox	1968
Pyrenean ibex	2000

Dodo

Siberian tiger

Found and lost: the Stephen's Island wren

David Lyall was a lighthouse keeper on Stephen's Island, a tiny island off New Zealand. One day in 1894 his cat brought in a dead bird. Mr Lyall didn't recognize the species, so he sent it to England to the famous ornithologist Lord Walter Rothschild. He identified it as an entirely new species, probably the only flightless songbird in the world. He named it in honour of Lyall as *Traversia lyalli*, or the Stephen's Island wren. But within a matter of weeks, the discovery was followed by the total annihilation of the species. The cat slaughtered all the rest of the wrens, making this the shortest recorded interval between discovery and extinction.

 See also

Environmental concerns: pages 70–71

Pollution fact file

Pollution happens when unwanted gases and other materials escape into the environment. It causes waste, financial losses, and damage to human, animal and plant health. Huge growth in industry and in the world's population in the last 100 years have led to more and more industrial processes and pollution. Deliberate dumping and accidents such as oil spillages have seriously affected the Earth's air, land and water.

Air pollution

Some gases and particles in the air may be dangerous to health if breathed in. Most air pollution comes from burning fossil fuels (coal, oil and gas) and solid waste, or from gases released into the air by different processes. One of the worst is carbon monoxide from vehicle exhausts. It is poisonous to humans because it prevents the absorption of oxygen. Another is nitrogen oxide, which reacts with sunlight to produce dense smog (a combination of smoke and fog). Tobacco smoke also damages health – even breathing in other people's smoke is harmful.

Acid rain

Acid rain was first identified in the 19th century. It is caused when nitrogen oxide, sulphur dioxide and other chemicals from volcanic eruptions and human sources combine with rain and fall as acid on land or into rivers and lakes. The strength of acidity in rain varies, but at its worst it can damage buildings, kill fish and harm trees and other plants.

Global warming

Global warming and the greenhouse effect were first described in 1896 by Swedish chemist Svante Arrhenius. Greenhouse gases in the Earth's atmosphere, such as carbon dioxide, nitrous oxide, water vapour and methane, help to trap heat and stop too much of it escaping into space. Without these gases, the Earth would not be warm enough for us to live on.

The problem is that more and more greenhouse gases are being released into the atmosphere from human activities, and too much heat is being trapped. The Earth became 0.5°C warmer during the 20th century and a further rise of even a couple of degrees will damage its natural balance. Polar icecaps will melt, sea levels will rise and many areas will be flooded. Changing climates will also affect plants and animals, which might not be able to adapt quickly enough to new conditions.

Land pollution

Soil can be damaged by the dumping of chemicals, toxic (poisonous), radioactive and other waste as well as the overuse of pesticides and fertilizers. Polluted land is unsafe for people or animals to live on and for growing food plants.

Water pollution

Increasing quantities of heavy metals such as mercury and lead, chemicals, sewage and oil spills are polluting lakes, rivers and oceans. Water in some places is unsafe to drink or even bathe in as a result, and animals are harmed or killed.

Reversing pollution

Many countries have become much more aware of pollution and the damage it can cause and are taking action to reduce it – for example, laws have been passed in Britain and other countries to reduce lead in petrol and paint. Clean air laws have reduced pollution in cities such as London, and scientists are looking at ways of making vehicles that do not burn fossil fuels. People and businesses are heavily fined for dumping waste and chemicals. However, pollution is still a huge problem and there is a lot more still to be done before it is solved.

Rush hour traffic queues in Paris, France

Worst oil tanker spills

About two million tonnes of oil are spilled into the sea every year from oil tankers, mostly during collisions or other accidents. Most spills are small (7 tonnes or less), but some are much more serious. When huge quantities of oil are discharged into the sea and washed up on shorelines they harm many birds and other creatures. The 1989 grounding of the *Exxon Valdez* in Prince William Sound, Alaska, caused the USA's worst oil spill. The amount spilled was much smaller in quantity than the spills listed (35,000 tonnes), but thousands of birds, fish, sea otters, seals and killer whales were killed.

Tanker/location	Year	Approx spillage (tonnes)
Atlantic Empress and *Aegean Captain*, off Tobago	1979	287,000
ABT Summer, off Angola	1991	260,000
Castillio de Bellver, off Saldanha Bay, South Africa	1983	252,000
Olympic Bravery, off Ushant, France	1976	250,000
Amoco Cadiz, off Finistère, France	1978	223,000

Workers cleaning up an oil spill in the Pacific

Destroying forests

Forests are often destroyed to obtain timber or to clear land so it can be used as pasture for animals, growing crops or other purposes. About 90,000sq km of forest is cut down every year worldwide. This is about the same area as a country the size of Portugal. Cutting down forests increases the amount of carbon dioxide in the atmosphere, which can affect climate and destroy the homes of many animals and plants.

Country	Average annual forest loss 1990-2000 (sq km)
Brazil	22,260
Indonesia	13,120
Sudan	9,590
Zambia	8,510
Mexico	6,310

Loggers cutting down rainforest in Borneo

Worst polluters

Carbon dioxide (CO_2) pollution enters the atmosphere from three main sources – burning fossil fuel (coal and oil), cement manufacturing and gas burning. These figures show the total amounts produced by some of the leading industrial countries in the 200 years from 1800 to 2000. CO_2 is produced naturally by animals, forest fires and other sources. But natural production has been overtaken by the amount produced by transport, manufacturing and other human activities. More carbon dioxide in the atmosphere increases the amount of heat absorbed, and this leads to global warming (see Pollution fact file).

Country	CO_2 emissions 1800–2000 (tonnes of carbon)
USA	301,279,000,000
Russia	86,705,000,000
Germany	75,606,000,000
China	72,615,000,000
UK	68,803,000,000
Japan	36,577,000,000
France	30,997,000,000
World total	**1,017,350,000,000**

See also

The world's energy sources: page 195

www.environment-agency.gov.uk

How much water?

People worldwide use 3,414,000,000,000,000 (3,414 trillion) litres of water every year. On average every person in the world uses 650,000 litres a year, or 1,781 litres a day. Of this total, 9 per cent (160 litres) a day is used in homes, 20 per cent (356 litres) by industry and 71 per cent (1,265 litres) by agriculture. In the UK we use 204,000 litres per head a year – 11,790,000,000,000 litres in total.

Countries that use the most water

Country	Litres per head per year	Total litres per year
USA	1,834,000	467,340,000,000,000
China	439,000	525,489,000,000,000
India	592,000	500,000,000,000,000
Pakistan	1,382,000	155,600,000,000,000

Household water usage

Activity	Litres
Brushing teeth (tap off)	2.5
Brushing teeth (tap on)	5
Toilet flush	5–20
Shower (per minute)	22
Washing machine	120
Bath (full)	170
Washing car	200
Watering garden (1 hour)	600–1,500

A brief history of rubbish

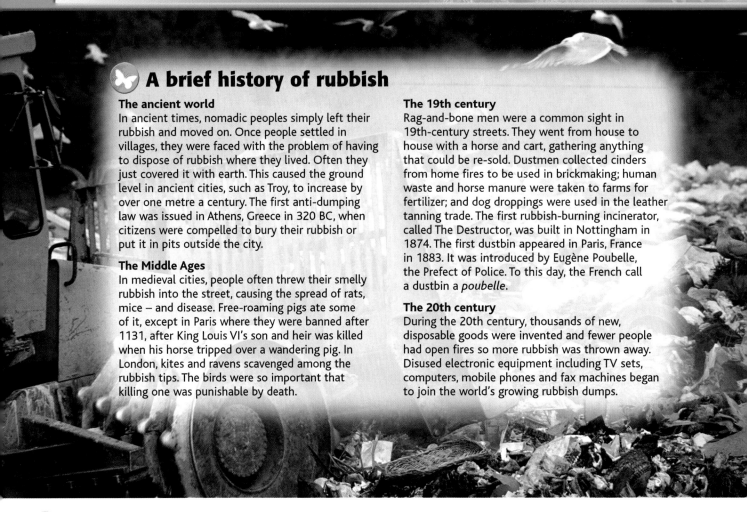

The ancient world
In ancient times, nomadic peoples simply left their rubbish and moved on. Once people settled in villages, they were faced with the problem of having to dispose of rubbish where they lived. Often they just covered it with earth. This caused the ground level in ancient cities, such as Troy, to increase by over one metre a century. The first anti-dumping law was issued in Athens, Greece in 320 BC, when citizens were compelled to bury their rubbish or put it in pits outside the city.

The Middle Ages
In medieval cities, people often threw their smelly rubbish into the street, causing the spread of rats, mice – and disease. Free-roaming pigs ate some of it, except in Paris where they were banned after 1131, after King Louis VI's son and heir was killed when his horse tripped over a wandering pig. In London, kites and ravens scavenged among the rubbish tips. The birds were so important that killing one was punishable by death.

The 19th century
Rag-and-bone men were a common sight in 19th-century streets. They went from house to house with a horse and cart, gathering anything that could be re-sold. Dustmen collected cinders from home fires to be used in brickmaking; human waste and horse manure were taken to farms for fertilizer; and dog droppings were used in the leather tanning trade. The first rubbish-burning incinerator, called The Destructor, was built in Nottingham in 1874. The first dustbin appeared in Paris, France in 1883. It was introduced by Eugène Poubelle, the Prefect of Police. To this day, the French call a dustbin a *poubelle*.

The 20th century
During the 20th century, thousands of new, disposable goods were invented and fewer people had open fires so more rubbish was thrown away. Disused electronic equipment including TV sets, computers, mobile phones and fax machines began to join the world's growing rubbish dumps.

Biggest rubbish producers

Country*	Household waste per person per year (kg)
USA	720
Australia	690
Iceland	650
Norway, Switzerland	600
France, Luxembourg	590
Belgium	580
Denmark, Ireland, The Netherlands	560
Austria	510
UK	502
Canada	500

*OECD countries only

How much rubbish is that?
Every person in the UK produces approximately half a tonne of household rubbish every year, which means that the UK as a whole produces 30 million tonnes. That's enough to fill dustbins stretching from the Earth to the Moon. But that's not all. Household rubbish makes up only 7 per cent of the yearly total. The rest comes from mining and quarrying (114 million tonnes), agriculture (86 million), demolition and construction – bricks, soil, etc (80 million), industrial waste (55 million), dredged spoils from rivers and harbours (34 million), commercial waste (25 million) and sewage (4 million).

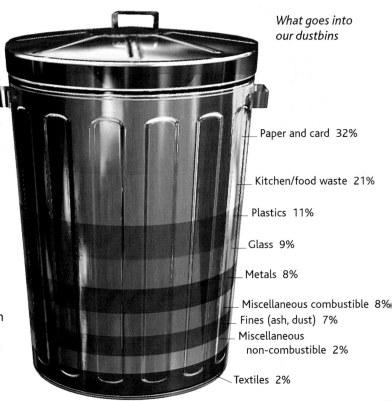

What goes into our dustbins

Paper and card 32%
Kitchen/food waste 21%
Plastics 11%
Glass 9%
Metals 8%
Miscellaneous combustible 8%
Fines (ash, dust) 7%
Miscellaneous non-combustible 2%
Textiles 2%

How long to rot

Cotton rags	1–5 months
Paper	2–5 months
Orange peel	up to 6 months
Wool socks	1–5 years
Cigarette ends	1–12 years
Plastic-coated drink cartons	5 years
Plastic bags	10–20 years
Photo film	20–30 years
Leather shoes	25–50 years
Artificial fibre clothes (nylon, etc)	30–40 years
Tin cans	50–100 years

A mountain of junk

More than 1,000 people have climbed Mount Everest, the world's highest peak, since it was conquered in 1953. They, and their support teams, have dropped more than 50 tonnes of rubbish, making Everest the world's highest rubbish dump. In 2001 Nepalese sherpas (local guides) collected more than six tonnes of paper bags, tents, ropes, clothes, aluminium ladders, batteries, oxygen bottles and plastic cans. Nepal now charges climbers a £3,000 deposit which is returned only if they remove all their rubbish.

Ways to reduce waste

1 Use a shopping bag and refuse unnecessary carrier bags

2 Buy refills

3 Buy fruits and vegetables loose, not pre-packed

4 Buy recycled goods

5 Buy reusable nappies

6 Buy soft drinks in large bottles and pour into smaller bottles for daily use

7 Reuse wrapping paper, packing materials and envelopes

8 Pack your lunch in a reusable box rather than foil or clingfilm

9 Choose durable products over disposable ones, eg rechargeable batteries

10 Donate unwanted clothes to charity shops or jumble sales

11 Donate unwanted furniture to a furniture recycling project

12 Buy drinks in glass bottles – they can be reused 20 times

13 If it's broken, mend it – don't throw it away!

14 Return clothes hangers to dry cleaners

15 Take glass, cans, paper and cardboard to recycling banks

16 Compost leftover food, garden waste, paper (in small amounts) and vacuum cleaner dust

Where does it go?

Landfills
Most waste ends up underground – in giant municipal pits, or landfill sites, where it can rot out of sight. These are usually lined to prevent dangerous chemicals seeping into the ground. However, many discarded objects take decades, even centuries to break down, and we are running out of suitable places to bury it.

Incineration
Burning rubbish is another solution. Burning gets rid of most kinds of waste and the heat can be converted into energy for other uses. The problem is that incineration releases harmful gases, some of which may contribute to global warming.

Recycling
Recycling uses old waste to make new products. It cuts down the amount of rubbish and saves natural resources by reducing the need for new raw materials. Items most suitable for recycling are organic matter (plant and animal) which can be composted and used as fertilizer, metals (such as aluminium cans), glass and paper.

Reduce and reuse
The most sustainable solution is to reduce the amount of waste we create. Compared with 50 years ago, food cans are 50 per cent lighter, yoghurt pots are 60 per cent lighter, glass bottles are 50 per cent lighter and plastic carrier bags are half as thick. Shoppers can help by choosing not to buy goods with lots of packaging or disposable containers, as these make up 10–20 per cent of all domestic rubbish.

www.wasteonline.org.uk

Cubes of compacted metal for recycling

Since humans made the first rough stone tools more than two million years ago, science and technology have advanced at astonishing speed. During the last 100 years, inventions such as the telephone, radar and most of all computers have had a dramatic impact on all our lives.

SCIENCE
AND TECHNOLOGY

How dense?

A cubic metre (m³) of pure water weighs 1,000kg or one tonne. Materials that have a density that is greater than water sink, and those that are less dense float. Lightweight metals such as aluminium and titanium are important to engineers – for example, for building aircraft that need to be strong but light enough to fly. These are the average densities of some of the substances around us.

Material	Weight of m³ (kg)	Material	Weight of m³ (kg)
Air at 0°C	1.29	Salt	2,165
Styrofoam	100	Carbon	2,267
Balsa wood	150	Chalk	2,300
Cork	240	China	2,300
Steam	600	Concrete	2,300
Petrol	730	Sand	2,500
Oak	750	Glass	2,600
Butter	900	Aluminium	2,700
Paper	900	Marble	2,700
Ice	920	Human tooth enamel	2,900
Olive oil	920	Diamonds	3,500
Rubber	940	Titanium	4,507
Wax	950	The Earth (average for whole planet)	5,520
Pure water at 0°C	1,000		
Milk	1,030	Iron	7,874
Sea water	1,030	Copper	8,920
Rubber	1,100	Silver	10,490
Ebony	1,200	Lead	11,340
Spider silk	1,260	Mercury	13,570
Coal	1,400	Tungsten	19,250
Bone	1,800	Gold	19,300
Brick	2,100	Platinum	21,090
		Osmium	22,610

Sound levels

The decibel (dB) is a way of measuring sound. Sounds of 80–90dB or more can damage hearing and it is dangerous for people to work in sound levels of more than 90dB. Sounds above 130dB become painful, and people should wear hearing protectors with sounds of more than 140dB. A decibel level of more than 150dB can cause permanent deafness.

Sound	dB	Sound	dB
Silence	0	Loud shout at 15m, lawnmower, chainsaw, blender	100
Rustle of leaves	10		
Quiet whisper at 5m, library	20–30		
Normal conversation, soft music	30	Heavy truck 1m away, orchestra playing Beethoven's Ninth Symphony	105
Sailing boat	35		
Quiet countryside, ticking watch	40	Circular saw at 1m, car horn at 5m	110
Inside average home	45–50	Shouting in someone's ear	114
Restaurant, office, loud conversation	50–60	Personal stereo	115
Background music, motorboat, department store	60	Loud scream, thunder, explosion, submarine engine room	120
Hairdryer	60–80	Loud rock music	120–130
Workshop	65	Racing car	125
Radio, telephone ring, busy traffic, orchestra, loud TV	70	Motorbike (without silencer)	130
Inside car, underground train	80	Banger, jumbo jet takeoff at 30m	140
Pneumatic drill at 15m, Niagara Falls, top limit of comfort	85	Rock music (peak at 5m from speaker)	150
Very loud snore	88	Level at ear of person firing powerful rifle	160
Heavy traffic at 15m, inside or 7m from bus or truck, roaring lion	90	Launch of *Saturn V* space rocket	172
		Blue whale call	188
		Volcanic eruption	272

Motorbike racer

→ See also

Conversions: pages 84–85

Strange studies

Name of study	Subject
Acarology	Mites and ticks
Anemology	Wind
Balneology	Bathing
Bryology	Mosses
Carpology	Fruits and seeds
Cetology	Whales and other aquatic mammals
Chorology	Geographical regions
Craniology	Skulls
Cryptology	Codes and ciphers
Dactylology	Fingerprints
Horology	Time and timepieces
Hypnology	Sleep
Ichnology	Fossilized footprints
Ichthyology	Fish
Melittology	Bees
Momilogy	Mummies
Mycology	Fungi
Myrmecology	Ants
Nidology	Birds' nests
Oikology	Housekeeping
Oneirology	Dreams
Oölogy	Eggs
Osmology	Smells
Otology	Ears
Polemology	Wars
Psephology	Elections
Pyrgology	Towers
Rhinology	Noses
Teratology	Monsters
Thelmatology	Swamps
Ufology	Unidentified flying objects
Vexillology	Flags

Spectrum colours

The electromagnetic spectrum includes all forms of light, from radio waves and microwaves at one end of the scale to X-rays and gamma rays at the other. In between is visible or white light, which is made up of a range of colours. We can see the individual colours when they are split up by water droplets and form a rainbow, or by passing white light through a prism. The colours of the spectrum are red, orange, yellow, green, blue, indigo and violet.

Light passing through a prism

Acids and alkalis

The pH (potential Hydrogen) system was invented in 1909 by Danish chemist Søren Sørensen (1868–1939). In this, pH is a measure of the concentration of hydrogen ions, which shows whether something is acid or base (also known as alkali). Pure water has a pH of 7.0. Substances that have a pH of less are acid. Substances with a pH of more than 7.0 are base (alkali). Acids make lemon juice and vinegar taste sharp, and acid rain harms trees and other plants. The traditional way of testing pH is by using litmus paper – acidic substances turn blue litmus red, while alkalis turn red litmus blue.

Substance	pH	Substance	pH
Hydrochloric acid	0	Wine/beer	4.0
Car battery acid	1.0	Tomato juice	4.3
Gastric (digestive) juices	1–3	Normal rainfall	5.6
Lime juice	2.3	Saliva	6.4–6.9
Lemon juice	2.4	Milk	6.6
Acid rain	2.4–3.6	Pure water	7.0
Apple	3.0	Human blood	7.4
Vinegar	3.0	Sea water	7.8–8.3
Grapefruit	3.2	Baking soda	8.5
Orange juice	3.7	Ammonia	12.0

Brightness scale

A candela is a unit of light intensity. It was originally equivalent to the amount given out by a candle, but is now more precise.

Source	Candelas per m²
Overcast sky	2,000
Moon	2,500
Clear sky (average)	8,000
Candle (brightest spot)	10,000
Domestic light bulb	100,000
Sun at Equator	1,600,000
Flash of lightning	80,000,000
Atom bomb	2,000,000,000

Flashes of lightning

What is an element?

The elements are sometimes called the building blocks of the Universe because everything in the Universe – including ourselves – is made of them. The nucleus of each element consists of atoms with the same number of protons. Each element is unique, although elements can exist in different forms – for example, carbon may be soft graphite or hard diamond. Elements cannot usually be broken down into any other substance.

There are about 118 elements altogether, and 91 occur naturally on Earth. Others can be created artificially in laboratories, but in minute quantities and they have very short lifespans of only thousandths of a second. Each element is also known by a one- or two-letter symbol as well as its name. Examples are *Fe* for iron and *Na* for sodium.

A chemical compound is a combination of two or more elements linked together, which can be broken down again into their constituent parts but no further. Water, for example, is made up of two hydrogen atoms linked to one oxygen atom. Salt, or sodium chloride, is a compound of sodium and chlorine.

Elements in sea water

A cubic kilometre (a billion tonnes) of sea water is a treasure chest of elements, but sodium and chlorine (combined as sodium chloride, or common salt) are the only two that are taken from it in large amounts. Other elements, such as gold, are too expensive to extract – even though there may be as much as 500kg of gold in a cubic kilometre of sea water.

Element	Mg per litre
1 Oxygen*	857,000
2 Hydrogen*	107,800
3 Chlorine	19,870
4 Sodium	11,050
5 Magnesium	1,326

* Combined as water

Elements on Earth

There is calcium in the Earth and sea in the form of calcium carbonate. Sodium exists in the form of sodium chloride, the salt in the sea and on our tables. The quantities of both calcium and sodium are so vast that these elements are considered unlimited. Some elements are mined and used in industry. Iron is the most common, followed by magnesium.

There are quite small amounts of some precious metals on Earth, which is why they are so valuable. For example, there are about one million tonnes of silver and 15,000 tonnes of gold. Elements are constantly being taken from Earth, but new discoveries are being made. We are still some way from running out of even the rarest elements.

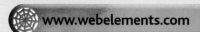

ONE AND ONLY

Element 98 was given the name Californium by the four scientists who discovered it in 1950. They were working at the University of California at Berkeley, and named the element for both the state and their university. One of them, Glen Theodore Seaborg (1912–99), received the Nobel Prize for Chemistry in 1951. The 106th element, Seaborgium, was named after him in 1994. It was the first to be named in honour of a living person.

The heaviest elements

Osmium
Osmium is the heaviest element of all (22.61g per cubic centimetre). It was discovered by the British chemist Smithson Tennant in 1803. He named it after the Greek word for smell because it smelt bad. Osmium is twice as heavy as lead – so heavy that a cubic foot (0.028317 cubic metres) weighs 640kg, as much as ten average people! A football made of osmium would weigh 126kg, or as much as two adults. Osmium is also very hard, and is used to make hard-wearing points, such as the nibs of fountain pens.

Platinum
Platinum was used before anyone realized that it was an element. It weighs almost as much as osmium (21.45g per cubic centimetre) and is used to make jewellery that is even more expensive than gold. It is also used in catalytic converters in cars to reduce the pollution from exhaust gases.

Plutonium
Plutonium was discovered in 1941 and is a heavy and highly radioactive metal. It is used as a nuclear fuel and in nuclear weapons – a kilogram of plutonium produces an explosion equivalent to 20,000 tonnes of TNT.

Gold
Gold is the best-known of all heavy metals – though at 19.29g per cubic centimetre it is less heavy than the others here. Gold has been prized since ancient times and has many uses beyond coins and jewellery.

Various weights of gold in a gold refinery

The Hindenburg, *a giant airship*

The lightest elements

Hydrogen

Hydrogen is the simplest and lightest element, and the most common in the entire Universe – 93 per cent of all atoms in the universe are hydrogen atoms. On Earth, it is relatively rare in the atmosphere – only 5 of every 100 million litres of air are hydrogen but hydrogen combined with oxygen forms all the water in the world's oceans, lakes and rivers. Hydrogen is very light. The air in a room with walls 4m long and 4m high would weigh 82.5kg, but if the same room were filled with hydrogen, it would weigh only 5.76kg. This is why it was used in balloons carrying human passengers: the second-ever flight, in Paris on 1 December 1783, was in a hydrogen balloon. Hydrogen was also used in giant airships until 6 May 1937, when the giant German airship *Hindenburg* exploded killing 36 people at Lakehurst, New Jersey, USA. Today, hydrogen fuel cells are used to power clean-energy cars.

Helium

Helium is twice as heavy as hydrogen, but it is still only one seventh the weight of air. Unlike hydrogen, helium does not burn, so it is used in modern airships.

Lithium

Lithium was discovered in 1817 by Swedish scientist Johan August Arfvedson. It takes its name from the Latin word for rock, although it is actually a metal. Lithium is so light (42 times lighter than the heaviest element, osmium) and so soft that it can be easily cut with a knife. It floats because it is half as heavy as water, and lighter than some types of wood. It is used to make lithium batteries.

Potassium and sodium

Both were discovered in 1807 by Sir Humphry Davy. Both are metals that are lighter than water. In a laboratory, potassium is usually kept in paraffin because if it comes into contact with water it releases hydrogen and generates so much heat that it catches fire. Sodium also has to be kept immersed in paraffin – if it is dropped into water it hurtles around on the surface before noisily bursting into flames. Potassium is vital for plant growth and human well-being – our bodies contain about 140g of it. Sodium is relatively common as part of a compound: in combination with chlorine it is ordinary table salt.

Highest melting points

Element	Melting point (°C)
1 Carbon	3,527
2 Tungsten	3,422
3 Rhenium	3,186
4 Osmium	3,033
5 Tantalum	3,017

For comparison, the surface of the Sun reaches 5,605°C, so no element could approach it and remain solid.

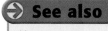

See also

Air transport
pages 216–17

Cowboy inventions

All these items, beloved of cowboys, are named after their inventors.

Levi jeans
Levi Strauss (1829–1902) was a Bavarian immigrant who arrived in San Francisco in 1850 at the height of the California gold rush. Strauss noticed that the gold miners needed strong trousers and began making them, first from tent canvas and later from denim with copper rivets to reinforce the seams. The hardwearing garment soon became standard clothing among cowboys, and the company has since become one of the world's largest clothing manufacturers.

Stetson hat
John Batterson Stetson (1830–1906) was a hat maker born in New Jersey. He established the John B. Stetson Manufacturing Company of Philadelphia, which made the famous ten-gallon hat worn by cowboys. The hat was often called a "John B" before acquiring its more familiar name of stetson.

Bowie knife
The large hunting knife was supposedly invented by Colonel James Bowie (1799–1836). Bowie was a Texan adventurer and slave trader who died during the siege of the Alamo fortress by Mexican soldiers, alongside his friend Davy Crockett. In fact, his older brother, Rezin Pleasant Bowie (1793–1841), may have invented the knife. The lethal weapon, jokingly called an Arkansas toothpick, had a blade of 25–38cm long, with a guard between the blade and the handle.

Colt revolver
The Colt was invented by Samuel Colt (1814–62), who is said to have whittled the original design in wood. Later, he perfected a working version that was patented in England and France in 1835 and in the United States the following year. Colts were used during the American Civil War, and the classic six-gun, the six-shot, single-action .45-calibre Peacemaker model introduced in 1873, made Samuel Colt a wealthy man.

100 years of everyday inventions

Date	Invention	Inventor
1903	Safety razor	King Camp Gillette
1904	Ice cream cone	Italo Marcioni
1906	Electric washing machine	Alva J. Fisher
1907	Vacuum cleaner with bag	J. Murray Spangler
1908	Cellophane	Jacques Edwin Brandenburger
1913	Crossword puzzle	Arthur Wynne
1913	Zip fastener	Gideon Sundback
1914	Aluminium foil bottle top	Josef Jonsson
1915	Pyrex glassware	Eugene G. Sulivan/ William C. Taylor
1924	Frozen food	Clarence Birdseye
1927	Pop-up toaster	Charles Strite
1928	Scotch Tape (Sellotape)	3M Company
1928	Elastoplast	Horatio Nelson Smith
1931	Electric razor	Col Jacob Schick
1938	Ballpoint pen	László Biro
1938	Instant coffee	Nestlé
1941	Aerosol spray	L.D. Goodhue/W.N. Sullivan
1945	Microwave oven	Percy LeBaron Spencer
1945	Tupperware (food containers)	Earl W. Tupper
1947	Polaroid camera	Edwin H. Land
1947	Long-playing record	Goldmark
1950	Credit card	Frank X. McNamara
1954	Non-stick pan (Teflon coated)	Du Pont (Teflon invented 1943)
1955	Lego	Gotfried Kirk Christiansen
1956	Velcro	Georges de Mestral
1958	Videotape	A.M. Poniatoff
1963	Ring-pull can	Alcoa
1971	Digital watch	George Theiss/Willy Crabtree
1974	Personal computer	MITS
1979	Post-it Notes	Spencer Silver/3M
1981	Compact disc	Philips
1982	Camcorder	Sony
1993	Bagless vacuum cleaner	James Dyson
2000	iPod digital music player	Apple Computer, Inc
2001	Self-cleaning glass	Kevin Sanderson

Stetson-wearing cowboys ride the range.

What is a patent?

A patent for an invention is granted by a government to the inventor. It gives him or her the right for a limited period – usually 20 years – to stop others from making, using or selling the invention without the inventor's permission. The invention is territorial and protected only in the country in which it is patented. The first patent was granted to Filippo Brunelleschi in Florence in 1421, for a barge crane to transport marble. In England the first was granted in 1449 by Henry VI to John of Utynam for making stained glass for the windows of Eton College.

The sport of windsurfing was invented by a 12-year-old boy.

Brainchildren: young inventors

Horatio Adams
Adams was only 16 when he assisted his father, Thomas, in his experiments with chicle, the dried sap of a Mexican jungle tree. This led to the invention of chewing gum.

Charles Babbage
Babbage was 19 when he first thought of the idea of the mechanical computer.

Louis Braille
He invented Braille, the raised-dot writing used by blind people, at the age of 15. Louis himself was blind.

Peter Chilvers
Chilvers was 12 when he invented boardsailing (windsurfing) in 1958 off Hayling Island, UK.

Frank Epperson
The Popsicle or ice lolly was invented by 11-year-old Frank Epperson of San Francisco, California, in 1905. He had the idea when he left a fruit drink out during a freezing winter night and originally called it the Epsicle. He did not apply for a patent until 1923, by which time his son had renamed it Popsicle.

Chester Greenwood
Greenwood of Farmington, Maine, USA, was aged 15 in 1873 when he invented earmuffs. He started Greenwood's Ear Protector Factory and made a fortune by supplying his product to US soldiers in World War I.

Walter Lines
British schoolboy Lines invented the scooter at the age of 15. He later founded Triang Toys, once Britain's leading toy manufacturer.

William Henry Perkin
During experiments in his garden shed, 18-year-old Perkin hit upon aniline dye, the first artificial dye, and patented it in 1856. It revolutionized the cloth industry and made Perkin immensely rich.

John J. Stone-Parker
In 1989 when he was only four years old, John and his sister, Elaine W. Stone-Parker, invented a star-shaped gadget to prevent ice from slipping out of a drinking-glass. He is the youngest-ever holder of a patent.

Leonardo da Vinci

Italian genius Leonardo da Vinci (1452–1519) is best known as a painter, anatomist, sculptor and architect. His paintings *The Last Supper* and *Mona Lisa* are among the most famous of all time. But he is also hailed as one of the greatest inventors who ever lived. Among his notebooks he left plans for countless advanced machines, often with descriptions written in secret mirror writing. Many of them were never built, but they anticipated modern inventions, often by hundreds of years. They include the following:

Air conditioner	Mechanical musical instruments
Alarm clock	Mileometer
Ball-bearings	Multi-barrelled machine gun
Chemical and biological warfare	One-person battleship
Clock with minute and hour hands	Parachute
Crane	Pedometer (for measuring walking distance)
Diving suit and diving bell	
Double-hull ship	Revolving stage
Dredging machine	Screw-making machine
Flying machine	Shrapnel bomb
Gas mask	Spectacles
Gears	Steam engine
Giant catapults and crossbows	Tank-like armoured vehicle
Helicopter	Telescope
Lifebelt	Water clock
Magnetic compass	Water turbine

Crazy inventions

There is no end to the extraordinary items dreamed up by inventors – a self-raising hat (1896) for the polite man with his arms full; spectacles for chickens to protect their eyes from other fowl that might attempt to peck them (1903); an automatic haircutter (1951); a motorized ice cream cone (1998) which rotates against the tongue. Here are some other interesting examples.

Rifle to shoot round corners, 1916
Jones Wister invented a rifle with a curved barrel for trench warfare: the soldier was able to take cover and fire it by using the periscopic sights.

Vacuum-cleaner dog, 1973
This was designed for cleaning up hairs after dog grooming without scaring the animal. In this invention by Anne Margaret Zeleskie, a vacuum cleaner is housed in a toy dog, with a suction hose built into its tail.

Anti-shark suit, 1989
Nelson C. Fox and Rosetta H.V.G. Fox of St Georges, Bermuda, were awarded a patent for a rubber suit (right) covered in spikes to protect its wearer from shark attack.

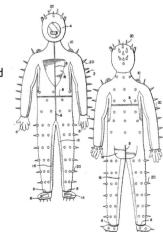

See also

Computer timeline: pages 86–87

Roman numerals

Roman numerals are made up from seven letters (I, V, X, L, C, M and D). A small numeral in front of a larger one is subtracted from it, so 90 is written as X (10) subtracted from C (100) – XC. A small number after a larger one is usually added to it – for example, XI (11).

This system was not very good for adding columns of figures and there was no way of showing zero. Despite these problems, Roman architects were able to work out the complicated sums needed when building some of the world's greatest structures, including the Pont du Gard.

Pont du Gard over the Gard River in the south of France, was built by the Romans

Roman	Arabic	Roman	Arabic	Roman	Arabic
I	1	XX	20	CCC	300
II	2	XXX	30	CCCC	400
III	3	XL	40	D	500
IV	4	L	50	DC	600
V	5	LX	60	DCC	700
VI	6	LXX	70	DCCC	800
VII	7	LXXX	80	CM	900
VIII	8	XC	90	M	1,000
IX	9	C	100	MM	2,000
X	10	CC	200		

Mathematical symbols

Symbol	Meaning	Symbol	Meaning
+	Plus or positive	%	Per cent
−	Minus or negative	>	Greater than
±	Plus or minus, positive or negative	<	Less than
		√	Square root
x	Multiplied by	Σ	Sum of
÷ or /	Divided by	π	Pi
=	Equal to	°	Degree
≠	Not equal to	∞	Infinity
~	Of the order of, similar to		

Mega multiples

Certain prefixes are used in the metric system. The prefixes are the same whether describing weight, such as a kilogram, distance, such as a kilometre, or other measurements.

Prefix	Name	Value
exa-	quintillion	1,000,000,000,000,000,000
peta-	quadrillion	1,000,000,000,000,000
tera-	trillion	1,000,000,000,000
giga-	billion	1,000,000,000
mega-	million	1,000,000
kilo-	thousand	1,000
hecto-	hundred	100
deca-	ten	10
	one	1
deci-	tenth	0.1
centi-	hundredth	0.01
milli-	thousandth	0.001
micro-	millionth	0.000,001
nano-	billionth	0.000,000,001
pico-	trillionth	0.000,000,000,001
femto-	quadrillionth	0.000,000,000,000,001
atto-	quintillionth	0.000,000,000,000,000,001

Useful mathematical formulae

Area of a rectangle	length x height
Area of a triangle	$\frac{1}{2}$ length x height
Area of a circle	π x radius^2
Diameter of a circle	radius x 2
Circumference of a circle	π x diameter
Volume of a sphere	$\frac{4}{3}\pi$ x radius^3
Surface of a sphere	$4 \times \pi^2$
Volume of a cylinder	π x radius^2 x height
Curved area of cylinder	$2 \times \pi$ x radius x height
Area of a cone	π x radius x length
Volume of a cone	$\frac{1}{3}\pi$ x radius^2 x height

π = pi, pi = 3.14159265

See also

Famous bridges: page 204

Big numbers

The terms used for big numbers differ between the UK and the USA and other parts of the world. Until recently, a billion was a million million in the UK, but a thousand million everywhere else. The UK has changed this definition to match the rest of the world, but other big numbers are still different.

Number	Equivalent to	Zeros US	Zeros UK
Thousand	10 hundreds	3	3
Million	1,000 thousand	6	6
Billion	1,000 million	9	9 (formerly 12)
Trillion	1,000 billion	12	18
Quadrillion	1,000 trillion	15	24
Quintillion	1,000 quadrillion	18	30
Sextillion	1,000 quintillion	21	36
Septillion	1,000 sextillion	24	42
Octillion	1,000 septillion	27	48
Nonillion	1,000 octillion	30	54
Decillion	1,000 nonillion	33	60
Undecillion	1,000 decillion	36	66
Duodecillion	1,000 undecillion	39	72
Tredecillion	1,000 duodecillion	42	78
Quattuordecillion	1,000 tredecillion	45	84
Quindecillion	1,000 quattuordecillion	48	90
Sexdecillion	1,000 quindecillion	51	96
Septendecillion	1,000 sexdecillion	54	102
Octodecillion	1,000 septendecillion	57	108
Novemdecillion	1,000 octodecillion	60	114
Vingtillion	1,000 novemdecillion	63	120
Centillion		303	600

There are names for even bigger numbers, including a trigent-billillion (60,000,003 zeros) and sextent-billillion (1,800,000,003 zeros).

In 1938, nine-year-old Milton Sirotta came up with the word googol, which means a one followed by 100 zeros. Milton was the nine-year-old nephew of an American mathematician called Edward Kasner (1878–1955).

A googolplex is an even bigger number – a one with a googol of zeros, or 10 to the googol power. This number is so vast that, as Kasner explained, "... there would not be enough room to write it, if one went to the furthest stars, touring all the nebulae in the Universe and putting down zeros every inch of the way."

There is no such number as a zillion – the word just means a huge amount.

Prime numbers

A prime number is a whole number that can be divided only by one and itself, and not by any other number. Examples include 2, 3, 5, 7,11 and 13. All prime numbers, except for two, are also odd numbers. There are 168 prime numbers under 1,000.

Regular polygons

A polygon is a shape enclosed by straight lines. Regular polygons have sides of equal length and the angles inside are all the same. A regular polygon fits inside a circle with all its points touching the circumference. An irregular polygon does not.

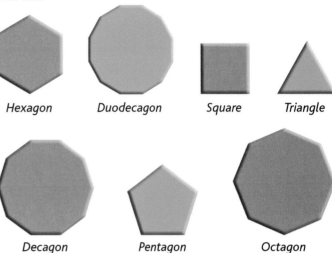

Hexagon *Duodecagon* *Square* *Triangle*

Decagon *Pentagon* *Octagon*

Polygon	Number of sides	Each internal angle	Sum of internal angles
Triangle	3	60°	180°
Square (or quadrilateral)	4	90°	360°
Pentagon	5	108°	540°
Hexagon	6	120°	720°
Heptagon	7	128.57°	900°
Octagon	8	135°	1,080°
Nonagon	9	140°	1,260°
Decagon	10	144°	1,440°
Undecagon	11	147.27°	1,620°
Duodecagon (or dodecagon)	12	150°	1,800°
Quindecagon	15	156°	2,340°
Icosagon	20	162°	3,240°

Regular solids

There are five types of regular solid. All faces on a regular solid are exactly the same shape. If you put a regular solid inside a sphere, all its points will touch the surface of the sphere.

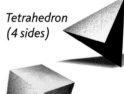

Tetrahedron (4 sides)

Cube (6 sides)

Octahedron (8 sides)

Dodecahedron (12 sides)

Isosahedron (20 sides)

Conversions

There are two systems of measuring length, area, weight, volume and so on – metric and imperial. Here's how to convert between the two different systems.

Length

From	To	Multiply by
Centimetres (cm)	Inches (in)	0.3937
Inches (in)	Centimetres (cm)	2.5400
Metres (m)	Feet (ft)	3.2808
Feet (ft)	Metres (m)	0.3048
Metres (m)	Yards (yd)	1.0936
Yards (yd)	Metres (m)	0.9144
Kilometres (km)	Miles (ml)	0.6214
Miles (ml)	Kilometres (km)	1.6093

Area

From	To	Multiply by
Square centimetres (cm²)	Square inches (in²)	0.1550
Square inches (in²)	Square centimetres (cm²)	6.4516
Square metres (m²)	Square feet (ft²)	10.7639
Square feet (ft²)	Square metres (m²)	0.0929
Square metres (m²)	Square yards (yd²)	1.1960
Square yards (yd²)	Square metres (m²)	0.8361
Square kilometres (km²)	Square miles (ml²)	0.3861
Square miles (ml²)	Square kilometres (km²)	2.5900
Hectares (ha)	Acres	2.4711
Acres	Hectares (ha)	0.4047

Speed

From	To	Multiply by
Metres per second (m/s)	Feet per second (ft/s)	3.2808
Feet per second (ft/s)	Metres per second (m/s)	0.3048
Kilometres per hour (km/h)	Miles per hour (mph)	0.6214
Miles per hour (mph)	Kilometres per hour (km/h)	1.6093

Weight

Grams (g)	Ounces (oz)	0.0353
Ounces (oz)	Grams (g)	28.3495
Kilograms (kg)	Pounds (lb)	2.2046
Pounds (lb)	Kilograms (kg)	0.4536
Stones	Kilograms (kg)	6.3503
Kilograms (kg)	Stones	0.1575
Hundredweight (cwt)	Kilograms (kg)	50.8024
Kilograms (kg)	Hundredweight (cwt)	0.0197
Tonnes	Tons (long)	0.9842
Tons (long)	Tonnes	1.0160
Tonnes	US short tons	1.1023
US short tons	Tonnes	0.9072

Temperature

Celsius (°C)	Fahrenheit (°F)	x 9 ÷ 5 + 32
Fahrenheit (°F)	Celsius (°C)	−32 x 5 ÷ 9

Volume

Cubic centimetres (cc)	Cubic inches (in³)	0.0610
Cubic inches (in³)	Cubic centimetres (cc)	16.3871
Cubic feet (ft³)	Cubic metres (m³)	0.0283
Cubic metres (m³)	Cubic feet (ft³)	35.3147
Cubic yards (yd³)	Cubic metres (m³)	1.3080
Cubic metres (m³)	Cubic yards (yd³)	0.7646
Cubic kilometres (km³)	Cubic miles (ml³)	0.2399
Cubic miles (ml³)	Cubic kilometres (km³)	4.1682
Litres (l)	Pints	1.7598
Pints	Litres (l)	0.5683
Litres (l)	UK gallons (gal)	0.2200
UK gallons (gal)	Litres (l)	4.5461
Litres (l)	US gallons (gal)	0.2642
US gallons (gal)	Litres (l)	3.78532

 ## Special measurements

Diamonds like this one are measured in carats.

Carat
The weight of diamonds and other valuable gems is measured in carats. The word comes from the carob bean, which has a consistent weight of 0.2 of a gram.

Hand
The height of horses is measured in hands. The measurement is usually taken from the front hoof to the highest point on the animal's shoulder. One hand is 10.16cm.

Knot
Speed at sea is measured in knots, which is the time it took a ship to travel the length of a knotted rope. A knot is now the same as a nautical mile, which is 1,852m.

Point
This measurement is used by typographers and printers and refers to the size of a letter such as an x. One point is equal to 0.3528mm, so the 6-point type in telephone directories is 2.116mm high.

Troy ounce
This measurement takes its name from the city of Troyes, France, where dealers in precious stones and metals gathered in medieval times. Gold and other rare metals are still measured in troy ounces (31.1035g). A standard international gold bar weighs 400 troy ounces (12.44kg).

Namesakes

These measurements were named after the men and women who discovered them.

Measurement	Measures	Named after
Ampere	Electrical current	André-Marie Ampère (French, 1775–1836)
Beaufort scale	Wind speed	Sir Francis Beaufort (British, 1774–1857
Bel/decibel	Sound	Alexander Graham Bell (Scots/USA, 1847–1922)
Celsius	Temperature	Anders Celsius (Swedish, 1701–44)
Curie	Radiation	Marie Curie (Polish/French, 1867–1934)
Fahrenheit	Temperature	Gabriel Fahrenheit (German, 1686–1736)
Joule	Energy	James Prescott Joule (British, 1818–89)
Kelvin	Temperature	William Thomson, Lord Kelvin (British, 1824–1907)
Mercalli scale	Earthquakes	Giuseppe Mercalli (Italian, 1850–1914)
Mohs' scale	Hardness	Friedrich Mohs (German, 1773–1839)
Ohm/Mho	Electrical resistance	Georg Simon Ohm (German, 1787–1854)
Richter scale	Earthquakes	Charles Richter (US, 1900–85)
Volt	Electromagnetic force	Alessandro Volta (Italian, 1745–1827)
Watt	Power	James Watt (British, 1736–1819)

Marie Curie in her laboratory

Weighty words

Acre
An acre describes an area of land and comes from the Old English word aecer, meaning a ploughed field. It was the area a team of oxen could plough in one day. In the UK in 1824, an acre was set as 4,840 square yards.

Celsius
A temperature scale invented in 1742 by Swedish astronomer Anders Celsius. A Celsius degree is 1/100th of the difference between the freezing and boiling points of water (0° and 100°).

Fahrenheit
This temperature scale was devised by German physicist Gabriel Fahrenheit. On this scale the freezing point of water is 32°.

Foot
Foot originally meant the average length of an adult foot, and has been used since ancient times. Before France invented the metric system, the French foot was based on the length of the Emperor Charlemagne's foot.

Gram/kilogram
Gram comes from the same ancient Greek word that gave us grammar, and means a marked-off division. A kilogram is 1,000 grams. Kilo comes from the Greek chilioi, meaning one thousand.

Hectare
This is used for measuring land areas and comes from the ancient Greek hekaton, meaning one hundred. One hectare is equivalent to 10,000 square metres or 2.4711 acres.

Hundredweight/ton
A hundredweight is 1/20th of a ton. A British or long hundredweight is 112 pounds, and a long ton is 2,240 pounds. An American or short hundredweight is 100 pounds. A short ton is 2,000 pounds.

Metre
Metre comes from the ancient Greek metron, meaning measure. The metre was introduced in France in June 1799 after the Revolution. The metre was first set as one ten-millionth of a quarter of the circumference of the Earth. A metre was later set as the distance between two lines on a metal bar which was kept in a special office in Sèvres, France. The distance is now calculated by a more precise method. It is the distance light travels in a vacuum in 1/299792458th of a second. A centimetre (from the French cent, meaning one hundred) is 1/100th of a metre. A millimetre is 1,000th of a metre and a kilometre is 1,000 metres.

The world's smallest

Aircraft
Bumble Bee Two, built in the USA, was just 2.69m long and had a wingspan of 1.68m. It was destroyed in a crash landing in 1988.

Banknote
The Romanian 10-bani note, issued in 1917, measured 27.5 x 38mm. It was barely larger than most postage stamps.

Bicycle
In 1988 Neville Patten of Australia rode a bicycle with wheels that were only 19mm in diameter.

Book
In 1985, copies of the children's story *Old King Cole* were printed in the UK. The books measured 1 x 1mm.

Dinosaur
Compsognathus, a dinosaur found in Germany, was less than 75cm long. That's about the size of a turkey.

Egg
The egg of the vervain hummingbird is less than 1cm long and weighs as little as 0.365g. It would take more than 60,000 of them to equal the weight of an ostrich egg.

Fish
The stout infantfish, discovered in Australia in 2004, is only 7mm long. That's shorter than most people's little fingernail. It is the smallest known fish and the smallest vertebrate animal.

Stout infantfish

Computer timeline

1642	Blaise Pascal, France, makes a numerical wheel calculator, an early mechanical adding machine.
1694	Gottfried von Leibniz, Germany, makes a machine that can multiply numbers.
1820	Charles Xavier de Colmar, France, makes an "Arithometer" that can add, subtract, multiply and divide.
1822	Charles Babbage, England, devises his Difference Engine.
1829	Wheatstone uses punched paper tape to store data.
1834	Babbage conceives the Analytical Engine.
1889	Hollerith's punch card machine used in US Census.
1928	IBM adopts 80-column punched card.
1944	Harvard's Mark I, first digital computer.
1952	Univac computer accurately predicts the US presidential election winner.
1953	First IBM electronic digital computer (IBM 701).
1956	First hard disk drive (IBM). Term "artificial intelligence" devised.
1958	First chess game between computer and human.
1960	USA has 6,000 computers.
1963	ASCII (American Standard Code for Information Interchange) introduced.
1967	IBM releases floppy disk.
1970	Douglas Engelbart patents first computer mouse.
1971	Intel builds the microprocessor, "computer on a chip". Wang 1200, world's first word processor.
1972	e-mail invented by Ray Tomlinson. First electronic video game, *Pong*.
1975	Microsoft founded by William H. Gates, later to become the world's richest person.
1976	First Apple computer. Cray-1, first supercomputer.
1979	Compuserve launches first commercial Bulletin Board (BBN) service.
1980	USA has more than one million computers. First laptop computers.
1981	First Nintendo home video game. Commercial introduction of the computer mouse. Microsoft introduces software for IBM personal computers.
1982	Worldwide, 200 computers connected to the Internet.
1983	USA has more than ten million computers.
1984	Apple Macintosh computers launched.
1985	Microsoft ships Windows 1.0.
1986	USA has more than 30 million computers.
1988	4.7 million microcomputers, 120,000 minicomputers and 11,500 mainframe computers sold in USA.
1989	100,000 hosts on the net.
1990	World Wide Web described by Tim Berners-Lee. First palmtop computers.
1991	First use of the phrase "surfing the net" by Jean Armour Polly.
1993	Mosaic, the first graphical Internet browser, launched.
1994	135 million PCs worldwide. First ads on the World Wide Web (ad for *Wired* magazine claimed as first).
1995	Amazon.com Internet bookseller founded. Microsoft's Internet Explorer browser launched.
1999	150 million people use Internet worldwide (more than half in USA).
2000	Dot-com crash.
2001	AOL subscribers reach 29 million worldwide.
2004	More than 2.8 million iPod digital music players sold.

Babbage's Difference Engine

iPod digital music player

Internet users

The Internet has become more popular, more quickly than anything else in the history of communications. In little over ten years, it has become a global phenomenon. In 1994 about 20 million people around the world used the Internet. This had grown to almost 500 million by 2000 and soon there will be one billion users. By the time you read this, the figures will have increased again.

Country	Internet users	Country	Internet users
USA	197,895,880	Germany	46,455,813
China	94,000,000	UK	35,309,524
Japan	67,677,944	World total	817,447,147

Computer use worldwide

In 1943 Thomas Watson, the chairman of IBM, made one of the least accurate predictions ever. He said, "I think there is a world market for maybe five computers."

There are now nearly one billion computers around the world. Forecasts for 2007 estimate that by then there will be 162 computers in use for every 1,000 people on the planet. The figure for some countries will be much higher. In the USA there may be as many as 831 per 1,000 people.

	1985	1990	1995	2000	2002	2007
PCs (total in millions)	31.4	98	226	523	663	1,069
PCs per 1,000 people	6.5	18.7	40	86.2	106.4	162.1

Internet milestones

1960s
During the 1960s scientists in the USA began trying to work out how organizations could keep in touch with one another after a nuclear attack. In 1965 ARPA (Advanced Research Projects Agency) suggested linking computers. In 1969 computers at four US universities were connected and were able to "talk" to each other for the first time.

1970s
The network was extended and in 1973 computers were connected between London and Norway. At the same time, electronic mail (e-mail) was being used more and more to send messages between computers. In 1976 Queen Elizabeth II became the first monarch to send an e-mail message. In 1979 the first Usenet newsgroups (online discussion groups) began.

1980s
By 1981 the ARPA network had 213 hosts (sites to which users could connect). A new host was added approximately every 20 days. In 1982 a common language called TCP/IP was invented which allowed all Internet computers to communicate with each other and the network was first called an Internet. In the 1980s many more people and businesses began to use computers. The Internet began to be used commercially, as well as by governments and universities.

1990s
In 1991 the World Wide Web (www) was created. It combined words, pictures and sounds in a system that ordinary people could easily understand and use. By 1994 approximately 40 million people were connected to the Internet. They could exchange information, sell goods, and work from any computer with a phone line. The Rolling Stones rock group even broadcast a concert over the Internet. Schools started using the Internet as an electronic library. By 1996 users in almost 150 countries around the world were connected to the Internet.

2000s
High-speed broadband and wireless access is now widespread and more and more businesses are using the Internet to promote and sell products and services. In 2001 there were 533 million Internet users worldwide. Experts predict that by 2007 about 1,460 million people will be using the Internet. Figures suggest that 236 million of these will be in the USA, 612 million in Asia-Pacific nations, and 290 million in Western Europe.

Computer class in an American high school

Computer speak

Storage	Equal to (bytes)
1 bit	0.125 (0 or 1/on or off)
1 nibble	0.5
8 bits	1
1 kilobyte	1,024
1 megabyte	1,018,576
1 gigabyte	1,073,741,824 (over 1 billion)
1 terabyte	1,099,511,627,776 (over 1 trillion)
1 petabyte	1,125,899,906,842,624 (over 1 quadrillion)
1 exabyte	1,152,921,504,606,846,976
1 zettabyte	1,180,591,620,717,411,303,424
1 yottabyte	1,208,925,819,614,629,174,706,176

What that means in data

Storage	Approximate equivalent
10 bytes	One word
2 kilobytes	One page of typewritten text
10 kilobytes	One page of a reference book
1 megabyte	A short novel
5 megabytes	The complete works of Shakespeare
100 megabytes	One metre of books on a shelf
250 megabytes	The total output of data per year for every person on Earth
500 megabytes	A CD-ROM
20 gigabytes	The complete works of Beethoven on CD
10 terabytes	All the printed works in the USA Library of Congress (the world's largest library)
200 petabytes	Everything ever printed
5 exabytes	Every word ever spoken

Telecom timeline

In the early years of telecommunications, the only way of linking one telephone with another was by fixed cables. Links between continents relied on cables under the sea. The invention of radio brought the first wireless communications, but because the surface of the Earth is curved these signals could not travel far.

Satellites changed everything. They sit at an exact height above the Earth's Equator (usually around 35,000km) and they rotate at the same speed as the Earth spins. This means that they stay in a fixed position. Telephone signals can be sent to the satellites and bounced back to Earth. Everywhere on the planet can be covered by only five or six satellites, except for the Poles and surrounding areas, which are out of their range.

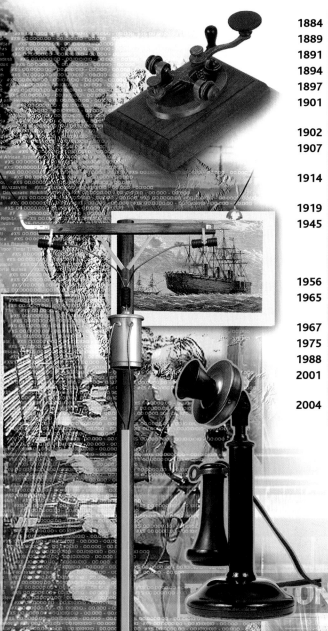

1793	Word "telegraph" first used (in France).
1837	Charles Wheatstone and William Cooke set up first electric telegraph in London.
1843	Morse code inventor Samuel Morse (USA) sends first telegraph message between Washington and Baltimore.
1850	Telegraph cable laid between England and France across English Channel, but fails; 12,000 miles of telegraph line in USA.
1851	Thomas Crampton lays successful Dover-Calais cable.
1852	First telegraph line in India; there are now 23,000 miles of telegraph line in USA.
1854	First Australian telegraph line (Melbourne to Williamstown).
1858	First transatlantic telegraph cable laid, but fails.
1861	First USA transcontinental telegraph.
1862	32,000 miles of telegraph line and more than 5 million messages sent in USA.
1867	First theory suggests using radio waves for telecommunication.
1876	Alexander Graham Bell patents the telephone – beating his rival Elisha Gray by a matter of hours. He make his historic first call to his assistant, Thomas Watson, who is in the next room: "Mr Watson, come here, I want to see you." The invention is demonstrated at the Centennial Exposition, Philadelphia, USA where Emperor Don Pedro of Brazil hears Bell recite the "To be or not to be" speech from *Hamlet* over the phone.
1877	Bell makes the first long-distance call between Boston and Salem, Massachusetts, 14 miles away.
1878	Bell demonstrates his telephone to Queen Victoria at Osborne House on the Isle of Wight. She becomes the first European monarch to use a phone.
1884	First telephone handset is launched.
1889	First coin-in-the-slot public phone, USA.
1891	France and England are connected by telephone cable.
1894	Guglielmo Marconi invents wireless telegraphy.
1897	There are seven phones per 1,000 people in the USA.
1901	The millionth phone in the USA is installed by the Bell network; Marconi sends a radio signal across the Atlantic.
1902	The trans-Pacific telephone cable connects Canada, New Zealand and Australia.
1907	There are an estimated 1,027,348 miles of land telecommunications lines and 233,823 miles of submarine cable worldwide.
1914	The first radio message is sent to an aircraft; the first transcontinental telephone call is made in the USA.
1919	Rotary dial telephones are invented.
1945	British writer Arthur C. Clarke proposes putting communications satellites in orbit above the Earth, which move at the same speed as the Earth spins; this means they stay in a fixed position, and communication with the ground is not interrupted.
1956	The first transatlantic telephone cable is laid.
1965	Intelsat I (*Early Bird*), the first commercial telecommunications satellite, is launched.
1967	The first cordless telephones go on sale.
1975	The first handheld mobile phones are sold.
1988	The first transatlantic fibre optic cable is laid.
2001	There are 990,728,000 telephone lines used around in the world: 316,850,000 are in Europe and 229,800,000 in North and South America.
2004	There are an estimated 1.598 billion mobile phone users worldwide. Some phones can be used for taking photos as well as making calls.

Countries with most telephones

Country	Telephone land lines
USA	202,176,000
China	136,800,000
Japan	74,100,000
Germany	51,157,000
UK	34,748,000

Telephone Bell

Alexander Graham Bell (1847–1922) is often called the father of the telephone. He was born in Edinburgh, Scotland, moved to Canada in 1870, and later to the USA. He became an expert on the science of speech and his first inventions helped deaf people to hear sounds. During his research, Bell developed a method of transmitting voice messages along a wire. In 1876 he patented the device, which he called the harmonic telegraph. This was the first telephone.

Cables under the sea

Soon after telegraph cables came into use in the 1840s, attempts were made to lay them across rivers and between islands and mainlands. Most didn't work. In 1850 the first cable was laid across the English Channel. The cable had to be strong enough to resist attack by salt water, ocean currents and water pressure, so had a thick, water-resistant cover made of steel. Inside were copper wires that carried the power and signal.

Technical improvements and the demand for faster communications encouraged companies to try laying cables over even greater distances. Several attempts to lay cables across the Atlantic failed when the cables snapped, but one was completed in 1858. To mark the occasion, Queen Victoria sent a telegraph message to President Buchanan in the USA. It took almost 18 hours to transmit her 99-word message! Attempts were made to increase the pace by raising the voltage, but this quickly burned out the cable. In 1865 the world's largest ship at the time, the *Great Eastern*, laid the first continuous cable across the Atlantic. It was the only ship able to carry a cable long enough.

During the 20th century, telegraph cables which transmitted Morse code were steadily replaced by telephone cables, which could transmit voices. Hundreds of thousands of kilometres of underwater cables were laid across the world's oceans and seas. These have now been replaced by fibre-optic cables, which offer faster transmission and many more connections. Along with satellites, they allow huge numbers of telephone messages and data to be sent across the world's telecommunications networks.

Alexander Graham Bell making the first call between New York and Chicago

Despite the advances of science, there is no machine in the world as complex as the human body. Our bodies are made up of 50 trillion cells and are extraordinarily adaptable. All the workings of the body are controlled by the brain, which is infinitely more complex than the most advanced computer.

HUMAN BODY

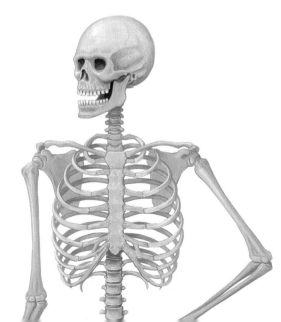

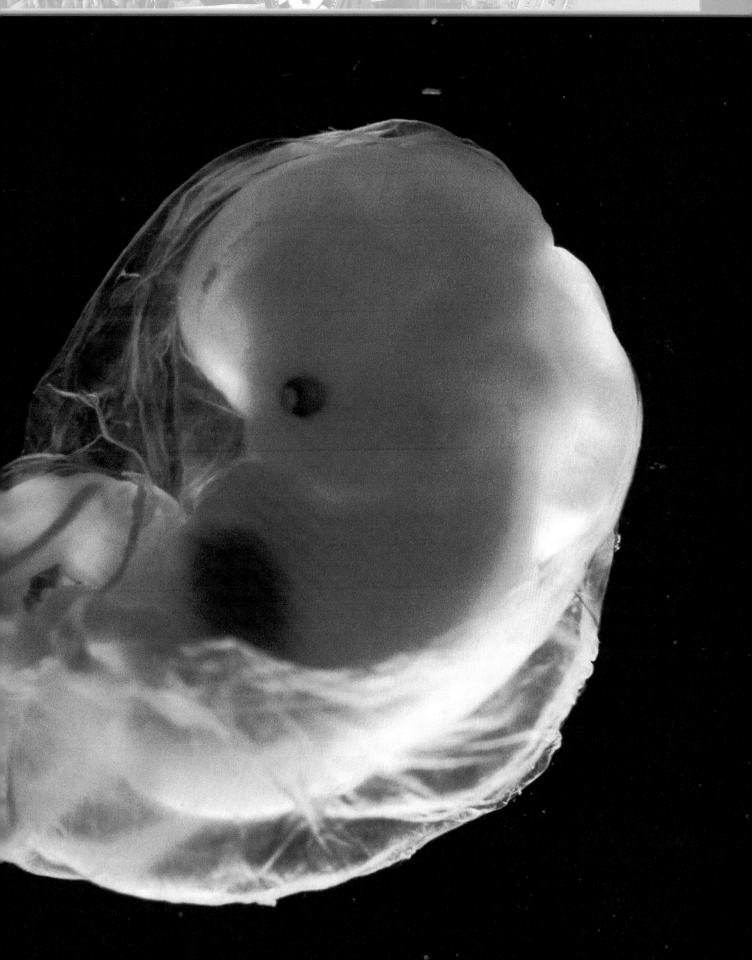

Your amazing body

Blood
An adult man's body contains about 5 litres of blood. A woman's contains about 4.3 litres. The blood travels along 100,000km of blood vessels which is equal to going 2.5 times round the Equator. It contains 25,000,000,000 to 30,000,000,000 red cells. The life span of red cells is only about 120 days, and 1,200,000 to 2,000,0000 of them are made every second. In a human lifetime you will make 0.5 tonne of red cells. Red cells are made and destroyed at a rate of 2–3 million per second.

Brain power
You lose 100,000 brain cells every day! Luckily you have 100 billion altogether. If the surface area of your brain could be ironed out it would measure 2,090sq cm.

Breathing
The average person inhales 6 litres of air per minute, or 8,640 litres a day. You take 13–17 breaths a minute when sitting still and up to 80 during vigorous exercise. If you average 20 breaths a minute, you breathe 28,800 times a day.

Cells
There are 50 trillion cells in your body and 3 billion of them die every minute (4,320,000,000,000 a day). Most of these are replaced. You make 10 billion new white blood cells each day. You have a total of 1,000,000,000,000 white cells, which help fight germs and infections.

Chemicals
There is enough carbon in your body to fill 900 pencils, enough fat to make 75 candles, enough phosphorus to make 220 match heads and enough iron to make a 7.5cm nail.

Digestive system
Your stomach produces up to 2 litres of hydrochloric acid a day. Stomach acid is strong enough to dissolve metals, but it does not have time to damage the stomach walls because 500,000 cells in your stomach lining are replaced every minute. The small intestine is about 5m long and is the longest part of your digestive system. The large intestine is a thicker tube, but is only about 1.5m long.

Eyes
You blink about 20,000 times a day.

Gas
On average, you will release 2 litres of gases from your intestines today as burps or farts.

Hair
Hair grows about 0.5mm a day.

Heartbeats
Your heart pumps 13,640 litres of blood around your body in a day – enough to fill nearly 40,000 drink cans. An average heartbeat pumps 59cc of blood. An average heartbeat rate of 70 beats a minute adds up to more than 100,000 beats a day.

Mouth
You will produce 37,800 litres of saliva in your lifetime.

Nails
Yours fingernails grow 0.05cm a week, which is four times faster than your toenails.

Nerves
There are about 13,000,000,000,000 nerve cells in your body, transmitting messages at speeds of 290 km/h – as fast as the world's speediest road cars.

Nose
Your sneezes can travel at 160km/h – as fast as a train.

Skin
Your skin weighs up to 4kg and covers an area of up to 1.3–1.7sq m. Getting dressed and undressed, rubbing body parts together, and even breathing cause microscopic flakes of skin to fall off at the rate of 50,000 flakes a minute. In a lifetime you will shed a total of 18kg of skin. Up to 80 per cent of household dust is made of dead human skin cells.

Sleep
In 7.5 hours of sleep, you will sleep lightly for 60 per cent of the time and deeply for 18 per cent. You will dream for 22 per cent of the time.

Sweat
You lose about 0.5 litres of water a day through 3,000,000 sweat glands. In hot climates you may lose as much as 13.5 litres a day.

Urine
You will pass between 400 and 2,000 millilitres of urine every day, depending on how old you are, your body size and the outside conditions, especially temperature.

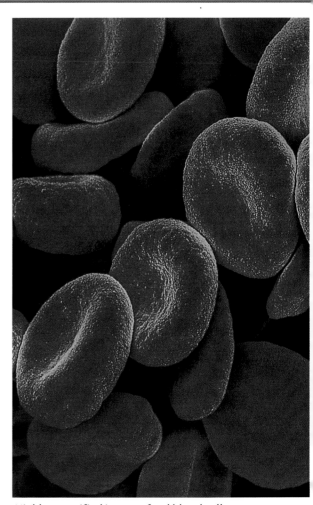

Highly magnified image of red blood cells

Largest human organs

The weights listed below are all averages, but sometimes organs are much larger. Some brains have weighed more than 2,000g, but that doesn't mean the owners were super-intelligent!

Organ		Average weight (grams)
Skin		10,886
Liver		1,560
Brain	male	1,408
	female	1,263
Lungs	right	580
	left	510
Heart	male	315
	female	265
Kidneys	left	150
	right	140
Spleen		170
Pancreas		98
Thyroid		35
Prostate	male only	20
Adrenals	left	6
	right	6

❤ Human skeleton

The skeleton is the body's framework. The bones of the skeleton support the body, protect the internal organs such as the heart and lungs, and allow you to move.

Longest bones in the body

These are the average measurements of the longest bones of an adult male. The same bones in the female skeleton are usually 6–13 per cent smaller, except the breastbone which is almost the same.

Bone	Average length (cm)
Femur (thighbone, upper leg)	50.50
Tibia (shinbone, inner lower leg)	43.03
Fibula (outer lower leg)	40.50
Humerus (upper arm)	36.46
Ulna (inner lower arm)	28.20
Radius (outer lower arm)	26.42
7th rib	24.00
8th rib	23.00
Hipbone (one half of pelvis)	18.50
Sternum (breastbone)	17.00

❤ What's your body made of?

Most of the human body is made up of water or H_2O, which is a combination of hydrogen and oxygen. As much as 99 per cent of the body is made up of oxygen, carbon, hydrogen, nitrogen, calcium and phosphorus. There are also small amounts of other elements.

Element	Average in 70kg person (g)	Element	Average in 70kg person (g)
Oxygen	43,000	Potassium	110–140
Carbon	16,000	Sodium	100
Hydrogen	7,000	Chlorine	95
Nitrogen	1,800	Magnesium	25
Calcium	1,200	Iron	4
Phosphorus	780	Zinc	2.3
Sulphur	140	Silicon	1

ONE AND ONLY

The only bone in the human body that is not connected to another bone is the hyoid bone, a U-shaped bone at the base of the tongue. It is supported by the muscles in the neck, but it is not connected to any other bone.

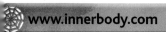
www.innerbody.com

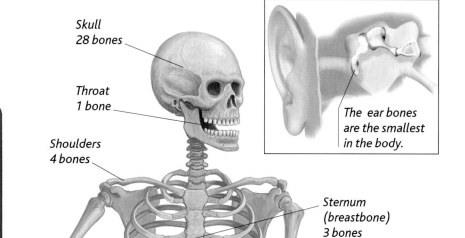

Skull
28 bones

Throat
1 bone

Shoulders
4 bones

The ear bones are the smallest in the body.

Sternum (breastbone)
3 bones

Ribs
24 bones

Vertebrae (backbone)
26 bones

Arms and hands
60 bones

Pelvis
2 bones

Legs and feet
58 bones

⚡ How many bones?

An adult human skeleton contains 206 bones. Amazingly, a baby has about 350 bones, but some some of them join together as the baby grows.

Body records

Longest nails
Shridhar Chillal of Pune, India (1937–) has not cut the nails on his left hand since 1952. By 2000 the total length of his nails on that hand was over 600cm.

Longest beard
Hans Langseth (1846–1927) had a beard that measured 5.33m. It has been in the Smithsonian Institution, Washington DC, USA, since 1967.

Hans Langseth

Longest moustache
Kalyan Ramji Sain of Sundargath, India, holds the record. His moustache measures 3.29m from tip to tip.

Longest hair
Swami Pandarasannadhi was the head of a monastery in Madras, India. When his hair was measured in 1949 it was 7.9m long.

Longest sneezing bout
Donna Griffiths of Pershore, Worcestershire, started sneezing on 13 January 1981 and continued for 978 days.

Longest hiccuping
Charles Osborne of Anthon, Iowa, USA, hiccupped from 1922 to 1990.

Maths genius
When he was only eight years old, American Zerah Colburn (1804–40) worked out how many seconds had elapsed since the birth of Christ. He did this in his head within seconds. When Zerah was asked whether 4,294,967,297 was a prime number (one that cannot be divided evenly by another number), he instantly replied that it was not – it is equal to 641 times 6,700,417.

Infant prodigy
By the age of four, Kim Ung-Yong of Korea (1963–) could speak fluent Korean, English, Japanese and German, and could solve calculus problems.

Memory
Gon Yang-ling of Harbin, China, has memorized more than 15,000 telephone numbers.

Weighty wonder

Daniel Lambert (1770–1809) was one of the heaviest British people of all time. At his largest, he weighed 330kg and measured 2.8m round his body and 94cm round his leg. Lambert used to charge visitors to his house a shilling (five pence) just to look at him. When he died in 1809, it took 34m of elm planking to make his coffin, which looked like a gigantic packing case. A window and part of the wall of his house had to be removed to get the coffin out, and it had to be mounted on wheels to trundle it to the cemetery.

Daniel Lambert

Amazing feats

- Basque strongman Mielxto Saralegi holds the world record for lifting a block of stone on to his shoulder. The stone weighed 327kg, as much as five adults.

- In 1996, at Sydney Airport, Australia, David Huxley pulled a Boeing 747-400 a distance of 54.7m. The plane weighed 187 tonnes and is one of the world's largest airliners.

- In 1992 Robert Galstyan dragged two railway wagons along a track in Moscow with his teeth. The wagons weighed 219.175 tonnes and he pulled them for 7m.

- In 1983, in Los Angeles, USA, Yogi Pandi supported the weight of a 3-tonne elephant on a board across his chest.

- In 1972 Walter Cornelius pushed a double-decker bus for a distance of 0.8km – with his head.

- In 1985 Mick Gooch of Chatham in Kent did 16 press-ups. He used only one finger, which was balanced on a coconut.

Left-handers
People called Kerr are likely to be left-handed. There were so many left-handers in the Kerr clan that they built spiral staircases in their castles which turned anticlockwise!

World's oldest people

Below is a list of the world's longest-living people, or supercentenarians. It includes only those for whom there are accurate records of their birth and death dates.

Name/dates	Country	Age
Jeanne Calment (1875–1997)	France	122 years and 164 days
Shigechiyo Izumi (1865–1986)	Japan	120 years and 237 days
Sarah DeRemer Knauss (1880–1999)	USA	119 years and 97 days
Lucy Hannah (1875–1993)	USA	117 years and 248 days
Marie-Louise Meilleur (1880–1998)	Canada	117 years and 229 days
Estella Jones (1881–1999)	USA	117 years and 229 days
Tane Ikai (1879–1995)	Japan	116 years and 175 days
Carrie White (1874–1991)	USA	116 years and 88 days
Kamato Hongo (1887–2003)	Japan	116 years and 45 days

Tallest real giants

These are the most reliable records. All are men, except Trijntje Keever and Jeng Jinlian.

Name/dates	Country	Height (m)
Robert Pershing Wadlow (1918–40)	USA	2.72
John Aasen (1887–1938)	USA	2.67
John William Rogan (1871–1905)	USA	2.64
John F. Carroll (1932–69)	USA	2.63.5
Al Tomaini (1918–62)	USA	2.55
Trijntje Keever (1616-33)	Netherlands	2.55
Väinö Myllyrinne (1909–63)	Finland	2.51.4
Bernard Coyne (1897–1921)	USA	2.48.9
Don Koehler (1925–81)	USA	2.48.9
Edouard Beaupre (1881–1904)	Canada	2.48.9
Jeng Jinlian (1964–82)	China	2.48
Patrick Cotter or O'Brien (c 1762–1806)	Ireland	2.46
Louis Moilanen (1885–1913)	Finland/USA	2.46

Robert Wadlow

Life expectancy

Life expectancy is the average number of years people are likely to live in different countries. Conditions can improve or sometimes get worse, so life expectancy can get higher or lower. The top 20 and lowest 20 countries are listed, together with figures for the USA and UK for comparison.

Highest life expectancy

Country	Years
Japan	81.5
Sweden	80.0
Iceland	79.7
Canada	79.3
Spain	79.2
Australia	79.1
Israel	79.1
Switzerland	79.1
France	78.9
Norway	78.9
Belgium	78.7
Italy	78.7
Austria	78.5
Luxembourg	78.3
Malta	78.3
Netherlands	78.3
Cyprus	78.2
Germany	78.2
Greece	78.2
New Zealand	78.2
UK	*78.1*
USA	*77.0*

Lowest life expectancy

Country	Years
Zambia	32.7
Zimbabwe	33.9
Sierra Leone	34.3
Swaziland	35.7
Lesotho	36.3
Malawi	37.8
Mozambique	38.5
Rwanda	38.9
Central African Republic	39.8
Angola	40.1
Burundi	40.8
Côte d'Ivoire	41.2
Botswana	41.4
Dem Rep of Congo	41.4
Tanzania	43.5
Chad	44.7
Guinea-Bissau	45.2
Kenya	45.2
Ethiopia	45.5
Uganda	45.7

Tom Thumb and friends

American showman Phineas T. Barnum first met Charles Sherwood Stratton (USA, 1838-83) when he was four years old. He was 61cm tall and weighed 6.8kg. Barnum persuaded Charles's parents to allow him to exhibit their son for a fee of $3 a week. He was advertised as "General Tom Thumb, a dwarf eleven years of age, just arrived from England". By the time he died, he had grown to 1m and weighed 32kg. Lavinia Warren (USA, 1841–1919) was 79cm tall. Her first husband was Tom Thumb.

"Commodore" Nutt (USA, 1844–81) was 74cm tall. Like Tom Thumb he was exhibited by Phineas T. Barnum.

Commodore Nutt, Miss Warren, normal-sized man and Tom Thumb

Calorie counts

A Calorie (with a capital C) is a unit that measures the amount of energy in foods. It is also known as a kilocalorie and is equal to 1,000 calories (with a small c). A calorie is the amount of heat needed to raise the temperature of 1 gram of water by 1°C. An adult might eat up to 3,000 Calories a day. Eating too many Calories that the body does not use for energy may make you fat. Nutritionists and scientists also use another unit, the kilojoule, for measuring the energy in food. One Calorie equals 0.004184 kilojoules. The figures below are based on the average number of Calories a 70kg adult burns when doing an activity for one hour. A lighter person uses fewer Calories and a heavier person more.

Activity	Calories used per hour
Squash	844
Rugby, skipping, swimming	704
Basketball, cycling, running, walking upstairs	563
Canoeing or rowing	493
Football, ice skating, roller skating, skiing, tennis	493
Aerobics	422
Mowing lawn	387
Cricket (batting or bowling), gardening, skateboarding	352
Dancing	317
Golf, table tennis	281
Housework, walking dog	246
Frisbee, surfing	211
Playing piano	176
Standing	120
Sitting	90
Sleeping	65

Common phobias

A phobia is a strong fear of a particular animal, object, situation or activity. The fear is often out of proportion to the reality and may make people vomit, sweat, tremble and even faint. People may go to great lengths to avoid the subjects of their phobias.

Most common phobias

Fear of	Phobia name
Spiders	Arachnephobia or arachnophobia
Snakes	Ophidiophobia
Flying	Aerophobia or aviatophobia
Open spaces	Agoraphobia, cenophobia or kenophobia
Confined spaces	Claustrophobia, cleisiophobia, cleithrophobia or clithrophobia
Heights	Acrophobia, altophobia, hypsophobia or hypsiphobia

Unusual phobias

Fear of	Phobia name	Fear of	Phobia name
Ants	Myrmecophobia	Hair	Chaetophobia
Bathing	Ablutophobia	Knees	Genuphobia
Beards	Pogonophobia	Mirrors	Eisoptrophobia
Chickens	Alektorophobia	Money	Chrometophobia
Dancing	Chorophobia	Number 13	Triskaidekaphobia
Dolls	Pediophobia	Opening your eyes	Optophobia
Fish	Ichthyophobia		
Frogs	Batrachophobia	Paper	Papyrophobia
Going to bed	Clinophobia	String	Linonophobia
		Teeth	Odontophobia

Keep fit

Experts say that these sports and activities are the best ways of keeping fit and making your body strong and supple. Current advice is that everyone needs to take at least a brisk 30-minute walk five times a week to stay healthy.

1 Swimming
2 Cycling
3 Rowing
4 Gymnastics
5 Judo
6 Dancing
7 Football
8 Jogging
9 Walking (briskly!)
10 Squash

Cycling is one of the best ways of keeping fit and uses about 563 Calories an hour.

Medical milestones

Milestone	Date	Inventor/discoverer	Country
First medical studies	c 460 BC	Hippocrates	Greece
Accurate anatomical drawings	AD 1543	Andreas Vesalius	Belgium
Blood circulation described	1628	William Harvey	UK
Bacteria described	1683	Antonie van Leeuwenhoek	Netherlands
Smallpox vaccination	1796	Edward Jenner	UK
Morphine (painkiller)	1805	Friedrich Sertürner	Germany
Homeopathy	1810	Samuel Hahnemann	Germany
Stethoscope	1816	René Laënnec	France
Blood transfusion	1818	Thomas Blundell	UK
Ether (anaesthetic)	1842	Crawford Long	USA
Nitrous oxide (laughing gas) anaesthetic	1844	Horace Wells	USA
Ether vapour (anaesthetic)	1846	William Morton	USA
Chloroform (anaesthetic)	1847	John Bell/James Simpson	UK
Red Cross founded	1864	Henri Dunant	Switzerland
Antiseptic surgery	1867	Joseph Lister	UK
Rabies vaccine	1885	Louis Pasteur	France
X-rays discovered	1895	William von Röntgen	Germany
Psychoanalysis	1895	Sigmund Freud	Austria
Aspirin	1898	Felix Hoffman	Germany
Blood groups identified	1901	Karl Landsteiner	Austria
Vitamins discovered	1906	Frederick Hopkins	UK
Insulin (diabetes treatment)	1922	Frederick Banting/ John Macleod/Charles Best	Canada/ Canada/USA
Iron lung	1927	Philip Drinker	USA
Penicillin discovered	1928	Alexander Fleming	UK
Penicillin used	1940	Howard Florey/ Ernest Chain	Australia/UK
Artificial heart valve	1952	Charles Hufnagel	USA
DNA structure identified	1953	Francis Crick/James Watson	UK/USA
Kidney dialysis	1955	Willem J. Kolff	Neths/USA
Heart pacemaker	1957	Clarence Lillehie	USA
Human heart transplant	1967	Christiaan Barnard	S. Africa
Artificial heart	1970	Robert Jarvik	USA
CAT scanner	1971	Godfrey Hounsfield	UK
Test-tube baby (Louise Brown)	1978	Patrick Steptoe	UK
Smallpox eradicated	1980	World Health Organization	International
Genetic fingerprinting	1984	Alec Jeffreys	UK
AIDS virus identified	1984	Centers for Disease Control	USA
First mammal cloning (Dolly, a sheep)	1996	Ian Wilmut, Roslin Institute	UK
Human DNA genome sequence completed	2000	—	International

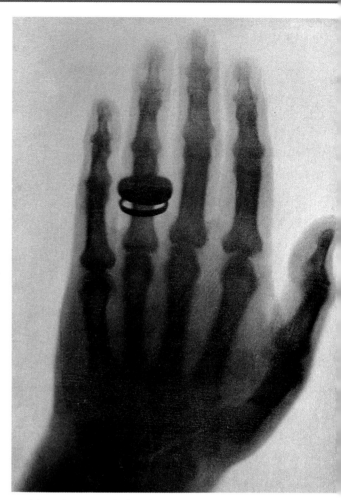

In this early X-ray of a hand, a ring can be seen on one finger.

Causes of death worldwide

There are very big differences between the causes of death in developing countries and in developed or Western countries. In developing countries, many more deaths are caused by infectious diseases and illnesses spread by insects such as malaria. In developed countries more people become ill from being overweight and eating rich diets. There are about 57,029,000 deaths a year worldwide.

Major causes of death	Approx number per year
Heart diseases	16,733,000
Cancers	7,121,000
Respiratory infections	3,963,000
Lung diseases	3,702,000
HIV/AIDS	2,777,000
Digestive diseases	1,968,000
Diarrhoeal diseases	1,798,000
Tuberculosis	1,566,000
Malaria	1,272,000
Road traffic injuries	1,192,000
Childhood diseases (measles, etc)	1,124,000
Neuropsychiatric disorders	1,112,000

Lou Gehrig's disease

Many diseases are named after the doctors who first identified them. Lou Gehrig's disease is unusual in that it was named after a famous sufferer, New York Yankees baseball player Henry Louis Gehrig (1903–41). It is also known as motor neurone disease. Other famous sufferers include physicist Stephen Hawking.

What we eat

How much food do you think you'll eat in a lifetime? Every few years the British government carries out a national survey to find out how much people eat. These latest figures show that the average person will eat more than 50 tonnes of food over an 80-year lifespan.

Food/drink	Amount eaten (kg)
Milk and cream	8,969
Soft drinks	7,255
Bread	3,261
Fresh fruit	3,166
Alcoholic drinks	3,058
Fresh potatoes	2,991
Processed vegetables	2,775
Other fresh vegetables	2,113
Cereals	2,092
Processed fruit and nuts	1,851
Cakes and biscuits	1,444
Poultry	1,140
Fresh green vegetables	1,023
Fats	836
Sugar and preserves (jam, etc)	720
Fish	678
Beef and veal	537
Sweets	532
Cheese	458
Eggs	404
Flour	304
Beverages	295
Pork	258
Mutton and lamb	204

Greedy people

"Diamond Jim" Brady

James "Diamond Jim" Buchanan Brady (1856–1917) was one of the richest – and greediest – men in the USA. He started his day with a huge breakfast washed down with several litres of orange juice. During the morning, he often ate two or three dozen oysters, then went on to lunch, which might be as many as six lobsters, a whole joint of beef, a few pastries and a big box of chocolates with another few litres of orange juice. At teatime he drank lemonade to wash down the enormous platter of seafood he guzzled. For dinner he would start with a few dozen oysters, followed by six crabs and two bowls of turtle soup, six or seven lobsters, two whole ducks and a few gigantic steaks – with yet more orange juice. A post-mortem showed that his stomach was six times normal size.

King Edward VII

Edward VII (1841–1910), Queen Victoria's eldest son, usually ate 14 courses for lunch and dinner. He could also eat hearty snacks between meals without ruining his appetite. At night a whole chicken was placed beside his bed – in the morning only the bones were left!

Honoré de Balzac

The French author (1799–1850) frequently scoffed 100 oysters, 12 lamb cutlets, a duck and a couple of partridges at a sitting.

Richard Owen's banquet was held inside a model of a dinosaur.

Extraordinary feasts

- Philip, Duke of Burgundy, gave a four-day banquet in 1454. The highlight came when a huge pie was brought into the room. The lid was raised to reveal 28 musicians playing inside the pie.

- On 23 October 1843, the statue of Lord Nelson was due to be hauled to the top of Nelson's Column in Trafalgar Square, London. Before this was done, 14 men sat down to a dinner of rump steak on the plinth on top of the column, 51m above the ground.

- On New Year's Eve 1853, dinosaur expert Professor Richard Owen held a banquet inside the framework of a model of a gigantic iguanodon dinosaur.

- A wealthy businessman called C.K.G. Billings gave a dinner at Sherry's restaurant in New York on 28 March 1903 to celebrate the completion of his new stables. All the 36 guests were on horseback. Their horses were brought to the ballroom by lift and the floor was laid with turf. The main course of pheasant was served out of nosebags, and the champagne in rubber buckets.

- American millionaire George A. Kessler held his birthday party at the Savoy Hotel in London on 30 June 1905. He had the courtyard flooded and decorated in Venetian style. His guests sat inside a gondola and were served by waiters dressed as gondoliers.

The birth of the burger

The name hamburger is nothing to do with ham, but comes from the German city of Hamburg. A burger was originally called a Hamburg steak. In 1889, the word hamburger first appeared in a restaurant review in the US newspaper *Walla Walla Union*. It was in a phrase that was itself a mouthful: "You are asked if you will have porkchopbeefsteakham andegghamburgersteak orliverandbacon."

Burger with all the trimmings

Who invented potato crisps?

Crisps were invented in Saratoga Springs, New York, in 1853 when a guest at Moon Lake Lodge complained that the French fries he was served were too thick. The chef, an American Indian named George Crum, made some wafer-thin crisps that were a huge success. Soon crisps were being made elsewhere in the USA and in other countries. Today the average person in the UK eats 3kg of crisps every year.

Bottles and barrels

The first bottles were made in sizes that were easy to carry. The 750ml bottle became the standard size for most types of wine in the 19th century. In the USA this has been the legal size since 1979, even though metric measurements are not widely used there. Some wine and champagne bottle sizes have Biblical names – the name Jeroboam was used for the four-bottle size as early as 1725 in Bordeaux, and others were soon named in the same way.

Bottle equivalents	Capacity (litres)	Champagne	Wine
½	0.375	Half-bottle	Half-bottle
Bottle	0.75	Bottle	Bottle
2	1.5	Magnum	Magnum
4	3	Double magnum	Jeroboam
6	4.5	Rehoboam	Jeroboam
8	6	Methuselah	Impériale
12	9	Salmanazar	-
16	12	Balthazar	-
20	15	Nebuchadnezzar	-
24	18	Melchior/Solomon	Melchior
36	27	Primat	-

The origins of the names used for bottles

- Jeroboam, the first king of Israel.
- Rehoboam, son of Solomon, the first king of Judah.
- Methuselah, a biblical leader reputed to have lived 969 years.
- Salmanazar, an Assyrian king.
- Balthazar, noted for serving wine at a great feast.
- Nebuchadnezzar, king of Babylon.
- Melchior, one of the Three Wise Men.

Barrels were invented during the Iron Age. They gradually replaced the pottery containers or amphorae the Ancient Greeks and Romans used for their wine, oil and other liquids. Barrels come in a range of different sizes, each with its own name.

Barrel	Gallons	Litres	Barrel	Gallons	Litres
Pin	4.5	20.5	Hogshead	54	245.5
Firkin	9	40.9	Puncheon	72	327.3
Kilderkin	18	81.8	Butt	108	491.0
Barrel	36	163.7	Tun	216	981.9

Bananas grow pointing upwards, not down.

Banana fact file

Bananas are one of the most popular of all fruits. Worldwide, people eat more than 70 million tonnes of bananas every year.

- Bananas grow on trees, but in botanical terms the banana is a herb.
- Bananas first grew in India and China, were then grown in Palestine and later in Africa. They were taken to the Caribbean in the 1500s.
- Bananas were imported into the USA from the early 19th century. They first became popular when they were exhibited at the Centennial Exposition, Philadelphia in 1876 – the same event at which Alexander Graham Bell's telephone was first demonstrated.
- The average British person will eat 882kg of bananas in a lifetime – more than 12 times the average adult body weight.
- India grows more than 16 million tonnes of bananas a year, which is more than any other country.
- Bananas are a tropical fruit, but more than 400,000 tonnes a year are grown in European countries, including Spain, Portugal, Cyprus and Italy.

⊘ See also

Trees and plants: pages 50–51

Prehistory is the time before writing, so what we know about this time comes from archaeology. More recently, history has been recorded so much more is known. Some major events (such as World War II) affected most of the world, but for much of the past, different regions have had quite separate histories.

WORLD HISTORY

Prehistoric ages

Prehistory is the time before events were written down and recorded. Human prehistory is usually divided into three periods.

Stone Age
The period when stone was used for tools. It is divided into two parts: Palaeolithic (Old Stone) from about 2 million to 10,000 BC and Neolithic (New Stone) from about 10,000 to 3300 BC.

Bronze Age (c 3300–c 2500 BC)
The period when people began to make things with bronze, which was more reliable and hardwearing than stone.

Iron Age (c 1200 BC–)
The period when iron was used for making tools. Bronze is a better material, but iron was more widely available, so cheaper.

Newgrange in Ireland is a famous prehistoric monument. It was made in about 3100 BC, and inside the stone and turf mound is a passage leading to a burial chamber.

Historical periods

History is usually divided into different periods to make it easier to study and talk about. The following are the main periods in the history of the Western world since the fall of the Roman Empire.

The early Middle Ages (Dark Ages)
This period came after the fall of the Roman Empire in AD 476, when so-called barbarians (Germanic tribes) took over areas that had been under Roman control. It became known as the Dark Ages because there was very little writing, science or culture during this time. The lack of writing also means that we do not know much about what happened. The early Middle Ages came to an end after the Norman Conquest when there was a revival in learning.

The Middle (Medieval) Ages
This was a very religious time. Most people believed in an all-powerful God, responsible for bringing order and prosperity. The Church was very influential and wealthy, and many great cathedrals and monasteries were built during this period. It was a great age of learning, and the first universities were founded in Bologna, then Paris and Oxford. Chartres Cathedral in France was built and the writings of Dante and Chaucer were published.

The Renaissance
The Renaissance began in Italy during the 14th century, and spread to northern Europe in the 16th century. The name Renaissance comes from the French word for rebirth; people looked back to Greek and Roman ideals in arts such as architecture and sculpture at this time. These ideas spread with the help of printing, which was invented by German Johannes Gutenberg in the mid-15th century. The Renaissance was marked by people's belief in progress and personal achievement. The playwright William Shakespeare and the artist Leonardo da Vinci lived and worked during this time.

The Reformation
In 16th-century Europe most people belonged to the Roman Catholic Church, which was headed by the Pope. Some were concerned that the Church was too involved with power and money. Leaders such as Erasmus and Martin Luther wanted people to reject the priests and return to the roots of Christianity and the Bible. This led to the start of Protestantism and its split from the Roman Catholic Church.

The age of colonialism
In 1492 Christopher Columbus discovered the Americas. This encouraged many European countries to invade and conquer other smaller or weaker countries so they could use their resources, trade with them or use them as stopping points for their ships. Portugal gained control of what is now Brazil, and Spain took most of Latin America, as well as large parts of what is now the United States. The Dutch gained the Indonesian islands and the French took Canada. Britain was the most powerful colonizing power. It gained 13 colonies in North America, plus Australasia, some Caribbean islands and, eventually, vast tracts of Africa and Asia, including India.

NORTH AMERICA

EUROPE

AFRICA

SOUTH AMERICA

Hetton Colliery, County Durham, 1822

The Industrial Revolution

The Industrial Revolution began with the invention of steam power and steam-driven machinery (mainly used in the textile industry) in 18th-century Britain. During the following century inventions such as steam-powered ships and railways spread throughout the world. This revolution led thousands of people to leave the countryside and move to crowded slum towns where there were large factories employing huge numbers of workers. The new industries needed better transport to bring supplies and deliver finished goods, so a huge network of roads and canals was built during the 18th century, followed by railways in the 19th. The Industrial Revolution also led to a growth in child labour and a widening divide between rich and poor people.

ASIA

AUSTRALIA

Extent of European colonialism 1815–1914

- Belgian
- British
- Dutch
- French
- German
- Italian
- Portuguese
- Russian
- Spanish

The modern age

During the 20th century advances in technology led to great changes in society and global politics. New weapons and military techniques changed the way wars were fought. Huge numbers of people died during World Wars I and II. During the Cold War between the USA and the USSR there was no fighting, but both sides were afraid of the nuclear weapons they were developing.

Factories began to mass-produce motorcars which ordinary people could afford. This allowed them to live further from their work places and led to the building of suburbs all over the Western world. Air travel, television and, most recently, the Internet have all enabled more people to experience the world beyond their own country. At the same time, cheap domestic appliances such as washing machines and dishwashers allow people more time to spend on activities such as entertainment and shopping.

Inside one of the huge shopping malls that have sprung up in suburban areas all over the USA and Europe

➡ **See also**

Inventions: pages 80-81

History timeline

Date	Event
753 BC	**Rome founded**
221 BC	Qin Shihuangdi becomes first Emperor of China
about AD 33	Jesus crucified
43	Emperor Claudius invades Britain
79	Pompeii in Italy destroyed by the eruption of Vesuvius volcano
476	Roman Empire ends when Goths invade
632	Death of Muhammad, founder of Islam
1066	Battle of Hastings; William the Conqueror becomes King of England
1086–7	Domesday Book records all land in England
1096–99	First Crusade – European Christians attempt to recover Jerusalem and the Holy Land from Muslim control
1215	King John signs Magna Carta, granting rights to English citizens
1347–80s	**Black Death kills 75 million in Asia and Europe**
1337–1453	100 Years War between England and France; France eventually wins
1415	Henry V of England defeats the French army at the Battle of Agincourt and goes on to conquer Normandy
1431	17-year-old French patriot Joan of Arc leads an army and defeats the English (1429), but is burned at the stake
1455–85	Wars of the Roses (civil war in England)
1476	Caxton begins printing in London
1478	Spanish Inquisition begins the persecution of non-Catholics
1492	Columbus sails from Palos, Spain, to Americas
1517	Reformation starts when Martin Luther publishes protests against Catholic Church
1519-22	Ferdinand Magellan's expedition circumnavigates the globe
1588	Spanish Armada defeated by the English fleet, fireships and storms
1618–48	Thirty Years War (Catholic v Protestant) in Europe

Black Death

This epidemic was probably caused by bacteria that were passed on by fleabites and by contact with infected sufferers. It was known as the Black Death because victims suffered from black blotches on their skin before dying. The plague swept across Asia and Europe in the 14th century, killing as many as a third of the people.

Date	Event
1620	The Pilgrim Fathers sail from Plymouth for America and found a new colony
1642–49	English Civil War
1649	King Charles I executed
1660	Restoration of the monarchy; Charles II becomes king
1664–65	The Great Plague kills 70,000 in London
1666	Great Fire of London
1707	Act of Union – Scotland and England unite
1776	**US Declaration of Independence**
1776–83	American War of Independence
1783	First balloon flight (Montgolfier brothers, France)
1788	First European settlers arrive in Australia
1789	**French Revolution**
1793	Louis XVI of France executed
1815	Battle of Waterloo; Wellington defeats Napoleon
1825	World's first public railway, Stockton to Darlington
1833	Slavery abolished in the British Empire
1853–56	Crimean War
1860–65	American Civil War
1863	First underground railway, London
1869	Suez Canal opens
1869	US transcontinental railway completed
1876	Alexander Graham Bell invents telephone
1901–10	Peak decade for immigration into USA (8.8 million immigrants)
1903	First aeroplane flights (Wright brothers, USA)
1903	Henry Ford begins mass production of cars
1914–18	World War I – 8,545,800 military deaths
1917	**Russian Revolution establishes Soviet Union**
1929–33	Great Depression (world economic crisis)
1939–45	World War II – 15,843,000 military deaths
1945	Atom bombs dropped on Hiroshima and Nagasaki, Japan
1945–90	Cold War between USSR and the West
1950–53	Korean War
1959–75	Vietnam War (US involved 1961–73)
1961	First man in space (Yuri Gagarin, USSR)
1961	Berlin Wall built, separating East and West Germany
1963	US President John F. Kennedy assassinated
1969	Neil Armstrong becomes first man on the Moon
1989	**Fall of the Berlin Wall marks the end of the Soviet Union**
1994	Nelson Mandela becomes president of South Africa
2001	World Trade Center, New York, destroyed by terrorists; US retaliates by invading Afghanistan
2003–	Iraq War; Saddam Hussein overthrown but violence continues
2004	**Tsunami kills thousands in Asia**

Fighting outside the Hotel de Ville, Paris, during the French Revolution

Declaration of Independence *by John Trumbull (1756–1843)*

 # 753 BC Rome founded

According to legend, Rome was founded by Romulus and Remus, the twin sons of the god Mars and priestess Rhea Silvia. The city is named after Romulus, who killed his brother and ruled as Rome's first king. Rome was the capital of the Roman Empire, which controlled the entire Mediterranean region and far beyond by 44 BC.

 # 1776 US Independence

The Declaration of Independence was prepared after years of tension between Britain and the American colonies over matters such as taxation. It listed the colonies' complaints and expressed the determination of the people of America to separate themselves from their British rulers. The declaration was signed on 4 July 1776. The armed conflict that followed ended with America's victory in 1781. In 1783 the Treaty of Paris recognized the country's independence.

 # 1789 French Revolution

The French people had many complaints against their system of government, especially the power of the monarchy and the land-owning aristocracy. These erupted in a revolution in which the Bastille prison was seized. The violent period that followed became known as the Reign of Terror, and King Louis XVI and many other members of the ruling class were executed.

 # 1917 Russian Revolution

The rule of the Russian royal family led by the Tsar ended with the February Revolution in 1917. The revolution was triggered by problems such as food shortages and Russia's involvement in World War I. The October Revolution followed later that year, when Soviet forces seized control. They murdered the Tsar and his family and attempted to create a Communist state under the leadership of Lenin. A civil war followed from 1918 to 1922. Soviet rule lasted until 1991.

 # 1989 Fall of Berlin Wall

After World War II, control of the East German city of Berlin was shared between West Germany (with American, British and French troops) and Soviet East Germany. In 1961 the East Germans built the Berlin Wall to stop its inhabitants fleeing to the West, and 192 people were shot while trying to defect. The wall was a symbol of the divide between the Soviet Union and the West. When the Soviet Union collapsed, the wall was torn down and East and West Germany were reunited, with Berlin as the new capital city.

East Berliners crossing into the West after the fall of the Berlin Wall

2004 Tsunami

The tsunami in December 2004 will go down in history as one of the worst natural disasters of modern times. It was caused by an undersea earthquake, which led to sudden and catastrophic flooding of coastal regions in Indonesia, Sri Lanka, Thailand, Myanmar, the Maldives, Malaysia and parts of Africa. More than 289,000 people were killed.

www.info-s.com/history.html

Mesopotamia/Sumeria

Mesopotamia was a region around the Tigris and Euphrates rivers, which is now part of Turkey, Syria and Iraq. The area was controlled by several different peoples, beginning with the Sumerians in around 3500 BC. They set up a number of city-states that constantly battled to control land and trade routes until they were united under one ruler in 2350 BC. The Sumerians are said to have invented the wheel and cuneiform script, which many people claim is the earliest form of writing. They finally became absorbed into other races around 2000 BC.

 ## Ancient Egypt

Egypt is an area in the Nile valley which was ruled as a single state from about 3200 BC. There were 30 dynasties, led by pharaohs who were both kings and gods. The pyramids were built during the fourth dynasty (2575–2467 BC) as tombs for the pharaohs of that time. The Great Pyramid of Giza was the world's tallest building for 4000 years, and it is the only wonder of the world that still stands. The Egyptians are also famous for their hieroglyphic writing and sea-going ships. Like other powerful empires, Ancient Egypt was weakened by invasions until it was taken over by Alexander the Great in 332 BC.

 ## Ancient Greece

Ancient Greece was called Hellas. The civilization was at its strongest in 500–400 BC, after Greece colonized Cyprus, parts of Italy, the Ukraine and the South of France. This era was known as the Golden Age. Some city-states, such as Athens and Sparta, became great centres of art, learning and politics. Many famous thinkers lived in Athens during this period, including Aristotle, Plato, Socrates and Aristophanes. The Ancient Greeks also created the idea of democracy: its citizens were encouraged to debate and then vote on issues. The Golden Age ended in wars between the city-states, which paved the way for King Philip of Macedonia to invade Greece, followed later by his son Alexander.

Greek empires
- Colonies of the Ancient Greeks
- Empire of Alexander the Great

 ## Alexander the Great's empire

Alexander III of Macedonia lived for only 33 years, from 356 to 323 BC. In that short time he built an empire covering Persia (modern Iraq, Iran, Syria and Turkey), Egypt, Greece and Babylon. It was difficult to keep this huge empire together, and it collapsed soon after his death.

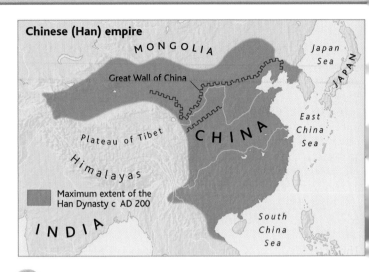

Chinese (Han) empire

Maximum extent of the Han Dynasty c AD 200

 ## Chinese empire

China was one of the first places where people are known to have lived. From 1600 BC it was made up of many small kingdoms which all united in 221 BC under one leader or emperor. Various dynasties ruled the empire, starting with the Qin dynasty. During this time, the Great Wall of China was built to keep invaders out. China was an extremely learned civilization, ahead of Europe in the arts and sciences by up to 200 years. The empire finally fell apart under the Han dynasty in AD 220 as a result of corruption and poverty.

 ## Roman empire

The Roman empire was formed in 31 BC under the leadership of Caesar Augustus, who ruled over every aspect of Roman life. Caesar Augustus brought peace, prosperity and culture. The empire expanded so much that by the 2nd century AD Rome had colonies which stretched from the Middle East to Spain, and from Great Britain to North Africa. The sheer size of the empire brought problems. There was not enough money to pay for an army spread across the world, which made the empire vulnerable to enemies. Constant attacks by German barbarians eventually defeated the army, and the empire fell in AD 476. The influence of Ancient Rome is staggering: Roman roads still cross Europe, the Roman legal system is still the model for countries in Europe and Latin America, and its language, Latin, is the basis of many languages spoken today.

Roman empire

Roman Empire c AD 200 during the reign of Emperor Trajan

Mayan empire

The Mayan empire was made up of city-states that stretched across southern Mexico and northern Central America. There have been Mayan people since 2000 BC but their greatest period was from AD 300 to 900, when architectural wonders such as Palenque and Uxmal were built. These structures and many others show that the Mayans had a very advanced knowledge of mathematics. The Mayan empire gradually declined after 900, and the Spanish invaded the area in the 15th century.

Inca empire

The Incas had a great empire that stretched 900,000sq km across South America and lasted from around 1200 until 1533. Their lands included Colombia, Bolivia and Argentina, with a capital, Cuzco, in Peru. Inca society was very organized: every person was told which job they had to do and where to do it. In return, the Incas were looked after by the state, and had basic benefits. Like the Aztecs, the Incas were brutally repressed by Spanish conquistadors in the 15th century.

Central and South American empires

- Aztec empire at about AD 1500
- Mayan empire c AD 300–900
- Maximum extent of the Inca empire

Aztec empire

The Aztecs were poor, nomadic people who arrived in Mexico in 1325 and founded the city of Tenochtitlán, on the site of Mexico City today. Tenochtitlán was a magnificent city, home to approximately 90,000 people. It showed the Aztecs' great skill in engineering and building, including a system of drainage that was far ahead of any in Europe. The Aztecs went on to conquer neighbouring city-states and extend their empire until it stretched from the Pacific to the Gulf of Mexico and into Guatemala. The empire ended when the Spanish, led by Hernán Cortés, invaded between 1519 and 1522.

Ottoman empire

The Ottoman empire was a mighty Islamic state from the 13th to 20th centuries, with lands that covered Turkey, parts of southwest Asia, southeast Europe and North Africa. The capital was Constantinople (now known as Istanbul). This was the most powerful empire in the world during the 1500s and 1600s. From then on the empire began to decline because its rulers refused to modernize and they lost lands in several wars. The empire was already weak when it allied with Germany in World War I. Defeat was the last straw, and the empire's remaining lands were divided up among the victors.

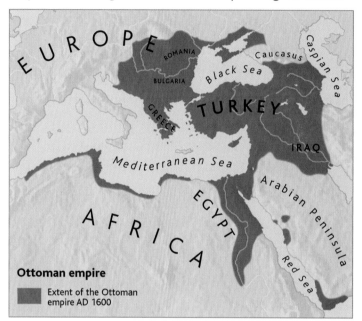

Ottoman empire

- Extent of the Ottoman empire AD 1600

Mogul empire

The Mogul empire was founded in AD 1526 in Northern India by a descendent of Genghis Khan. This was a hugely wealthy civilization and the Moguls greatly valued education, culture and art. The Taj Mahal was built by Moguls from 1632–53. This beautiful mausoleum was made for Emperor Shah Jahan's favourite wife, Mumtaz Mahal, and is built of marble with exquisite inlaid decoration. The empire's Muslim leaders wanted the people to keep Muslim ways, but many of its subjects were Hindu. In 1691 the empire was torn apart by bloody battles between Muslims and Hindus. The Mogul empire was finally overthrown by the British in 1857.

British empire

At the beginning of the 20th century, about a quarter of the world's people lived under British rule. The British had been expanding their empire since the 15th century, and by 1900 its lands included South Africa, Kenya, Egypt, Hong Kong, India, Iraq, Nepal, Singapore, Malta, Australia, New Zealand and Canada. Most of Britain's former colonies have now won or been granted independence. Many belong to the Commonwealth, which is a voluntary association of independent states founded in 1931 (see map on pages 102–103).

US presidents

US presidents are elected for a term of four years. George Washington was the first president of the USA and he served two terms. Only Franklin Delano Roosevelt served three terms. He was elected for a fourth term, but died shortly afterwards. In 1951 the 22nd Amendment to the US Constitution ruled that two terms are the most any president may serve. The two main political parties in the USA today are the Democratic Party and the Republican Party.

Bill Clinton, President of the USA 1993–2001

	Name	Party	First elected president
1	George Washington	Federalist	1789
2	John Adams	Federalist	1797
3	Thomas Jefferson	Dem-Rep	1801
4	James Madison	Dem-Rep	1809
5	James Monroe	Dem-Rep	1817
6	John Quincy Adams	Dem-Rep	1825
7	Andrew Jackson	Democrat	1829
8	Martin Van Buren	Democrat	1837
9	William Henry Harrison	Whig	1841
10	John Tyler	Whig	1841
11	James Knox Polk	Democrat	1845
12	Zachary Taylor	Whig	1849
13	Millard Fillmore	Whig	1850
14	Franklin Pierce	Democrat	1853
15	James Buchanan	Democrat	1857
16	Abraham Lincoln	Republican	1861
17	Andrew Johnson	Democrat	1865
18	Ulysses Simpson Grant	Republican	1869
19	Rutherford Birchard Hayes	Republican	1877
20	James Abram Garfield	Republican	1881
21	Chester Alan Arthur	Republican	1881
22	Grover Cleveland	Democrat	1885
23	Benjamin Harrison	Republican	1889
24	Grover Cleveland	Democrat	1893
25	William McKinley	Republican	1897
26	Theodore Roosevelt	Republican	1901
27	William Howard Taft	Republican	1909
28	Woodrow Wilson	Democrat	1913
29	Warren Gamaliel Harding	Republican	1921
30	Calvin Coolidge	Republican	1923
31	Herbert Clark Hoover	Republican	1929
32	Franklin Delano Roosevelt	Democrat	1933
33	Harry S. Truman	Democrat	1945
34	Dwight David Eisenhower	Republican	1953
35	John Fitzgerald Kennedy	Democrat	1961
36	Lyndon Baines Johnson	Democrat	1963
37	Richard Milhous Nixon	Republican	1969
38	Gerald Rudolph Ford	Republican	1974
39	Jimmy Carter	Democrat	1977
40	Ronald Reagan	Republican	1981
41	George Bush	Republican	1989
42	Bill Clinton	Democrat	1993
43	George W. Bush	Republican	2001

World monarchies

A monarchy is a country where the head of state is a king, queen or other hereditary ruler – someone who inherits the throne from a family member. But in some countries, such as Malaysia and the United Arab Emirates, the monarch is elected.

Country	Monarch	Year succeeded to throne
Bahrain	Shaikh Hamad bin Isa al-Khalifa	1999
Belgium	King Albert II	1993
Bhutan	King Jigme Singye Wangchuck	1972
Brunei	Sultan Haji Hassanal Bolkiah	1967
Cambodia	King Norodom Sihanouk	1993
Denmark	Queen Margrethe II	1972
Japan	Emperor Akihito	1989
Jordan	King Abdullah II	1999
Kuwait	Shaikh Jabir al-Ahmad al-Jabir al-Sabah	1977
Lesotho	King Letsie III	1996
Liechtenstein	Prince Hans Adam II	1989
Luxembourg	Grand Duke Henri	2000
Malaysia	Sultan Tuanku Syed Sirajuddin Putra Jamalullail	2001
Monaco	Prince Rainier III	1949
Morocco	King Mohammed VI	1999
Nepal	King Gyanendra Bir Bikram Shah Dev	2001
Netherlands	Queen Beatrix	1980
Norway	King Harald V	1991
Oman	Sultan Qaboos Bin Said al-Said	1970
Qatar	Shaikh Hamad bin Kaalifa al-Thani	1995
Samoa	King Susaga Malietoa Tanumafili II	1963
Saudi Arabia	King Fahd ibn Abdul Aziz al-Saud	1982
Spain	King Juan Carlos I	1975
Swaziland	King Mswati III	1986
Sweden	King Carl XVI Gustaf	1973
Thailand	King Bhumibol Adulyadej	1946
Tonga	King Taufa'ahau Tupou IV	1965
United Arab Emirates	Sheikh Zayed bin Sultan al-Nahyan	1971
United Kingdom	Queen Elizabeth II	1952

Kings and queens of Britain

Britain's royal rulers are all related, but come from different branches of the family. Some of the names of these branches – Windsor, Hanover and so on – are based on places, others on symbols. Plantagenet, for example, comes from the broom flower (*Planta genesta*) which family members wore as an emblem. The only time Britain has been without a monarch since 1066 was after the Civil War and the execution of Charles I. The government was led by Oliver Cromwell – one of the leaders in the Civil War – until the monarchy was brought back and Charles II took the throne.

Monarch	Ruled
Norman	
William I	1066–87
William II	1087–1100
Henry I	1100–35
Blois	
Stephen	1135–54
Plantagenet	
Henry II	1154–89
Richard I	1189–99
John	1199–1216
Henry III	1216–72
Edward I	1272–1307
Edward II	1307–27
Edward III	1327–77
Richard II	1377–99
Lancaster	
Henry IV	1399–1413
Henry V	1413–22
Henry VI	1422–61
York	
Edward IV	1461–70
Lancaster	
Henry VI (restored)	1470–71
York	
Edward IV (restored)	1471–83
Edward V	1483
Richard III	1483–85
Tudor	
Henry VII	1485–1509
Henry VIII	1509–47
Edward VI	1547–53
Jane	1553
Mary I	1553–58
Elizabeth I	1558–1603
Stuart	
James I	1603–25
Charles I	1625–49
Commonwealth	
Council of State	1649–53
Oliver Cromwell	1653–58
Richard Cromwell	1658–59

Monarch	Ruled
Stuart	
Charles II	1660–85
James II	1685–88
Mary II	1689–84
William III (jointly with Mary)	1689–84
William III (alone)	1694–1702
Anne	1702–14
Hanover	
George I	1714–27
George II	1727–60
George III	1760–1820
George IV	1820–30
William IV	1830–37
Victoria	1837–1901
Saxe-Coburg	
Edward VII	1901–10
Windsor	
George V	1910–36
Edward VIII	1936
George VI	1936–52
Elizabeth II	1952–

Henry VIII

Youngest prime minister

William Pitt was the youngest British prime minister. Pitt was born on 28 May 1759. He went to Cambridge University at the age of 14, became a Member of Parliament at 22 and Chancellor of the Exchequer at 23. He was elected Prime Minister in 1783 when he was only 24 and served until 1801, when he resigned. He returned in 1804 but died in 1806.

Amazing monarchs

Oldest monarch to ascend the British throne
William IV (ruled 1830–37) was 64 when he was crowned.

British monarchs with the most children
Edward I had 16 children (6 sons and 10 daughters). Both George III and James II had 15.

Most-married British monarch
Henry VIII had six wives who suffered various fates. They were: Catherine of Aragon (divorced), Anne Boleyn (beheaded), Jane Seymour (died 1537), Anne of Cleves (divorced), Catherine Howard (beheaded) and Catherine Parr, who survived Henry.

Youngest British monarchs
Henry VI was just eight months old when he became king on 1 September 1422 after the death of his father, Henry V. When his grandfather, Charles VI, died 50 days later on 21 October 1422, Henry also became King of France.

Shortest-reigning British monarchs
Queen Jane (Lady Jane Grey), ruled for only nine days in 1553, before being sent to the Tower of London. She was executed the following year. Edward V ruled for 75 days. He was one of the Princes in the Tower, who were allegedly murdered on the orders of their uncle, Richard III. Edward VIII abdicated (gave up the throne) on 11 December 1936, before his coronation. He had ruled for just 325 days.

Longest-reigning world monarch
King Louis XIV of France became king at the age of five. He ruled for 72 years, from 1643–1715.

Longest-reigning British monarch
Queen Victoria was 18 years old when she became queen in 1837 and she ruled for 63 years.

Richest world ruler
King Fahd ibn Abdul Aziz al-Saud of Saudi Arabia is reckoned to have assets worth more than $30 billion.

Monarchies with the most rulers
Japan's monarchy dates from 40 BC. Since then, it has had 125 rulers.

See also
Types of government: page 111

Women campaigning for the vote in New York

Votes for women

The Isle of Man was the first place to give women the vote in 1880, but the island is part of the UK and not a separate country. Until 1920 the only European countries that allowed women to vote were Sweden (1919) and Czechoslovakia (1920). In the USA women were granted the vote in 1920, although some states allowed it earlier – Wyoming in 1869, Colorado in 1894, Utah in 1895 and Idaho in 1896. A number of countries, such as France and Italy, did not give women the vote until 1945. Switzerland did not allow women to vote in elections to the Federal Council until 1971, and Liechtenstein was one of the last, in 1984. In some countries, such as Saudi Arabia, women are not allowed to vote at all – but neither can men.

	Country	Year
1	New Zealand	1893
2	Australia (women had the vote in South Australia in 1894 and in Western Australia in 1898 before the separate states were united in 1901)	1902
3	Finland (then a Grand Duchy under the Russian Crown)	1906
4	Norway (some women only; all women over 25 in 1913)	1907
5	Denmark and Iceland (a Danish dependency until 1918)	1915
6=	Netherlands	1917
=	USSR	1917
8=	Austria	1918
=	Canada	1918
=	Germany	1918
=	Great Britain and Ireland (in Ireland, part of UK until 1921, only women over 30 got the vote in 1918; lowered to 21 in 1928)	1918
=	Poland	1918

Women in parliament

There are 39 countries with at least 20 per cent of their parliament made up of women – but a number of countries still do not have any women representatives at all. The countries listed below have the highest percentages of women in parliament. These figures are based on the most recent general election results.

Parliament/ election date	Women members	Total members	Percentage women
Rwanda, 2003	39	80	48.8
Sweden, 2002	158	349	45.3
Denmark, 2001	68	179	38.0
Finland, 2003	75	200	37.5
Netherlands, 2003	55	150	36.7

* As at 29 February 2004

Roosevelt's Four Freedoms

On 6 January 1941 during World War II, US President Roosevelt made a famous speech to the US Congress. He proclaimed that four freedoms are essential to a flourishing democracy: freedom of speech, freedom of worship, freedom from want, and freedom from fear. He looked forward to these freedoms being possible after the defeat of Hitler and the Axis powers. In 1997 a memorial park was opened in Washington DC, honouring Roosevelt and his presidency. The Four Freedoms fountain in the park is a symbol of the ideas he expressed in his great speech.

Four Freedoms fountain, Washington DC

Major international organizations

A number of international organizations have been set up to deal with issues that concern the world in general, rather than the interests of individual countries. These organizations are not linked to political parties but often become involved in political matters.

Amnesty International (AI)
Amnesty International is a charitable organization set up in 1961. It campaigns for human rights throughout the world and against the detention of political prisoners.

Food and Agriculture Organization (FAO)
The FAO was set up in 1945 and is a United Nations agency based in Rome. Its main aim is to encourage the efficient production and distribution of food in the world.

International Labour Organization (ILO)
This organization was founded in 1919 and is based in Switzerland. Its aims are to improve the conditions of workers worldwide.

International Monetary Fund (IMF)
The IMF was established in 1944 and promotes world trade. It has 184 member countries.

International Red Cross and Red Crescent Movement
These organizations help the victims of such events as warfare and natural disasters.

Organization for Economic Co-operation and Development (OECD)
The OECD was formed in 1961. It aims to encourage economic and social development in industrialized countries and provide aid to developing countries.

United Nations
The UN was founded in 1945. Most countries of the world – a total of 191 – are members. The General Assembly of the UN meets at the New York headquarters and makes decisions about peacekeeping and human rights. Many other special organizations operate under the control of the UN.

United Nations Children's Fund (UNICEF)
UNICEF was set up in 1947. It works to improve the health and welfare of children and mothers in developing countries.

United Nations Educational, Scientific and Cultural Organization (UNESCO)
UNESCO was set up in 1946. It encourages countries to get together on matters such as education, culture and science.

World Bank
The World Bank was founded in 1944 and has 183 member countries. It helps developing countries by giving loans.

World Health Organization
The WHO is part of the UN. It promotes health matters worldwide and aims to raise medical standards and monitor diseases.

World Trade Organization (WTO)
The Swiss-based WTO encourages international trade by establishing trade agreements between countries.

World Wildlife Fund (WWF)
The WWF was set up in 1961 and is the world's largest conservation organization. Its main aims are to protect endangered animals and the places where they live.

Fidel Castro has ruled Cuba since 1959.

Types of government

There have been many different types of government around the world throughout history. Many of the names for them end in -cracy, from a Greek word meaning power.

Aristocracy
Rule by a small group of members of a privileged class.

Autocracy
Government by one person with unrestricted power; also known as despotism and dictatorship.

Communist
Government of a classless state in which private ownership is abolished and the state controls all means of production, as in China and Cuba.

Democracy
Government by the people directly or through elected representatives, as in the UK and USA.

Meritocracy
Government by leaders selected according to their ability.

Monarchy
Government in which power is held by a king (or queen, emperor or empress) who can pass power on to their heirs.

Oligarchy
Government by a small group of people.

Plutocracy
A government or state in which wealthy people rule.

Theocracy
Government ruled by or subject to religious authority.

The world is divided into 192 countries, although this number changes as countries divide, gain independence or take over other countries. This section looks at all the world's nations, from the biggest (Russia) to the smallest (Vatican City) and lists statistics such as population, capital city and currency.

COUNTRIES OF THE WORLD

ARCTIC OCEAN

Greenland
(DENMARK)

Beaufort Sea

Baffin
Bay

Arctic Circle

Alaska
(USA)

ICELAND

Bering
Sea

Hudson
Bay

Labrador
Sea

UNITED
KINGDO

Gulf of
Alaska

CANADA

IRELAND

PACIFIC
OCEAN

UNITED STATES

ATLANTIC
OCEAN

PORTUGA

Canary Islands
(SPAIN)

MO

Gulf of
Mexico

Tropic of Cancer

Western
Sahara
(MOROCCO)

M

E

X

I

C

O

BAHAMAS

CAPE
VERDE

MAURITAN

Hawaii
(USA)

CUBA

DOMINICAN
REPUBLIC

JAMAICA

HAITI

Puerto Rico (USA)

ANTIGUA & BARBUDA

BELIZE

ST CHRISTOPHER
& NEVIS

DOMINICA

SEN

GUATEMALA

HONDURAS

ST VINCENT & THE
GRENADINES

ST LUCIA
BARBADOS

GAMBIA

GUINEA

M

Caribbean Sea

EL SALVADOR

NICARAGUA

GRENADA

GUINEA-BISSAU

TRINIDAD &
TOBAGO

SIERRA
LEONE

COSTA RICA

PANAMA

VENEZUELA

French Guiana
(FRANCE)

LIBERIA

COLOMBIA

GUYANA

SURINAME

Equator

Galapagos Islands
(ECUADOR)

ECUADOR

B R A Z I L

PERU

Easter Island
(CHILE)

BOLIVIA

PACIFIC
OCEAN

PARAGUAY

C

H

I

L

E

A

R

G

E

N

T

I

N

A

URUGUAY

ATLANTIC
OCEAN

Falkland Islands
(UNITED KINGDOM)

Antarctica

Key to numbered countries

EUROPE
1 NETHERLANDS
2 LUXEMBOURG
3 ANDORRA
4 MONACO
5 LIECHTENSTEIN
6 VATICAN CITY STATE
7 SAN MARINO
8 SLOVENIA
9 BOSNIA-HERZEGOVINA
10 SERBIA AND MONTENEGRO
11 MACEDONIA

AFRICA
12 REPUBLIC OF CONGO-BRAZZAVILLE

ASIA
13 SINGAPORE

ARCTIC OCEAN

Svalbard
(NORWAY)

Barents Sea

Kara
Sea

Arctic Circle

NORWAY
SWEDEN
FINLAND
Baltic Sea
ESTONIA
LATVIA
LITHUANIA
RUSSIA
ARK
GERMANY
POLAND
BELARUS
CZECH
REP.
SLOVAKIA
AUSTRIA
HUNGARY
UKRAINE
MOLDOVA
ROMANIA
CROATIA
ITALY
ALBANIA
BULGARIA
Black Sea
GEORGIA
ARMENIA
AZERBAIJAN
Sardinia
(ITALY)
GREECE
TURKEY
CYPRUS
Caspian Sea
Aral
Sea
KAZAKHSTAN
UZBEKISTAN
KYRGYZSTAN
TURKMENISTAN
TAJIKISTAN
MONGOLIA

Sea of
Okhotsk

NORTH
KOREA
Sea of
Japan
SOUTH
KOREA
JAPAN

CHINA

TUNISIA
MALTA
Mediterranean Sea
LEBANON
ISRAEL
SYRIA
JORDAN
IRAQ
KUWAIT
IRAN
AFGHANISTAN
PAKISTAN
NEPAL
BHUTAN
BAHRAIN
QATAR

PACIFIC
OCEAN

Tropic of Cancer

LIBYA
EGYPT
SAUDI
ARABIA
UNITED ARAB
EMIRATES
Red Sea
YEMEN
OMAN
INDIA

TAIWAN
Philippine
Sea

GER
CHAD
SUDAN
ERITREA
DJIBOUTI
Arabian
Sea
BANGLADESH
MYANMAR
LAOS
THAILAND
South
China
Sea
PHILIPPINES

MARSHALL
ISLANDS

ERIA
CAMEROON
CENTRAL AFRICAN
REPUBLIC
ETHIOPIA
SOMALIA
Bay of
Bengal
CAMBODIA
VIETNAM
MICRONESIA

PALAU

RIAL
EA
GABON
12
DEMOCRATIC
REPUBLIC OF
CONGO
UGANDA
KENYA
SRI LANKA
MALDIVES
BRUNEI
MALAYSIA
13
Equator

ngola
RWANDA
BURUNDI
TANZANIA
SEYCHELLES
INDONESIA
PAPUA
NEW
GUINEA
NAURU
KIRIBATI

ANGOLA
ZAMBIA
MALAWI
COMOROS
EAST TIMOR
SOLOMON
ISLANDS
TUVALU

ZIMBABWE
MOZAMBIQUE
MADAGASCAR
MAURITIUS
INDIAN
OCEAN
Coral Sea
VANUATU
NEW ZEALAND
SAMOA
FIJI
TONGA

NAMIBIA
BOTSWANA
AUSTRALIA
New Caledonia
(FRANCE)
Tropic of Capricorn

SWAZILAND
LESOTHO
SOUTH
AFRICA

Tasman Sea

NEW
ZEALAND

SOUTHERN OCEAN

Antarctic Circle

Antarctica

Largest countries

These figures are based on total land area but do not include inland water, such as lakes and rivers. If the water area was included, Canada would be the second largest country at 9,976,140sq km and China the third at 9,598,077sq km.

St Peter's, Vatican City

Largest countries

Country	Area (sq km)
Russia	16,888,500
China	9,327,400
Canada	9,221,000
USA	9,159,000
Brazil	8,456,500
Australia	7,682,300

Smallest countries

Country	Area (sq km)
Vatican City	0.44
Monaco	2
Nauru	21
Tuvalu	26
San Marino	61
Liechtenstein	160

Longest and shortest frontiers

A country's frontier is made up of the combined length of all its land borders.

Longest		Shortest	
Country	Frontiers (km)	Country	Frontiers (km)
China	22,143	Gibraltar	1.2
Russia	20,139	Vatican City	4.0
Brazil	14,691	Monaco	4.4
India	14,103	Cuba	29.0
USA	12,248	San Marino	39.0

Longest and shortest coastlines

The figures below include both the mainland and all the islands that belong to a country.

Longest

Country	Total coastline (km)
Canada	265,523
USA	133,312
Russia	110,310
Indonesia	95,181
Chile	78,563

Shortest

Monaco	4
Bosnia-Herzegovina	20
Tuvalu	24
Jordan	26
Nauru	30

Grassy beach on the Newfoundland coast, Canada

Biggest landlocked countries

A landlocked country has no coastline. This means that it has no direct access to the sea and fishing. Also, people and goods travelling to and from the country must go through another country. This may be difficult or expensive.

There are more than 40 landlocked countries in the world. The largest, Kazakhstan, has a coast on the Caspian Sea – which is a landlocked sea. The largest landlocked European country is Hungary (92,300sq km). Europe also contains the world's smallest landlocked countries – Andorra, Liechtenstein, San Marino and Vatican City. All are less than 500sq km in size. Liechtenstein and Uzbekistan are both double-landlocked. This means that they are surrounded by other landlocked countries.

Country	Area (sq km)
Kazakhstan	2,699,700
Mongolia	1,566,500
Chad	1,284,000
Niger	1,267,000
Mali	1,240,192
Ethiopia	1,127,130
Bolivia	1,084,400

Country development

These rankings from the United Nations are based on a range of factors, including how long people can expect to live, how much money they earn, education level and quality of life.

Most developed	Least developed
1 Norway	1 Sierra Leone
2 Sweden	2 Niger
3 Australia	3 Burkina Faso
4 Canada	4 Mali
5 Netherlands	5 Burundi
6 Belgium	6 Guinea-Bissau
7 Iceland	7 Mozambique
8 USA	8 Ethiopia
9 Japan	9 Central African Republic
10 Ireland	10 Democratic Republic of Congo
11 Switzerland	11 Chad
12 UK	12 Angola

Population density

In densely populated countries lots of people live on a small amount of land, usually in cities. The least densely populated countries are usually difficult for people to live in. The climate may be very cold or very hot, or there may be large areas of mountain, desert or forest.

Most densely populated countries

Country	Area (sq km)	Population	Pop per sq km
Monaco	2	35,000	17,500
Singapore	648	4,326,000	6,676
Malta	316	402,000	1,272
Maldives	298	329,000	1,104
Bahrain	694	727,000	1,047

Least densely populated countries

Country	Area (sq km)	Population	Pop per sq km
Mongolia	1,566,500	2,646,000	1.69
Namibia	823,300	2,031,000	2.47
Australia	7,682,300	20,155,000	2.62
Iceland	103,000	295,000	2.86
Botswana	600,300	1,765,000	2.94

Monaco

Crowded shopping street in Shanghai, China

Biggest and smallest populations

In most countries, more people are born every day than die, so population figures are going up all the time. China has the biggest population, but India is catching up fast.

Biggest population

Country	Population
China	1,315,844,000
India	1,103,371,000
USA	298,213,000
Indonesia	222,781,000
Brazil	186,405,000
Pakistan	157,935,000
Russia	143,202,000
Bangladesh	141,822,000
Nigeria	131,530,000
Japan	128,085,000

Smallest population

Country	Population
Vatican City	1,000
Tuvalu	10,000
Nauru	14,000
Palau	20,000
San Marino	28,000
Liechtenstein	35,000
Monaco	35,000
St Christopher and Nevis	43,000
Marshall Islands	62,000
Bermuda	64,000

www.census.gov/main/www/popclock.html

Cities with the most people

City/country	Est population, 2005*
1 Tokyo, Japan	34,000,000
2 Mexico City, Mexico	22,350,000
3 Seoul, South Korea	22,050,000
4 New York, USA	21,800,000
5 São Paulo, Brazil	20,000,000
6 Mumbai (Bombay), India	19,400,000
7 Delhi, India	19,000,000
8 Los Angeles, USA	17,750,000
9 Jakarta, Indonesia	16,850,000
10 Osaka, Japan	16,750,000
11 Calcutta, India	15,350,000
12 Cairo, Egypt	15,250,000

* Figures for city and adjoining populated areas

What is a city?

City
A large town. In some countries, a city has a special status. In the UK it may have been given a royal charter. In the USA it is an urban area with its own government.

Town
A densely populated area with a defined boundary and its own government. A town is smaller than a city and larger than a village.

Village
A small group of houses and other buildings in a country area.

Hamlet
A small village or a cluster of houses in a country area. In the UK a village is a hamlet if it does not have a church.

Settlement
A small group of inhabited buildings, or a small countryside community, such as a ranch or farm with a few dwellings.

Changing names

Many cities change their names after the countries they are in become independent. Others are renamed after political changes, such as those ending the former Soviet Union. Some changes come from variations in the way in which foreign languages are translated from one alphabet to another.

Was called/country	Now called (since)
Batavia, Indonesia	Jakarta (1949)
Christiania, Norway	Oslo (1924)
Ciudad Trujillo, Dominican Republic	Santo Domingo (1961)
Byzantium/Constantinople, Turkey	Istanbul (1930)
Danzig, Poland	Gdansk (1945)
Leningrad, USSR	St Petersburg, Russia (1991)
Léopoldville, Belgian Congo	Kinshasa, Zaire (1960)
New Amsterdam, America	New York, USA (1664)
Rangoon, Burma	Yangon, Myanmar (1989)
Saigon, Vietnam	Ho Chi Minh City, Vietnam (1975)
Salisbury, Rhodesia	Harare, Zimbabwe (1980)
Santa Isabel, Equatorial Guinea	Malabo (1973)
Tsaritsyn/Stalingrad, USSR	Volgograd, Russia (1961)

Highest towns and cities

Some towns and cities are in surprisingly high places. The Chinese city of Wenchuan, founded in 1955, is at more than half the height of Everest. Even the towns and cities at the bottom of this list are at more than a third the height of Everest.

	City	Country	Height (m)
1	Wenchuan	China	5,099
2	Potosí	Bolivia	3,976
3	Oruro	Bolivia	3,702
4	La Paz	Bolivia	3,632
5	Lhasa	China	3,684
6	Cuzco	Peru	3,399
7	Huancayo	Peru	3,249
8	Sucre	Bolivia	2,835
9	Tunja	Colombia	2,820
10	Quito	Ecuador	2,819

La Paz, the world's highest capital city

🌐 Lost cities

There are some cities that were very famous in the past but have since been destroyed or abandoned.

Angkor, Cambodia
Angkor was once the largest city in the world and more than a million people lived there. The city had an area of more than 78sq km and was surrounded by a water-filled moat. It was abandoned in about AD 1100. French naturalist Henri Mouhot was the first westerner to discover the city, in 1861.

Atlantis
Some people believe that there was a city and island of Atlantis, perhaps in the Mediterranean, that was destroyed by an earthquake and flooding almost 12,000 years ago. No one knows exactly where it was or even whether it really existed.

Chichén Itzá, Mexico
Chichén Itzá was once the centre of the Mayan empire. It was built in about AD 400 and had many buildings used in Mayan rituals. The city was abandoned in AD 1200.

Cliff Palace (Mesa Verde), Colorado, USA
This Native American Indian city was built on a cliff side, but was abandoned during a long drought in the late 13th century. It lay unknown until 18 December 1888, when Richard Wetherill, a local farmer, spotted it while looking for stray cattle.

Machu Picchu, Peru
The fortified Inca city on top of a mountain was stumbled on in 1911 by American explorer Hiram Bingham. He was searching for Vilcabamba, another lost Inca city.

Pompeii, Italy
The entire city was buried by volcanic ash when Mount Vesuvius erupted in AD 79. Nearby Herculaneum was buried at the same time. Excavations began in 1748, and many treasures have been uncovered, including beautifully preserved murals (wall paintings). Plaster casts have been made of the bodies of inhabitants who were buried beneath the debris.

Troy, Turkey
Troy was once thought to have existed only in legends, but its site was discovered in the 1870s.

Ur, Iraq
Ur was once one of the greatest cities in the world, but was abandoned in the 4th century BC. Its magnificent royal tombs and other sites were excavated by archaeologists in 1922–34 and many treasures discovered.

ONE AND ONLY

The only city in two continents
Istanbul, Turkey, is partly in Europe and partly in Asia.

The only city centre with no cars
Venice. Its only traffic is boats on the canals.

The only non-US capital city named after a US president
Monrovia, the capital of Liberia, in Africa, was named after the fifth US president, James Monroe.

Grand Canal, Venice

The great temple complex of Angkor Wat in Cambodia is all that remains of the ancient city.

➡ **See also**
World civilizations and empires: pages 106–107

Canada

Area	9,221,000sq km
Country population	32,268,000
Capital city (pop)	Ottawa (1,063,664)
Languages	French/English
Currency	Canadian dollar

Canada is the third largest country in the world, after Russia and China. Almost half of Canada's land area is covered by forest and it exports more timber, pulp and newsprint than any other country. Canada also has a successful fishing industry and lots of natural resources, such as minerals and metals. Its varied landscape attracts millions of tourists each year. Famous Canadian landmarks include Niagara Falls and the Rocky Mountains.

United States

Area	9,159,000sq km
Country population	298,213,000
Capital city (pop)	Washington DC (4,923,153)
Language	English
Currency	US dollar

The USA is made up of 50 states (including Alaska and Hawaii) and the District of Columbia, which contains the capital city of Washington. It includes a huge variety of landscapes, from hot deserts to snow-covered mountains. The country was once a colony under British rule but has been independent since 1776. It has become the world's wealthiest country and a leader in industry. It is now the greatest economic and military superpower.

Mexico

Area	1,908,700sq km
Country population	107,029,000
Capital city (pop)	Mexico City (8,591,309)
Language	Spanish
Currency	Peso

Some of the world's oldest civilizations have lived in Mexico, such as the Aztecs and Mayans. Nowadays, many tourists visit and it has plenty of natural resources. However, almost half the people are very poor and many try to cross the border into the USA every year. Some of them are arrested by border patrols.

Banff National Park, Canada

Guatemala

Area	108,400sq km
Country population	12,599,000
Capital city (pop)	Guatemala City (1,675,589)
Language	Spanish
Currency	Quetzal

Guatemala is one of Central America's most beautiful countries, with a dramatic landscape of forests, lakes and volcanoes. It is also one of the poorest and most violent. The country is still suffering from the after-effects of a long civil war (1960-96). Two-thirds of Guatemalan children live in poverty.

Belize

Area	22,800sq km
Country population	270,000
Capital city (pop)	Belmopan (8,130)
Language	English
Currency	Belize dollar

Belize was a British colony called British Honduras, but became independent in 1981. Queen Elizabeth II is still the head of state. The coral reef off the coast is the world's second largest after Australia's Great Barrier Reef. Belize is now very popular with tourists.

Honduras

Area	112,088sq km
Country population	7,205,000
Capital city (pop)	Tegucigalpa (850,445)
Language	Spanish
Currency	Lempira

Honduras lies in Central America between the Caribbean Sea and the Atlantic Ocean. It is one of the world's poorest countries, although it has valuable stocks of timber. In 1998 Hurricane Mitch caused four billion dollars' worth of damage.

El Salvador

Area	20,700sq km
Country population	6,881,000
Capital city (pop)	San Salvador (1,985,294)
Language	Spanish
Currency	US dollar

The tiny country of El Salvador is on Central America's Pacific coast. It is a poor country and often suffers hurricanes and earthquakes. Coffee is a major crop, but El Salvador relies heavily on aid money from other countries.

Nicaragua

Area	130,000sq km
Country population	5,487,000
Capital city (pop)	Managua (864,201)
Language	Spanish
Currency	Córdoba

Nicaragua is the largest country in Central America. It is one of the poorest countries in the Western world and half its people are very poor indeed. In 1998, Hurricane Mitch caused great damage and left 20 per cent of Nicaraguans homeless.

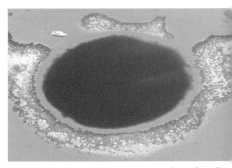

Coral reef, Belize

Costa Rica

Area	51,100sq km
Country population	4,327,000
Capital city (pop)	San José (1,982,339)
Language	Spanish
Currency	Costa Rican colón

Costa Rica is one of the most successful Central American countries and has a good standard of living. Its landscape is beautiful, with many mountains and tropical forests, and tourism is increasing. However, the country is also becoming more and more involved in the drugs trade.

Panama

Area	74,400sq km
Country population	3,232,000
Capital city (pop)	Panama City (464,928)
Language	Spanish
Currency	Balboa

Panama is a narrow strip of land stretching between North and South America. It has coastlines on the Atlantic Ocean and the Pacific Ocean, and is known for its canal, which connects the two oceans. Panama receives money from the many ships that use the canal each year and has other successful industries, but nearly 40 per cent of the people are very poor.

Cuba

Area	109,800sq km
Country population	11,269,000
Capital city (pop)	Havana (2,184,990)
Language	Spanish
Currency	Cuban peso

Cuba is just 150km south of Florida and is the largest island in the Caribbean. It is one of the few places in the world with a Communist government, which has been led by Fidel Castro since 1959. Cuba attracts more and more tourists, but the collapse of the Soviet Union and trade restrictions put on Cuba by the USA have caused financial problems.

Jamaica

Area	10,800sq km
Country population	2,651,000
Capital city (pop)	Kingston (524,638)
Language	English
Currency	Jamaican dollar

The Caribbean island of Jamaica became independent of Britain in 1962 but has remained in the Commonwealth. Tourism is its main industry, but many visitors are put off by the island's poverty and violence. Jamaica has one of the world's highest murder rates.

The Bahamas

Area	13,939sq km
Country population	323,000
Capital city (pop)	Nassau (172,196)
Language	English
Currency	Bahamian dollar

The Bahamas is made up of more than 700 islands, which lie southeast of Florida in the Atlantic Ocean. The islands were owned by the British, but became independent in 1973. Queen Elizabeth II is still the head of state. About 40 per cent of people work in tourism, but banking and finance are also important.

Haïti

Area	27,750sq km
Country population	8,528,000
Capital city (pop)	Port-au-Prince (884,472)
Languages	Haïtian Creole/French
Currency	Gourde

Haïti shares the island of Hispaniola with the Dominican Republic. In 1804, Haïti was the first Caribbean state to become independent. Now Haïti is the poorest country in the Americas, after years of dictatorship and violence. Financial help from the EU and US was stopped in 2000 after unfair elections, and drug-trafficking is a big problem.

Dominican Republic

Area	48,400sq km
Country population	8,895,000
Capital city (pop)	Santo Domingo (2,134,779)
Language	Spanish
Currency	Dominican Republic peso

The Dominican Republic makes up the eastern two-thirds of the island of Hispaniola, sharing it with Haïti. It is the oldest European settlement in America. The Dominican Republic is one of the Caribbean's poorest countries, but it is now very popular with tourists.

St Christopher and Nevis

Area	262sq km
Country population	43,000
Capital city (pop)	Basseterre (12,200)
Language	English
Currency	East Caribbean dollar

The Caribbean islands of St Christopher (also known as St Kitts) and Nevis became independent of Britain in 1983. Most of the people are descended from slaves brought from West Africa to work on the islands. Sugar has always been the island's main crop, but tourism and financial services are now important industries.

Antigua and Barbuda

Area	443sq km
Country population	81,000
Capital city (pop)	St John's (24,226)
Language	English
Currency	East Caribbean dollar

The Caribbean islands of Antigua and Barbuda were settled by the Spanish, the French and the British before becoming independent in 1981. They are still part of the Commonwealth, and Queen Elizabeth II is the head of state. The islands are popular with tourists.

Street scene in Havana, Cuba

Dominica

Area	750sq km
Country population	79,000
Capital city (pop)	Roseau (16,243)
Language	English
Currency	East Caribbean dollar

This tropical, mountainous Caribbean island was once under British rule. It became independent in 1978. Dominica's main exports are bananas and fruit juices, but the crops are often destroyed by hurricanes.

 St Lucia

Area	616sq km
Country population	161,000
Capital city (pop)	Castries (62,967)
Language	English
Currency	East Caribbean dollar

This mountainous island lies between the Atlantic Ocean and the Caribbean Sea. It is famous for its two large, cone-shaped peaks known as the Pitons. Bananas are the island's main crop, but banking and tourism are also important.

St Vincent and the Grenadines

Area	388sq km
Country population	119,000
Capital city (pop)	Kingstown (13,857)
Language	English
Currency	East Caribbean dollar

This Caribbean nation includes 33 small islands. It became independent from Britain in 1979, but it is still a member of the Commonwealth. Bananas are the main crop. Many tourists visit the islands.

 Barbados

Area	431sq km
Country population	270,000
Capital city (pop)	Bridgetown (108,000)
Language	English
Currency	Barbados dollar

This Caribbean island became an independent state in 1966 but it remains part of the Commonwealth. Queen Elizabeth II is the head of state. The main industries are tourism and sugar manufacturing.

 Grenada

Area	345sq km
Country population	103,000
Capital city (pop)	St George's (4,788)
Language	English
Currency	East Caribbean dollar

Grenada lies between the Caribbean Sea and the Atlantic Ocean, north of Trinidad and Tobago. Nearly 400,000 tourists visit Grenada every year. The island exports spices, and about a quarter of the world's nutmegs come from there.

 Trinidad and Tobago

Area	5,100sq km
Country population	1,305,000
Capital city (pop)	Port of Spain (49,031)
Language	English
Currency	Trinidad and Tobago dollar

The Caribbean islands of Trinidad and Tobago lie northwest of Venezuela. They have large reserves of oil and natural gas and are among the richest of all Caribbean nations. Tobago is quieter than Trinidad and popular with tourists.

South America

 Venezuela

Area	882,100sq km
Country population	26,649,000
Capital city (pop)	Caracas (3,435,795)
Language	Spanish
Currency	Bolívar

Venezuela is a land of great natural beauty in northern South America. Angel Falls is the world's highest waterfall, and Maracaibo is the largest lake in South America. Venezuela has large reserves of oil, coal and gold, but almost half of Venezuelans live in poverty.

 Guyana

Area	214,969sq km
Country population	751,000
Capital city (pop)	Georgetown (250,000)
Language	English
Currency	Guyana dollar

Guyana is South America's only English-speaking country. Its natural resources include gold and diamonds, but it is very poor and has political problems. The country has many fascinating animals and plants and is popular with tourists interested in nature.

 Suriname

Area	163,265sq km
Country population	449,000
Capital city (pop)	Paramaribo (213,836)
Language	Dutch
Currency	Suriname guilder

This is the smallest independent nation in South America. It was owned by the Netherlands but became independent in 1975. Suriname has large amounts of timber as well as bauxite and gold, but 70 per cent of the people are still very poor.

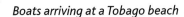

Boats arriving at a Tobago beach

Colombia

Area	1,038,700sq km
Country population	45,600,000
Capital city (pop)	Bogotá (6,712,247)
Language	Spanish
Currency	Columbian peso

Colombia is in the northwest of South America. The main crops are coffee, bananas and sugar, and the country has oil and mineral reserves. Colombia is also the world's leading producer of cocaine.

Ecuador

Area	276,800sq km
Country population	13,228,000
Capital city (pop)	Quito (1,399,814)
Language	Spanish
Currency	US dollar

Ecuador lies on the Equator and stretches across the Andes Mountains. The country's main exports are fish, bananas, cocoa and coffee. Oil was discovered there in 1972.

Peru

Area	1,280,000sq km
Country population	27,968,000
Capital city (pop)	Lima (6,723,130)
Languages	Spanish/Quechua
Currency	New sol (Nuevo sol)

Peru lies on South America's Pacific coast. It has been home to famous ancient civilizations, including the Inca Empire. Peru has important natural resources, including gold and oil, but they have not yet been developed.

Bolivia

Area	1,084,400sq km
Country population	9,182,000
Capital city (pop)	La Paz (739,453)
Languages	Spanish/Quechua/Aymará
Currency	Boliviano

The Andes mountain range crosses Bolivia. The Bolivian capital La Paz is in the Andes and is the highest capital city in the world. Bolivia is one of only two landlocked countries in South America.

Brasilia Cathedral, Brazil

Brazil

Area	8,456,500sq km
Country population	186,405,000
Capital city (pop)	Brasília (1,737,813)
Language	Portuguese
Currency	Real

Brazil covers nearly half of South America. It contains the world's second longest river, the Amazon, and vast tropical rainforests. About 82 per cent of Brazil's population lives in cities, which are mostly on the coast in the south and southeast of the country. Brazil is the leading nation in South America but there are wide divisions between rich and poor.

Uruguay

Area	175,000sq km
Country population	3,463,000
Capital city (pop)	Montevideo (1,303,182)
Language	Spanish
Currency	Uruguayan peso

Uruguay is the second smallest country in South America. It is wealthier than most South American nations because of its livestock, tourism and banking industries. It has a good welfare system and its people are well educated.

Paraguay

Area	397,300sq km
Country population	6,158,000
Capital city (pop)	Asunción (550,060)
Languages	Spanish/Guaraní
Currency	Guaraní

The Republic of Paraguay is landlocked. It has one of the smallest populations of any South American country. Alfredo Stroessner, the region's longest-ruling dictator, was overthrown in 1989, but Paraguay is still struggling with political and financial problems.

Chile

Area	748,800sq km
Country population	16,295,000
Capital city (pop)	Santiago (4,690,684)
Language	Spanish
Currency	Chilean peso

Chile is an extremely long, narrow country, which lies between the Andes Mountains and the Pacific Ocean. It is one of the most successful nations in South America and has many natural resources, including minerals and timber, as well as thriving agriculture and fishing industries.

Argentina

Area	2,736,700sq km
Country population	38,747,000
Capital city (pop)	Buenos Aires (11,453,725)
Language	Spanish
Currency	Argentinian peso

Argentina was once owned by Spain, but it became independent in 1816. This South American country is famous for its beef and has large mineral deposits.

Cattle market, Argentina

Iceland

Area	103,000sq km
Country population	295,000
Capital city (pop)	Reykjavík (113,387)
Language	Icelandic
Currency	Icelandic króna

Iceland is a volcanic island and is the furthest west country in Europe. Its capital city is the furthest north in the world. Iceland is a wealthy country with low unemployment and a good welfare system. Fishing provides 70 per cent of its exports, which could cause problems as fish stocks decline.

Bathers in a volcanic hot spring, Iceland

Denmark

Area	42,400sq km
Country population	5,431,000
Capital city (pop)	Copenhagen (1,081,673)
Language	Danish
Currency	Danish krone

Denmark shares a border with Germany and is the smallest, most southerly Scandinavian nation. It is a wealthy, high-tech country and has all the oil and natural gas it needs. The standard of living is high. Denmark is a monarchy and the kingdom includes the Faeroe Islands and Greenland.

Norway

Area	306,800sq km
Country population	4,620,000
Capital city (pop)	Oslo (508,726)
Language	Norwegian
Currency	Krone

Norway has one of the world's longest coastlines. The population is small and has a very good standard of living, thanks to the country's plentiful natural resources. Only Russia and Saudi Arabia export more oil than Norway, and it is the world's biggest exporter of seafood.

Sweden

Area	411,600sq km
Country population	9,041,000
Capital city (pop)	Stockholm (1,684,420)
Language	Swedish
Currency	Swedish krona

Sweden is a rich country with a high standard of living. Swedes have one of the world's longest life expectancies. The country has many natural resources including iron ore, lead, granite, zinc and forests. Forests cover about half the land and there are important timber and paper industries.

Finland

Area	304,600sq km
Country population	5,249,000
Capital city (pop)	Helsinki (1,163,000)
Languages	Finnish/Swedish
Currency	Euro

Since the end of World War II, Finland has changed from being a rural country covered with dense forest into a modern nation. It has very successful industries and an excellent welfare system. Finland joined the European Union in 1995 and adopted the Euro as its currency in 2002.

Ireland

Area	68,900sq km
Country population	4,148,000
Capital city (pop)	Dublin (1,122,600)
Languages	Irish/English
Currency	Euro

Ireland is separated from Scotland by the North Channel and from England and Wales by the Irish Sea and St George's Channel. It was divided in the 1920s, when 26 counties in the south gained independence from the United Kingdom. Since then there has been conflict in Northern Ireland between those who want to remain part of the United Kingdom and those who want a united, independent Ireland. Since Ireland joined the European Community in 1973 it has become a modern, high-tech nation with successful industry. Ireland began using the Euro in January 1999 along with ten other EU nations.

Dingle Harbour, Ireland

United Kingdom

Area	242,910sq km
Country population	59,668,000
Capital city (pop)	London (7,074,265)
Language	English
Currency	British pound

The United Kingdom is made up of Great Britain (England, Scotland and Wales) and Northern Ireland. Although it is a small country, the UK has had a huge influence on the world because of its cultural, military and industrial strengths. At one time, it controlled a vast empire of lands across the globe and was the world's leading industrial nation. Traditional manufacturing industries are now less important. In the 21st century the UK's main industries are technology, tourism and services such as banking, and it is still an important economic power.

The Netherlands

Area	33,900sq km
Country population	16,299,000
Capital city (pop)	Amsterdam (736,538)
Languages	Dutch/Frisian
Currency	Euro

Almost one-fifth of the Netherlands is water, and nearly a quarter of its land lies below sea level. It is a very rich country and is the sixth largest exporter in the world. Banking, shipping and fishing are all important industries.

Luxembourg

Area	2,586sq km
Country population	465,000
Capital city (pop)	Luxembourg (77,400)
Language	

Luxembourgish is the main spoken language. French and German are the official languages for written purposes, and French is the language of administration.

Currency	Euro

Luxembourg is landlocked by Belgium, Germany and France. It is by far the world's richest country, with an amazingly high standard of living. Steel was once the main industry, but financial services have now become more important.

Heidelberg, Germany

Germany

Area	356,700sq km
Country population	82,689,000
Capital city (pop)	Berlin (3,388,434)
Language	German
Currency	Euro

Germany was divided after World War II. The Soviet Union and Poland claimed the East, and the USA, UK and France controlled the West. The East became a Communist state and the West became a democracy. Thousands of East Germans fled to the West. The Berlin Wall was built in 1961 to close the border and stop the flow of people. The decline of the USSR led to the fall of the Berlin Wall in 1989 and Germany was reunited in 1990. Today, 80 per cent of Germany's people live in the West, and the effects of Communism are still felt in the East.

Belgium

Area	30,200sq km
Country population	10,419,000
Capital city (pop)	Brussels (978,384)
Languages	Flemish/French/German
Currency	Euro

Belgium is divided into Flanders (in the northwest), and Wallonia (in the southeast). Brussels is the headquarters of the European Union. This has brought wealth to the country as multinational companies have settled in the city. Belgium is well known for its fine chocolates and beer – and Tintin!

France

Area	550,100sq km
Country population	60,496,000
Capital city (pop)	Paris (9,644,507)
Language	French
Currency	Euro

France is the largest country in Western Europe and a key member of the European Union. It has a varied landscape ranging from coastal plains to the Alps in the southeast. Farms and forests cover a large proportion of the country, and agricultural products – particularly wine and liqueurs – are major exports. France once had one of the world's largest empires. Most of its former colonies are now independent, but French Guiana, Guadeloupe, Martinique, Réunion, Mayotte, St Pierre and Miquelon, French Polynesia, New Caledonia, Wallis and Futuna and the Southern and Antarctic Territories all still have links with France.

Monaco

Area	2sq km
Country population	35,000
Capital city	Monaco
Language	French
Currency	Euro

Monaco is a principality – it is ruled by a prince. It is surrounded by France and is the second smallest independent state in the world. It has no income tax and low business taxes so rich people flock there to escape taxes.

Andorra

Area	464sq km
Country population	75,000
Capital city (pop)	Andorra la Vella (20,724)
Language	Catalan
Currency	Euro

Andorra is a small principality (a state ruled by a prince), which dates from 1278. It lies in the mountains between France and Spain. Tourism is its main industry, but financial services are also becoming important.

Spain

Area	499,400sq km
Country population	43,064,000
Capital city (pop)	Madrid (5,086,635)
Language	

Castilian Spanish is the official language. Basque, Catalan, Galician and Valencian (a variation of Catalan) are spoken in different regions

Currency	Euro

Spain covers most of the Iberian peninsula. The country has many cultures and there are 17 regions with their own elected authorities. This has led to a campaign for independence by the Basque region in the north. Spain is the world's second most popular tourist destination (after France) and has more than 50 million visitors every year. The fishing industry is one of the biggest in Europe, but unemployment is high: more than one in ten Spaniards is unemployed.

Portugal

Area	91,500sq km
Country population	10,495,000
Capital city (pop)	Lisbon (1,878,006)
Language	Portuguese
Currency	Euro

Portugal lies to the west of Spain on the Iberian peninsula and borders the Atlantic Ocean. It is one of the European Union's least developed countries and has the highest number of people working on the land. Portugal's economy has grown rapidly since it joined the European Union in 1986. Tourism is one of its fastest growing industries. Portugal once had a vast empire, stretching across the Americas, Africa and Asia. About 176 million people worldwide speak Portuguese.

Malta

Area	316sq km
Country population	402,000
Capital city (pop)	Valletta (7,048)
Languages	Maltese/English
Currency	Maltese lira

Malta, which includes the neighbouring island of Gozo, used to be under British rule. It became independent in 1964, but remains a part of the Commonwealth. Malta became the European Union's smallest new member in 2004. Tourism is the island's most important industry and Malta has more than a million visitors every year.

Italy

Area	294,100sq km
Country population	58,093,000
Capital city (pop)	Rome (2,459,776)
Language	Italian
Currency	Euro

Italy is a long, narrow country reaching into the Mediterranean Sea. It includes the islands of Sicily and Sardinia among others. Italy can be divided into two: the wealthy, industrial north, and the poorer south. In the south, most people work on the land and around 20 per cent of the population is unemployed. About 40 million foreign tourists visit Italy every year, many of them to see its beautiful cities, which include Rome, Venice and Florence.

San Marino

Area	61sq km
Country population	28,000
Capital city (pop)	San Marino (4,357)
Language	Italian
Currency	Euro

San Marino is entirely surrounded by Italy and it is the third smallest state in Europe. The tiny republic attracts about three million tourists every year. San Marino's inhabitants (known as Sammarinese) enjoy the world's sixth highest income per person.

Vatican City State

Area	0.44sq km
Country population	1,000
Capital city (pop)	Vatican City (766)
Languages	Latin/Italian
Currency	Euro

The Vatican City is the smallest country in the world, both in area and population. It is entirely surrounded by the city of Rome. The Vatican is home to the Pope and it is the spiritual centre of the Roman Catholic Church. It depends on contributions from Roman Catholics all over the world for its income, as well as the sale of souvenirs and publications.

Andalucia, southern Spain

Switzerland

Area	39,600sq km
Country population	7,252,000
Capital city (pop)	Bern (317,367)
Languages German/French/Italian/Romansch	
Currency	Swiss franc

Switzerland is the most mountainous country in Europe. The Alps occupy 60 per cent of its land area. It has a very high income per person, low unemployment and its people have a long life expectancy. Switzerland was not involved in either World War and has not joined the European Union.

New Year concert in Vienna

Austria

Area	82,700sq km
Country population	8,189,000
Capital city (pop)	Vienna (1,550,123)
Language	German
Currency	Euro

Austria is a small mountainous country. It is landlocked by the Czech Republic, Slovakia, Italy, Slovenia, Hungary, Germany, Switzerland and Liechtenstein. It was once the centre of the powerful Austro-Hungarian empire until its defeat in World War I. It was occupied by Nazi Germany and then by the Allies after World War II. Since the war Austria has flourished, and it is now a popular holiday spot.

Liechtenstein

Area	160sq km
Country population	35,000
Capital city (pop)	Vaduz (5,038)
Language	German
Currency	Swiss franc

Liechtenstein is the sixth smallest country in the world. Its low taxes have encouraged extraordinary economic growth, and thousands of foreign companies have bank accounts there.

Belarus

Area	207,500sq km
Country population	9,755,000
Capital city (pop)	Minsk (1,725,100)
Languages	Belarusian/Russian
Currency	Russian rouble

Belarus became independent when the Soviet Union collapsed in 1991. In 1996 it agreed to form the Commonwealth of Independent states with Russia. In January 2005 the Russian rouble became the single currency of the Commonwealth.

Lithuania

Area	64,800sq km
Country population	3,431,000
Capital city (pop)	Vilnius (542,287)
Language	Lithuanian
Currency	Litas

Lithuania became independent of the Soviet Union in 1991. It used to depend on Russia, but more recently it has developed trade links with the West. It joined the European Union in 2004.

Latvia

Area	62,100sq km
Country population	2,307,000
Capital city (pop)	Riga (747,157)
Language	Latvian
Currency	Lats

Latvia is bounded by the Baltic Sea, Estonia, Lithuania, Belarus and Russia. It became independent of the Soviet Union in 1991 and in 2004 it was accepted into the European Union.

Tallinn, Estonia

Estonia

Area	42,300sq km
Country population	1,330,000
Capital city (pop)	Tallinn (404,000)
Language	Estonian
Currency	Kroon

The small Baltic state of Estonia regained its independence in 1991 when the Soviet Union collapsed. It was one of the Eastern European nations that joined the European Union in 2004.

Poland

Area	304,400sq km
Country population	38,530,000
Capital city (pop)	Warsaw (1,609,780)
Language	Polish
Currency	Zloty

Poland is the largest nation in Central Europe and has the highest population. It was devastated by World War II, when more than six million people died – more than in any other country. In 1989 Poland was the first Eastern European nation to topple its Communist leaders. In May 2004 it joined the European Union.

Czech Republic

Area	77,300sq km
Country population	10,220,000
Capital city (pop)	Prague (1,178,576)
Language	Czech
Currency	Koruna

The Czech Republic was part of Czechoslovakia until it split from Slovakia in 1993. It now attracts investment from other countries and has a thriving tourism industry. The country joined the European Union in 2004.

Slovakia

Area	48,100sq km
Country population	5,401,000
Capital city (pop)	Bratislava (428,672)
Language	Slovak
Currency	Koruna

Slovakia is landlocked and mountainous. It became independent in 1993, when Czechoslovakia divided into the Czech Republic and Slovakia. It joined the European Union in 2004.

Hungary

Area	92,300sq km
Country population	10,098,000
Capital city (pop)	Budapest (1,775,203)
Language	Hungarian
Currency	Forint

Hungary became Communist after World War II. In the 1990s, it defied the Soviet Union and began some free trade with the West. This central European country has flourished since the Soviet Union's collapse and it entered the European Union in 2004.

Ukraine

Area	579,400sq km
Country population	46,481,000
Capital city (pop)	Kiev (2,602,000)
Language	Ukrainian
Currency	Hryvna

Ukraine is a vast area between Poland and Russia. It became independent after the collapse of the Soviet Union in 1991. Ukraine has successful manufacturing, petrochemical, mining and agricultural industries.

Moldova

Area	33,851sq km
Country population	4,206,000
Capital city (pop)	Chisinau (655,940)
Language	Moldovan
Currency	Moldovan leu

Moldova is Europe's poorest country. It has no natural resources and imports all its energy supplies from Russia, from which it became independent in 1991.

Market stall in Budapest, Hungary

Georgia

Area	69,700sq km
Country population	4,474,000
Capital city (pop)	Tbilisi (1,253,100)
Language	Georgian
Currency	Lari

Georgia lies in a key position east of the Black Sea between Russia and Turkey. It has coal deposits, but they have not yet been exploited. The country relies on farming – particularly grapes from which wine is made.

Armenia

Area	29,800sq km
Country population	3,016,000
Capital city (pop)	Yerevan (1,254,400)
Language	Armenian
Currency	Dram

Armenia was the first country formally to adopt Christianity in AD 301. This mountainous country is bordered by Azerbaijan, Georgia, Iran and Turkey. Its key position between Europe and Asia led to invasions by the Persian, Ottoman, Roman and Byzantine empires, among others.

Azerbaijan

Area	86,600sq km
Country population	8,411,000
Capital city (pop)	Baki/Baku (1,817,900)
Language	Azerbaijani
Currency	Manat

Azerbaijan regained its independence from the Soviet Union in 1991. The country has rich mineral resources as well as oil and natural gas. However, conflict and corruption have kept it from developing a healthy economy.

Slovenia

Area	20,100sq km
Country population	1,967,000
Capital city (pop)	Ljubljana (257,338)
Language	Slovene
Currency	Tolar

Slovenia is the third most forested country in Europe. About half the country is covered by forest. Slovenia became independent from Yugoslavia in 1991. Its people now have a reasonably good standard of living, and the country joined the European Union in 2004.

Croatia

Area	55,900sq km
Country population	4,551,000
Capital city (pop)	Zagreb (867,717)
Language	Croatian
Currency	Kuna

Croatia declared its independence from Yugoslavia in 1991. It had been one of Yugoslavia's most advanced and prosperous areas. The country borders the Adriatic Sea. Its coast was popular with tourists before the Yugoslavian conflict of 1991–95. Visitors are now returning to Croatia.

Bosnia-Herzegovina

Area	51,197sq km
Country population	3,907,000
Capital city (pop)	Sarajevo (529,021)
Language	Bosnian
Currency	Convertible marka

Bosnia-Herzegovina was recognized as an independent state in 1992 after Yugoslavia collapsed in 1991. Since then clashes between Bosnia's Croats, Serbs and Muslims have caused civil war, which is still not resolved. Despite this, more tourists are beginning to visit the country again.

Albania

Area	28,748sq km
Country population	3,130,000
Capital city (pop)	Tirana (244,153)
Languages	Albanian
Currency	Lek

Albania depends mostly on farming, and its main crops are wheat, maize, sugar beet, potatoes and fruit. It has borders with Serbia and Montenegro, Kosovo, Macedonia and Greece.

Macedonia

Area	25,713sq km
Country population	2,034,000
Capital city (pop)	Skopje (429,964)
Languages	Macedonian/Albanian
Currency	Denar

Macedonia's full name is the Former Yugoslav Republic of Macedonia (FYROM), not to be confused with the Greek region of Macedonia. Macedonia became independent in 1991. Since then there have been clashes between the country's large Albanian minority and its Macedonian majority.

Serbia and Montenegro

Area	102,100sq km
Country population	10,503,000
Capital city (pop)	Belgrade (1,574,050)
Language	Serbian
Currency	New dinar

The country of Serbia and Montenegro came into being in February 2003. The Serbian province of Kosovo has been under the control of the United Nations since 1999, when there was violent conflict between Kosovo's ethnic Albanians and the Serbian police force. There is a federal government, but the two republics of Serbia and Montenegro are semi-independent. Both depend mostly on farming.

Romania

Area	230,300sq km
Country population	21,711,000
Capital city (pop)	Bucharest (2,066,723)
Language	Romanian
Currency	Leu

The mountainous Republic of Romania is the largest Balkan nation. The Communist regime was overthrown in 1989 when the dictator Nicolae Ceausescu was executed. The country is still very poor, with almost half of Romanians living in poverty. It is working towards membership of the European Union in 2007.

Bulgaria

Area	110,600sq km
Country population	7,726,000
Capital city (pop)	Sofia (1,096,389)
Language	Bulgarian
Currency	Lev

Bulgaria was Communist until 1990, when it became a democracy. It is now moving towards joining the European Union in 2007, despite organized crime, corruption, inflation and unemployment. Bulgaria is becoming popular with tourists, especially the historic capital city of Sofia.

Dubrovnik, Croatia

The island of Santorini, Greece

Greece

Area	128,900sq km
Country population	11,120,000
Capital city (pop)	Athens (3,072,922)
Language	Greek
Currency	Euro

The ancient country of Greece lies in an important position between Europe, Asia and Africa. It includes about 2,000 islands as well as the mainland. About 14 million tourists visit Greece every year. However, it has few natural resources and relies on money from the European Union.

Cyprus

Area	9,200sq km
Country population	835,000
Capital city (pop)	Nicosia (195,300)
Languages	Greek/Turkish
Currency	Cyprus pound

The Mediterranean island of Cyprus has been divided since Turkey invaded the north of the island in 1974. The Turkish Republic of Northern Cyprus is recognized only by Turkey. Greek Cyprus attracts many tourists and was accepted into the European Union in 2004. The Turkish part depends heavily on loans from Turkey.

Morocco

Area	446,300sq km
Country population	31,478,000
Capital city (pop)	Rabat (1,385,872)
Language	Arabic
Currency	Dirham

The kingdom of Morocco lies on the northwestern tip of Africa. It is separated from the rest of the continent by the Atlas Mountains and the Sahara Desert. Morocco has rich mineral deposits and nearly three-quarters of the world's phosphate. It also has a successful fishing industry. Almost half the people work on the land.

Casbah (a type of castle) in the Atlas Mountains, Morocco

Algeria

Area	2,381,700sq km
Country population	32,854,000
Capital city (pop)	Algiers (1,507,241)
Language	Arabic
Currency	Algerian dinar

Algeria is a North African country. It became independent from France in 1962 and is now struggling to control its religious militants and to improve its weak economy.

Tunisia

Area	155,400sq km
Country population	10,102,000
Capital city (pop)	Tunis (929,500)
Language	Arabic
Currency	Tunisian dinar

The North African country of Tunisia shares borders with Algeria and Libya and has a Mediterranean coastline. About one-fifth of the people live by farming and fishing. Tunisia's industries include oil, gas, tourism and electronics.

Libya

Area	1,759,500sq km
Country population	5,853,000
Capital city (pop)	Tripoli (1,000,000)
Language	Arabic
Currency	Libyan dinar

Libya has large oil reserves, but its economy has suffered from sanctions imposed by the United Nations. These were in response to the bombing of an airliner over Lockerbie in Scotland in 1988. Sanctions have now been lifted and Libya's leader, Colonel Gaddafi, has promised to bring his country back into the international community.

Egypt

Area	995,500sq km
Country population	74,033,000
Capital city (pop)	Cairo (7,200,000)
Language	Arabic
Currency	Egyptian pound

Egypt lies in a key position. It has a coastline on both the Mediterranean and Red Seas, and borders with the Sudan, Libya, Israel and the Gaza Strip. Egypt also controls the vital Suez Canal. This allows about 15,000 ships each year to travel between the Mediterranean and the Indian Ocean without sailing around Africa. Famous landmarks include the pyramids.

Camel and rider near the Great Pyramid in Egypt

Sudan

Area	2,376,000sq km
Country population	36,233,000
Capital city (pop)	Khartoum (947,483)
Language	Arabic
Currency	Sudanese dinar

Sudan is the largest country in Africa. The country has suffered from civil war since its independence in 1956. This war has been going on longer than any other war in Africa. About two million people have died and thousands more have lost their homes. There are large oil reserves, which have been exploited since 1999. Farming is Sudan's biggest industry, although it is often badly affected by drought.

Ethiopia

Area	1,127,130sq km
Country population	77,431,000
Capital city (pop)	Addis Ababa (2,495,000)
Language	
There is no official language, but Amharic is the most widely used of the 70 languages	
Currency	Ethiopian birr

Ethiopia is Africa's oldest independent country. It has suffered many droughts and famines. These, combined with civil war and a border dispute with Eritrea, have made Ethiopia one of Africa's poorest nations. Its natural resources are underdeveloped, and 85 per cent of the people still depend upon the land for a living.

General store in Nouakchott, Mauritania

★ Somalia

Area	637,657sq km
Country population	8,228,000
Capital city (pop)	Mogadishu (525,000)
Languages	Somali/Arabic
Currency	Somali shilling

Somalia is one of the world's poorest countries and there has been conflict between different groups. The north declared independence under the name Somaliland, but is not recognized by any foreign government.

Djibouti

Area	23,200sq km
Country population	793,000
Capital city (pop)	Djibouti (62,000)
Languages	Arabic/French
Currency	Djibouti franc

Djibouti lies in a key position between Ethiopia and the Red Sea. The country provides refuelling facilities for ships and operates a free port, which bring money into Djibouti.

Eritrea

Area	117,600sq km
Country population	4,401,000
Capital city (pop)	Asmara (450,000)
Languages	
No official language; Arabic, Tigrinya and English are the main working languages. Italian is also spoken.	
Currency	Nakfa

Eritrea is in Eastern Africa and has had violent border disputes with Ethiopia since 1998. The conflict has affected Eritrea's economy, but the government continues to improve the country's roads, schools and transport systems. Its Red Sea ports are an important source of income.

Mauritania

Area	1,025,520sq km
Country population	3,069,000
Capital city (pop)	Nouakchott (850,000)
Language	Arabic
Currency	Ouguiya

Mauritania is mainly desert and lies between the Middle East and Africa. There is conflict between the black population and its Arab majority. Mauritania has rich mineral deposits but these have not yet been exploited.

Niger

Area	1,267,000sq km
Country population	13,957,000
Capital city (pop)	Niamey (627,400)
Language	French
Currency	CFA franc

Niger is the largest nation in West Africa. It is also one of the hottest and poorest countries in the world. Niger borders the Sahara Desert and droughts often kill much of the country's vital livestock. Niger has one of the lowest literacy rates in the world.

Mali

Area	1,240,192sq km
Country population	13,518,000
Capital city (pop)	Bamako (809,552)
Language	French
Currency	CFA franc

Mali's first democratically elected government came to power in 1992 after more than 20 years of dictatorship. This West African nation is one of the world's poorest countries. About 80 per cent of the people depend on farming for a living.

★ Senegal

Area	196,722sq km
Country population	11,658,000
Capital city (pop)	Dakar (1,641,358)
Language	French
Currency	CFA franc

Senegal is almost divided into two by The Gambia. It became independent from France in 1960. It is now popular with tourists, but has few natural resources, high unemployment and more than half its people live in poverty.

Gambia

Area	11,295sq km
Country population	1,517,000
Capital city (pop)	Banjul (42,407)
Language	English
Currency	Dalasi

The Gambia is a sliver of land and the smallest country in Africa. About 80 per cent of Gambians work on the land. Groundnuts are one of the few crops that will grow there and they are Gambia's most important export.

Cape Verde

Area	4,033sq km
Country population	507,000
Capital city (pop)	Praia (61,644)
Languages	Portuguese
Currency	Cape Verdean escudo

Cape Verde is made up of the Windward Islands and the Leeward Islands in the Atlantic Ocean off the west coast of Africa. Their main exports are bananas and coffee.

Guinea

Area	245,857sq km
Country population	9,402,000
Capital city (pop)	Conakry (763,000)
Language	French
Currency	Guinean franc

Guinea has been placed under great strain by thousands of refugees from its war-torn neighbours, Liberia and Sierra Leone. Guinea has natural resources, including iron ore, gold and diamonds.

Guinea-Bissau

Area	36,125sq km
Country population	1,586,000
Capital city (pop)	Bissau (195,400)
Language	Portuguese
Currency	CFA franc

Guinea-Bissau is one of the poorest countries in the world. A civil war in 1998 destroyed many of its roads, schools and hospitals, and ruined its economy. Most people live by fishing and farming. Cashew nuts are the main crop.

Sierra Leone

Area	71,740sq km
Country population	5,525,000
Capital city (pop)	Freetown (469,776)
Language	

English is the official language but is spoken by very few. Mende is the main language in the south, and Temne in the north. Krio, an English-based Creole language, is the language used and understood across the country

Currency	Leone

Sierra Leone's civil war of 1991–2002 killed many thousands of people, and many others had to move from their homes. Sierra Leone has diamond and gold deposits, but its political problems have made it one of the world's poorest countries, along with Somalia and East Timor. About three-quarters of its people live on less than $2 a day.

Traditional wedding in Ghana

Liberia

Area	111,369sq km
Country population	3,283,000
Capital city (pop)	Monrovia (421,000)
Language	English
Currency	Liberian dollar

The West African country of Liberia was founded by freed American slaves. It has been independent since 1847. The civil war that began in 1990 ended in 2003, but the country is struggling to recover.

Côte d'Ivoire

Area	318,000sq km
Country population	18,154,000
Capital city (pop)	Yamoussoukro (126,191)
Language	French
Currency	CFA Franc

Côte d'Ivoire became independent from France in 1960. It was a peaceful, prosperous African country until its first military coup in 1999. Trouble then began between rebels and the government which is still going on.

Ghana

Area	227,500sq km
Country population	22,113,000
Capital city (pop)	Accra (1,445,515)
Language	English
Currency	Cedi

Ghana was a British colony, but in 1957 it became the first African country to become independent. It contains Lake Volta, the world's largest artificial lake, and it is one of the world's top ten gold producers.

Burkina Faso

Area	274,000sq km
Country population	13,228,000
Capital city (pop)	Ouagadougou (1,000,000)
Language	French
Currency	CFA Franc

Burkina Faso is an inland country in West Africa that was called Upper Volta. It is one of the world's poorest nations. About 90 per cent of people work on the land.

Togo

Area	56,785sq km
Country population	6,145,000
Capital city (pop)	Lomé (700,000)
Language	French
Currency	CFA franc

Togo was the French territory of Togoland until it became independent in 1960. More than half the people work on the land. Cotton, coffee and cocoa are the main exports. Nearly a third of the people are very poor.

Nigeria

Area	910,800sq km
Country population	131,530,000
Capital city (pop)	Abuja (378,671)
Language	English
Currency	Naira

Nigeria has the biggest population of any African country. It is the leading oil producer south of the Sahara, but is extremely poor. About 60 per cent of Nigerians live in poverty because of corruption, unequal distribution of money and a rapidly growing population.

Benin

Area	112,622sq km
Country population	8,439,000
Capital city (pop)	Porto Novo (232,756)
Languages	French
Currency	CFA Franc

The African country of Benin became fully independent from France in 1960. It now has a thriving tourist industry, which provides much-needed money.

Transporting dried grasses by river in Chad

Cameroon

Area	465,400sq km
Country population	16,322,000
Capital city (pop)	Yaoundé (653,670)
Languages	French/English
Currency	CFA Franc

Cameroon in West Africa became an independent republic in 1972. It has good natural resources, including bauxite and aluminium, and grows crops such as cocoa, coffee and rubber.

Central African Republic

Area	622,984sq km
Country population	4,038,000
Capital city (pop)	Bangui (473,817)
Language	French
	(national language: Sangho)
Currency	CFA Franc

The Central African Republic became independent from France in 1960. Since then there have been almost constant political problems and it is now a very poor country. It exports some timber and diamonds, but most people work on the land.

Equatorial Guinea

Area	28,051sq km
Country population	504,000
Capital city (pop)	Malabo (30,418)
Languages	Spanish/French
Currency	CFA franc

Equatorial Guinea is made up of five islands and part of the African mainland. It became independent from Spain in 1968 and is one of the smallest countries in Africa. Many people work on the land, but gas and oil have been found and so the country is becoming wealthier.

Chad

Area	1,284,000sq km
Country population	9,749,000
Capital city (pop)	N'Djaména (530,100)
Languages	Arabic/French
Currency	CFA Franc

The Sahara desert covers much of Chad. The country became independent from France in 1960 and since then has suffered conflict with its neighbour Libya. Most of its people work on the land. Oil has been found in Chad and is now being exported.

São Tomé and Príncipe

Area	964sq km
Country population	157,000
Capital city (pop)	São Tomé (43,420)
Language	Portuguese
Currency	Dobra

The islands of São Tomé and Príncipe lie on the Equator in the Gulf of Guinea and make up Africa's smallest country. Cocoa was the main crop, but São Tomé and Príncipe now has other sources of income, such as newly-discovered oil.

Gabon

Area	257,700sq km
Country population	1,384,000
Capital city (pop)	Libreville (362,400)
Language	French
Currency	CFA franc

Gabon has a small population and good oil and mineral reserves. It is one of Africa's richest nations. However, many of its people are very poor because its wealth has been mismanaged and is unequally distributed.

Republic of Congo – Brazzaville

Area	342,000sq km
Country population	3,999,000
Capital city (pop)	Brazzaville (937,579)
Language	French
Currency	CFA franc

The region of Middle Congo became independent from France in 1960 and was renamed the Republic of Congo. The country has large oil deposits and is one of Africa's largest producers of petroleum.

Democratic Republic of Congo

Area	2,344,858sq km
Country population	57,549,000
Capital city (pop)	Kinshasa (4,655,313)
Languages	French/English
Currency	Congolese franc

The Democratic Republic of Congo, which was called Zaïre, is Africa's third largest country. In 2003 a five-year struggle between government forces and rebels ended and since then it has been fairly peaceful. The country has good natural resources but has been very poor since the war.

Agricultural land in the Democratic Republic of Congo

Uganda

Area	197,100sq km
Country population	28,816,000
Capital city (pop)	Kampala (774,241)
Language	English
Currency	Uganda shilling

Uganda is a landlocked West African nation on the shores of Lake Victoria. It is now a fairly peaceful country after a devastating civil war and a military dictatorship. The land is fertile and it has natural resources, but Uganda is still being held back by a large international debt.

Burundi

Area	27,834sq km
Country population	7,548,000
Capital city (pop)	Bujumbura (235,440)
Languages	Kirundi/French
Currency	Burundi franc

Burundi gained independence in the 1960s. Since then it has been devastated by fighting between the two main tribes, the Hutus and the Tutsis. Burundi lies between the politically troubled countries of Rwanda and the Democratic Republic of Congo, and is being held back by uncertainty over its future.

Rwanda

Area	26,338sq km
Country population	9,038,000
Capital city (pop)	Kigali (608,141)
Languages	Kinyarwanda/French/English
Currency	Rwanda franc

Rwanda is a densely populated country in Central Africa. It is still suffering the effects of a civil war that began in 1990 and lasted for four years. At least 60 per cent of the people live in poverty.

Mount Kilimanjaro, Tanzania, is the highest mountain in Africa.

Masai woman, Kenya

Kenya

Area	569,100sq km
Country population	34,256,000
Capital city (pop)	Nairobi (2,143,254)
Languages	Swahili/English
Currency	Kenya shilling

Kenya lies on the Equator on the east coast of Africa. It has some of the most fertile land in Africa, and 75 per cent of the people work in farming. Kenya has also been one of Africa's most popular tourist destinations, but since 2002 fears of terrorism have put off many visitors.

Tanzania

Area	883,600sq km
Country population	38,329,000
Capital city (pop)	Dodoma (1,502,344)
Languages	Swahili/English
Currency	Tanzanian shilling

Tanzania is made up of the country that used to be called Tanganyika on the eastern African mainland, and the island of Zanzibar, which is in the Indian Ocean just off the coast of Tanganyika. The two nations joined in 1964 after becoming independent. The country contains Lake Victoria and Mount Kilimanjaro.

Malawi

Area	118,484sq km
Country population	12,884,000
Capital city (pop)	Lilongwe (505,200)
Languages	Chichewa/English
Currency	Kwacha

In 1964, the British territory of Nyasaland in southeastern Africa became Malawi, which is an independent republic. The country has had many natural disasters and depends on aid from other countries. About 15 per cent of the adult population has HIV or AIDS, and Malawi now has one of the world's lowest life expectancies.

Zambia

Area	743,400sq km
Country population	11,668,000
Capital city (pop)	Lusaka (1,269,848)
Language	English
Currency	Kwacha

The landlocked country of Zambia in Central Africa has a small population. Copper is its chief export, but demand for copper has fallen and Zambia is now one of the world's poorest countries. Almost 90 per cent of its people live on less than a dollar a day.

Angola

Area	1,246,700sq km
Country population	15,941,000
Capital city (pop)	Luanda (1,822,407)
Language	Portuguese
Currency	Kwanza

Angola became independent from Portugal in 1975. Since then, there has been a civil war almost all the time. The country has valuable oil and diamond deposits, but has many financial problems.

Botswana

Area	600,300sq km
Country population	1,765,000
Capital city (pop)	Gaborone (186,007)
Language	English
	(national language: Setswana)
Currency	Pula

Botswana used to be called the British Protectorate of Bechuanaland, but in 1966 became an independent Commonwealth republic. It has done well and is now one of the most thriving countries in Africa. Botswana has many natural resources and is one of the world's largest producers of diamonds.

Namibia

Area	823,300sq km
Country population	2,031,000
Capital city (pop)	Windhoek (147,056)
Language	English
Currency	Namibian dollar

Namibia was a British colony but became independent in 1990. Almost half the people work on the land, but the country often suffers from drought so much of its food has to be imported from other countries. Namibia is an important producer of diamonds, but the wealth from this is unevenly distributed. Half of all Namibians are living in poverty.

Zimbabwe

Area	386,900sq km
Country population	13,010,000
Capital city (pop)	Harare (1,189,103)
Language	English
Currency	Zimbabwe dollar

Zimbabwe was previously the British colony of Rhodesia. It used to be a fairly well-off country, but since 2000 has suffered a series of political problems and upsets. Zimbabweans now have an extremely low standard of living: one-third have HIV/AIDS and 70 per cent live in poverty. Average life expectancy is just 33.9 years.

Mozambique

Area	784,100sq km
Country population	19,792,000
Capital city (pop)	Maputo (1,039,700)
Language	Portuguese
Currency	Metical

Mozambique used to be a Portuguese colony. It gained independence in 1975, became a republic in 1990, and held its first free elections in 1994. It is one of the world's poorest countries and about 70 per cent of its people live in poverty. But since the beginning of the 21st century, things have begun to improve and other countries have started to invest in Mozambique.

Madagascar

Area	587,041sq km
Country population	18,606,000
Capital city (pop)	Antananarivo (2,000,000)
Languages	Malagasy/French
Currency	Malagasy franc

Madagascar is in the Indian Ocean off the coast of Africa. It is the fourth largest island in the world. More than 80 per cent of people work on the land. The country has often suffered natural disasters, however. In 2000 most of its rice crop was destroyed by cyclones.

Baobab trees, Madagascar

South Africa

Area	1,221,000sq km
Country population	47,432,000

Capital city (pop)
The seat of government is Pretoria (1,800,000); the seat of the legislature is Cape Town (3,088,028); the seat of the judiciary is Bloemfontein (467,400)

Languages
11 official languages, including Afrikaans, English, Ndebele, Pedi, Sotho, Swazi, Tsonga, Tswana, Venda, Xhosa, Zulu

Currency	Rand

South Africa lies on the southern tip of the continent. Until 1994 the country was ruled by its white minority and had an apartheid policy. This segregated the races – kept black and white apart – and denied black citizens the vote. Because of this many other countries refused to trade with South Africa. The African National Congress won South Africa's first inclusive elections in 1994, and it has been in power ever since.

Swaziland

Area	17,364sq km
Country population	1,032,000
Capital city (pop)	Mbabane (67,200)
Languages	English/Swazi
Currency	Lilangeni
(South African currency is also in circulation)	

Swaziland is one of the world's few absolute monarchies – political parties were banned by the king in 1973. Most of the people work on the land and the country relies on South Africa for trade. About 40 per cent of the people live on less than one dollar a day.

Lesotho

Area	30,355sq km
Country population	1,795,000
Capital city (pop)	Maseru (367,000)
Languages	Sotho/English
Currency	Loti

The Kingdom of Lesotho was once called Basutoland and became independent from the UK in 1966. It is entirely surrounded by South Africa. Lesotho has diamond mines but few other resources. Most people work on the land or in South African mines.

The Kremlin, Moscow, Russia

Russia

Area	16,888,500sq km
Country population	143,202,000
Capital city (pop)	Moscow (10,101,500)
Language	Russian
Currency	Rouble

The Russian Federation is the largest country in the world, almost twice the size of the United States. It stretches from Europe to Asia and covers 13 per cent of the world's total land area. Russia was the chief republic of the former Soviet Union, which in 1991 was split into 15 separate republics. Since then Russia has gradually been establishing free trade. Oil, natural gas, timber and metals make up more than 80 per cent of its exports. The country is still held back by poor transport and other systems. It also suffers from violent conflict in the Chechnya region.

Turkey

Area	769,600sq km
Country population	73,193,000
Capital city (pop)	Ankara (3,203,362)
Language	Turkish
Currency	Turkish lira

Turkey is in a key position between Europe and Asia. The territory west of the Bosphorus strait is in Europe, while the much larger area to the east is in Asia. Turkey is popular with tourists, and between seven and ten million people every year visit its coastline and the historic city of Istanbul.

Syria

Area	183,800sq km
Country population	19,043,000
Capital city (pop)	Damascus (1,549,000)
Language	Arabic
Currency	Syrian pound

Syria has been home to some of the world's oldest civilizations, and Damascus is probably the oldest city in the world. Syria became independent from France in 1946. Its people come from many different ethnic groups and religions, including Arabs, Kurds, Assyrians and Armenians, and Muslims, Christians and Jews.

Israel

Area	20,600sq km
Country population	6,725,000
Capital city (pop)	Jerusalem (758,000)

Jerusalem is the seat of government but is not recognized as the capital by the UN because East Jerusalem is part of the Occupied Territories captured in 1967. The UN considers Tel Aviv (1,919,700) to be the capital.

Languages	Hebrew/Arabic
Currency	Shekel

After World War II, Israel was created in Palestine as a homeland for Jews. When Britain left the area in 1948 the State of Israel was proclaimed, and there was immediate conflict between the Jewish settlers and the Arabs who were living there. The State of Israel gained a great deal of land in the conflict, and many Palestinians were made homeless. There have been many attempts to make peace between the two sides, but the conflict continues.

The Wailing Wall and Mosque of Omar, Jerusalem

Lebanon

Area	10,200sq km
Country population	3,577,000
Capital city (pop)	Beirut (1,100,000)
Language	Arabic
Currency	Lebanese pound

Lebanon is a small country bordering the Mediterranean Sea. It became independent from France in 1943. Since Lebanon's civil war of 1975–91 huge sums have been spent on rebuilding the country and it is heavily in debt.

Jordan

Area	88,900sq km
Country population	5,703,000
Capital city (pop)	Amman (1,270,000)
Language	Arabic
Currency	Jordanian dinar

Jordan shares borders with Syria, Israel, the West Bank, Saudi Arabia and Iraq. Despite the problems of its neighbours the country is relatively peaceful. It doesn't have many natural resources, and its vital supplies of Iraqi oil were halted by the Iraq war of 2003.

Iraq

Area	437,400sq km
Country population	28,807,000
Capital city (pop)	Baghdad (3,841,268)
Language	Arabic
Currency	Iraqi dinar

Iraq has had a violent recent history. From 1979 to 2003, Iraq was controlled by the dictator President Saddam Hussein. The USA, supported by the UK, Spain, Australia, Poland and Denmark, removed Hussein from power in 2003, and continues to occupy Iraq.

Iran

Area	1,622,000sq km
Country population	69,515,000
Capital city (pop)	Tehran (6,758,845)
Language	Farsi
Currency	Rial

Iran is a mountainous Middle Eastern country. Until 1935 it was known as Persia. It shares borders with several of the world's most troubled nations, including Iraq, Afghanistan and Pakistan. This discourages investment from other countries and tourism, and Iran's economy depends on oil.

Saudi Arabia

Area	2,149,700sq km
Country population	24,573,000
Capital city (pop)	Riyadh (4,761,000)
Language	Arabic
Currency	Saudi riyal

Saudi Arabia is a monarchy. It is ruled by the sons and grandsons of Abdul Aziz ibn Saud, who founded the kingdom. Saudi Arabia is one of the richest countries in the Middle East. It has the largest reserves of petroleum in the world and exports more than any other country. It is about the same size as Western Europe and includes an area called the Empty Quarter, the world's largest sand desert. Saudi Arabia is a Muslim country and includes the city of Makkah (or Mecca). This was the birthplace of the Prophet Muhammad and millions of Muslims make a pilgrimage there every year.

Kuwait

Area	17,800sq km
Country population	2,687,000
Capital city (pop)	Kuwait City (388,663)
Language	Arabic
Currency	Kuwaiti dinar

Kuwait has large oil reserves that make up more than eight per cent of the world's total. The country's economy was almost destroyed when Iraqi forces invaded in 1990 and burned oil wells as they retreated. The Kuwaiti government has spent billions of dollars on repairs, and oil production is now higher than it was before the invasion.

Bahrain

Area	694sq km
Country population	727,000
Capital city (pop)	Manama (140,401)
Language	Arabic
Currency	Bahraini dinar

The island state of Bahrain is 32km off the east coast of Saudi Arabia. Oil is its main source of income, but the country is also a centre for offshore banking.

United Arab Emirates

Area	83,600sq km
Country population	4,496,000
Capital city (pop)	Abu Dhabi (450,000)
Language	Arabic
Currency	UAE dirham

The UAE is a group of seven Middle Eastern states and is one of the wealthiest countries in the area. It used to be a very poor country where most people lived by fishing, but is now the Gulf's third largest oil producer.

Qatar

Area	11,000sq km
Country population	813,000
Capital city (pop)	Doha (285,000)
Language	Arabic
Currency	Qatar riyal

Qatar became independent from Britain in 1971 and has changed from being a poor country dependent on pearl fishing to one of the Gulf's richest states. It has large reserves of oil and gas, which have brought great wealth.

Oman

Area	212,500sq km
Country population	2,567,000
Capital city (pop)	Muscat (540,000)
Language	Arabic
Currency	Omani rial

Oman borders Yemen, Saudi Arabia and the United Arab Emirates so is in a key position for the transportation of oil. Oil makes up more than 80 per cent of Oman's exports, but the government wants to encourage tourism and information technology.

Hotel in Dubai, United Arab Emirates

Yemen

Area	527,968sq km
Country population	20,975,000
Capital city (pop)	Sana'a' (1,590,624)
Language	Arabic
Currency	Riyal

In 1990 North and South Yemen were formally joined as the Republic of Yemen after years of conflict. Yemen is a poor country, affected by drought, political problems and a fast-growing population.

Kazakhstan

Area	2,699,700sq km
Country population	14,825,000
Capital city (pop)	Astana (320,000)
Language	Kazakh
Currency	Tenge

Kazakhstan is an enormous, landlocked nation almost four times the size of Texas. It was part of the former Soviet Union. Kazakhstan is rich in minerals and fossil fuels, including oil, coal, natural gas, gold, silver and lead.

Uzbekistan

Area	414,200sq km
Country population	26,593,000
Capital city (pop)	Tashkent (2,142,700)
Language	Uzbek
Currency	Soum

Uzbekistan has the largest population in Central Asia. It has been independent of the Soviet Union since 1991. It is the second largest exporter of cotton in the world and has mineral deposits. However, its people are poor because the wealth is distributed unequally.

Tajikistan

Area	143,100sq km
Country population	6,507,000
Capital city (pop)	Dushanbe (509,300)
Language	Tajik
Currency	Somoni

Tajikistan lies west of China in Central Asia. It was part of the former Soviet Republic and is one of the world's poorest nations. About 50,000 people died in the civil war of 1992–97 and the country is still violent and unsettled.

Turkmenistan

Area	488,100sq km
Country population	4,833,000
Capital city (pop)	Ashgabat (604,700)
Languages	Turkmen/Russian
Currency	Manat

Turkmenistan borders the Caspian Sea in Central Asia. About 90 per cent of its land is desert. It has the fifth largest oil and natural gas reserves in the world, but is crippled by debt to other countries.

Kyrgyzstan

Area	199,900sq km
Country population	5,264,000
Capital city (pop)	Bishkek (589,400)
Languages	Kyrgyz/Russian
Currency	Som

Kyrgyzstan is a picturesque country of mountains, glaciers and lakes. This small nation became independent from the former Soviet Union in 1991. It now has a modern, active government.

Yurts (tents) in a nomad camp, Uzbekistan

Afghanistan

Area	652,090sq km
Country population	25,863,000
Capital city (pop)	Kabul (1,424,400)
Languages	Dari (Persian)/Pashto
Currency	Afghani

Afghanistan is a mountainous country in Central Asia. It has been through more than 20 years of political upheaval, and instead of working in farming and silk making, many people are now involved in the narcotics trade. One million people in the country may be close to starvation.

Pakistan

Area	770,900sq km
Country population	157,935,000
Capital city (pop)	Islamabad (350,000)
Language	Urdu
(Punjabi is the most commonly used language, and English is used in business, government and higher education)	
Currency	Pakistan rupee

Pakistan lies between India, China, Iran, Afghanistan and Kashmir. It was created in 1947 as a home for Indian Muslims, and was divided into Pakistan and Bangladesh in 1972. The country is in dispute with India over ownership of the state of Kashmir. This has led to fears of an arms race, as both countries have nuclear weapons.

Bangladesh

Area	130,200sq km
Country population	141,822,000
Capital city (pop)	Dhaka (9,912,908)
Language	Bengali
Currency	Taka

Bangladesh was divided from Pakistan in 1972. About 70 per cent of the people work in farming and the country produces all its own food. The main industries include cotton, tea, leather, sugar and natural gas, and its leading export is clothing.

Rickshaw traffic jam in Dhaka, Bangladesh

India

Area	2,973,200sq km
Country population	1,103,371,000
Capital city (pop)	New Delhi (9,817,439)
Languages	Hindi/English
Currency	Indian rupee

India is the largest democracy in the world. It became independent from Britain in 1947. The division of the country that followed has led to three wars between India and Pakistan. The economy is seriously weakened by overpopulation, and about 25 per cent of Indians cannot afford to feed themselves. Most people still live by farming, but India has a booming information technology industry.

Sri Lanka

Area	64,600sq km
Country population	20,743,000
Capital city (pop)	Colombo (642,163)
Language	
Sinhala is the official language, Tamil is a national language, and English is used in government	
Currency	Sri Lankan rupee

Sri Lanka was called Ceylon until 1948, when it became independent from the UK. It is a tropical island in the Indian Ocean, only 20km from the south coast of India. The country has textile, food processing and telecommunications industries. It is held back, however, by nearly 20 years of conflict between some of its people, the Tamils, who want independence, and the government.

Nepal

Area	147,181sq km
Country population	27,133,000
Capital city (pop)	Kathmandu (535,000)
Language	Nepali
Currency	Nepalese rupee

Nepal lies between India and China. It is one of the poorest countries in the world. Nepal is home to Everest, the world's highest mountain, and tourism brings vital money into the country. In 2001, Nepal's Crown Prince murdered ten members of the royal family before taking his own life.

The Taj Mahal, India's most famous building

Bhutan

Area	47,000sq km
Country population	2,163,000
Capital city (pop)	Thimphu (30,340)
Language	Dzongkha
Currency	Ngultrum

The mountainous kingdom of Bhutan lies between Tibet (China) and India in the eastern Himalayas. Its main exports are rice, machinery and diesel oil, but tourism is also important.

China

Area	9,327,400sq km
Country population	1,315,844,000
Capital city (pop)	Beijing (7,362,426)
Language	Mandarin Chinese
Currency	Renminbi (also known as the yuan)

For centuries China led the world in the arts and sciences. The 19th and 20th centuries were troubled times because of foreign occupation, civil unrest and the policies of leader Mao Zedong. After his death in 1976 the situation began to improve and China now has the world's fastest-growing economy.

Taiwan

Area	36,175sq km
Country population	22,350,000
Capital city (pop)	Taipei (2,646,474)
Language	Chinese
(Taiwanese is spoken by 85 per cent of the population)	
Currency	New Taiwan dollar

The island of Taiwan lies 150km from mainland China. China sees Taiwan as one of its provinces. Taiwan has a thriving electronics industry. It is one of the world's leading producers of computer technology.

Mongolia

Area	1,566,500sq km
Country population	2,646,000
Capital city (pop)	Ulaanbaatar (515,100)
Language	Khalkha Mongolian
Currency	Tugrik

Mongolia is a landlocked nation between Russia and China. It is three times the size of France and is a land of deserts, grasslands, forests and mountains. Temperatures range from summer highs of 40°C in the Gobi Desert to -40°C during the winter. More than half the population are nomads – they move from place to place with their livestock. Gers (moveable tent-like huts) are the most common form of shelter, even in cities.

South Korea

Area	98,700sq km
Country population	47,817,000
Capital city (pop)	Seoul (10,321,000)
Language	Korean
Currency	Won

During the three-year Korean War in 1953 North Korea attacked the South with Chinese support. The Korean Peninsula was then divided into two. South Korea is a democratic country and has a thriving, high-tech economy and a growing tourism industry.

North Korea

Area	120,400sq km
Country population	22,488,000
Capital city (pop)	Pyongyang (2,741,260)
Language	Korean
Currency	Won

North Korea is one of the world's few remaining Communist states. As many as three million North Koreans have probably died of starvation because of famine and financial mishandling, while the regime spends money on military equipment. North Korea's nuclear programme threatens the international food aid that keeps the population going at present.

Capsule hotel in Osaka, Japan

Japan

Area	364,500sq km
Country population	128,085,000
Capital city (pop)	Tokyo (12,310,000)
Language	Japanese
Currency	Yen

Japan is made up of four large islands and many smaller islands. This mountainous and volcanic country is one of the world's most densely populated places, and there are more people in Tokyo than any other city in the world. Japan is a wealthy country and a world leader in the electronics, robotics and car production industries.

Thailand

Area	510,900sq km
Country population	64,233,000
Capital city (pop)	Bangkok (5,882,000)
Language	Thai
Currency	Baht

Until 1939, Thailand was called Siam. It is the only country in Southeast Asia never to have been under the control of a European power. About ten million tourists visit Bangkok and the country's beautiful coasts each year. Farming is important and about half the people still work on the land.

Myanmar

Area	676,578sq km
Country population	50,519,000
Capital city (pop)	Rangoon (2,513,023)
Language	Burmese
Currency	Kyat

Myanmar used to be called Burma. The country is ruled by an undemocratic military government and has been accused by foreign governments of severe human rights abuses. It may also be the world's largest producer of heroin. These things have led both the European Union and the USA to limit trade with the country.

Vietnam

Area	325,500sq km
Country population	84,328,000
Capital city (pop)	Hanoi (1,073,760)
Language	Vietnamese
Currency	Dông

North and South Vietnam were rejoined in 1976 after 30 years of war. At first the war was between the Communists and the French colonialists, and later between the Communist North Vietnam and the South, which was supported by the USA. Nearly four million people died and much of Vietnam's landscape was destroyed. There is now a Communist socialist government. Vietnam is now one of the world's leading rice exporters, and the country's oil production has increased.

Rice farm in Vietnam

Cambodia

Area	181,035sq km
Country population	14,071,000
Capital city (pop)	Phnom Penh (1,200,000)
Language	Khmer
Currency	Riel

1999 was Cambodia's first full year of peace after more than 20 years of conflict. In 1975 Phnom Penh was captured by Communist Khmer Rouge forces, who executed millions of Cambodians. The country is still very poor. Farming and fishing are the main occupations, but tourism has become more important.

Laos

Area	236,800sq km
Country population	5,924,000
Capital city (pop)	Vientiane (555,100)
Language	Lao
Currency	Kip

Laos is a landlocked, mountainous country bordered by China, Vietnam, Cambodia, Thailand and Myanmar. It is one of the world's last remaining Communist states. Laos is popular with adventurous tourists, but it is extremely primitive. There are few paved roads and no railways.

Malaysia

Area	328,600sq km
Country population	25,347,000
Capital city (pop)	Kuala Lumpur (1,297,526)
Language	Bahasa Malaysia (Malay)
Currency	Malaysian dollar (Ringgit)

Malaysia is made up of two regions, which are separated by about 1,030km of the South China Sea. The country used to rely on farming and exports of raw materials, but it is now a leading producer and exporter of high-tech, electronic merchandise.

Singapore

Area	648sq km
Country population	4,326,000
Languages	Malay/Mandarin/Tamil/English
Currency	Singapore dollar

The city state of Singapore in Southeast Asia is one of the richest nations in the world. Its people have one of the world's highest standards of living. Singapore's thriving manufacturing industry includes shipbuilding, electronics and pharmaceuticals.

Indonesia

Area	1,811,600sq km
Country population	222,781,000
Capital city (pop)	Jakarta (8,347,083)
Language	Indonesian
Currency	Rupiah

Indonesia includes more than 17,000 islands. The world's largest Muslim population lives on about 6,000 of these. Indonesia is rich in minerals, and it exports petroleum, textiles, timber, natural gas and rubber.

East Timor

Area	14,874sq km
Country population	947,000
Capital city (pop)	Dili (56,000)
Languages	Portuguese/Tetum
Currency	US dollar

East Timor became independent from Indonesia in 2002. It is Southeast Asia's youngest nation and the world's newest democracy. East Timor is a very poor country and often suffers floods.

Brunei

Area	5,300sq km
Country population	374,000
Capital city (pop)	Bandar Seri Begawan (46,000)
Language	Malay
Currency	Brunei dollar

Brunei gained full independence from Britain in 1984. It is ruled by the Sultan, whose family have reigned for six centuries. Brunei is enormously wealthy because of its natural gas and oil fields.

Gamelan orchestra in Bali, Indonesia

The Philippines

Area	298,200sq km
Country population	83,054,000
Capital city (pop)	Manila (9,906,048)
Languages	Filipino/English
Currency	Philippine peso

The Philippines is made up of more than 7,000 islands in Southeast Asia. More than 80 per cent of the population is Roman Catholic – the Philippines is the only Asian nation that is mainly Christian. It suffers from natural disasters, such as volcanic eruptions and typhoons, as well as a very high birth rate. Many Filipinos go to work abroad and their country depends on the $6–7 billion they send home each year.

Maldives

Area	298sq km
Country population	329,000
Capital city (pop)	Malé (74,069)
Language	Maldivian Dhivehi
Currency	Rufiyaa

The Maldives are a chain of 1,190 coral islands. The chief industries are fishing and tourism. Nearly half a million tourists a year visit the islands. Few crops can be grown there and almost all food must be imported.

Aerial view of a Maldive island

The Comoros

Area	2,235sq km
Country population	798,000
Capital city (pop)	Moroni (30,365)
Languages	Arabic/French (most people speak Comoran)
Currency	Comorian franc

The Comoros is a group of islands between Madagascar and Mozambique. It is one of the world's poorest countries. The Comoros exports vanilla, cloves and essential oils, but also depends on aid from other countries.

Mauritius

Area	1,864sq km
Country population	1,245,000
Capital city (pop)	Port Louis (146,499)
Languages	English/French
Currency	Mauritius rupee

Mauritius is an island in the Indian Ocean. It has had a stable government, and Mauritians have some of the highest incomes in Asia. The island exports sugar cane, tea and tobacco and has a thriving tourism industry.

Seychelles

Area	455sq km
Country population	81,000
Capital city (pop)	Victoria (71,000)
Languages	English/French
Currency	Seychelles rupee

The Seychelles is made up of 155 islands in the Indian Ocean, east of mainland Africa. It became independent from Britain in 1976. About 90 per cent of the islands' people live on the main island of Mahé and are reasonably well off, thanks to successful tourism and tuna fishing industries.

Purnululu National Park, Australia

Micronesia

Area	702sq km
Country population	110,000
Capital city (pop)	Palikir (10,000)
Language	English
Currency	US dollar

The Federated States of Micronesia is a group of more than 600 islands in the North Pacific Ocean. It gained independence from the USA in 1986, but the USA has kept the right to have military bases on the islands. This agreement brings Micronesia billions of dollars of financial aid.

Nauru

Area	21sq km
Country population	14,000
Capital city (pop)	no official capital
Languages	Nauruan/English
Currency	Australian dollar

The island of Nauru lies 53km south of the Equator in the Pacific Ocean. It is the smallest independent republic in the world. At present, the people have one of the highest incomes per head in the world, thanks to the export of phosphates (fertilizer). However, Nauru's phosphate reserves are expected to run out during 2005, and it has few other resources.

Australia

Area	7,682,300sq km
Country population	20,155,000
Capital city (pop)	Canberra (322,500)
Language	English
Currency	Australian dollar

Australia was discovered by Captain James Cook in 1770. It became independent within the British Empire in 1931 and Queen Elizabeth II remains the head of state. Australia is the world's sixth largest country. It has important mineral resources and there are vast areas given over to sheep and cattle farming. Some famous landmarks include the Great Barrier Reef and Uluru.

Papua New Guinea

Area	452,900sq km
Country population	5,887,000
Capital city (pop)	Port Moresby (173,500)
Language	English
Currency	Kina

Papua New Guinea is made up of many small islands and one half of New Guinea, the world's second largest island. It has mineral deposits such as gold and copper, as well as oil and natural gas. It has been difficult to use these to the full because the country lacks good roads and transport, and there are large areas of rainforest.

New Zealand

Area	268,000sq km
Country population	4,028,000
Capital city (pop)	Wellington (340,719)
Languages	English/Maori
Currency	New Zealand dollar

New Zealand lies in the Pacific Ocean, about 1,600km east of Australia. It is made up of two main islands and several smaller ones. New Zealand is one of the most isolated countries in the world, and Wellington lies further south than any other capital city. New Zealand is mountainous and relatively unspoilt, and is becoming more and more popular with tourists from all over the world.

The bay of Auckland, New Zealand

Palau

Area	458sq km
Country population	20,000
Capital city (pop)	Koror (13,303)
Languages	Palauan/English
Currency	US dollar

The Republic of Palau is made up of 340 islands in the Pacific Ocean, southeast of the Philippines. It became independent in 1994 and is one of the world's youngest nations. The islands rely mainly on tourism. The waters around Palau are rich in marine life, and visitors come to snorkel and scuba-dive. The islands also export fish, shellfish and coconuts.

Solomon Islands

Area	28,896sq km
Country population	478,000
Capital city (pop)	Honiara (49,107)
Language	English
Currency	Solomon Islands dollar

The Solomon Islands include several densely forested volcanic islands in the South Pacific. It is one of the world's poorest countries. People live by farming, forestry and fishing, but since 1998 there has been conflict between different groups in the population. Law and order has broken down, and the islanders' average income has been halved. A peacekeeping force led by Australia arrived in 2003.

Vanuatu

Area	12,189sq km
Country population	211,000
Capital city (pop)	Port Vila (29,356)
Languages	Bislama/English/French
Currency	Vatu

Vanuatu is a chain of 83 volcanic islands in the South Pacific Ocean, between Hawaii and Australia. About 65 per cent of the people work on the land, but offshore banking and tourism are growing industries. However, the islands sometimes suffer earthquakes, tsunamis and cyclones, which may limit the growth of tourism.

Fiji

Area	18,274sq km
Country population	848,000
Capital city (pop)	Suva (77,366)
Languages	

There is no official language, but the main languages are Fijian and Hindi

Currency	Fiji dollar

Fiji is made up of more than 300 volcanic islands in the South Pacific Ocean, about 1,770km north of New Zealand. Fiji's main export is sugar, and it has a flourishing tourism industry. However, political problems from time to time have discouraged other countries from investing in the islands, and Fiji is a poor country.

Tuvalu

Area	26sq km
Country population	10,000
Capital city (pop)	Funafuti (3,856)
Languages	Tuvaluan/English
Currency	

Australian dollar of 100 cents is legal tender. In addition there are Tuvalu dollar and cent coins in circulation

Tuvalu is a group of nine coral atolls in the South Pacific Ocean. It is the second lowest country in the world, has no known natural resources, and receives fewer than 1,000 tourists a year. The islanders rely on exporting fish, stamps and handicrafts, as well as the money sent home from Tuvaluans working abroad.

Tonga

Area	650sq km
Country population	102,000
Capital city (pop)	Nuku'alofa (34,000)
Languages	Tongan/English
Currency	Pa'anga

Tonga is a group of 169 islands in the southern Pacific Ocean. It is the only country ruled by a monarchy in the Pacific. The islands have no natural resources and people rely on farming. Tonga exports products such as coconuts, vanilla and yams. Around half of the Tongan people live abroad, particularly in the USA and Australasia.

Traditional houses, Fiji

Samoa

Area	2,831sq km
Country population	185,000
Capital city (pop)	Apia (38,836)
Languages	Samoan/English
Currency	Tala

Samoa is a group of islands in the South Pacific Ocean. Samoa's beaches and rainforests have led to a booming tourism industry. This now brings in a quarter of the islands' income.

Kiribati

Area	726sq km
Country population	99,000
Capital city (pop)	Tarawa (36,717)
Language	English
Currency	Australian dollar

Kiribati is made up of 33 islands in the Pacific Ocean, halfway between Hawaii and Australia. Kiribati's main exports are coconuts and fish.

Marshall Islands

Area	181sq km
Country population	62,000
Capital city (pop)	Dalap-Uliga-Darrit (20,000)
Languages	Marshallese/English
Currency	US dollar

The Marshall Islands lie in the central Pacific. The islands were occupied by the USA after World War II until 1986, and were used for nuclear weapons testing. About half the people work in farming. Coconut oil is the main export.

Which do you think are the most common surnames around the world? Where do the most weddings take place? And who has changed the course of history? Find the answers to these and many other questions about people – young and old, celebrities and unknowns – in the following pages.

PEOPLE

Surnames around the world

Surnames were not used in Britain until after the Norman Conquest in 1066. Until then, most people were known only by their first name. People started to add extra names in order to tell one William from another. Some surnames came from where a person lived or the person's father's name – so the son of someone called John was known as Johnson. Others were based on a person's occupation (a blacksmith would be called Smith) or their appearance (a brown-haired person might be called Brown). The origins of some surnames have been forgotten.

Most common surnames

UK	Denmark
1 Smith	1 Jensen
2 Jones	2 Nielsen
3 Williams	3 Hansen
4 Taylor	4 Pedersen
5 Brown	5 Andersen
6 Davies	6 Christensen
7 Evans	7 Larsen
8 Wilson	8 Sørensen
9 Thomas	9 Rasmussen
10 Johnson	10 Jørgensen

USA	France
1 Smith	1 Martin
2 Johnson	2 Bernard
3 Williams	3 Thomas
4 Jones	4 Petit
5 Brown	5 Robert
6 Davis	6 Richard
7 Miller	7 Durand
8 Wilson	8 Dubois
9 Moore	9 Moreau
10 Taylor	10 Laurent

Belgium	Germany
1 Peeters	1 Müller
2 Janssens	2 Schmidt
3 Maes	3 Schneider
4 Jacobs	4 Fischer
5 Mertens	5 Meyer
6 Willems	6 Weber
7 Claes	7 Schulz
8 Goossens	8 Wagner
9 Wouters	9 Becker
10 De Smet	10 Hoffmann

China	India
1 Zhang	1 Singh
2 Whang	2 Kumar
3 Li	3 Sharma/Sarma
4 Zhao	4 Patel
5 Chen	5 Shah
6 Yang	6 Lal
7 Wu	7 Gupta
8 Liu	8 Bhat
9 Huang	9 Rao
10 Zhou	10 Reddy

Ireland	Russia
1 Murphy	1 Ivanov
2 Kelly	2 Smirnov
3 O'Sullivan	3 Vasilev
4 Walsh	4 Petrov
5 Smith	5 Kyznetsov
6 O'Brien	6 Fedorov
7 Byrne	7 Mikhailov
8 Ryan	8 Sokolov
9 O'Connor	9 Pavlov
10 O'Neill	10 Semenov

Japan	Scotland
1 Sato	1 Smith
2 Suzuki	2 Brown
3 Takahashi	3 Wilson
4 Tanaka	4 Campbell
5 Watanabe	5 Stewart
6 Ito	6 Thomson
7 Yamamoto	7 Robertson
8 Nakamura	8 Anderson
9 Kobayashi	9 Macdonald
10 Saito	10 Scott

Netherlands	Spain
1 De Jong	1 García
2 De Vries	2 Fernández
3 Jansen	3 González
4 Van den Berg/ Van der Berg/ Van de Berg	4 Rodríguez
5 Bakker	5 López
6 Van Dijk	6 Martínez
7 Visser	7 Sánchez
8 Janssen	8 Pérez
9 Smit	9 Martín
10 Meijer/Meyer	10 Gómez

Norway	Sweden
1 Hansen	1 Johansson
2 Olsen	2 Andersson
3 Johansen	3 Karlsson
4 Larsen	4 Nilsson
5 Andersen	5 Eriksson
6 Nilsen	6 Larsson
7 Pedersen	7 Olsson
8 Kristiansen	8 Persson
9 Jensen	9 Svensson
10 Karlsen	10 Gustafsson

Popular first names

First name fashions change – especially those for girls. Some traditional names remain popular but new names come into use. Chloe, for example, was not in the top 100 until the 1980s, but has been in the top ten since 1997. These are the most popular names now and 100 years ago in the UK and USA.

UK

Girls	Boys
1 Emily	Jack
2 Ellie	Joshua
3 Jessica	Thomas
4 Sophie	James
5 Chloe	Daniel
6 Lucy	Samuel
7 Olivia	Oliver
8 Charlotte	William
9 Katie	Benjamin
10 Megan	Joseph

UK 100 years ago

Girls	Boys
1 Mary	William
2 Florence	John
3 Doris	George
4 Edith	Thomas
5 Dorothy	Arthur
6 Annie	James
7 Margaret	Charles
8 Alice	Frederick
9 Elizabeth	Albert
10 Elsie	Ernest

USA

Girls	Boys
1 Emily	Jacob
2 Madison	Michael
3 Hannah	Joshua
4 Emma	Matthew
5 Alexis	Ethan
6 Ashley	Joseph
7 Abigail	Andrew
8 Sarah	Christopher
9 Samantha	Daniel
10 Olivia	Nicholas

USA 100 years ago

Girls	Boys
1 Mary	John
2 Helen	William
3 Margaret	George
4 Ruth	James
5 Anna	Joseph
6 Dorothy	Charles
7 Elizabeth	Robert
8 Marie	Frank
9 Alice	Edward
10 Florence	Walter

Long names

Anna Pepper was born in Derby, England, on 19 December 1882. She was given 26 first names, one for each letter of the alphabet, in alphabetical order: Anna Bertha Cecilia Diana Emily Fanny Gertrude Hypatia Inez Jane Kate Louisa Maud Nora Ophelia Prudence Quince Rebecca Starkey Teresa Ulysis Venus Winifred Xenophon Yetty Zeus Pepper.

Louis Jullien (1812–1860) was a French conductor and composer, born in Sisteron, France. His parents were persuaded by the 36 members of the local Philharmonic Society that they should all be godfathers, and Louis received all their names.

www.anzwers.org/free/jhpn

Brazilian footballer Ronaldo

Initial impressions

These famous people are known by their initials and surnames, rather than their full first names.

Initials	Full names	Surname	Famous as
W.H.	Wystan Hugh	Auden	Poet
Rev W.	Wilbert	Awdry	*Thomas the Tank Engine* author
P.T.	Phineas Taylor	Barnum	Circus proprietor
J.M.	James Matthew	Barrie	*Peter Pan* author
T.S.	Thomas Stearns	Eliot	Author of the book on which the musical *Cats* was based
W.C.	William Claude	Fields	Film actor
W.G.	William Gilbert	Grace	Cricketer
H.J.	Henry John	Heinz	Food manufacturer
k.d.	Kathryn Dawwn	Lang	Singer
D.H.	David Herbert	Lawrence	Writer
T.E.	Thomas Edward	Lawrence	Soldier/writer (Lawrence of Arabia)
C.S.	Clive Staples	Lewis	*The Lion, the Witch and the Wardrobe* author
A.A.	Alan Alexander	Milne	*Winnie the Pooh* author
E.	Edith	Nesbit	*The Phoenix and the Carpet* author
J.K.	Joanne Kathleen	Rowling	*Harry Potter* author
O.J.	Orenthal James	Simpson	Footballer
R.L.	Robert Lawrence	Stine	*Goosebumps* author
J.R.R.	John Roland Ruel	Tolkien	*Lord of the Rings* author
J.M.W.	Joseph Mallord William	Turner	Painter
H.G.	Herbert George	Wells	Science-fiction author
E.B.	Elwyn Brooks	White	*Charlotte's Web* and *Stuart Little* author
F.W.	Frank Winfield	Woolworth	Retailer

Known by one name

Some people are so famous they are instantly recognizable by just one name.

Aaliyah	US singer/actress Aaliyah Haughton, 1979–2001
Barbie	US doll Barbara Millicent Roberts, 1959–
Beyoncé	US singer Beyoncé Knowles, 1981–
Björk	Icelandic singer/actress Björk Gudmundsdóttir, 1965–
Bono	Irish rock band U2 singer Paul Hewson, 1960–
Canaletto	Italian painter Giovanni Antonio Canale, 1697–1768
Cher	US singer Cherilyn Sarkasian, 1946–
Colette	French writer Sidonie-Gabrielle Colette, 1873–1954
Dido	UK singer Dido Armstrong, 1971–
Eminem	US rap singer Marshall Mathers, 1972–
Enya	Irish singer Eithne ní Bhraonáin, 1961–
Evita	Argentinean politician Eva Peron, 1919–52
Flea	US Red Hot Chili Peppers bass guitarist Michael Peter Balzary, 1962–
Hergé	Belgian Tintin cartoonist Georges Rémi, 1907–83
Houdini	US magician Erich Weiss, 1874–1926
Jewel	US singer Jewel Kilcher, 1974–
Lulu	UK singer Marie McDonald McLaughlin, 1948–
Madonna	US singer Madonna Louise Ciccone, 1958–
Meatloaf	US singer Marvin/Michael Lee Aday, 1947–
Michelangelo	Italian painter Michelangelo Buonarroti, 1475–1564
Moby	US musician Richard Melville Hall, 1965–
Pelé	Brazilian footballer Edson Arantes Nascimento, 1940–
Pink	US singer Alecia Moore, 1979–
Ronaldo	Brazilian footballer Ronaldo Luiz Nazario de Lima, 1976–
Shaggy	Jamaican singer Orville Richard Burrell, 1968–
Sting	UK singer Gordon Matthew Sumner, 1951–

J.K.Rowling, author of the Harry Potter *books*

Who's who in the family?

We all know who's who in our immediate family – our mothers, fathers, grandparents, aunts and uncles, sisters and brothers. But how do you identify a second cousin or a cousin once removed?

Nephew
Son of your sister or brother.

Niece
Daughter of your sister or brother.

Cousin, or first cousin
Child of your aunt and uncle.

Second cousin
Child of your first cousin. Second cousins have the same great-grandparents as you, but not the same grandparents. Third cousins have the same great-great-grandparents, fourth cousins have the same great-great-great-grandparents, and so on.

Removed
A child of your first cousin is described as "once removed". Removed shows that people are from different generations. Once removed is one generation, twice removed is two generations, and so on.

Step
Stepmother, stepfather, stepsister, stepbrother, stepson or stepdaughter is a person who is related to you only by the remarriage of someone in your immediate family after death or divorce. For example, if a woman marries again, her new husband will be her children's stepfather but has no blood relationship with them.

Half
A half-sister or half-brother has either the same mother or father as you, but not both.

In-law
A relative by marriage – so the wife of your son is your daughter-in-law or the wife of your brother is your sister-in-law. It refers only to immediate members of your family (your own marriage, that of your brothers and sisters, and your children).

Wedding on a Pacific island beach

 # Weddings around the world

The number of people marrying every year varies from country to country. Some tropical islands have particularly high marriage rates because couples go there specially to have a romantic wedding.

Country	Marriages per 1,000 per year*	Country	Marriages per 1,000 per year*
High rates		**Low rates**	
Barbados	13.1	United Arab Emirates	2.5
Liechtenstein	12.8	Georgia	2.9
Cyprus	12.3	Peru	3.2
Seychelles	11.5	Saudi Arabia	3.2
Medium rates			
USA	8.2	* In those countries for which data available	
Australia	5.9		
UK	5.1		
Canada	5.1		

 # Divorce around the world

The number of divorces varies greatly from country to country, according to the legal system and religion.

Country	Divorces per 1,000 per year*	Country	Divorces per 1,000 per year*
High rates		**Low rates**	
Belarus	4.71	Guatemala	0.12
USA	4.19	Libya	0.25
Russia	3.66	Mongolia	0.34
Estonia	3.09	Armenia	0.35
		Georgia	0.35
Medium rates			
UK	2.59	* In those countries for which data available	
Australia	2.61		
Canada	2.28		

Four generations of one family

Till death do us part...

Longest marriages

- Cousins Sir Temulji Bhicaji Nariman and Lady Nariman of Mumbai (Bombay), India were married in 1853 when they were both five years old. They remained married until Sir Temulji's death in 1940 – a total of 86 years.
- Lazarus Rowe and Molly Weber were allegedly married in Greenland, New Hampshire, USA, in 1743. They remained married for 86 years until 1829 when Lazarus died.
- In the UK, James Frederick Burgess and Sarah Ann Gregory were married for 82 years from 1883 to 1965, when Sarah died.

Most marriages

- In the Bible, we are told that King Solomon had 700 wives and 300 concubines (partners to whom he was not married).
- King Mongkut of Siam (1804–68) had 39 wives and 82 children. The musical *The King and I* was about King Mongkut.
- American Glynn "Scotty" de Moss Wolfe (1908–97) was married 29 times, which is a US record. His 29th and last wedding was on 20 June 1996 to Linda Essex. It was her 23rd wedding – another US record.
- US asbestos millionaire Tommy Manville (1894–1967) was married 13 times.
- In the UK, Sir Francis Ferdinand Maurice Cook (1907–78) was married seven times.

Anniversary gifts

There is a very old tradition of celebrating wedding anniversaries by presenting special types of gift. For example, for a 25th anniversary people give gifts made of silver. In the UK and USA most people celebrate only the milestone anniversaries: the 25th, 30th, 40th, 50th and 60th. The 75th anniversary was traditionally the diamond but few married couples live long enough to celebrate it. Since Queen Victoria's Diamond Jubilee was held to mark her 60 years on the throne, the 60th wedding anniversary has become the diamond celebration.

Anniversary	Gift
1st	Cotton (UK); paper (US)
2nd	Paper (UK); cotton, calico (US)
3rd	Leather
4th	Fruit, flowers (UK); linen, silk (US)
5th	Wood
6th	Sugar, sweets, iron
7th	Wool, copper
8th	Bronze
9th	Pottery, willow
10th	Tin, aluminium
11th	Steel

Anniversary	Gift
12th	Silk, linen
13th	Lace
14th	Ivory
15th	Crystal, glass
20th	China
25th	Silver
30th	Pearls
35th	Coral, jade
40th	Rubies
45th	Sapphires
50th	Gold
55th	Emeralds
60th	Diamonds
70th	Platinum
75th	Diamonds (again)

Coat of arms

A coat of arms is the symbol or badge of a family, person or even organization. The idea started in Europe in the Middle Ages, when knights began to add decoration to their armour. This helped soldiers tell the difference between their own army and the enemy on a battlefield. It also helped people to tell knights apart in jousting contests. The designs on a coat of arms symbolized the achievements of the family, and were passed on from generation to generation. A coat of arms is still put together by people called heralds, and the process is known as heraldry.

Parts of a coat of arms
Each coat of arms has a unique combination of colours and symbols. The positions of the different features are described in special terms, such as sinister (left) and dexter (right).

Ordinaries
The geometric designs in a coat of arms are called ordinaries.

Colours
The background or field uses one of two metals: Gold, (known as or, in the language of heraldry), represented by yellow, and Silver (argent), shown as white. There are five basic colours: Gules (red), Azure (blue), Sable (black), Vert (green) and Purpure (purple). Patterns called furs, such as ermine, are also used. Each colour or pattern symbolizes a special feature, such as red for bravery. Special rules dictate how these devices are used: a metal may not be placed on metal, and so on.

Charge, supporters and other features
An object on the body of a shield is called a charge. It may include real and imaginary animals, often lions, eagles or dragons. At each side of the shield are the supporters, which may be animals, birds, or people. There may also be other features such as a family motto in a banner above the shield and a crest or helmet which may feature the same animals used as the charge or supporters.

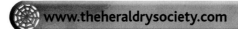
www.theheraldrysociety.com

Christopher Columbus landing in the New World

Christopher Columbus (1451–1506) Italian

Christopher Columbus is one of the most famous of all explorers. He believed he could reach Asia by sailing west across the Atlantic Ocean and in 1492 he set sail in the *Santa Maria* to prove his theory. Instead, he landed on the islands now known as the West Indies. His discoveries led to the European exploration and settlement of the Americas.

William Shakespeare (1564–1616) English

William Shakespeare is generally agreed to be the greatest playwright in the English language. He began as an actor and wrote at least 154 love poems and 37 plays, including *Hamlet*, *King Lear*, *Romeo and Juliet* and *Macbeth*. Shakespeare also probably introduced more than 1,700 new words to the English language.

Charles Darwin (1809–82) English

Naturalist Charles Darwin established the theory of evolution. He began forming his ideas when he served as official naturalist on a world voyage on *HMS Beagle* (1831–36) and spent the rest of his life back in England developing them. When his famous book *The Origin of Species by Means of Natural Selection* was published in 1859 there were violent reactions against it. Darwin challenged the Bible's account of creation, and explained that human beings are descended from an ape-like ancestor. Another English naturalist, Alfred Russel Wallace, independently developed very similar ideas at the same time as Darwin.

Charles Darwin

Karl Marx (1818–83) German

Karl Marx's ideas on economic history and sociology changed the world. Marx was a social philosopher who attacked the state and predicted a future in which everyone was equal. He explained his theories in the *Communist Manifesto* (compiled with Friedrich Engels and published in 1848) and *Das Kapital* (1867–94). His ideas eventually led to the Russian Revolution and communism. By 1950 almost half of the world's people lived under communist regimes.

Emmeline Pankhurst (1858–1928) English

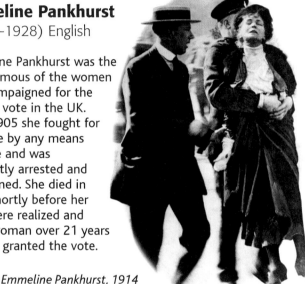

Emmeline Pankhurst was the most famous of the women who campaigned for the right to vote in the UK. From 1905 she fought for the vote by any means possible and was frequently arrested and imprisoned. She died in 1928 shortly before her aims were realized and every woman over 21 years old was granted the vote.

Emmeline Pankhurst, 1914

Mahatma Gandhi (1869–1948) Indian

Gandhi began his career as a lawyer but became a great political and spiritual leader. He led the peaceful civil disobedience of Indians against British rule in India and negotiated with the British government until 1947, when India was granted independence. Gandhi became the first icon of a people's struggle against oppression. His simple lifestyle and his belief in religious tolerance have made him a symbol of decency and peace ever since.

Albert Einstein (1879–1955) German/American

Einstein was one of the greatest of all physicists and his name has become a symbol of genius. When his most famous work, the General Theory of Relativity, was proven in 1919, Einstein became the most celebrated scientist in the world, and he won the Nobel Prize for Physics in 1921. Einstein was a firm believer in pacifism, but his scientific theories helped his adopted country, the USA, to develop the atomic bomb. A week before he died Einstein wrote to Bertrand Russell, a British philosopher and leading anti-nuclear campaigner, asking to put his name to a manifesto urging all countries to give up their nuclear weapons.

Adolf Hitler (1889–1945) Austrian

Adolf Hitler was Germany's leader from 1933 to 1945, during which time he led the world into the most devastating war in history. Hitler's hatred of Jewish people and his desire for a blue-eyed, blond-haired master race led to the murder of six million people during World War II; most died in concentration camps in Eastern Europe.

Mao Zedong/Mao Tse-tung/Chairman Mao
(1893–1976) Chinese

Mao Zedong was one of the founders of the Chinese Communist Party and the first chairman of the People's Republic of China in 1949. He had an enormous influence on his country and was greatly admired for founding the Chinese republic and for changes in the early years of his rule. His later policies were less successful. During his rule, Mao's image was displayed everywhere – in every school, home, factory and workplace.

Nelson Mandela (1918–)
South African

Nelson Mandela dedicated his life to the fight against apartheid – a policy which kept black and white South Africans apart and denied black citizens the vote. He was imprisoned in 1964 for his aggressive opposition to South Africa's racist government and was held for 26 years. In 1990, after his release, Mandela was elected president of the African National Congress. In 1993 he won the Nobel Peace Prize for his work to end apartheid.

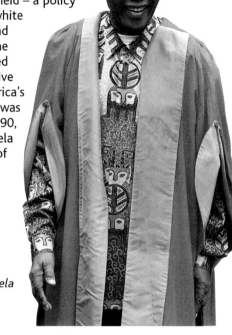

Nelson Mandela

James Watson (1928–) American
and Francis Crick (1916–2004) English

American biologist James Watson and English scientist Francis Crick discovered the molecular structure of DNA, using theories already written by Maurice Wilkins. Their theory helps to explain how DNA carries hereditary information and their discoveries have revolutionized our understanding of genetics and the study of disease.

Martin Luther King, Jr (1929–68) American

Martin Luther King was a Baptist minister who campaigned against the segregation of blacks in the southern states of the United States. He was influenced by Gandhi and believed in peaceful protest. He won the Nobel Peace Prize in 1964. King was assassinated in 1968, but will always be remembered for his dignified, passive resistance to an unjust society.

Bill Gates (1955–) American

Bill Gates created his first computer program while still at high school, and became convinced that computers would eventually be used in every office in the world. He co-founded Microsoft in 1977, and Microsoft operating systems now run more than 90 per cent of the world's personal computers. Gates is now one of the richest people in the world.

*A portrait of
Chairman Mao
in Beijing*

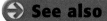
See also

History timeline :
page 104

Explorers and travellers

Today there are few places that have not been explored, but this was not always so. America was unknown to Europeans until little over 500 years ago, and Australia was scarcely known by the rest of the world until the late 18th century. These are some of the people who made Europeans aware of the rest of the world.

Marco Polo (c 1254–1324)
Italian traveller Marco Polo was one of the first Europeans to visit China and other Far Eastern territories. His reports were not believed, but he encouraged the idea of trading with the East.

John Cabot (1450–98)
Italian-born explorer John and his son Sebastian Cabot were employed by British merchants to seek a western route to Asia. During their travels they discovered parts of the northeast coast of America.

Christopher Columbus (1451–1506)
Italian explorer Columbus discovered North, Central and South America and the islands of the West Indies.

Vasco da Gama (c 1460–1524)
Portuguese explorer Vasco da Gama travelled round the Cape of Good Hope and up the East coast of Africa. He discovered a trade route to India.

Ferdinand Magellan (1480–1521)
Magellan was a Portuguese explorer who led the first voyage round the world. He discovered the Strait of Magellan, near the tip of South America.

Abel Tasman (1603–59)
Abel Tasman, a Dutchman, explored Australia. In 1642 he discovered Van Diemans Land (later called Tasmania) and New Zealand.

Henry Hudson (c 1550–1611)
Henry Hudson was an English navigator who searched for a Northwest Passage (a route to the East by travelling north of America). He discovered Hudson's Bay.

James Cook (1728–79)
British Captain James Cook led several major expeditions. He explored the coasts of Australia, New Zealand and North America.

David Livingstone (1813–73)
Livingstone was a Scottish missionary and explorer of Africa. He discovered and named the Victoria Falls after Queen Victoria.

Sir Richard Burton (1821–90)
Burton was one of the first Europeans to travel to Arabia. With John Hanning Speke he discovered Lake Tanganyika in Africa.

John Hanning Speke (1827–64)
Speke discoverered Lake Tanganyika with Burton. He also discovered Lake Victoria, believed to be the source of the River Nile.

Sir Henry Morton Stanley (1841–1904)
Stanley was a British explorer of Africa and was involved in the search for Livingstone.

Top of the world
The first people to succeed in climbing Everest, the world's highest mountain, were Edmund Hillary from New Zealand and Tenzing Norgay from Nepal. They reached the summit on 29 May 1953.

Polar exploration firsts

The North and South Poles are two of the most difficult places on Earth to reach and so have been great challenges for explorers. These are some of the people who reached the Poles by one means or another.

Liv Arnesen at the North Pole

First to reach the North Pole?
American adventurer Frederick Albert Cook (1865–1940) claimed he and two Eskimo companions reached the North Pole on 21 April 1908, but he probably faked his journey. Another American, Robert Edwin Peary (1856–1920), his companion Matthew Alexander Henson (1866–1955) and four Eskimos were first at the Pole on 6 April 1909.

First to reach the South Pole
Norwegian explorer Roald Amundsen (1872–1928) and four companions reached the South Pole on 14 December 1911. They just beat British explorer Robert Falcon Scott and his team, who got there on 17 January 1912 but died on their return journey.

First to fly over the North and South Poles
Two Americans, Richard Evelyn Byrd and Floyd Bennett, flew over the North Pole on 9 May 1926 in a three-engined Fokker F.VIII-3m plane named *Josephine Ford* after motor magnate Henry Ford's granddaughter. Ford had given some of the money to fund the flight. On 29 November 1929, Byrd also became the first person to fly over the South Pole.

First solo overland journey to the North Pole
Japanese explorer Naomi Uemura reached the Pole on 1 May 1978. He travelled by dog sled, but was then picked up by an aircraft. Frenchman Jean-Louis Etienne made the first solo journey without dogs. He reached the North Pole on 11 May 1986.

First to the North Pole on skis
Dmitry Shparo (USSR) and six others skied to the Pole, arriving on 31 May 1979.

First pole-to-pole expedition
British explorer Sir Ranulph Fiennes and his partner Charles Burton were the first people to walk from pole to pole. They walked over the North Pole on 10 April 1982, having crossed the South Pole on 15 December 1980.

First to the North Pole on a motorcycle
Fukashi Kazami of Japan arrived at the North Pole on 20 April 1987 on a specially adapted 250cc motorcycle. He was picked up and brought back by aeroplane.

First woman to reach the South Pole solo
Norwegian Liv Arnesen trekked to the South Pole unaided in 50 days, arriving on 25 December 1994. British woman Fiona Thornewill did so in a record 42 days, arriving on 12 January 2004.

Women adventurers

These are just some of the intrepid women who went where no other woman – or, in some cases, no man – had gone before.

Amelia Earhart in the cockpit of her plane

- Jeanne Labrosse (France, 1775–1847) was the first woman to use a parachute. She jumped from a balloon on 12 October 1799. She later married pioneer parachutist André-Jacques Garnerin.

- French novelist Jules Verne's novel *Around the World in 80 Days* inspired American journalist Nellie Bly (real name Elizabeth Cochrane, 1864–1922) to beat this time. She set out in 1889, and returned to New York on 25 January 1890 – a record round-the-world trip of 72 days, 6 hours, 11 minutes and 14 seconds.

- Amelia Earhart (USA, 1898–1937) became the first woman to fly solo across the Atlantic in 1932.

- Cosmonaut Valentina Tereshkova (USSR, 1937–) was the first woman in space. She went into orbit on 16 June 1963.

- Sheila Scott (UK, 1927–88) was the first woman to fly round the world solo, in 1971. She was also the first woman to pilot a plane over the North Pole.

- Clare Francis (UK, 1946–) became the first woman to sail solo across the Atlantic in 1973.

- Ellen MacArthur (UK, 1978–) set a new world record for the fastest single-handed, round-the-world voyage of 71 days 14 hours 18 minutes 33 seconds, on 7 February 2005.

First cat to sail round the world

Trim, the cat belonging to Captain Matthew Flinders, was born on board *HMS Reliance* in 1799 on the journey to Australia. The following year he sailed to England and back to Australia.

First round the world

Since the first voyage round the world almost 500 years ago, people have been looking for different ways of circumnavigating (travelling right round) the planet by land, sea or air.

First circumnavigation
Juan Sebastian de Elcano and his crew of 17 on board *Vittoria* sailed from Spain in 1519 and returned 1,079 days later. The expedition was led by Ferdinand Magellan, but he did not survive the voyage. He was murdered in the Philippines on 27 April 1521.

First British circumnavigation
Sir Francis Drake and his crew of 50 left Plymouth, England on the *Golden Hind* in 1577 and returned to Plymouth on 26 September 1580.

First solo sailing
Canadian-born sailor Captain Joshua Slocum (1844–1910) sailed round the world alone in *Spray*, an oyster boat he built himself. He left the US on 24 April 1895 and returned on 27 June 1898.

First walk
George Matthew Schilling (USA) claimed to have walked round the world between 1897 and 1904, but his journey has not been verified. David Kunst (USA) made the first confirmed journey from 20 June 1970 to 5 October 1974. He took 20 million steps and wore out 21 pairs of shoes during his 23,250km walk.

First non-stop flight
USAF B-50A bomber *Lucky Lady II* piloted by Capt James Gallagher flew from Fort Worth Texas on 26 February 1949. The journey took 94 hours 1 minute and the plane was refuelled four times in mid-air.

First underwater
US Navy nuclear submarine *Triton* travelled round the world underwater between 16 February and 25 April 1960.

First non-stop solo voyage
British yachtsman Robin Knox-Johnston sailed from and returned to Falmouth, UK, in *Suhali* between 14 June 1968 and 22 April 1969.

A replica of Sir Francis Drake's ship, the Golden Hind

First in a wheelchair
Rick Hansen (Canada) went round the world in a wheelchair between 21 March 1985 and 22 May 1987. He travelled through 34 countries.

First balloon flight
Brian Jones (UK) and Bertrand Piccard (Switzerland) made a round-the-world voyage in the *Breitling Orbiter 3*. They left on 1 March 1999 and their journey took three weeks.

First solo flight
On 7 March 2005 Steve Fossett (USA) achieved the first solo round-the-world flight without refuelling in *Virgin Atlantic Global Flyer*, covering a total distance of 36,818km in a flight time of 67 hours 2 minutes and 38 seconds.

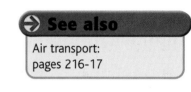

See also

Air transport: pages 216-17

Awards

Awards are presented in almost every area of achievement. The ones that receive the most attention in newspapers and on television are those given to famous film stars, writers, artists and singers. Among the best known are the following.

Academy Awards (Oscars)
These are the most famous of all film awards. The Oscar presentations are now watched on television by more than a billion people worldwide. The Academy Awards – also called the Oscars after the statuette that winners receive – were first presented in 1929. Walt Disney has won the most, a total of 20.

BAFTA Awards
The British Academy of Film and Television Arts awards began in 1947. British actress Judi Dench has won eight awards for film and television roles.

Booker Prize
This British book prize was set up in 1968 and is awarded each year for a novel published in the previous 12 months. It is now known as the Man Booker Prize. The first winner, in 1969, was P.H. Newby for *Something to Answer For*. Only two authors, Peter Carey and J.M. Coetzee, have so far won the prize twice.

Golden Globe Awards
These US film awards began in 1943. Julia Roberts has been nominated five times and won three awards, and Tom Hanks has won four of the six awards for which he was nominated.

Prix Goncourt
This prize has been awarded yearly since 1903 for the best new work in French literature. Marcel Proust won in 1919 for the second volume of his great work *In Search of Lost Time*.

Grammy Awards
The US music awards have been presented since 1959. The classical awards have been dominated by conductor Sir Georg Solti, who won 38 Grammys. Stevie Wonder gained an unrivalled 22 awards for popular music, while Beyoncé won in five categories in 2003.

Nobel Prize
These international awards are named after Alfred Nobel, the inventor of dynamite, and were first presented in 1901. There are now six categories – Physics, Chemistry, Medicine, Literature, Peace and Economics. Famous winners include Winston Churchill (Literature, 1953) and Mother Theresa (Peace, 1979).

Pulitzer Prizes
These US awards are given for a range of achievements in journalism, writing (fiction, non-fiction and poetry) and music. They are named after publisher Joseph Pulitzer and began in 1917.

Tony Awards
These US theatre awards were started in 1947 and named after actress, director and producer Antoinette Perry. Tonys have been won by many actors also known for their film roles, including Paul Newman and Sidney Poitier.

Turner Prize
This British art prize is named after landscape painter J.M.W. Turner and was established in 1984. The winning works are often controversial, and usually not conventional paintings. Damien Hirst is a recent winner.

Stevie Wonder, 22 times a Grammy winner

Gandhi – Time's person of the year in 1930

In the news

Every year the editors of *Time* magazine nominate a person of the year – the individual or group who has most influenced world events during the year. The winner may not always have had a good influence – Adolf Hitler was nominated in 1938. Nominees may be a man, a couple (Chinese leaders General and Madame Chiang Kai-shek in 1937), a woman (Queen Elizabeth II in 1952), a group of people (three astronauts in 1968), even a machine (a computer in 1982). Here are just some of the winners.

Date	Time's person of the year
2003	The American Soldier
2000/04	George W. Bush (US president)
1999	Jeff Bezos (founder of Amazon.com)
1994	Pope John Paul II
1992/98	Bill Clinton (US president)
1987/89	Mikhail Gorbachev (Soviet leader)
1966	Young people
1963	Martin Luther King, Jr (civil rights campaigner)
1961	John F. Kennedy (US president)
1958	Charles De Gaulle (French president)
1949	Winston Churchill (British prime minister)
1935	Haile Selassie (Ethiopian ruler)
1930	Mohandas Gandhi (Indian leader)
1927	Charles Lindbergh (transatlantic aviator)

Golden Raspberry Awards
The Golden Raspberries, founded in 1980, are joke awards presented to the worst films and actors! Madonna was a notable winner. She also received the Razzies award as Worst Actress of the 20th century.

 Against all odds

All these people triumphed over their disabilities to achieve fame.

Douglas Bader (1910–82) became a British war hero and flying ace, despite losing both his legs in a plane crash.

Ludwig van Beethoven (1770–1827) was one of the world's greatest composers. He continued to compose music even after he became totally deaf in 1817.

Sarah Bernhardt (1844–1923) a French actress, lost a leg in 1914 but continued acting.

David Blunkett (1947–) British MP and former minister, is blind and attends the House of Commons accompanied by his guide dog.

Louis Braille (1809–1852) was blind and invented the Braille system of printing with raised dots to enable blind people to read.

Miguel de Cervantes (1547–1616) Spanish author of *Don Quixote*, lost an arm in a battle.

Frederick Delius (1862–1934) was a British musician. Although he was crippled and blind for the last ten years of his life he continued to compose by dictating his music.

Stephen Hawking (1942–) a British physicist and celebrated author of *A Brief History of Time*, suffers from motor neurone disease. He is confined to a wheelchair and speaks with the aid of a voice synthesizer.

Jack Hawkins (1910–73) was a British film actor who lost his voice after suffering from cancer of the larynx. He continued to act, with others speaking his parts.

Helen Keller (1880–1968) was a famed author and lecturer despite being blind and deaf.

Lord Horatio Nelson (1758–1805) was a British admiral. He lost one arm and an eye, but won many naval victories, including the Battle of Trafalgar in 1805.

Joseph Pulitzer (1847–1911) US publisher and founder of the prestigious Pulitzer Prizes, was blind from the age of 40.

Franklin D. Roosevelt (1882–1945) was crippled by polio and spent much of his life in a wheelchair, but was elected US president four times.

Henri de Toulouse-Lautrec (1864–1901) Impressionist painter, suffered from a disability that prevented his legs from growing.

Stevie Wonder (1950–) US singer, has been blind from birth, but is one of the world's most popular entertainers.

Geoffrey Winthrop Young (1876–1958) was a British writer and mountaineer. He lost a leg during World War I, but continued to climb Alpine peaks.

Actress Sarah Bernhardt, who had only one leg

ONE AND ONLY

At the age of 82 Irish playwright George Bernard Shaw won an Oscar for Best Screenplay for *Pygmalion* (1938). He had already won the Nobel Prize for Literature in 1925, so became the only person ever to win both a Nobel and an Oscar.

Late success

As people live longer, many continue to work well into what was once thought of as extreme old age. These are all famous people who continued to make great achievements in their eighties and beyond.

Celebrity	Achievement	Age
Grandma (Anna Mary) Moses, US painter	Painted *The Rainbow*, her last work (1961)	101
George Burns, US film actor	Appeared in his last film, *Radioland Murders* (1994)	98
Pablo Casals, Spanish musician	Conducted the Israel Festival Youth Orchestra	96
Frank Lloyd Wright, US architect	Completed his design for the Guggenheim Museum, New York	89
Michelangelo, Italian artist	Produced his Rondandini *Pietà* sculpture	88
Claude Monet, French painter	Completed his water-lily paintings	84
Winston Churchill, UK prime minister	Finished writing his *History of the English-Speaking Peoples*	83
Benjamin Franklin, American statesman	Helped write the US Constitution	81
George Cukor, US film director	Directed film *Rich and Famous* (1981)	81
Jessica Tandy, US actress	Oldest Best Actress Oscar win (*Driving Miss Daisy*, 1989)	80

 www.amillionlives.com

Where are the children?

In countries such as India, where people have large families and relatively short lives, there are more children than older people. In the US and UK there are more middle-aged and older people. Most people have smaller families so there are fewer young people. In the UK there are 10,720,283 children.

Country	No of children (0–14)
India	337,566,907
China	279,180,343
Indonesia	70,414,087
Pakistan	64,348,608
Nigeria	60,899,349
USA	60,799,722
Brazil	48,632,210
Bangladesh	47,752,627
Mexico	33,003,911
Philippines	31,125,224

Population pyramids show the proportions of older and younger people in a country. In countries such as India with lots of children and low life expectancy, the population pyramid is wide at the bottom and narrower at the top. In the United States and Europe, the age groups are more evenly distributed.

Schoolchildren in India taking part in a physical education class

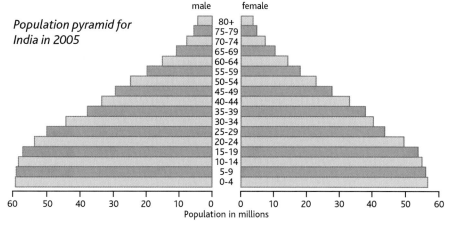

Population pyramid for India in 2005

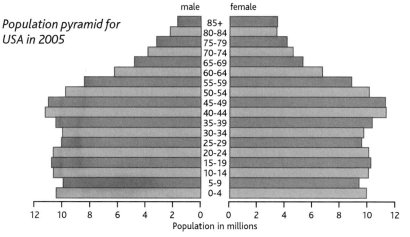

Population pyramid for USA in 2005

 # Young populations

Countries with a lot of people under 15 usually have high birth rates and high death rates. In countries where families have many children who are too young to work and adults die relatively young, there are not enough people of working age to earn money to feed and take care of the families. As a result, these countries tend to be among the world's poorest.

	Country	Percentage under 15
1	Uganda	50.3
2	Democratic Republic of Congo	48.1
3	Chad	47.9
4	São Tomé and Príncipe	47.6
5	Niger	47.3
	World average	**27.8**

By comparison the USA, Canada and UK have a lower than average proportion of children.

USA	20.6
Canada	17.9
UK	17.7

The UN Convention on the Rights of the Child

The United Nations issued its Declaration on the Rights of the Child in 1959 in an attempt to relieve the suffering of children in poor and war-torn countries. It came into force as a convention in 1990 and has been agreed to by 191 countries. Only Somalia and the USA have not signed.

All the countries who have signed the convention agree to make sure that children aged under 18 have certain basic rights, such as housing and medical care. Recent optional additions include one to make sure that children will not have to serve in military action.

The Convention on the Rights of the Child states that all children have the right to:

- a name and nationality
- affection, love, understanding and material security
- adequate nutrition, housing and medical services
- special care if disabled – physically, mentally or socially
- be among the first to receive protection and relief in all circumstances
- be protected against all forms of neglect, cruelty and exploitation
- full opportunity for play and recreation and equal opportunity to free and compulsory education, to enable the child to develop his/her individual abilities and to become a useful member of society
- develop his/her full potential in conditions of freedom and dignity
- be brought up in a spirit of understanding, tolerance, friendship among peoples, peace and universal brotherhood
- enjoy these rights regardless of race, colour, sex, religion, political or other opinion, national or social origin and property, birth or other status.

Danielle Mitterrand, former First Lady of France, and a group of children present a children's rights charter to the United Nations.

www.unicef.org/crc/crc.htm

Early success

Wolfgang Amadeus Mozart (Austria, 1756–91) began composing music at the age of five, and a year later began a concert tour across Europe.

William James Sidis (USA, 1898–1944) went to Harvard University to study mathematics at the age of 11.

Balamurali Ambati (USA, 1977–) graduated from university at the age of 13 and from medical school at the age of 17, becoming the world's youngest qualified doctor.

Sergey Karjakin (Ukraine, 1990–) became the youngest ever chess grandmaster at the age of 12.

Youngest self-made millionaire

US film actress Shirley Temple (1928–) became the first self-made child millionaire (one who earned her money, rather than inheriting a fortune) by making more than $1 million before the age of ten.

International youth organizations

Scouts and Cub Scouts
Sir Robert Baden-Powell (1857–1941) a former general in the British army, launched the scouting movement in 1907. Today there are scouts in almost every country in the world – a total of 28 million. More than six million are in the USA and half a million in the UK, but the leading scouting country is Indonesia, with almost nine million members. Scouting is forbidden in some countries, including Cuba and North Korea. The junior division for boys under 11 is called the Cub Scouts (formerly Wolf Cubs in the UK) and was founded in 1930.

Girl Guides/Girl Scouts and Brownies
The Girl Guide Movement was started in 1910 by Sir Robert Baden-Powell and his sister Agnes (1858–1945). Today the World Association of Girl Guides and Girl Scouts (WAGGGS) has 144 member organizations with a total membership of ten million. It is the largest international organization for girls and young women. The junior division, for girls under 11, is called the Brownies.

YMCA and YWCA
The YMCA (Young Men's Christian Association) was founded by George Williams in the UK in 1844 and in the USA in 1851. Its aim was to provide shelter and other support for young men who came into cities to find work. The organization now has branches in 122 countries. Its sister body, the YWCA (Young Women's Christian Association), was founded in the UK in 1855 and in the USA in 1858.

Humans have always sought answers to the mysteries of life and many believe in the existence of a sacred or supernatural power that guides life on Earth. This section looks at the most important religions today, as well as the myths and legends of ancient cultures.

BELIEFS AND IDEAS

Gods and goddesses

In most of the world's major religions today only one god is worshipped. But in many ancient religions followers worshipped a group of gods. Each god had special characteristics and responsibilities, and some could appear in a variety of forms. The myths and legends of ancient cultures and the range of gods worshipped often changed over thousands of years as different gods and goddesses rose or fell in importance. Those listed on these pages are a selection of the most revered and long-standing gods of some of the world's ancient cultures.

Chinese gods

The Chinese worshipped a large range of gods for more than 4,000 years, up to the coming of Chinese communism in the 20th century. Some Chinese people continue to worship these gods – often in secret – today.

God	Role
Dragon Kings	Ao-Shin (North), Ao-chin (South), Ao-kuang (East) and Ao-jun (West), the gods of rain, rivers and seas
Fu-xi	God of arts and creativity
Guan-yin	God and goddess of compassion
Guan-yu	God of war
Meng-po	Goddess of the underworld
Nu-gua	Serpent goddess of creation
Pan-gu	Giant creator god
Qi-yu	God of the rain (half bull, half giant)
Three Pure Ones	Supreme trinity of Yuan-shi-tian-zong, Ling-bao-tian-song and Lao-jun
Xi-he	Goddess of light
Xi-wangmu	Goddess of immortality
Yi-di	God of wine
Zao-jun	God of the household

Greek and Roman gods

The Ancient Greeks had 12 major gods and goddesses. They believed the gods all lived on Mount Olympus and influenced the well-being of all humans. As the Greek civilization declined and the Roman empire grew, the Romans renamed the Greek gods and took them as their own.

Greek	Roman	Role
Hera	Juno	Chief goddess – marriage
Aphrodite	Venus	Goddess of beauty
Artemis	Diana	Goddess of hunting
Athena	Minerva	Goddess of wisdom
Demeter	Ceres	Goddess of the harvest, nature
Hestia	Vesta	Goddess of the hearth
Zeus	Jupiter	Chief god – sky and air
Apollon	Apollo	God of poetry, music, Sun
Ares	Mars	God of war
Hephaistos	Vulcan	God of blacksmiths
Hermes	Mercury	Messenger of the gods
Poseidon	Neptune	God of the sea

Ancient Egyptian gods

Egyptian religion dates back about 5,000 years and lasted until the coming of Christianity and Islam. Its huge range of gods and goddesses were believed to control almost every aspect of people's lives.

God	Role
Amun-Ra	King of the gods
Anubis	The jackal god of death and Egyptian mummies
Aten	God of the sun-disc
Bast/Bastet	Cat goddess of fertility
Bes	Lion-like domestic god
Hathor	Cow-headed goddess of happiness
Horus	Falcon-headed sky god
Isis	Wife of Osiris, mother of Horus, goddess of motherhood and royalty
Month	Falcon-headed god of war
Nefertum	God of the sacred blue lotus and the rising sun
Osiris	God of the underworld and agriculture
Ptah	Creator god and patron of craftsmen
Ra	Sun-god, Ancient Egypt's most important god
Reshef	God of war and thunder
Sekhmet/Sakhmet	Lion-headed goddess of war and destruction
Seth	God of storms and violence
Thoth	Ibis-headed god of the Moon, arts and sciences

Ancient Egyptian goddess Hathor and god Horus

Mayan gods

The Mayan civilization and neighbouring Olmec culture date back 3,000 years. Descendants of the Mayans still live in southern Mexico, Belize and Guatemala.

God	Role
Bacabs	Gods of the four directions – Mulac (north), Cauac (south), Kan (east) and Ix (west)
Balu-chabtan	God of war and sacrifice
Chak	God of rain, fertility and agriculture
Hunahau	God of death
Itzamna	Reptile creator god
Ix-chel	Moon goddess
Kinichi-ahau	Sun god
Kukulcan	Feathered serpent god
Xbalanque	God of the jaguar
Yum-kaax	Corn god

See also

World civilizations and empires: pages 106-107
Time: pages 14-16

Statue of the Aztec god Xochipilli, made between the 14th and 16th centuries

Inca gods

The Inca people lived in the part of South America that is now Peru from about 1200 to 1533. Inca gods were thought to influence natural events.

God	Role
Apocatequil	God of lightning
Apu Illapu	God of thunder
Chasca Coyllur	God of flowers
Copacati	Lake goddess
Ilyap'a	Weather god
Inti	Sun god
Kon	God of rain and the southern wind
Mama Oello	Mother goddess, daughter of Inti and Mama Quilla
Mama Quilla	Moon goddess, daughter of Viracocha and wife of Inti
Manco Capac	Creator god, sun and fire
Pachacamac	Earth god
Punchau	Sun god
Vichaama	God of death
Viracocha	Supreme god of creation

Aztec gods

The Aztecs were based in central Mexico. They flourished from the 14th century up to their conquest by Spanish invaders in 1522. The Aztec religion demanded human sacrifices to the gods, who were believed to control daily life and agriculture.

God	Role
Chalchiuhtlicue	Goddess of lakes and streams, youth and beauty
Cinteotl	God of maize
Coyolxauhqui	Goddess of the Moon
Ehecatl	God of the wind and weather
Huehueteotl	God of the hearth, the fire of life
Huitzilopochtli	War god to whom humans were sacrificed
Ilamatecuhtli	Goddess of the Earth, death and the Milky Way
Itztlacoliuhqui	God of stone and the Morning Star
Mayahuel	Goddess of alcohol and the maguey plant (from which alcoholic drinks were made)
Mictlantecuhtli	God of death
Quetzalcoatl	Creator god – and bringer of chocolate!
Tepeyollotl	God of caves and earthquakes
Tezcatlipoca	God of night and death
Tlahuizcalpantecuhtli	God of dawn
Tonacatecuhtli	God of food
Xipe-totec	God of spring and agriculture, patron of goldsmiths
Xochipilli	God of love, flowers, singing and dancing
Xochiquetzal	Goddess of love

The 12 Norse gods

The Norse people lived in ancient and medieval Scandinavia (modern Norway, Sweden, Finland, Iceland and Denmark). The 12 Norse, or Scandinavian, gods were together called the Aesir, and their homeland was Asgard. There was also a second group of gods called the Vanir, who fought the Aesir. Later some Vanir gods, including Frey and his sister Freya, became Aesir.

- Odin, or Woden, chief god in Norse mythology
- Thor, red-haired and bearded son of Odin and Jord, god of war (his name gave us Thursday – Thor's day)
- Tyr, Tiu or Tiw, another son of Odin, god of warfare and battle (his name is commemorated in Tuesday)
- Balder or Baldur, god of sunlight
- Brag or Bragi, god of poetry
- Vidar, god of silence, stealth and revenge
- Hoder the blind
- Hermód or Hermoder the Brave, Odin's son and his messenger
- Hönir or Hoenir, a minor god
- Odnir, husband of Freya
- Loki, god of strife or mischief, capable of changing shape and performing tricks
- Vali, Odin's youngest son by Rind, a giantess. He slew Hod, who had murdered his brother Balder

Holy places

A holy place is somewhere that is especially revered by the followers of a religion. Examples include the birthplace of the founder of a religion, shrines, and places of pilgrimage. There has been conflict in some of these holy places when members of other religions have claimed or attacked the sites.

Amritsar, India
This city is the Sikh religion's spiritual centre. The Golden Temple is the main shrine.

Athos, Greece
This is a holy mountain for the Greek Orthodox Church where there are many monasteries. Women are forbidden to go on to the mountain.

Benares, India
This Hindu holy city is dedicated to the god Shiva.

Bethlehem, Israel
The birthplace of Jesus.

Canterbury, UK
The city was once England's most important pilgrimage centre.

Ganges, India
The Ganges river is sacred to Hindus, who bathe here and scatter the ashes of their dead in its waters.

Jerusalem, Israel
A holy city for Christians, Muslims and Jews. Sites include the Western Wall, Dome of the Rock and Church of the Holy Sepulchre.

Karbala, Iraq
This city is the centre of Shi'a Islam and contains the shrine of the prophet Muhammad's grandson al-Husain.

Lhasa, Tibet (China)
The centre of Tibetan Buddhism. The monastery here was once the home of the Dalai Lama.

Lourdes, France
In 1858 Bernadette Soubirous (later St Bernadette) saw visions of the Virgin Mary in a grotto at Lourdes. Since then Catholics have made pilgrimages there, seeking cures for their illnesses.

Makkah (Mecca), Saudi Arabia
Every year, millions of Muslims go on pilgrimage to this city. They also turn to face Makkah when they pray.

Medina, Saudi Arabia
This is the site of the tomb of the prophet Muhammad.

Olympus, Greece
The Ancient Greeks believed the mountain to be the home of Zeus and other gods.

Salt Lake City, Utah, USA
The headquarters of the Church of Latter-Day Saints (Mormons).

Santiago de Compostela, Spain
In the 9th century a tomb believed to belong to the apostle James the Greater was discovered here. Christians make pilgrimages to a shrine made on the site.

Mount Shasta, California, USA
A dormant volcano and a sacred site for Native Americans.

Vatican City
The city-state in Rome, Italy, is the centre of the Roman Catholic faith.

The five pillars of Islam

The following are the five most important aspects of the Muslim faith.

1 ash-Shahada – profession of faith in Allah and his prophet Muhammad

2 salat – prayer five times a day, facing Makkah

3 zakat – giving alms to the poor and needy

4 sawm – fasting between dawn and dusk during Ramadan

5 hajj – pilgrimage to Makkah, at least once in one's lifetime

Jihad, meaning holy war, is sometimes added as an extra pillar.

Major world religious beliefs

Religion	Followers (2004)
Christians	2,090,763,000
Muslims	1,271,884,000
Hindus	841,078,000
Chinese folk-religions	400,600,000
Buddhists	376,574,000
Sikhs	24,402,000
Jews	14,956,000

The Golden Temple at Amritsar, India

Hindu gods and goddesses

About 80 per cent of the people of India are Hindus. Most believe that God takes many different forms, so the Hindu religion has a range of gods and goddesses. Brahma, Vishnu and Shiva are the most important.

Gods of the Vedas (sacred books)

Indra   Thunder god of battle
Varuna   Guardian of order
Agni   God of fire
Surya   Sun deity

Other Hindu gods

Brahma   The creator
Vishnu   The preserver, who has ten incarnations:
          Matsya, the fish
          Kurma, the tortoise
          Varah, the boar
          Nrisinha, half-man, half-lion
          Vamana, the dwarf
          Parasurama, Rama bearing the axe
          Ramachandra, Rama with bow and arrows
          Krishna, god of the Bhagavadgita
          Buddha, teacher
          Kalki, "the one to come"

Shiva   God of destruction
Ganesh   Elephant-headed god
Hanuman Monkey warrior god

Hindu goddesses

Durga   Or Amba, warrior god
Parvati   Wife of Shiva
Kali   Goddess of destruction
Lakshmi   Wife of Vishnu, goddess of beauty, wealth and fortune
Saraswati Goddess of learning, arts and music

A Mongolian rock shrine, visited by Mongolians at festival times

Religious buildings

Abbey – a building occupied by monks or nuns and run by an abbot or abbess

Basilica – a type of early Christian church

Cathedral – the main church in an area and the seat of the bishop

Chapel – a place of worship within a larger building, or a nonconformist Christian religious building

Church – a building used for public worship by Christians

Convent or nunnery – the home of a community of nuns

Dagoba – a Buddhist shrine

Friary – home to friars, members of a religious order

Meeting house – a place where certain religious groups, such as Quakers, gather

Monastery – the home to a religious community of monks

Mosque – a Muslim place of worship

Pagoda – an Eastern temple

Priory – a religious house run by a prior; it may be under the control of an abbey

Shrine – a place of worship connected with a sacred person or saint. It may contain sacred objects or relics

Synagogue – a building for Jewish religious services

Tabernacle – a house or tent used for worship, named after the tent used by the Israelites to cover the Ark of the Covenant

Temple – a place of worship dedicated to a particular god or gods. Also sometimes used instead of synagogue

An image of Hindu god Shiva in a temple in Singapore

Sacred books

The Koran (Islam)

Allah is the Islamic name for God. Muslims believe that He revealed His wishes for the world to a man called Muhammad. These messages were later collected together as the Koran (also written Qur'an). Muslims believe that the words of the Koran are the exact words of Allah. It is said that it has not been altered since it first appeared in AD 632. The Koran is written in Arabic, the language which Muhammad spoke, and it contains the main teachings of Islam.

The Torah (Judaism)

The Torah is Judaism's most sacred text. It includes the first five books of the Bible, also known as the Pentateuch. These include the laws that God revealed to Moses on Mount Sinai. The Jewish scriptures also include the books of the prophets, historical writings and the Talmud. The Talmud contains instructions for following a Jewish way of life and understanding Jewish laws.

The Cairo Koran, made for the Sultan of Morocco in the 18th century

The Vedas (Hinduism)

The four books of the Vedas contain the earliest Hindu beliefs and they have also influenced Buddhism, Sikhism and Jainism. The *Rig Veda* is the oldest of the Vedas. It was composed about 1500 BC, although it was not written down until around 300 BC. The Vedas include rituals and hymns that give us a glimpse of life in ancient India. Another important Hindu text is the *Bhagavad Gita*, or Song of the Lord. This is one section of a very long epic poem called the *Mahabharata*. The *Bhagavad Gita* is about 700 verses long and sets out Hindu philosophy, explaining the importance of selflessness, duty, devotion and meditation.

The Pali Canon (Buddhism)

The Pali Canon is a collection of sacred texts followed by the Theravada school of Buddhism. The teachings of the Buddha were first passed on through the spoken word and were not written down until the 1st century BC. The Pali Canon is written in the Pali language, and is also known as the Tripitaka, meaning three baskets. The texts are divided into three sections which were originally written on palm leaf scrolls and kept in three different baskets. They include rules for Buddhist monks and nuns, tales of the Buddha's life and teachings, stories and philosophical arguments.

Guru Granth Sahib (Sikhism)

Sikhs believe that the Guru Granth Sahib is the supreme spiritual authority and head of the Sikh religion, rather than any living person. The original version was compiled by Guru Arjan Dev, the fifth Sikh guru, in 1604. He collected the compositions of previous gurus over a number of years. The text includes almost 6,000 hymns and poems composed at different times and in different languages, which makes it very difficult to translate. It also includes Hindu and Muslim writings, reflecting the religious tolerance of the gurus.

Boy reading from the Torah at a bar mitzvah ceremony

The Bible

The Christian sacred book is called the Bible. It is made up of two parts – the Old Testament and the New Testament. The Old Testament describes the history of the Israelites and contains books of history, law, poetry and wisdom. It was written by different people, probably between 1100 and 200 BC. The New Testament describes the story of Jesus' life and his importance for Christians, and also contains writings by some important early Christians. It was probably written between AD 50 and 150. Passages from the Bible are read at Christian church services, and Christians also see the Bible as containing a code to live by and guidance in following their faith.

Animals in the Bible

There are many animals mentioned in the Bible. Sheep and lambs are referred to most often, probably because they were important for their meat and wool. The lion appears because it is a symbol of power, strength and wisdom.

Animal	OT*	NT*	Total
1 Sheep	155	45	200
2 Lamb	153	35	188
3 Lion	167	9	176
4 Ox	156	10	166
5 Ram	165	0	165
6 Horse	137	27	164

* Occurrences in verses in the King James Bible
OT: Old Testament, NT: New Testament

The Ten Commandments

The commandments are the divine law handed down to Moses by God on Mount Sinai. They are key to both Christian and Jewish religions. The commandments appear in the books of Exodus and Deuteronomy in the Old Testament, but are also described by Jesus in Matthew's Gospel in the New Testament, where he shortens them to just two – Love God, Love your neighbour.

1 Thou shalt have no other gods before me
2 Thou shalt not make unto thee any graven image
3 Thou shalt not take the name of the Lord thy God in vain
4 Remember the sabbath day, to keep it holy
5 Honour thy father and thy mother
6 Thou shalt not kill
7 Thou shalt not commit adultery
8 Thou shalt not steal
9 Thou shalt not bear false witness against thy neighbour
10 Thou shalt not covet thy neighbour's house, thou shalt not covet thy neighbour's wife, nor his manservant, nor his maidservant, nor his ox, nor his ass, nor any thing that is thy neighbour's (Exodus xx.3)

The 12 disciples (Jesus' guests at the Last Supper)

The New Testament describes the Last Supper, which took place the day before Jesus was crucified. Jesus' followers, called disciples, were all there. They were the original apostles and the first Christians. Except for Judas, they acted as missionaries, spreading Jesus' message after his death.

- Andrew
- Bartholomew
- James the Greater
- James the Lesser
- John
- Judas
- Jude
- Matthew
- Peter
- Philip
- Simon
- Thomas

The Last Supper, painted by Pomponio Amalteo in 1574

Bible sales

No one really knows how many copies of the Bible have been printed in the past 500 years. The Bible Society (an organization that distributes Bibles worldwide) came up with a figure of 2,458,000,000 for the years 1816 to 1975. A survey up to 1992 puts the all-time figure at nearly six billion copies in more than 2,000 languages and dialects. That is one Bible for almost everyone on the planet. The Gideons International, a missionary organization, gives away almost 60 million bibles every year.

Bible fast facts

The word "Lord" is used almost 8,000 times in the Bible, making it more common than the words "a", "they" and "is". "God" is referred to on 4,105 occasions. The name "David" is mentioned more than twice as often as "Jesus", making 1,064 appearances.

The longest verse in the Bible is Esther viii.9, totalling 90 words. John xi.35 is the shortest. It has just two words: "Jesus wept".

See also

Bestsellers: page 230

Christianity timeline

c 6–4 BC	Birth of Jesus Christ, Bethlehem
AD c 33	Christ crucified
c 60–100	Gospels written
c 64	Persecution of Christians by Roman Emperor Nero
312	Emperor Constantine converts to Christianity, leading to it becoming sole religion in the Roman Empire
324	Building of St Peter's Basilica, Vatican, Rome, begun on site of Circus of Nero
c 380	Final agreement on which books should be in the Christian Bible
635	Jerusalem and most of Middle East conquered by Muslims
999	Most of Europe converted to Christianity
1054	Christian church splits into Western (Catholic) and Eastern (Orthodox)
1095–1272	Crusades (series of wars by Christians to take holy sites in Middle East away from Muslim control)
1187	Jerusalem captured by Saladin
1209	Franciscan order of monks started
1382	John Wycliffe translates Bible into English
1456	First printed Bible (Johannes Gutenberg, Germany)
1479	Spanish Inquisition begins to persecute heretics
1517	Martin Luther begins Protestant Reformation, Germany
1534	Henry VIII breaks with Rome; leads to the founding of the Church of England
1610–1795	Baptist, Congregationalist, Presbyterian, Quaker (Society of Friends) and Methodist Churches founded
1611	King James Bible published
1800–1900	The Age of the Mission. Western Churches send missionaries to every country in the world. Number of Christians doubles by the end of the century
1830	Church of the Latter-Day Saints (Mormons) founded, Fayette, New York, USA
1872	Jehovah's Witnesses founded by Charles Taze Russell, USA (named 1931)
1878	Salvation Army founded by William Booth, UK
1910	International Missionary Conference in Edinburgh marks first attempt in nearly 1000 years to reunite churches
1948	World Council of Churches founded
1962–65	Second Vatican Council radically reforms the Catholic Church worldwide
1992	Church of England votes to allow women priests

World's largest Christian populations

Country	Total Christian population (2004)
1 USA	246,543,000
2 Brazil	164,122,000
3 China	106,902,000
4 Mexico	101,541,000
5 Russia	85,234,000
6 Philippines	73,862,000
7 India	68,125,000

Longest-serving popes

Popes are usually chosen from among senior cardinals. They rarely live long enough to serve more than about 20 years. However, Pope Benedict IX is said to have been only 12 years old when he was elected in 1033! Pius IX was the longest-serving pope. He was 85 years old when he died. Leo XIII was even older at 93. The shortest-serving pope was Urban VII, who died of malaria 12 days after his election in 1590.

Pope	Period in office	Years
Pius IX	16 June 1846–7 February 1878	31
John Paul II	16 October 1978–2 April 2005	26
Leo XIII	20 February 1878–20 July 1903	25
Peter	c 42–67	c 25
Pius VI	15 February 1775–29 August 1799	24
Adrian I	1 February 772–25 December 795	23
Pius VII	14 March 1800–20 August 1823	23

ONE AND ONLY

English Pope

Nicolas Breakspear was born at Abbots Langley near St Albans in Hertfordshire, England, in about 1100. He entered a monastery in France and became abbot in 1137. He was appointed cardinal-bishop of Albano in 1146 and worked for a time in Norway until the death of Pope Anastasius IV in 1154. Breakspear was then elected pope, taking the name Adrian or Hadrian IV. He served for less than five years and died in 1159.

World's largest Christian denominations

Denomination	Members
1 Roman Catholic	981,703,000
2 Orthodox	140,300,000
3 Pentecostal	128,405,000
4 Lutheran	82,271,000
5 Anglican	79,177,000
6 Baptist	73,383,000
7 Presbyterian	49,630,000
8 Methodist	26,576,000

Patron saints

A patron saint is a saint chosen to be the protector of a particular person or group of people, or associated with a particular problem or situation. Many more saints are called upon for help with problems than are linked with pleasant events. For example, at least 26 saints are connected with difficult marriages, but only one (Saint Valentine) with happy marriages.

Patron saints for special problems

Problem	Saint
Appendicitis	Erasmus
Arthritis/rheumatism	James the Greater
Broken bones	Drogo+
Cold weather	Sebaldus
Coughs	Blaise+
Dog bites	Vitus
Earache	Cornelius+
Famine	Walburga
Floods	Christopher+
Headaches	Acacius+
Insect bites	Felix+
Knee problems	Roch+
Lost articles	Anne+
Natural disasters	Agatha
Poisoning	Benedict+
Shipwreck	Anthony of Padua
Snake bites	Hilary of Poitiers+
Storms	Scholastica+
Toothache	Apollonia+

Patron saints with animal associations

Animal	Saint
Bees	Ambrose of Milan
Birds, geese	Gall
Blackbirds	Kevin
Cats	Gertrude of Nivelles
Cattle	Brigid of Ireland+
Dogs	Hubert+
Domestic animals (pets)	Cornelius+
Doves	David of Wales
Fish	Neot
Horses	Anthony of Padua+
Lambs	John the Baptist
Lions	Mark the Evangelist
Pigs	Anthony the Abbot
Salmon	Kentigern
Sheep	Drogo
Swans	Hugh of Lincoln
Whales	Brendan the Navigator
Wolves	Edmund of East Anglia

Patron saints of professions and groups

Group	Saint
Accountants	Matthew the Apostle
Actors	Genesius of Rome+
Air travellers	Joseph of Cupertino
Ambulance drivers	Michael the Archangel
Architects	Barbara+
Artists	Luke the Apostle+
Astronauts	Joseph of Cupertino
Athletes	Sebastian
Authors	Francis de Sales
Bakers	Elizabeth of Hungary+
Beekeepers	Ambrose of Milan+
Booksellers	John of God+
Boys	John Bosco+
Bricklayers	Stephen of Hungary
Broadcasters	Gabriel the Archangel
Cab drivers	Christopher+
Carpenters	Joseph+
Children	Nicholas of Myra+
Comedians	Vitus+
Cooks	Martha+
Dentists	Apollonia
Doctors	Cosmas+
Farmers	Isidore the Farmer+
Fathers	Joseph
Firefighters	Florian+
Fishermen	Andrew the Apostle+
Gardeners	Adelard
Girls	Agnes of Rome+
Hairdressers	Cosmas+
Librarians	Jerome+
Mathematicians	Barbara
Mothers	Monica+
Motorcyclists	Our Lady of Grace
Musicians	Cecilia+
Nurses	Agatha+
Plumbers	Vincent Ferrer
Poets	David+
Police officers	Michael the Archangel+
Postal workers	Gabriel the Archangel
Printers	Augustine of Hippo+
Prisoners	Dismas
Sailors	Francis of Paola+
Scientists	Albertus Magnus+
Sculptors	Claude de la Columbiere+
Soldiers	George+
Teachers	Catherine of Alexandria+

+ More than one saint

See also

History timeline:
page 104

St Apollonia (in red) with St Genevieve in a painting by Lucas Cranach the Elder (1472–1553)

Largest church bells

The largest church bell in the world is the Tsar Kolokol, which was cast in 1735 in Moscow, Russia. It weighs 196.6 tonnes and measures 6.14m high and 6.6m in diameter. It cracked in a fire before it was installed and has remained outside the Kremlin, unrung, ever since. A companion bell, the Tsarsky Kolokol, was originally cast in 1748, but re-cast in 2004. It weighs 72 tonnes and is the largest bell that can be rung. The 18.54-tonne bourdon bell (the one sounding the lowest note) at New York's Riverside Church is the largest ever cast in England. It measures 3.10m in diameter.

Buddhist festivals

There are a number of Buddhist traditions, and Buddhists in different countries have their own festivals on different dates. These are the most important Buddhist festivals.

- Wesak, held on the full moon in May, is the most important Buddhist festival and celebrates the birth of Buddha.

- Dharma Day celebrates Buddha's teaching and is held on the full moon of July. On Dharma Day there are readings from Buddhist scriptures, and people spend time reflecting on what they mean.

- Sangha Day is held on the full moon in November and celebrates the spiritual Buddhist community. Buddhists traditionally give presents on this day.

- Parinirvana Day, also known as Nirvana Day, marks the death of Buddha. Celebrations vary from place to place, but generally Buddhists go to temples or monasteries on this day, or meditate.

- Losar is a Tibetan Buddhist festival. It is held in February and marks the New Year. The festival lasts for three days, when people go to monasteries, visit friends and family and exchange gifts.

Tibetan monks blow horns to celebrate the Buddhist festival of Losar.

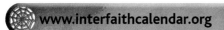
www.interfaithcalendar.org

Christian festivals

Epiphany (also known as Twelfth Night)
6 January (18 January in Russia; 1 February in Ethiopia). The Epiphany (Epiphaneia: Greek for manifestation) celebrates three events that are all thought to have happened on this day: Jesus' appearance as a newborn to the Magi (three wise men); Jesus' baptism, when God acknowledged his son; Jesus' first public miracle, when he turned water to wine in Galilee.

Ash Wednesday
The first day of Lent (see below). Ash Wednesday is a day of repentance for Christians, when they make amends for the year's sins before the fasting of Lent. Anglican and Roman Catholic churches hold ceremonies at which churchgoers' foreheads are marked with crosses using ash.

Lent
The 44 days before Good Friday (including Sundays). Lent is a period of fasting when Christians identify with Jesus Christ's suffering. The day before the start of Lent is known as Shrove Tuesday or "Fat Tuesday" (Mardi Gras), when Christians traditionally eat up any leftover animal products (often in the form of pancakes), as these cannot be eaten during Lent.

Palm Sunday
The Sunday before Easter Sunday and the first day of Holy Week. Palm Sunday commemorates Jesus' arrival in Jerusalem, when the crowd threw palm leaves in front of his donkey. Later that week, many in the cheering crowd were calling for Christ's execution.

Maundy (or Holy) Thursday
The Thursday before Easter Sunday. Maundy Thursday commemorates the Last Supper, which established the ceremony of Holy Communion, when bread and wine became identified with Jesus' body and blood. It was also the day when Jesus washed the feet of his disciples. At Roman Catholic church services on Maundy Thursday the priest ceremonially washes 12 people's feet.

Good Friday
The Friday before Easter Sunday. Good Friday ("good" meant "holy" in Early Modern English) commemorates the day when Jesus Christ was crucified. The symbol of the cross is an important part of church services on Good Friday, and churchgoers read the psalms and the gospels to remember Christ's experience.

Easter Sunday
The Sunday that follows the first full moon after the 21 March (the spring equinox). Easter always falls between March 22 and April 25 in the Western calendar. Easter is up to two weeks later in Orthodox Churches. Easter Sunday is the most important day in the Christian calendar, as it celebrates Jesus' resurrection from the dead. Easter Sunday is a day of joy for Christians.

Pentecost/Whitsunday
Fifty days after Easter Sunday. Pentecost celebrates the day the Holy Spirit entered the Apostles, enabling them to speak many new languages and spread the word of God. This event is considered by most Christians to mark the birth of the Church.

Christmas
Christmas is the celebration of the birth of Jesus on 25 December (6 January in Russia and 17 January in Ethiopia). It comes in midwinter, a time of the year when many faiths hold festivities.

Jewish festivals

The main Jewish festivals celebrate the great events in the history of the people of Israel. The Jewish month in which they fall is given, with an approximate equivalent in the Gregorian calendar.

Tishri (September/October)
Rosh Hashana: New Year
Yom Kippur: Day of Atonement
Sukkoth: Feast of Tabernacles
Shemini Atzeret: 8th Day of the Solemn Assembly
Simhat Torah: Rejoicing of the Law

Kislev (November/December)
Hanukkah: Feast of Dedication

Adar (February/March)
Tanrit Esther: Fast of Esther
Purim: Feast of Lots

Nisan (March/April)
Pesach (Passover)
Holocaust Remembrance Day

Iyar (April/May)
Lag B'Omer: Counting Day of Barley Sheaves

Sivan (May/June)
Shavuoth: Feast of Weeks

Tammuz (June/July)
Shiva Asar be-Tammuz: Fast of 17th Tammuz

Av (July/August)
Tisha be-Av: Fast of 9th Av

Hindu festivals

These are the main Hindu festivals, held in honour of gods as well as to celebrate important events in mythology and in the heavens. The Hindu month in which they fall is given, with an approximate equivalent in the Gregorian calendar.

Chaitra (March/April)
Ramanavami: Birthday of Lord Rama

Asadha (June/July)
Rathayatra: Pilgrimage of the Chariot at Jaggannath

Sravana (July/August)
Jhulanayatra: Swinging the Lord Krishna
Rakshabandhana: Tying on Lucky Threads

Bhadrapada (August/September)
Janamashtami: Birthday of Lord Krishna

Asvina (September/October)
Durga-puja: Homage to Goddess Durga
Navaratri: Festival of Nine Nights
Lakshmi-puja: Homage to Goddess Lakshmi
Diwali, Dipavali: String of Lights

Magha (January/February)
Sarasvati-puja: Homage to Goddess Sarasvati
Maha-sivaratri: Great Night of Lord Shiva

Phalguna (February/March)
Holi: Festival of Fire
Dolayatra: Swing Festival

Muslims at the Grand Mosque in Makkah before pilgrimage (Hajj) month

Islamic festivals

Most Islamic festivals commemorate events in the life of the Prophet Muhammad. New Year's Day, for example, marks the day on which he set out from Makkah to Medina in the year 622. The month of the Islamic calendar in which the festival falls is given. Every month starts approximately on the day of a new moon, or when a crescent is first seen after a new moon, so the calendar shifts and these festivals fall at different times every year according to the Gregorian calendar.

Festival	Date
New Year's Day	1 Muharram
Birthday of Muhammad, AD 572	12 Rabi I
Night of Ascent (of Muhammad to Heaven)	27 Rajab
Month of fasting during daylight hours	1 Ramadan
Night of Power (sending down the Koran to Muhammad)	27 Ramadan
Feast of Breaking of the Fast (Eid Ul Fitr)	1 Shawwal (end of Ramadan)
Pilgrimage (Hajj) month;	8-13 Dhu-al-Hijja ceremonies at Makkah
Feast of the Sacrifice	10 Dhu-al-Hijja

Children light lamps for Diwali in Chandrigarh, India.

Heroes of legend

King Arthur
Legend says that Arthur, king of the Britons, won the throne by pulling a sword – the famous Excalibur – from a stone. This was a feat that only the true king was able to achieve. Arthur ruled during a period of peace and prosperity in Britain. Some folk tales say that if Britain is in danger, Arthur will return with his knights to defend the nation.

Beowulf
Beowulf was a Scandinavian warrior and the hero of *Beowulf*, the oldest poem in the English language. Beowulf was loyal to his king and also extremely brave. He killed Grendel the ogre, Grendel's mother and finally a fearsome dragon that cost him his own life.

Paul Bunyan
The lumberjack Paul Bunyan is a famous character in American folklore. It is said that he was so enormous, he created the Grand Canyon by dragging his pick behind him, and his giant footsteps formed the lakes of Minnesota. The legend came from stories told by the lumberjacks of the northern United States.

El Cid
El Cid really did exist and many legends have grown up around him. He was also known as El Cid Campeador (meaning my lord, the champion). His real name was Rodrigo Díaz de Vivar and he was a Spanish nobleman who was born in about 1040 and died in 1099. El Cid is a national hero in Spain because he is seen as a brave and accomplished warrior who fought to take control of Spain from the Muslims. Legend suggests that El Cid fought for both sides at different times.

St George
St George was a soldier for the Roman Empire who refused to take part in the Empire's persecution of Christians. He was executed for treachery and became a Christian martyr. Later, King Edward III made him the patron saint of England. St George is the hero of a legend in which he slays a man-eating dragon that was guarding a city's water supply. The city's inhabitants were so grateful that they converted from paganism to George's Christianity.

Heracles/Hercules
According to Greek and Roman mythology, Hercules was born with superhuman strength. By the time he reached adulthood he had killed a lion. Hercules had a jealous stepmother, who drove him to madness. While in this state, Hercules killed his wife and children. In order to regain his honour, Hercules had to perform 12 difficult tasks (see box).

Robin Hood
The Robin Hood of folklore was an English nobleman whose land was seized while King Richard the Lionheart was away fighting in the Crusades (1188–92). He became an outlaw in Sherwood Forest and led a band of Merry Men (and Maid Marian, his true love). They robbed the nobility who travelled through the forest and passed on the valuables they stole to the poor and needy. Robin Hood was a master of disguise and many stories describe how he dressed as somebody else in order to trick his enemies or rescue his friends.

The Labours of Hercules
The Greek hero Hercules killed his wife Megara and some of their children after being driven mad by his stepmother, the goddess Hera. As a punishment he had to perform 12 dangerous tasks or labours. When he succeeded in all of them, he was granted immortality.

1 Slay the Nemean lion (its skin resisted weapons, so he strangled it)
2 Kill the Hydra (a many-headed monster) of Lerna
3 Catch the Arcadian stag
4 Destroy the giant Erymanthian boar
5 Clean the Augean stables
6 Destroy the cannibal birds of the Lake Stymphalis
7 Capture the fire-breathing Cretan bull
8 Catch the horses of the Thracian king Diomedes
9 Seize the girdle of Hippolyta, Queen of the Amazons
10 Capture the oxen of the monster Geryon
11 Obtain the golden apples of the Hesperides
12 Bring Cerberus from Hades (hell)

Hercules battling with the Hydra of Lerna

Mythical creatures

Almost every culture on Earth has legends of imaginary beasts. Some are like humans with supernatural powers; some are part human, part animal; while others are unlike anything we know.

Centaurs

A centaur is half-horse and half-man, with the head and arms of a man and the body of a horse. It is one of the best known of all Greek mythological creatures and is said to have come from Thessaly in northern Greece. The myth may have arisen because of the skilful horsemanship of the people there.

Dragons

Dragons appear in the myths of many cultures, especially China, where the dragon was a symbol of the emperor. A typical dragon has a serpent-like body covered with scales, large wings, and can breathe fire. In legends, dragons often guard a cave of treasure.

Fairies

Fairies also feature in many tales. They are usually sweet, kindly creatures. In the Middle Ages, however, people believed that fairies stole children and replaced them with fairy beings known as changelings.

Giants

Giants or ogres are enormous human-shaped creatures. They are usually seen as fearsome but stupid monsters that feed on human flesh. Famous giants include Goliath in the Bible, and Cyclops, Atlas and the Titans in Greek mythology.

Leprechauns

Leprechauns are small Irish fairies who bring good luck. They are helpful creatures, usually shown wearing green clothes, with an apron, buckled shoes and a red cap. Their fun-loving nature means that leprechauns are fond of alcohol, music and sport, but they are also mischievous and love practical jokes. Other "little people", including dwarfs, elves, gnomes and pixies, appear in many European fairy stories.

Centaur

Troll

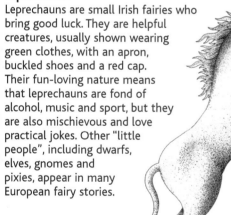

Unicorn

Dragon

Mermaids

Mermaids are beautiful creatures with the head and body of a woman and the tail of a fish. The first mermaid legend is thought to have been the story of Atargatis, a Syrian moon goddess of about 1000 BC. Atargatis had a child with a human. She then killed her lover, abandoned the child and jumped into a lake, where she took the form of a mermaid.

Trolls

Trolls are grotesque, malicious and rather dim-witted creatures in Scandinavian folklore. They are said to steal sleeping children, sometimes replacing them with one of their own. Trolls have poor eyesight, and are active only at night because sunlight turns them to stone.

Unicorns

A unicorn has the body of a horse, a lion's tail, a goat's beard, an antelope's legs and a single, often twisted, horn growing from its forehead. The unicorn is a popular subject in medieval stories; it is ferocious but good, and can purify water – or neutralize poison – by dipping its horn into it. The way to catch a unicorn is to use a young girl as bait, as a unicorn will lie down peacefully next to a maiden.

Vampires

Vampires are the "undead" who drink the blood of the living to survive. Ideas about vampires include the belief that plunging a wooden stake through a vampire's heart can destroy it. Some people also think that you can protect yourself against vampires with garlic, holy water, crosses and Bibles, and that a vampire cannot enter a home unless invited.

Werewolves

Werewolves, or lycanthropes, are mythical creatures in the folk tales of many cultures. They usually appear as men by day, but may turn into wolves on the night of a full moon. The werewolf is bloodthirsty and ruthless. It devours its prey and shows none of the remorse that it might have felt in human form.

See also

Monsters in the movies: page 273

Black cats are seen as lucky in the UK, but unlucky in the USA.

 # Good and bad luck signs

Black cats
In the UK, people think black cats are lucky, particularly if they cross your path. The opposite is true in the USA and several European countries, where a black cat is seen as a bad omen. In the USA a white cat is very good luck, while in the UK it is a sign of bad luck.

Horseshoes
A horseshoe is a piece of metal fixed to a horse's foot. Some people think that if you find a horseshoe and the open space is facing you it will bring you luck. Traditionally, people also hang horseshoes above the doorway of their home to bring good luck. In many European countries, the horseshoe is hung downwards – that's believed to let the luck flow out into the house. In Britain and Ireland, the shoe must be hung with the opening at the top to keep the good fortune.

Clovers
Four-leaf clovers are very rare. Anyone who finds one is said to be able to recognize evil influences and avoid them.

Ladders
A ladder leaning against a wall forms a triangle. Some people believe it is disrespectful, and unlucky, to walk underneath one because triangles symbolize the Holy Trinity. The bad luck is supposed to be warded off by crossing the fingers or making a wish while under the ladder.

Magpies
Magpies are generally thought to be unlucky. This belief is said to come from the Bible, as the magpie was the only bird that refused to enter Noah's Ark. In China, however, the magpie is a good omen, and should never be killed.

Mirrors
Breaking a mirror is said to bring seven years' bad luck. This idea may come from the old belief that your reflection is an image of your soul, so anything that changes the reflection may bring evil. The length of the period of bad luck may come from the Roman belief that life renews itself every seven years.

Number 13

The belief that the number 13 is unlucky is very ancient. The Romans believed the number 13 was a symbol of death and destruction. Norse legends claimed that the thirteenth guest at a banquet is the spirit of evil. The Christian belief that the number brings bad luck is often said to come from the Last Supper, when Christ sat down with his 12 disciples – making 13 people. Some people think that the first person to leave a dinner table at which there are 13 diners will die before the end of the year.

Unlucky for some?
- The thirteenth Apollo space mission was known as Apollo 13. On 13 April 1970, there was an explosion on board and the spacecraft began to leak oxygen. This happened two days after it took off at 13:13 (1:13 pm). The spacecraft only just made it back to Earth.
- On Friday 13 September 1928, a hurricane killed 2,000 people in Puerto Rico, Florida and the Virgin Islands, and caused approximately $25 million in damage.
- There is no building in Paris that bears the number 13.
- Italy omits the number 13 from its national lottery.
- The 13th of the month costs the USA about $1 billion a year through cancellations on trains and planes, absenteeism from work, and reduced business activity.

Lucky for others?
- The number 13 was sacred for the Mayans and Aztecs of Central America, and it is traditionally a lucky number in China.
- Buddhists pay homage to 13 Buddhas, and the orthodox Jewish prayerbook holds 13 principles of faith.

Predictions that were wrong

"It's only a toy."
Gardiner Green Hubbard, a founder of the National Geographic Society, on seeing Alexander Graham Bell's telephone, 1876

"Television won't matter in your lifetime or mine."
Rex Lambert in The Listener, *1936*

"There is no reason anyone would want a computer in their home."
Ken Olson, president, chairman and founder of Digital Equipment Corp, 1977

"I have not the smallest molecule of faith in aerial navigation [flying] other than by ballooning."
Lord Kelvin, President of the Royal Society, 1896 (the Wright brothers first flew in 1903)

"We don't like their sound, they sound too much like the Shadows, and guitar music is on the way out."
The Decca Recording Company rejects the Beatles, 1962

"Speaking movies are impossible. When a century has passed, all thought of so-called speaking movies will have been abandoned. It will never be possible to synchronize the voice with the picture."
D.W. Griffith, director, early 1920s

The signs of the zodiac

In Western astrology the zodiac has 12 parts. Each is named after a constellation and corresponds to a different time of year. Astrologers believe that the movements of the planets influence what happens on Earth, and that people born under the different signs have certain characteristics.

Aries, the ram   *21 March–19 April*
Creative, impatient, masculine, competitive, warrior-like, independent, outspoken

Taurus, the bull   *20 April–20 May*
Determined, resourceful, materialistic, touchy, ruthless, entrepreneurial

Gemini, the twins   *21 May–21 June*
Intellectual, shallow, inquisitive, selfish, talkative, witty, indecisive, irritable

Cancer, the crab   *22 June–22 July*
Emotional, sympathetic, moody, sensitive, home-loving, romantic, loyal, tactless

Leo, the lion   *23 July–22 August*
Generous, creative, broad-minded, patronising, bossy, extroverted, idealistic, arrogant

Virgo, the virgin   *23 August–23 September*
Diligent, intelligent, modest, conservative, overcritical, pedantic, affectionate, methodical

Libra, the scales   *24 September–23 October*
Charming, sociable, gullible, flirtatious, attractive, objective, artistic

Scorpio, the scorpion   *24 October–22 November*
Forceful, passionate, jealous, obsessive, secretive, intense, outspoken, extreme, rebellious

Sagittarius, the archer   *23 November–21 December*
Optimistic, honest, philosophical, careless, irresponsible, energetic, adventurous

Capricorn, the goat   *22 December–20 January*
Disciplined, economical, patient, reserved, pessimistic, serious, organized, rational

Aquarius, the water bearer   *21 January–19 February*
Inventive, friendly, independent, unpredictable, serious, intelligent, eccentric

Pisces, the fishes   *20 February–20 March*
Imaginative, compassionate, vague, gentle, sensitive, creative, spiritual, easygoing

Palmistry

Palmistry is the art of telling the future from the lines on the palms of your hands. The lines are unique to each person and are said to show the person's character and what will happen in the future. Palmistry began in India thousands of years ago as a form of counselling.

The heart, head and life lines are especially important. They are judged by their length and strength. The life line shows how healthy you are and how much you enjoy life. The head line shows how intelligent you are, and the heart line reveals the physical condition of the heart, as well as a person's sexual and emotional nature.

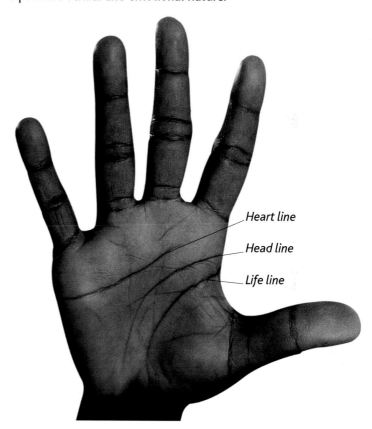

Heart line
Head line
Life line

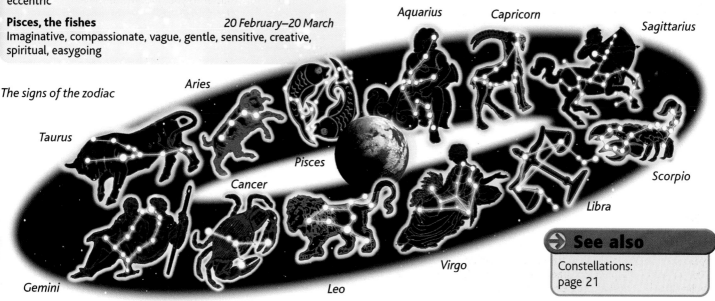

The signs of the zodiac

Aquarius   Capricorn   Sagittarius
Aries
Taurus   Pisces   Scorpio
Cancer   Libra
Virgo
Gemini   Leo

See also

Constellations: page 21

Mysterious places

Stonehenge

Stonehenge is a circle of 17 upright stones called sarsens which stand on Salisbury Plain in southwest England. The stones weigh up to 50 tonnes and have other stones, called lintels, laid across the top. There is also an inner circle of smaller bluestones weighing up to four tonnes each. Stonehenge is the only stone circle in the world with lintels across the top of the stones, and experts think it was completed in about 1500 BC. They believe that the sarsen stones were transported from 32km away and the bluestones came from an incredible 250km away. At least 600 men would have been needed to move each sarsen stone on some of the steepest parts of the journey. Nobody knows exactly why Stonehenge was built, but it may have been a druids' temple or even a kind of astronomical calendar.

Stonehenge

Easter Island

Easter Island (or Rapa Nui) lies in the South Pacific between Chile and Tahiti, and is one of the most isolated islands in the world. By the 16th century, Easter Island had nearly 10,000 inhabitants, who made huge statues known as *moai*. The 887 *moai* were carved from the island's volcanic rock and have long, angular faces. Some have eyes made from coral. The average *moai* was about 4m tall and weighed over 14 tonnes, so they would have been extremely difficult for the islanders to transport. Archaeologists believe that the statues symbolize the spirits of Easter Island's most important inhabitants.

Four of the huge moai *figures on Easter Island*

The Bermuda Triangle

The Bermuda Triangle is an area of the Atlantic Ocean off the coast of Florida. It is famous for being the supposed site of many unexplained disappearances. The three points of the triangle are Miami, Bermuda and San Juan in Puerto Rico. In the 15th century, Christopher Columbus claimed to have seen a "great flame of fire" falling into the ocean in the area. The mystery of the Bermuda Triangle first began to attract attention in 1945, when Flight 19, a training mission of five US bombers, vanished off the Florida coast. The plane that was sent to find them also disappeared, and around 100 boats and aircraft have also been lost there. Explanations include magnetic fields, sea monsters and abduction by aliens, but most experts agree the disappearances are caused by bad navigation and/or extreme weather conditions.

The Nazca Lines

The Nazca Lines are enormous drawings on the ground (called geoglyphs) that stretch across the Nazca Desert in southern Peru. They show more than 300 geometric patterns, spirals and animals. The lines are so vast (one extends 65km) that they can only be seen properly from a height of about 300m. The lines were first noticed when commercial aeroplanes began to fly over Peru in the 1920s. Most experts agree that they were made by the Nazca Indians who lived in the region between 300 BC and AD 800, but there are many questions yet to be answered about them. For example, why were the pictures made and how are they so precise if their makers had no means to view them from the sky?

Teotihuacán

In AD 600 Teotihuacán in Mexico was the sixth largest city in the world and about 200,000 people lived there. Just 150 years later, Teotihuacán was almost deserted, and plants had begun to grow over the city's huge pyramids. Nobody knows why Teotihuacán was abandoned, but it may have been devastated by a huge fire in AD 650.

See also

Aztec empire: page 107

A crop circle on Salisbury Plain

Crop circles

Crop circles are complicated geometric patterns, usually in wheat fields. Some people believe that the patterns are left by the imprint of an extra-terrestrial craft, or that they are a message from extra-terrestrials themselves. Another theory is that natural forces such as tornadoes, heat or strong winds create the patterns by flattening the crops, but the regular shapes of most crop circles makes this unlikely.

The most likely explanation is that the circles are made by people as a hoax. They gradually build up a design by flattening the wheat, using very basic equipment such as rope and planks of wood.

Mysterious monsters

The Loch Ness Monster

The Loch Ness Monster, nicknamed Nessie, is said to live in Loch Ness in Scotland. The monster is generally thought to be a long-necked creature with flippers, like a prehistoric reptile. Many people have reported seeing Nessie, but there is no real evidence that the creature exists.

Yeti

The Yeti, also called the Abominable Snowman, is believed to live in the Himalaya mountains. People say this legendary creature measures up to 1.4m, is covered in long brown hair, and walks upright like a human being. Everest mountaineers, including Sir Edmund Hillary and Sherpa Tenzing Norgay, have reported seeing mysterious footprints in the snow.

Bigfoot

Another legendary creature is said to live in the northwest of North America. People who claim to have seen Bigfoot say it is a large hairy creature that walks upright like the Yeti. There is no firm evidence that Bigfoot exists, but there are some fuzzy photos and videos that are supposed to to show this mystery monster.

Lincoln/Kennedy coincidences

There are more than 100 coincidences relating to the US presidents Abraham Lincoln and John F. Kennedy, who were both assassinated. These are all historical facts.

- Abraham Lincoln was elected to Congress in 1846. John F. Kennedy was elected to Congress in 1946.
- Abraham Lincoln was elected president in 1860. John F. Kennedy was elected president in 1960.
- John Wilkes Booth, who assassinated Lincoln, was born in 1839. Lee Harvey Oswald, who assassinated Kennedy, was born in 1939.
- Both assassins were known by three names, John Wilkes Booth and Lee Harvey Oswald; both names contain 15 letters.
- Both presidents were shot on a Friday, in the presence of their wives.
- Both presidents were shot in the head, from behind.
- Lincoln was killed in Ford's Theater. Kennedy met his death while riding in a Lincoln car made by the Ford Motor Company.
- Booth ran from the theatre and was caught in a warehouse. Oswald ran from a warehouse and was caught in a theatre.
- Booth and Oswald were assassinated before their trials.
- Lincoln had sons named Edward and Robert; Kennedy had brothers named Edward and Robert.
- Both presidents were shot by southerners and were succeeded by southerners named Johnson.
- Andrew Johnson, who succeeded Lincoln, was born in 1808. Lyndon Johnson, who succeeded Kennedy, was born in 1908.
- Both successors died ten years later: Abraham Lincoln died in 1865; Andrew Johnson died in 1875. John F. Kennedy died in 1963; Lyndon Johnson died in 1973.

Amazing coincidence?

On 5 December 1664, a ship sank in the Menai Strait. The only one of the 81 people on board to survive was a man named Hugh Williams. On 5 December 1785, another ship, carrying 60 passengers, sank in the same area. The only survivor was named Hugh Williams. On 5 December 1860, a third ship sank in in the Menai Strait. The only survivor of the 25 on board? Hugh Williams.

Menai Strait between the island of Anglesey and Wales

Conflict has been part of human life since time began, and war has shaped the world's history. This section looks at some important wars and battles, as well as the weapons used in them. It also focuses on aspects of crime, punishment and the legal system.

CONFLICT AND CRIME

Weapons milestones

Date	Weapon
500,000 BC	Spears
250,000 BC	Stone axes
25,000 BC	Boomerang-like weapons (Poland)
	Knives
15,000 BC	Spear-throwers
3000 BC	Bows and arrows
	Shields
	War chariots
2000 BC	Armour
	Swords
865 BC	Battering rams and other siege engines (Assyria)
3rd C BC	Galleys, Crete
397 BC	Catapults propelling darts
332 BC	Catapults throwing stones
7th century	Gunpowder (China)
8th century	Viking longships
11th century	Chain mail
	Crossbows
1150	Longbows
1221	Bombs (China)
1242	English monk Roger Bacon first describes gunpowder
1288	First guns (China)
1324	Cannon used at Battle of Metz
1346	Cannon (siege of Calais)
1370s	Arbalests (crossbows)
1492	Leonardo da Vinci invents giant siege crossbows
1514	Man-of-war
1515	Wheel-lock muskets
1590	Bayonets made at Bayonne, France
1776	Submarine torpedoes
1784	Shrapnel shells
1835	Revolvers, Samuel Colt (US)
1838	Breech-loading rifles
1847	Guncotton, invented by Christian Friedrick Schönbein
1847	Nitroglycerine (explosive) invented by Ascanio Solaro
1850	Battleships
1860	Repeating rifle invented by Christopher Spencer (US)
1861	Metal gun cartridges
	Sea mines
1862	Gatling machine guns
	Winchester repeating rifles
1866	Dynamite invented by Alfred Nobel (Sweden)
1872	Automatic pistols
1884	Maxim machine guns
1897	Dum-dum bullets (banned 1908)
1898	Lüger pistols
1901	Modern submarines
1902	Armoured cars
1911	Aircraft carriers
	Bombers
1914	Zeppelin airships and large multi-engined aircraft able to carry heavy bombs used in aerial warfare
1914	Flechéttes first used – steel darts, designed to be dropped from aircraft on the enemy beneath
1915	Aircraft machine gun invented by German manufacturer Anthony Fokker

Date	Weapon
1915	Poisonous gases, such as mustard gas, chlorine, and tear gas, first used by German army at Ypres. Gas masks invented to combat them
1915	Rifles with periscopic sights (allowing users to remain hidden) invented by an Australian soldier.
1917	Water-cooled Browning machine guns invented by John Browning
	Tanks introduced as a way of getting through enemy barbed wire, and increasingly as a battlefield weapon
1936	Nerve gas (Tabun)
	Spitfire fighter aircraft
1939	Military helicopters
1940	Bazookas
	Radar
1942	Napalm
	V2 rockets
1942	Dam-buster bombs
1943	Jet bombers and fighters
1945	Atomic bomb
1952	Hydrogen bomb
1955	Nuclear submarines
1960	Harrier jump jets
1970	Exocet missiles
1982	Air-launched cruise missiles
1984	Stun guns
1988	Stealth bombers
1988	IMINT (Imagery Intelligence) satellites
2001	Heckler and Koch MP7 submachine guns
2003	Multiple JDAM (Joint Direct Attack Munition) air-launched smart bombs

B-2 Stealth Bomber

Countries with nuclear weapons

The numbers of nuclear warheads owned by these countries are as estimated by the Carnegie Endowment for International Peace. The total for Israel is not officially acknowledged.

Country	Warheads
Russia	17,000
USA	10,000
China	410
France	350
UK	185
Israel	100
India	50–90
Pakistan	30–50
World total:	*28,185*

Largest armed forces

The armed forces listed below are all active forces, but some countries have many reserves (soldiers who can be called for service if needed). South Korea may have as many as 4.5 million reserve forces, Vietnam may have 3 to 4 million and China 800,000. Figures for the UK are given for comparison.

Estimated active forces

	Country	Army	Navy	Air	Total
1	China	1,600,000	255,000	400,000	2,255,000
2	India	1,100,000	55,000	170,000	1,325,000
3	USA	502,000	400,000	379,500	1,281,500
4	North Korea	1,106,000	46,000	110,000	1,262,000
5	Russia	360,000	155,000	184,600	699,600
	UK	*116,760*	*40,630*	*48,500*	*205,890*

Parade of Chinese military forces

Weird weapons

Biological warfare

The aim of biological warfare is to infect enemies with deadly diseases. It is a modern form of warfare. However, in 1500 Leonardo da Vinci suggested using bombs containing saliva from mad dogs or pigs, or the venom of poisonous animals such as toads or spiders. The rotting carcasses of horses and other animals were also catapulted into enemy castles to infect the inhabitants.

Combined gun and plough

This was patented in 1862 by C.M. French and W.H. Fancher of Waterloo, New York. It was designed to be used by farmers so they could quickly turn their ploughs into powerful guns if they were attacked while ploughing.

Hard cheese

In 1865 during a war between Uruguay and Brazil, a Uruguayan ship ran out of cannon balls. Instead they fired stale Dutch cheeses, one of which dismasted an enemy vessel and killed two sailors.

Boomerang bullets

These bullets were invented in the USA in 1870, and were designed to fire in a curved line. The danger was that if they travelled in a complete circle, they could kill the person who fired them.

Weapons named after people

Big Bertha

Big Bertha was a 144-tonne cannon used by the German army to shell Paris from a distance of 122km during World War I. The name came from Bertha Krupp von Bohlen und Halbach (1886–1957), who inherited the German Krupp armaments business from her father, Friedrich Alfred Krupp.

Congreve rocket

This rocket was named after British inventor Sir William Congreve (1772–1828). It was used in battles against Napoleon in the early years of the 19th century.

Kalashnikov

This machine gun is named after its inventor, Russian Mikhail Kalashnikov (1922–). More than 70 million have been made.

Lüger

Gunmaker Georg Lüger (1849–1923) pioneered the P-08 pistol that bears his name in 1898. It was adopted by the German army and was widely used during both World Wars.

Mauser

The Mauser bolt-action rifle was developed in 1898 by German brothers Wilhelm (1834–82) and Peter Paul Mauser (1838–1914). They also invented an automatic pistol.

Mills grenade

This hand grenade was designed in 1915 by William Mills (1856–1932). An estimated 70 million were used by the British during World War I. Mills was knighted in 1922.

Molotov cocktail

This was a crude but effective bomb made with a petrol-filled bottle and fuse. It was given its name by the Finns in about 1940 who used it during the war against Russia. They called it a cocktail for Molotov: Vyacheslav Mikhailovich Molotov (1890–1986) was the Soviet prime minister at the time.

Shrapnel

This name was originally given to the exploding shells invented by British officer Henry Shrapnel (1761–1842). Fragments of bombs are also often called shrapnel.

Sten gun

The name comes from the initial letters of the surnames of the weapon's inventors, Major Reginald V. Shepherd and Harold J. Turpin, combined with the first two letters of England (or, according to some authorities, Enfield), where it was first made.

Tommy gun

The Thompson sub-machine gun was invented by American army general John Taliaferro Thompson and US Navy commander John N. Blish. It became known as the Tommy gun and was popular with gangsters during the 1920s.

Krupp's Big Bertha gun being fired

Major wars

Date	War	Principal combatants
431–404 BC	Peloponnesian War	Sparta v Athens
264–146 BC	Punic Wars	Rome v Carthage
1095–1291	Crusades	Christians v Muslims
1337–1543	Hundred Years War	England v France
1455–85	Wars of the Roses	York v Lancaster
1618–48	Thirty Years War	Catholic v Protestant forces in Europe
1642–51	English Civil War	Crown v Parliament
1701–14	War of the Spanish Succession	France v Grand Alliance (of other European countries)
1740–48	War of the Austrian Succession	France, Spain, Bavaria, Prussia v Britain, Netherlands, Savoy
1756–63	Seven Years War	Austria, Russia, France, Sweden, Poland v Prussia, Britain, Portugal
1775–83	American War of Independence	America v Britain
1792–1815	Napoleonic Wars	Britain, Austria, Russia, Sweden, Naples v France
1812–15	War of 1812	USA v Britain
1846–48	Mexico-American War	Mexico v USA
1853–56	Crimean War	Russia v Turkey, Britain, France, Sardinia
1861–65	American Civil War	North v Confederate (Southern) states
1870–71	Franco-Prussian War	France v Germany
1894–95	Chinese-Japanese War	China v Japan
1898	Spanish-American War	Spain v USA
1899–1902	Boer War	Boers (South Africa) v Britain
1904–05	Russo-Japanese War	Russia v Japan
1914–18	World War I	Allies v Germany and others
1931–33	Chinese-Japanese War	China v Japan
1936–39	Spanish Civil War	Nationalists v Republicans
1937–45	Chinese-Japanese War	China v Japan
1939–45	World War II	Allies v Germany and others (Axis powers)
1950–53	Korean War	North Korea (with Chinese aid) v South Korea (supported by USA)
1957–75	Vietnam War	North Vietnam v South Vietnam (with US aid)
1982	Falklands War	Argentina v Britain
1991	Gulf War	Iraq v Allied forces
2001–	War on Terrorism	USA and allies v al-Qaida, Taliban in Afghanistan
2003	Iraq War	USA and allies v Iraq

Largest armed forces of the World Wars

Largest armed forces of World War I

Country	Personnel*
1 Russia	12,000,000
2 Germany	11,000,000
3 British Empire	8,904,467
4 France	8,410,000
5 Austria-Hungary	7,800,000
USA	*4,355,000*

* Total at peak strength

Largest armed forces of World War II

Country	Personnel*
1 USSR	12,500,000
2 USA	12,364,000
3 Germany	10,000,000
4 Japan	6,095,000
5 France	5,700,000
UK	*4,683,000*

* Total at peak strength

Youngest medal winners

UK
Andrew Fitzgibbon, an Irish hospital apprentice, was awarded Britain's highest military honour, the Victoria Cross, when he was only 15. He won the medal for bravery during action at Taku Forts, China, on 21 August 1860.

US
William Johnston was a drummer who won the Congressional Medal of Honor, America's highest military award, when he was 12. The award was for bravery in action during the Seven Day Battle and Peninsular Campaign of 1862.

Worst battles

The Battle of Stalingrad was one of the longest and bloodiest battles of all time. It was fought between German and Soviet forces and continued from 19 August 1942 to 2 February 1943. The total number of casualties can only be estimated.

Battle	War	Casualties*
1 Stalingrad	World War II, 1942–43	2,000,000
2 Somme River	World War I, 1916	1,000,000
3 Po Valley	World War II, 1945	740,000
4 Moscow	World War II, 1941–42	700,000
5 Gallipoli	World War I, 1915–16	500,000

* Estimated total of military and civilian dead, wounded and missing

Russian troops in action during the battle for Stalingrad

Great land battles

Marathon, Greece, September 490 BC
The Athenians defeated an invading Persian army during the Battle of Marathon.

Hastings, England, 14 October 1066
In the last successful invasion of England, the Norman and French army under William, Duke of Normandy, defeated the Saxons under King Harold. Harold was killed and William, who became known as William the Conqueror, was crowned King of England.

Crécy, France, 26 August 1346
During the Hundred Years War, 9,000 English soldiers under Edward III defeated a French army of 30,000 under the command of King Philip IV of France.

Agincourt, France, 25 October 1415
The English army under King Henry V defeated the French decisively although heavily outnumbered (5,700 against 25,000). This gained them control of much of France.

Naseby, England, 14 June 1645
In the English Civil War Oliver Cromwell's New Model Army defeated the Royalist army of King Charles I, who was later taken prisoner and executed.

Blenheim, Bavaria, 13 August 1704
This battle took place in the War of the Spanish Succession. English and Dutch troops crossed Germany and defeated the Franco-Bavarian army. The English and Dutch were led by John Churchill, later Duke of Marlborough.

Yorktown, America, 6–19 October 1781
In the American War of Independence, the British were forced to surrender by the American army. The Americans were led by General George Washington, later the first president of the USA.

Waterloo, Belgium, 18 June 1815
During the Napoleonic Wars the Emperor Napoleon's army fought against the British and allies under the Duke of Wellington. Britain and the allies won and Napoleon was sent into exile.

Gettysburg, USA, 1–3 July 1863
During this important American Civil War battle the Confederate (Southern) army under General Robert E. Lee was defeated by the Union army.

Somme, France, 1 July–18 November 1916
During World War I the British army under General Sir Douglas Haig attempted to end the stalemate of trench warfare against the German army. This led to the first of two battles of the Somme river. Neither side gained any advantage, and both suffered massive casualties.

El Alamein, Egypt, 1–27 July and 23 October–4 November 1942
These two World War II battles were fought in the desert when the British 8th Army under Lieutenant-General Bernard Montgomery eventually crushed the German and Italian armies under Field Marshal Erwin Rommel.

Stalingrad, USSR, 19 August 1942–2 February 1943
During World War II the German 6th Army was surrounded by the Soviet army in Stalingrad (now Volgograd) and suffered huge casualties in an extended siege.

Desert Shield/Storm/Sabre, Iraq/Kuwait, 16 January–27 February 1991
These Gulf War campaigns were a response to Iraq's invasion of Kuwait. Coalition forces led by the USA drove the Iraqis out through a combination of air and land attack.

The Battle of Trafalgar, *painted by John Callow, 1875*

Great sea battles

Salamis, 20 October 480 BC (Greco-Persian Wars)
The Greeks overcame a Persian fleet, saving Greece from conquest.

Aegosopotami, 405 BC (Peloponnesian War)
In this battle 180 Athenian triremes were faced with 170 Peloponnesian ships. The Athenians were conquered, and the Peloponnesian War ended.

Actium, 2 September 31 BC (Wars of the Second Triumvirate)
Mark Antony and the Egyptian fleet were defeated by the Romans during this battle.

Lepanto, 7 October 1571 (Cyprus War)
The Spanish force defeated the Turkish fleet, which lost 25,000 sailors in 250 galleys.

Spanish Armada, 29 July 1588 (Anglo-Spanish War)
In July 1588, 130 Spanish ships with 2,500 guns and 30,000 troops set out to attack England. The English fleet badly damaged the Spanish ships with their guns, and the rest of the fleet was destroyed by bad weather.

Trafalgar, 21 October 1805 (Napoleonic Wars)
The British fleet under Lord Nelson won this sea battle against the French, although Nelson was killed.

Jutland, 31 May 1916 (World War I)
During this engagement the Royal Navy took on the German fleet, which withdrew.

Guadalcanal, 9 August–30 November 1942 (World War II)
This series of six naval engagements between the USA and Japanese resulted in heavy losses on both sides.

Coral Sea, 8 May 1942 (World War II)
The US Navy took on the Japanese in the first major battle fought using aircraft from carriers.

Leyte Gulf, 22–27 October 1944 (World War II)
The USA defeated the Japanese in this battle. The Japanese lost three battleships, four aircraft carriers, ten cruisers and nine destroyers.

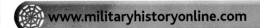

Legal language

accessory	Someone who assists a criminal
accomplice	A criminal's partner in crime
acquit	To free or release from a charge, find not guilty
affidavit	A written statement
arson	Deliberately setting a building on fire
assault	Inflicting harm on another person
bail	A sum of money paid to ensure a person appears in court. The money is forfeited if they fail to appear
battery	Unlawful assault
blackmail	Attempting to obtain money by threats
burglary	Breaking into a building to commit theft
capital crime	A crime for which the penalty is death (abolished in the UK in 1965)
civil law	Disputes between individuals
criminal law	Deals with acts considered harmful to the community
damages	Money paid as compensation for injury or loss
defamation	Harming a person's reputation by libel or slander
evidence	Information presented to a court to prove or disprove a legal issue, such as a defendant's guilt or innocence
fraud	Deception to gain money, etc
homicide	The unlawful killing of another person
indictment	A written accusation
kidnap	Illegally carrying off a person, for example, to obtain ransom payment
libel	Defamation in writing, such as in a newspaper article
manslaughter	Taking another person's life without deliberate intent
murder	The deliberate killing of another person
oath	A promise to tell the truth in court, often sworn on a holy book such as the Bible
perjury	A false statement made while under oath in a court
probation	Placing an offender under the supervision of a probation officer
receiving	Taking goods knowing that they are stolen
robbery	Theft with force or threat of violence
slander	Defamation of a person in spoken language
sue	To bring legal proceedings against a person, organization, etc
summons	An official order to attend court
trespass	Illegal entry of another person's property
trial	The examination of a case in a court of law
vandalism	Deliberate damage to another's property
verdict	The outcome of a trial – whether the accused is guilty or not guilty
warrant	A legal document allowing for someone's arrest, the search of their property, etc

A statue of justice holding scales and sword at Dublin Castle

Law courts

This is the court system in England and Wales. The system differs in Scotland. Some countries follow the English system, but most have their own procedures. In many court rooms in the UK and elsewhere there is an image of justice as a woman, which dates from Roman times. It traditionally shows her holding scales in one hand, to show that she is impartial, and a sword to represent the power of the law. Sometimes she is blindfolded to show that justice cannot be influenced.

County Court
Civil (non-criminal) cases are heard by a judge in a County Court.

Magistrates' Court
Criminal and civil cases are held before Justices of the Peace or District Judges, without a jury. There are limits on the sentences and fines they can impose. Youth Courts are part of Magistrates' Courts and hear cases involving young people between 10 and 17 years of age.

Crown Court
These hold trials by judge and jury for more serious criminal cases.

High Court
The High Court tries civil cases and hears appeals in criminal cases.

Court of Appeal
These hear appeals against civil and criminal cases following High Court and Crown Court convictions.

House of Lords
The House of Lords is the highest court in the land and hears appeals against judgements of the Court of Appeal.

Coroners' Courts
Coroners' courts investigate violent and unnatural deaths or sudden deaths in which the cause is unknown.

US court room

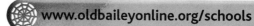

www.oldbaileyonline.org/schools

 Who's who in court

accused	A person charged with an offence
barrister	A lawyer qualified to appear in higher courts
defence	A barrister or solicitor who represents the defendant
defendant	A person accused of a crime
dock officer	An official who accompanies the defendant during a trial
judge	The public official in charge of a trial
jury	A group of 12 members of the public (jurors) chosen to hear the evidence and decide whether the defendant is guilty or not guilty
logger	A person who records the court proceedings using a stenograph or other equipment
magistrate/Justice of the Peace (JP)	A non-professional person qualified to try certain cases
plaintiff	A person bringing a civil action to court
prosecution	A barrister or solicitor who presents evidence against the defendant and has to prove his/her guilt beyond reasonable doubt (cases may be "not proven" in Scotland)
solicitor	A lawyer who advises clients and prepares cases for barristers
usher	A court assistant who guides the jury and witnesses in and out of court and administers oaths
witness	A person who gives evidence in court – someone who saw the offence, a police officer, or a specialist such as a medical expert

Strange laws

- Members of Parliament are not allowed to wear suits of armour in the House of Commons.
- A law passed by Oliver Cromwell banning the eating of mince pies on Christmas Day has not yet been repealed.
- Wyoming State Legislature banned the photographing of rabbits during January, February, March and April without an official permit.
- Anyone detonating a nuclear weapon within the city limits of Chico, California, USA, is liable to a $500 fine.
- In Arkansas, USA, it is illegal to extract the teeth of a bear or otherwise surgically alter it.
- Owners of monkeys in Indonesia must have an identity card for the animal, complete with a photo of the monkey.
- In France, no pig may be called Napoleon.
- No one may eat a rattlesnake in public on a Sunday in Kansas, USA.
- It is illegal to sell a teddy bear or play with a yo-yo on a Sunday in Memphis, Tennessee, USA.
- A law in Alderson, West Virginia, USA, says that "No lions shall be allowed to run wild on the streets".
- In Spades, Indiana, USA, you may not open a can with a revolver.
- In England it is illegal to impersonate a Chelsea Pensioner.

Scottish law

Scottish law differs from English law in a number of ways. The Procurator Fiscal presents the case for the prosecution in Sheriff Courts and in District Courts (where minor cases are tried). Advocates, instead of barristers, appear in Scottish courts. In Scottish law, if a person is charged with a criminal offence, they must be brought to trial within 110 days. If that does not happen, they are set free. In English courts juries can only find defendants guilty or not guilty, but in Scotland they may find a case "not proven".

 Ways of execution

Methods used around the world include shooting (China, Vietnam), hanging (Iran, Singapore), beheading (Saudi Arabia), lethal injection and electric chair (USA).

The electric chair at the State Penitentiary in Virginia, USA

The death penalty

The death penalty was once the most common punishment for murder and other serious crimes. It has been abolished in more than half the world's countries.

- 82 countries have abolished the death penalty for all crimes
- 14 countries have abolished the death penalty for ordinary crimes, but keep it for exceptional crimes such as treason and war crimes
- 22 countries keep the death penalty in law but have not carried out any executions for the past ten years or more
- 78 other countries and territories officially have the death penalty, but fewer than 30 of these use it

China probably executes the largest number of people every year for offences from drug trafficking to murder. The USA executed 59 people in 2004, and on 3 March 2004 Marcus Cotton became the 900th person executed since the death penalty was re-introduced in 1977. More than one-third of all US executions take place in the state of Texas.

Punishments

In most countries people who break the law are either fined or imprisoned, but through the ages there have been many other forms of punishment. Whipping was once common: mutinous sailors were whipped with a cat-o'-nine-tails or keelhauled (dragged beneath a ship on the end of a rope). Not so long ago schoolchildren who misbehaved were caned. These are just some of the punishments once used.

Scold's bridle
Nagging women or scolds were punished with the scold's bridle. This was a metal frame that fitted over the victim's head, making it impossible to speak.

Pillory
Like the stocks, the pillory held victims in place – but by the neck and wrists. The pillory was worse than the stocks as people could not use their hands to protect their faces from things thrown at them, and could be blinded or even killed. The last person to be pilloried in England was Peter James Bossy in London on 22 June 1830. The pillory was abolished in 1837. A Chinese version, a sort of heavy wooden collar, was known as the Winged Tiger.

Stocks
Stocks were wooden structures which held the seated victim by the ankles. People threw things at them and ridiculed them – they were literally made a laughing stock. The last time stocks were used was in Rugby in 1865.

Ducking stool
This punishment was used in England and America. The victims were usually women. They were strapped into a special chair and plunged into a river or pond. The last person to be punished this way in England was Jenny Pipes in Leominster, Herefordshire, in 1809.

A ducking stool in action

Burning at the stake

Many famous people were burned at the stake, including the French patriot Joan of Arc in 1431 and Protestant martyrs in England. In Germany up to 100,000 people accused of witchcraft and other crimes were burned during the 16th, 17th and 18th centuries. In 1589 133 people were burned in a single day. Witches were rarely burned in England, and never in America, where hanging was the usual punishment.

Prison fact file

| World prison population | | Prisoners per | |
Country	Total prisoners	100,000 people	
1 USA	2,085,620	1 USA	714
2 China	1,548,498	2 Belarus	532
3 Russia	763,054	= Bermuda	532
4 Brazil	330,642	= Russia	532
5 India	313,635	5 Palau	523
England and Wales	*74,103*	*England and Wales*	*140*

Longest jail sentence
In Thailand on 27 July 1989, fraudster Chamoy Thipyaso and her seven accomplices were each sentenced to 141,078 years.

Longest in jail
Paul Geidel, a New York State prisoner, was sentenced for murder on 5 September 1911 at the age of 17. He was released on 7 May 1980 at the age of 85, having served 68 years 245 days.

Great robberies

Crown jewels
On 9 May 1671, Colonel Thomas Blood entered the Tower of London disguised as a priest and stole the Crown Jewels. He was captured, but pardoned by Charles I, who admired his daring.

Mona Lisa
Leonardo da Vinci's famous painting was stolen from the Louvre Museum, Paris, on 21 August 1911 by Vicenzo Peruggia. He kept it for two years, but when he tried to sell it he was caught and jailed.

Great Train Robbery
A gang of 12 robbers stole £2.6 million from the Glasgow to London mail train on 8 August 1963. They were caught and jailed, but one, Ronald Biggs, escaped and lived for many years in Brazil.

Brinks Mat bullion robbery
The biggest armed robbery in British history took place on 25 November 1983, when a gang stole 6,800 gold bars worth £26 million from a warehouse in Heathrow. Not all the gang members were caught.

Art theft
On 18 March 1990 two thieves disguised as policemen stole 12 works of art by Rembrandt, Degas, Vermeer and others from the Isabella Stewart Gardner Museum, Boston. The paintings were valued at $300 million and have never been recovered.

See also

History timeline:
page 104

Alcatraz, in the bay of San Francisco, is no longer used as a prison.

 # Famous prisons

Newgate
This was once London's most notorious prison. Public hangings took place outside its gates, and it features in several of Charles Dickens' novels. Newgate was rebuilt several times, and finally demolished in 1902. The Central Criminal Court (Old Bailey) was built on the site of the prison.

Dartmoor
Dartmoor was first used for prisoners of war during the Napoleonic Wars and has served as a high-security, long-term prison ever since. The prison is miles from anywhere on a bleak Devon moor so if prisoners escape, they are usually recaptured quickly.

Devil's Island
France's worst criminals and political prisoners were sent to this prison off the coast of French Guiana from 1852 until 1938. Henri Charrière, known as Papillon, is one of the few inmates ever to escape. Conditions on the island were very harsh and many prisoners died of disease.

Alcatraz
This island in San Francisco Bay, California, USA, is often known as The Rock, but was originally called Isla de los Alcatraces (Isle of the Pelicans). It was first used as a military prison, but then became a prison for the country's most dangerous criminals, among them Al Capone. Robert Stroud, a bird expert who became famous as the Birdman of Alcatraz, spent many years there.

Sing Sing
This New York prison was named after the Sin Sinck Native Americans who originally lived there. It was built from 1825 to 1828, and from 1891 onwards many murderers were electrocuted in the electric chair at Sing Sing. In 1969 the prison was renamed Ossining Correctional Facility.

 # Science and crime detection
Modern detectives use a wide range of scientific techniques to help them identify and catch criminals.

Fingerprinting
No two humans have the same fingerprints – not even identical twins. Fingerprints have been used for more than 100 years to prove whether someone was at a crime scene or held a weapon. Experts dust areas for hidden prints, which can also be revealed under special lights or on contact with certain chemicals. Faint prints can be improved by laser image enhancement.

DNA testing
Detectives have long been able to identify any blood at the scene of a crime. Now forensic scientists use DNA testing or genetic fingerprinting to prove or disprove a suspect's connection with a crime. Everyone's DNA is unique and even the smallest samples – a single hair or a trace of saliva – can provide evidence.

Psychological profiling
Experts prepare profiles that suggest certain features of the killer, based on the nature of their murders. The profile may give likely age, background and habits. This builds a portrait of the criminal and helps detectives track him or her down.

Ballistics
All guns have a unique "fingerprint" – the marks made on a bullet as it leaves the barrel. Ballistics specialists examine these with microscopes and compare bullets used in crimes with those fired from a suspect's gun to find out whether they are identical.

Identikit
The Identikit system was developed in the USA in the 1940s by Hugh C. McDonald of the Los Angeles Police. It originally used transparent layers to build up a picture of a suspect based on witnesses' descriptions. Facial features, such as eye colour and hair styles, were laid over a basic face shape. Modern developments from this include Photofit and computerized E-fit (Electronic Facial Identification Technique).

Surveillance
Crime-fighters increasingly use electronic methods to spy on suspects. They can plant bugs (hidden microphones and video cameras) and intercept telephone calls and computer data.

A police control room with surveillance screens

 www.institutions.org.uk/prisons

Did you know that the first washing machine was made more than 300 years ago? Or that the first vacuum cleaner was so big it had to be pulled by a horse? Which country do you think produces the most oil and which relies most on nuclear power? Find all this information and much more on the following pages.

WORK
AND HOME

The first vacuum cleaner

In 1901, Englishman Hubert Cecil Booth invented the first successful vacuum cleaner. The machine worked well and was popular with rich people. It was also used in places such as Westminster Abbey, Buckingham Palace and Windsor Castle. Booth's cleaner was so large that it had to be pulled along by a horse, and six people were needed to operate it. The machines were only hired out, never sold.

The upright vacuum cleaner was invented by an American named James Murray Spangler in 1907. Spangler realized that his asthma was made worse by dust, and wanted to find a more effective way of sweeping. He made the first upright vacuum cleaner with the help of a pillowcase tied to a broom handle and an electrical pump. Spangler sold the patent to his cousin William H. Hoover, who improved the invention and started a very successful business selling vacuum cleaners.

Hoover advertisement

Amazing beds

One of the largest beds in the world is the Great Bed of Ware. It is 3.26m wide, 3.38m long and was made in about 1580. The bed is mentioned by Shakespeare in *Twelfth Night*. It is now in the Victoria and Albert Museum in London.

In 1882 an Indian maharajah had a bed made of solid silver. At each corner of the bed there was a life-sized statue of a naked woman holding a fan. When the maharajah lay on the bed, his weight started a mechanism that made the women wave their fans.

Great Bed of Ware

Fussy sleepers

British statesman Winston Churchill and American Benjamin Franklin always slept in rooms with two beds. They both liked to move into a fresh bed during the night. Charles Dickens always placed his bed north to south, and carried a pocket compass so that he could adjust it.

In the kitchen

The first washing machine
A washing machine was made in about 1677 by an Englishman named John Hoskin. Fellow Englishman William Bailey made a more efficient version in 1758. The first mass-produced washing machine was invented by American Alva J. Fisher in 1907, and was called the Thor.

The first microwave oven
The Raytheon Company in the USA began using microwave ovens in 1947 to cook food commercially. The idea came from one of their scientists, Percy Spencer. He had been standing near a microwave tube and noticed that a chocolate bar in his pocket had melted, although he had not felt any heat. The first home microwave appeared in 1952 and cost $1,295.

The first refrigerator
People used to pickle, smoke, dry and salt food so they could store it. During the 19th century some households began to use large boxes filled with blocks of ice, and the first electric fridge was made in 1913. It was called the Domelre (Domestic Electric Refrigerator) and was for home use, although it was very bulky. Refrigerators did not really become popular until after World War II, when the design was improved.

The first pop-up toaster
Charles Strite, a US mechanic, invented the pop-up toaster in 1919. There were toasting machines before then, but they had to be watched carefully all the time so the toast didn't burn. Strite worked out a way to put a timer and springs into the design. His first toasters were large machines, used by restaurants, but in 1926 he launched a smaller version called the Toastmaster.

www.geffrye-museum.org.uk/kidszone

Bath and toilet fact file

- Bathing was originally a group activity; the Greeks and Romans built large, luxurious bathhouses which were like modern health spas. During the Middle Ages communal bathing stopped.
- In the Middle Ages people used chamber pots which they emptied out of the window. In castles there would be a garderobe – a small cupboard with a hole that allowed waste out into the moat. But throwing waste out of windows into the street, or rivers that provided drinking water, spread disease. The worst epidemic was the Black Death during the 14th century, which killed about a quarter of the people in Europe.
- In the Middle Ages people stank and used perfume to cover up the smells. During the 16th and 17th centuries it was good manners for a gentleman to walk closest to the street when escorting a lady. This meant that he was more likely to be in the path of sewage as it was thrown into the street!
- In London a gigantic cesspit was built under 200,000 houses, and often overflowed into them. Cesspits in London were abolished in 1847 and every home had to have a lavatory. Sewage was still diverted into the River Thames, which resulted in the "Great Stink" in the summer of 1858 – the worst smell in the city's history.
- Many of Europe's major cities and the biggest cities in the USA started building sewers in the 19th century. Many of these early systems are still in use today.

Building a London sewer, 1862

- When running water was first piped into houses it rarely reached above the ground floor, so most people bathed in the kitchen, often in a tin bath in front of the fire. It was time-consuming and expensive to heat water, so people often shared bath water and bathed only once a week.
- Showers became popular towards the end of the 19th century as a more efficient alternative to baths, Throughout the 20th century shower design was improved, making the "stand up bath" an essential feature of the modern bathroom.

Toilets and toilet paper

- Before the invention of toilet paper, people improvised with many different things. The rich used wool or lace, but the poor used anything they could find, including wood shavings, grass, stone, sand, leaves, corn cobs, moss, seashells, water or snow, as well as their hands. Later people began to use newspapers or telephone directories as toilet paper.

- Chinese emperors used toilet paper in the 14th century, but the first commercial toilet paper was produced in 1857 by Joseph Gayetty, an American businessman. Gayetty's paper was sold as individual sheets with his name on them.

- Every person in the UK spends an average of $25.93 on toilet paper every year, compared with the average American's $19.46. The world average is $3.41 per person.

Home accidents

We think of our homes and gardens as safe places, but a surprising number of accidents are caused by everyday things. These UK figures record the number of people in a year who needed hospital treatment after accidents at home.

Accidents involving animals

Dogs	66,915
Cats	16,126
Bees and wasps	11,123
Rabbits, hamsters, etc	3,264
Wild birds	745
Pet birds	692
Snakes and other reptiles	426
Pet fish	106

Accidents with containers or packaging

Boxes (cardboard or wood)	8,764
Glass bottles	8,249
Plastic bottles	2,448
Corned beef tins	2,147
Plastic bags	2,111
Aerosols	1,348
Tubes	745
Ring pulls	621
Lollipop sticks	160
Paper bags	18

Accidents with sport or leisure equipment

Footballs and basketballs	13,695
Swings	6,528
Slides	5,801
Climbing frames	3,743
Bouncy castles	3,690
Rollerblades	2,874
Skateboards	2,643
Cricket bats	621
Cricket balls	461
Golf balls	355
Tennis racquets	337
Table tennis balls	142

Accidents involving clothing or personal effects

Trainers	60,830
Slippers	60,493
Jewellery	13,695
Socks, tights, etc	11,726
Wellington boots	4,364
Trousers	3,885
Shirts/T-shirts	1,472
Coats	1,401
Hairbrushes	1,224
Toothbrushes	763
False teeth	532

Valuable toys

Some wealthy collectors prize rare toys, especially those that are in good condition – in their original box, and never played with. These are just some of the toys that may have cost very little when they were made, but now sell for high prices.

- A Kämmer and Reinhardt doll was sold at Sotheby's, London on 8 February 1994 for £188,500 ($277,981).

- Titania's Palace, a doll's house with 2,000 items of furniture, was sold at Christie's, London in 1978 for £135,000 ($258,728).

- Dingley Hall, a doll's house dating from 1877, was sold at Christie's, London in 2003 for £124,750 ($211,938).

- A 1906 train set made by German toymaker Märklin was sold at Christie's, London in 2001 for £113,750 ($165,290).

- "Teddy Girl" is a teddy bear made by the German manufacturer Steiff in 1904. It was sold at Christie's, London on 5 December 1994 for a record £110,000 ($171,600). A Japanese collector named Yoshiro Sekiguchi bought the bear for his teddy bear museum near Tokyo.

- A black mohair Steiff teddy bear, made in about 1912, was sold at Christie's, London in 2000 for £91,750 ($132,157). It was one of only 494 black Steiff bears made as a mark of respect after the sinking of the *Titanic*. They are known as "mourning teddies".

- A tinplate clockwork motorcycle with Mickey Mouse and Minnie from about 1930, was sold at Christie's, London in 1997 for £51,000 ($83,650).

- A Machine Man robot, made by Japanese manufacturer Masudaya in about 1955, sold at Sotheby's, New York in 1996 for $42,550 (£25,891).

"Teddy Girl" teddy bear made in 1904

Birth of Barbie

The first Barbie doll appeared in February 1959. It was made by Ruth and Elliot Handler, co-founders of American toy manufacturers Mattel, and they named the doll after their daughter Barbara. The doll was dressed in a black and white striped swimsuit, with sunglasses, high heels and gold hoop earrings. In the first year a total of 351,000 Barbies were sold at $3 each, and the doll went on to become one of the bestselling toys of all time.

The first Barbie dolls in the Barbie Museum, Palo Alto, California

Top toy-buying countries

The amount spent on toys worldwide is about $11 (£6) a year for every person on the planet, or an average of $32 (£18) for every child. There are huge differences between countries. In North America people spend an average of $328 each. Europeans spend $100 and in Africa, they spend only $2.

	Country	$ per person	Total $
1	USA	120.9	35,115,300,000
2	Japan	69.3	8,811,570,000
3	UK	112.5	6,758,620,000
4	Germany	63.3	5,213,810,000
5	France	70.8	4,259,480,000
	World total		**69,493,000,000**

Scrabble

Scrabble was invented in the USA during the 1930s by an unemployed architect named Alfred Mosher Butts. First he called it Lexiko, then It and Criss-Cross, before hitting on the name Scrabble. Well over 100 million sets have been sold in more than 130 countries. The numbers of letters included vary according to the language. In Dutch, for example, there are 18 Es, 10 Ns and two Js. The Slovak version has 41 different letters – more than any other version.

Monopoly®

Monopoly was invented in 1934 by an unemployed engineer called Charles Darrow, who lived in Philadelphia, USA. In his first version of the game he used street names from Atlantic City in New Jersey because he dreamed of going there, but could not afford the fare. The game was so successful that Darrow became a millionaire and spent the rest of his life travelling and growing rare orchids. Monopoly was soon adapted for other countries, using street names from their main cities. The British version, for example, uses London place names and Mayfair is the most expensive street. There are also versions of Monopoly based on popular TV series, such as *The Simpsons*. Parkers, the US manufacturers of the game, print more Monopoly money than the US Treasury prints dollars.

Monopoly® around the world

Country	City*	Mayfair becomes
Australia	Canberra + state capitals	Kings Avenue
Canada	Vancouver, etc	Robson Street
China	Hong Kong	Victoria Peak
Egypt	Cairo	Shari Qasr El Nil
France	Paris	Rue de la Paix
Germany	Munich	Schlossallee
Ireland	Dublin	Shrewsbury Road
Netherlands	Amsterdam	Kalverstraat
New Zealand	Auckland	Queen Street
Portugal	Lisbon	Rossio
Russia	Moscow	Arbat
Singapore	Singapore	Queen Astrid Park
South Africa	Johannesburg	Eloff Street/Eloffstraat
Spain	Madrid	Paseo Del Prado
Switzerland	Zurich, etc	Paradeplatz
US	Atlantic City	Boardwalk

* Some feature streets from more than one city

Russian Monopoly board

Playing cards

- Playing cards were invented in China some time before AD 969.

- Cards were first used in Europe in the 12th–13th centuries and were common in France by 1254.

- Tarot cards, used in fortune-telling, were introduced in 14th-century Italy and France.

- Playing cards were printed from woodblocks in Germany by 1402 – before book printing was invented.

- The four suits (hearts, clubs, spades and diamonds) were created in France in about 1440.

- The most expensive deck of cards ever sold was hand-painted in the Netherlands in 1470–80. It was auctioned for £99,000 ($143,104) at Sotheby's, London, in 1983, and is now in the Metropolitan Museum, New York.

- Cribbage (a game that uses cards and a peg board) was probably invented in England in the early 17th century by English poet Sir John Suckling. He adapted it from a traditional game called Noddy and made a fortune by challenging people to play against him.

Early 19th-century playing cards

Money facts

The first coins
Coins made from gold and silver were used in Lydia, an ancient Middle Eastern kingdom, in about 687–652 BC. The coins were known as staters.

Largest coins
Swedish 10-daler copper coins (made in 1644) weighed 19.71kg.

Smallest coins
The silver quarter-jawa was made in Nepal in about 1740 and weighed only 0.002g. You would need half a million of them to equal a kilogram.

Most coins made
The US Mint makes more than 12 billion coins every year. Almost 7 billion of them are 1 cent coins. There are nearly 25 billion UK coins in circulation, worth a total of over £3 billion.

Banknotes
Paper money was first made in China in the 13th century. The first European notes were made in Sweden in 1548. Banknotes were issued in America in 1690 and in England in 1695.

Largest banknotes
One-guan Chinese notes from the late 14th century measured 22.8 x 33cm – bigger than a page of this book.

Smallest banknotes
Romanian 10-bani notes of 1917 had a printed area of just 27.5 x 38mm, which is not much bigger than a postage stamp.

Cheques
The first cheque was issued in London on 22 April 1659. It was for £10 and made payable to the bearer by Nicholas Vanacker. It was drawn on the bank of Clayton & Morris. The original cheque was sold for £1,300 at Sotheby's, London in 1976.

Credit cards
The first credit card was invented by Frank X. McNamara in the USA and issued in 1950 by Diner's Club. Holograms were first used for security on Visa cards in the US in 1984. Smart cards (cards with built-in microchips) were introduced in France in 1975. There are about 120 million credit and debit cards in the UK, about four for each adult.

Travellers' cheques
The first were issued by American Express in the USA as early as 1891.

ATM
The world's first ATM (Automated Teller Machine, or cashpoint) began operation on 27 June 1967 at Barclays Bank, Enfield, London.

Euro
The new European currency was introduced in 1999 and was taken up by most European Union countries on 1 January 2002.

US $20 gold coins

British Imperial State Crown

Diamond fact file

- The weight of diamonds is measured in carats. The word comes from carob which is a bean that grows on the *Ceratonia siliqua* tree. The bean has an amazingly consistent weight of 0.2g. There are five carats to a gram and about 142 carats to the ounce.

- Fewer than 1,000 rough diamonds weighing more than 100 carats have ever been found.

- The first ever reference to diamonds is in the Bible in Exodus xxviii.18 and xxxix.11. It mentions a diamond mounted on a priest's breastplate.

- In 1796, Smithson Tennant (1761–1815), a British scientist, was the first person to show that diamonds are made of carbon. The diamond is the only gem in the world made of a single element.

- Diamonds are 180 times harder than emeralds.

- Diamonds melt at 6,900°C, which is two and a half times the temperature needed to melt steel.

- Diamonds come from a rock called kimberlite. About 200 tonnes of kimberlite are mined for every carat of polished diamond.

- The largest diamond ever found is called the Cullinan after Thomas Cullinan, who was president of the famous diamond company De Beers. The stone weighed 3,106 carats (621g) and was found in South Africa in about 1905. It was presented to King Edward VII, who had it cut to make 105 separate diamonds. One of the largest of these weighs 317.4 carats and is set in the British Imperial State Crown.

What's a million?

If you earned £100 (or $100) a week, it would take you 192 years to earn £1 million/$1 million.

The UK no longer has £1 notes, but £1 million in £1 coins would weigh 9.5 tonnes. If they were put in a line edge to edge they would stretch 225km. £1 million in 1p coins would weigh 356 tonnes. $1 million in $1 bills would weigh exactly 1 tonne. $1 million in one-cent coins would weigh 250 tonnes.

Gold mask of Tutankhamen

Golden treasures

Tutankhamen's mask

Tutankhamen was king of Ancient Egypt in the 14th century BC. In 1923 fabulous treasures were found in his tomb by archaeologist Howard Carter. They are now in the Cairo Museum, Egypt. They include a magnificent gold mask, which weighs 10.23kg. It was found inside a solid gold coffin weighing 110.4kg.

Buddha statue

A 15th-century statue of Buddha is the largest gold object in the world. It is in the Wat Traimit temple, Bangkok, Thailand, stands 3m tall and weighs 5.5 tonnes.

Gold salt cellar

This was made by Benvenuto Cellini for Francis I of France in about 1540. It is made of solid gold, elaborately decorated, and is one of the greatest works of the goldsmith's art. It is now in the Kunsthistorisches Museum, Vienna.

Fort Knox

The vaults of Fort Knox, Kentucky, USA, contain the largest amount of gold in one place anywhere in the world. They hold more than half the country's total reserves – mostly in gold bars.

Golden wonder

Probably less than 150,000 tonnes of gold have ever been mined. If it were made into one cube, it would have sides measuring 19.8m and fill an area only slightly bigger than a tennis court. If all the gold was stretched into a wire it would circle the Earth nine million times.

Gold fact file

- People have prized gold since ancient times. It is easy to work with and makes beautiful objects that do not corrode. Even coins and jewellery that have been buried for thousands of years are as bright as the day they were made.

- Gold is rare – it is only the 73rd commonest element in Earth's crust. There are more than ten million tonnes of gold in the world's seas, but it would cost too much to get it out.

- Gold is very heavy. A cup of gold would weigh 19.3 times as much as the same cup filled with water.

- Gold can be stretched into very thin wire. Just one gram of gold makes a wire 2.4km long and 5 microns (5 millionths of a metre) thick.

- More than 90 per cent of all the gold mined in the past 6,000 years has been extracted since 1848.

- Gold is used for making coins and jewellery. It is also used in electronics, dentistry and for making special products such as the coating on astronauts' visors that protects them against harmful radiation.

- The largest gold nugget ever was found at Moliagul, Australia, in 1869. It is known as Welcome Stranger and weighs 70.92kg.

- Gold bars like those seen in films about bank robberies are known as "London Good Delivery Bars". They measure 17.8 x 8.2 x 4.4cm and weigh 12.5kg, about six times as much as an average house brick.

Top gold producers

Country	2003 production (tonnes)
1 South Africa	375.8
2 USA	285.2
3 Australia	283.6
4 China	213.1
World total	**2,593.1**

Countries with the most gold

Gold reserves are the amount of gold held by the government in each country – usually far more than the amount owned by any individuals. The price of gold varies a great deal, but recently has been about £6,800 a kilo.

Country	Gold reserves 2005 (tonnes)
1 USA	8,135.1
2 Germany	3,433.2
3 France	2,993.4
4 Italy	2,451.8
5 Switzerland	1,347.1
UK	*312.3*
World total	**31,587.1**

www.gold.org

Top energy users

These countries guzzle more energy than any others in the world. The figures below show the amount of gas, coal or other power needed to produce the same amount of energy as a tonne of oil. This is the standard way of comparing energy produced and consumed from different sources.

Energy consumption 2003

Country	Oil	Gas	Coal	Nuclear	HEP	Total
USA	914.3	566.8	573.9	181.9	60.9	2297.8
China	275.2	29.5	799.7	9.8	64	1178.3
Russia	124.7	365.2	111.3	34.0	35.6	670.8
Japan	248.7	68.9	112.2	52.2	22.8	504.8
Germany	125.1	77.0	87.1	37.3	5.7	332.2
India	113.3	27.1	185.3	4.1	15.6	345.3
Canada	96.4	78.7	31.0	16.8	68.6	291.4
France	94.2	39.4	12.4	99.8	14.8	260.6
UK	76.8	85.7	39.1	20.1	1.3	223.2
World total	**3636.6**	**2331.9**	**2578.4**	**598.8**	**595.4**	**9741.1**

Oil well pump in Louisiana, USA

Top coal producers

Country	2003 production (tonnes oil equivalent)
1 China	842,600,000
2 USA	551,300,000
3 Australia	188,700,000
4 India	172,700,000
5 South Africa	134,600,000
UK	*17,200,000*
World total	**2,518,700,000**

Top oil producers

Country	2003 production (tonnes)
1 Saudi Arabia	474,800,000
2 Russia	421,400,000
3 USA	341,100,000
4 Iran	190,100,000
5 Mexico	188,800,000
UK	*105,600,000*
World total	**3,697,000,000**

Top natural gas producers

Country	2003 production (tonnes oil equivalent)
1 Russia	578,600,000
2 USA	549,500,000
3 Canada	180,500,000
4 UK	102,700,000
5 Algeria	82,800,00
World total	**2,618,500,000**

Nuclear power

The following countries are those that rely most on nuclear power.

Country	Nuclear electricity as percentage of total energy (2003)
1 Lithuania	79.9
2 France	77.1
3 Slovakia	57.4
4 Belgium	55.5
5 Sweden	49.6
UK	*23.7*
USA	*19.9*
World average	**16.0**

Hydroelectricity

Country	2003 production (% of world total)
1 Brazil	11.6
2 Canada	11.5
3 China	10.8
4 USA	10.2
5 Russia	6.0
UK	*0.2*

Wind farm in California, USA

 # How much power?

All electrical appliances use energy. The amount depends on their size and purpose: an electric heater might use ten times as much energy as a single light bulb. The energy an appliance uses is measured in watts. These are named in honour of Scottish engineer James Watt (1736–1819), who first worked out how to measure energy.

Appliance	Watts
Air conditioner	2500–3000
Central heating pump	800
Coffee percolator	500–750
Computer	400
Cooker	10,000
Deep freeze	1000–2000
Dishwasher	2000–2500
Electric blanket	50–150
Electric kettle	2200–3000
Electric razor	6
Fan	50–100
Fluorescent light	60
Food mixer	450
Hair dryer	1000–1500
Iron	1000–1500
Light bulb	100
Microwave oven	1500
Photocopier	1500
Printer	350
Radiator (oil filled)	1000–2000
Radio, CD player, etc	40–200
Refrigerator	1000
Sewing machine	100
Toaster	750–1500
Tumble dryer	2400
TV (colour)	250
Vacuum cleaner	800–1400
Washing machine	3000–4000

 # The world's energy sources

A century ago, few homes had electricity and cars were a rare sight. Today, much of the world's energy is turned into electricity for homes, to power equipment in factories, and to fuel our cars, buses, aircraft and other transport. These are some of the main sources of this energy.

Oil

The first oil wells were drilled less than 150 years ago but oil, and petroleum which comes from it, has become the most important energy source. Almost 40 per cent of the world's energy supply comes from oil. Most oil is found in the Middle East and has to be taken by tankers or pipelines to places where it is used around the world.

Coal

Coal is the world's second most important source of energy. It makes up about 27 per cent of the total. Coal is a fossil fuel and is made from plants that lived and died in swamps 300 million years ago. The world's coal reserves will last about another 192 years. This is nearly three times as long as gas (67 years) and almost five times as long as oil (41 years).

Natural gas

The third main source of power comes from gas that occurs naturally beneath the Earth's surface. It accounts for 23 per cent of the world total. The gas is mainly methane, with some ethane, propane and other gases. It is collected and taken to where it is needed by pipelines, and has replaced the highly polluting coal gas that used to be made by burning coal.

Nuclear power

The fourth most important power source (7% of the world total) is nuclear power. A nuclear reaction releases huge amounts of heat which in turn heats water or other liquid and drives a turbine to produce electricity. The first nuclear power station to produce electricity for public use was Calder Hall, UK, which opened in 1956.

Hydropower

Flowing water has been used as a power source since the Middle Ages and water mills were once a common sight. Modern hydropower uses water flowing through turbines in dams to produce electricity.

Solar energy

The Sun's warmth can be stored to produce energy. Mirrors and glass were used to collect heat in ancient times, but the first houses to use solar heating were not built until 1955. Solar energy is becoming more popular and the technology is getting better all the time. The world's largest solar energy generating plants are in the Mohave Desert, California, USA. They are designed to use the Sun's rays to heat oil which drives a generator. It creates enough electricity for a small town.

Wind energy

Windmills were used in Persia (now Iran) in the 7th century, and in Europe since the 12th century, but they were first used for making electricity in the late 19th century. Today, California, USA, is the world's leading area for wind-generated electricity. Tehachapi Wind Resource, California, produces as much wind energy as the rest of the USA combined.

Tidal energy

Using waves and marine currents to release energy is expensive and as yet small-scale. The first and largest tidal power station on the Rance river, St Malo, France was completed in 1967. It can produce enough energy every year to supply power to 120,000 households.

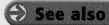 ## See also

Pollution fact file: page 70

The earliest humans lived in caves or rough shelters. About 10,000 years ago people began to build places in which to live, worship and work. Some of the world's most famous buildings are centuries old. Today's architects strive to build structures that are bigger, taller and more impressive than ever.

BUILDINGS
AND
STRUCTURES

Western architecture

Below are the main styles of Western architecture, from prehistory to the present day and famous examples of each. Styles did not stop and start abruptly; one style blended into another, so all dates are approximate. Before the Renaissance most buildings had several architects or the architect's name was not recorded. The names of the architects of more recent buildings are given in brackets.

Prehistoric
Wooden post buildings, simple stone buildings, stone circles
• Stonehenge, Wiltshire, UK

Ancient 3000–337 BC
Ancient Egyptian pyramids, tombs and temples
• Great Pyramid, Egypt

Etruscan 700–200 BC
• Alatri Temple, Villa Giulia, Rome, Italy

Greek 600–100 BC
• Parthenon, Athens, Greece

Roman 100 BC–AD 370
• The Baths of Caracalla, Rome, Italy
• The Pantheon, Rome, Italy
• The Colosseum, Rome, Italy
• Maison Carrée, Nîmes, France

Byzantine 330–1450
• Hagia Sophia, Istanbul, Turkey
• St Mark's, Venice, Italy

Pre-Columbian 300–1540
Mayan, Aztec, Inca South and Central American
• Mayan temples at Tikal, Guatemala

Carolingian 751–987
• Chapel Palatine (now part of cathedral), Aachen, Germany

Romanesque 800 to 1200
• St James, Santiago de Compostela, Spain
• Tournai Cathedral, Belgium

Moorish/Islamic from 8th century
• Great Mosque, Cordoba, Spain

Norman 1045–1180
• Durham Cathedral, Durham, UK
• Ely Cathedral, Ely, UK

Gothic 1140–1534
• Cologne Cathedral, Cologne, Germany
• Notre Dame Cathedral, Paris, France
• Chartres Cathedral, Chartres, France
• Salisbury Cathedral, Salisbury, UK

Greek
The Parthenon, Athens, Greece, 447–438 BC. Doric is the first and simplest classical Greek building style and this is the finest Doric building still standing. When it was first built the Parthenon was decorated with marble sculptures painted in bright colours. Some of these, known as the Elgin Marbles, were removed and are now displayed in the British Museum, London.

Gothic
Chartres Cathedral, Chartres, France, 1194–1220. Chartres is one of the most famous and beautiful cathedrals in the world. It also contains some of the best medieval sculpture and stained glass. The cathedral has 176 windows, many of which contain the original medieval glass.

Renaissance 1400–1600
• Hampton Court Palace, London, UK
• Little Moreton Hall, Cheshire, UK
• Florence Cathedral, Florence, Italy (Filippo Brunelleschi)
• Ducal Palace, Urbino, Italy (Luciano Laurana)
• Château de Chambord, France (Domenico da Cortona)

Baroque 1585–1750
• St Paul's Cathedral, London, UK (Sir Christopher Wren)
• Versailles Palace, France (Louis Le Vau and Jules Hardouin Mansart)
• Greenwich Hospital (Royal Naval College), London, UK (Inigo Jones and Sir Christopher Wren)
• Blenheim Palace, Oxfordshire, UK (Sir John Vanbrugh)

American Colonial 1600–1780
• Governor's Palace, Williamsburg, Virginia, USA (rebuilt 1930)

Jacobean 1618–25
• Ham House, Twickenham, Middlesex, UK
• Blickling Hall, Norfolk, UK

➔ See also
Mysterious places: page 174

Rococo 1650–1790

- Vierzehnheiligen Church, Banz, Germany (Johann Balthasar Neumann

Georgian 1714–1837

- The Circus, Bath, UK (John Wood, Sr and Jr)
- Charlotte Square, Edinburgh, UK (Robert Adam)

Neoclassical/Federalist US 1750–1880

- Panthéon, Paris, France (Germain Soufflot)
- Brighton Pavilion, Brighton, UK (John Nash)
- University of Virginia, Charlottesville, Virginia, USA (Thomas Jefferson)

Victorian 1837–1901

- Houses of Parliament, London, UK (Sir Charles Barry and A.W.N. Pugin)
- Crystal Palace, London, UK (Joseph Paxton)
- American Surety Building, New York, USA (Bruce Price)

Arts and Crafts 1860–1900

- The Red House, Kent, UK (Philip Webb)

Art Deco

Chrysler Building, New York, USA, 1930. The Chrysler is one of the best-known art deco buildings. The gleaming metal spire was based on the Chrysler cars of the time and skyscrapers are still a key feature of the New York skyline.

Art Nouveau 1890–1905

- Glasgow Art School, Glasgow, UK (Charles Rennie Macintosh)
- Paris Metro stations (Hector Guimard)
- La Sagrada Familia, Barcelona, Spain (Antonio Gaudí)
- Secession Building, Vienna, Austria (Joseph Maria Olbrich)

Art Deco 1925–35

- Chrysler Building, New York, USA (William Van Alen)

Bauhaus 1919–37

- Bauhaus, Dessau, Germany (Walter Gropius)

International Modernism 1920–50

- Fallingwater, Pennsylvania, USA (Frank Lloyd Wright)

Brutalism 1950s

- Unité d'Habitation, Marseilles, France (Le Corbusier)
- Seagram Building, New York, USA (Mies van der Rohe)

High-tech

Swiss Re Building (The Gherkin), London, 2004. This building is London's first eco-friendly skyscraper. Its shape allows maximum natural light and ventilation inside so it uses only half the amount of energy consumed by a normal office block.

High-Tech 1970s–

- Centre Georges Pompidou, Paris, France (Richard Rogers and Renzo Piano)
- Swiss Re Building (The Gherkin), London, UK (Norman Foster)

Post–Modern 1970s

- Staatsgalerie, Stuttgart, Germany (James Stirling)

Deconstruction 1990s–

- Guggenheim Museum, Bilbao, Spain (Frank Gehry)

Japanese architecture

Eastern countries, such as Japan, had their own strong traditions of architecture. The Katsura Palace in Kyoto was built in the early 17th century, at the time of baroque and Jacobean architecture in Europe. It is a simple, elegant building and one of the most perfect examples of traditional Japanese architecture.

American Colonial

Governor's Palace, Williamsburg, Virginia, USA, 1722. European settlers in the New World used architectural ideas from their home countries. The historic district of Williamsburg in Virginia has some of the most famous colonial buildings, dating from before the War of American Independence. The Governor's Palace is one of the finest.

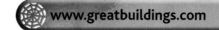
www.greatbuildings.com

Great religious buildings

The world's major religions, including Christianity, Islam, Judaism, Buddhism, Hinduism and Sikhism, have inspired many of the world's greatest buildings. Some are shrines to the religion's founders. Others are places of pilgrimage. Several are among the world's largest structures.

Tallest churches

Church/location	Year completed	Height m
1 Chicago Methodist Temple*, Chicago, USA	1924	173
2 Ulm Cathedral, Ulm, Germany	1890	161
3 Notre Dame de la Paix, Yamoussoukro, Côte d'Ivoire	1989	158
4 Cologne Cathedral, Cologne, Germany	1880	156
5 Rouen Cathedral, Rouen, France	1876	148

* Built on top of a 25-storey 100m building

- The UK's tallest church is Salisbury cathedral, built in 1310. Its spire measures 123m. The height to the top of the dome of St Paul's Cathedral, London (completed in 1710) is 112m.

- Spanish architect Antonio Gaudi's Sagrada Familia cathedral in Barcelona, Spain, was begun in 1883, but is not yet completed. Its tallest spires are planned to reach 170m.

Sagrada Familia, Barcelona

Largest churches
Salt Lake Temple, Utah, USA (1893) has a floor area of 23,506sq m. St Peter's in the Vatican (1612), the centre of the Roman Catholic church, is 218.7m long and covers an area of 23,000sq m. It was the largest Christian cathedral in the world until 1989, when it was overtaken by the 30,000sq m basilica in Yamoussoukro, Côte d'Ivoire.

Tallest mosques
The Great Hassan II Mosque, Casablanca, Morocco (1993) is the tallest mosque at 210m. The Saddam Mosque, Baghdad, Iraq was designed to be the largest in the Middle East, with a record-breaking 280m minaret, but it has not been completed.

Largest mosque
The Masjid al Haram is the holy mosque of Makkah (formerly Mecca), the birthplace of the prophet Muhammad. Millions of Muslim pilgrims visit the mosque every year. The mosque covers 82,000sq m and the surrounding yards cover another 985,000sq m. Together they can accommodate up to 1.2 million worshippers.

Largest Buddhist temple
The largest Buddhist temple in the world is Borobudur (many Buddhas), near Yogyakarta, Java, Indonesia. It was built between AD 750 and 842. The temple covers 60,000sq m and contains 56,634cu m of stone.

Largest Hindu temple
Angkor Wat, Cambodia, built between 879 and 1191, is the largest religious structure in the world. The complex of buildings inside its walls and moat covers 83,110sq m.

Largest synagogue
The world's largest synagogue is Temple Emanu-El, New York City, USA. It opened in 1929 and occupies an area of 3,523sq m.

Lighthouses

Tallest in the world
The biggest lighthouse ever built was the Pharos of Alexandria, which stood 124m tall. It was one of the Seven Wonders of the world. The world's tallest lighthouse today is in Yamashita Park, Yokohama, Japan, and is 106m tall.

Tallest in the UK
The Bishop Rock lighthouse off the Scilly Isles, built in 1858, is 49m tall and has a helipad on top. The equally tall Eddystone lighthouse, off Plymouth, was originally made of wood. The one there now is the fifth on the site, and was opened in 1882.

Tallest in the US
The Cape Hatteras lighthouse in North Carolina was built in 1870. It is the tallest in the USA at 59.7m. The lighthouse was being eroded by the sea so between 1999 and 2000 the entire 2,540-tonne building was moved 884m inland, very slowly, on tracks.

→ See also

Holy places: page 162

Domes and roofs

Building	Year completed	Diameter m
Wembley Stadium, London	2006	315
When completed, the single-span roof (supported only at the sides) will measure 315m, the largest in the world.		
Millennium Dome, Greenwich, London	1999	358
The span is supported by steel masts that project through the dome.		
Georgia Superdome, Atlanta, Georgia, USA,	1992	256
The world's largest cable-supported fabric roof		
Houston Astrodome, Houston, Texas, USA	1966	
exterior		216
interior		196
Louisiana Superdome, New Orleans, Louisiana, USA	1975	207
SkyDome, Toronto, Canada	1989	205
The world's largest retractable roof		
Notre Dame de la Paix, Yamoussoukro, Côte d'Ivoire	1989	90
Royal Albert Hall, London	1871	68
South Pole Scientific Station, Antarctic	1972	50
Duomo, Florence, Italy	1434	45.5
Pantheon, Rome, Italy	AD 123	43.3
British Museum, London	1857	43
St Peter's, Vatican City	1626	42
Reichstag, Berlin, Germany	1999	40
St Paul's Cathedral, London	1710	33
Hagia Sophia, Istanbul, Turkey	537	31
Capitol, Washington DC, USA	1824	29
Taj Mahal, Agra, India	1641	17.7

Florence Cathedral, usually known as the Duomo

Obelisks and columns

Obelisks are stone columns that were made in Ancient Egypt almost 4,000 years ago. Some were taken away as trophies by invading armies and are now in cities such as Rome, London, Paris, New York and Istanbul. More recently, people have built memorials based on the design of obelisks.

- A column commemorating the battle of San Jacinto (1836) near Houston, Texas, USA, is the world's tallest monument at 174m. It was completed in 1939.

- The Washington Monument, Washington DC, USA, was completed in 1884. It is 169m tall, made of 36,491 stone blocks on an iron frame and weighs 82,421 tonnes. It was the world's tallest structure for five years until it was overtaken by the Eiffel Tower in 1889.

- The Wellington Monument in Dublin, Ireland is a stone obelisk made to celebrate the victories of the Duke of Wellington. It was completed in 1861 and is Europe's tallest obelisk at 63m.

- The Monument in London commemorates the Great Fire of London in 1666. It was built in 1667 and is 62m tall.

- Nelson's Column in Trafalgar Square, London, was completed in 1842 to celebrate Britain's great naval commander. The column is 44m high and has a 5m statue of Nelson on top.

- The tallest Egyptian obelisk is in the Piazza San Giovanni in Laterano, Rome, Italy. It measures 32m. The tallest still in Egypt is in Karnak and is 30m tall. The Ancient Egyptian obelisk in New York is 22m and the London obelisk, Cleopatra's Needle, is 21m.

Modern pyramids

The Ancient Egyptian pyramids are the best known, but this style of building has also been used in modern times.

"Mad Jack" Fuller's tomb, Brightling, East Sussex
Jack Fuller (1757–1834), an eccentric landowner and Member of Parliament, had his own 8m pyramid tomb built in 1811. There is a legend that his body is seated inside, wearing a top hat!

Louvre Museum Pyramid, Paris, France (below)
The Chinese-born American architect I. M. Pei designed the 22m glass pyramid which was built in 1989 as the main entrance to the Louvre Museum, Paris, France.

Christa McAuliffe Planetarium, Concord, New Hampshire, USA
Christa McAuliffe was killed in the *Challenger* space shuttle disaster. The pyramid-shaped planetarium named after her opened in 1990.

Luxor Hotel and Casino, Las Vegas, Nevada, USA
This hotel was opened in 1993 at a cost of $375 million. It is 107m tall and its entrance is guarded by a sphinx that shoots laser beams from its eyes.

Rainforest Pyramid, Galveston, Texas, USA
This 38m-tall pyramid was completed in 1993 and houses one of the world's largest indoor rainforests.

Rock and Roll Hall of Fame, Cleveland, Ohio, USA
The museum, designed by I.M. Pei, architect of the Louvre Pyramid, opened in 1998.

Tallest skyscrapers over the last 100 years

New York's 119.2m Park Row Building was the tallest office or apartment building in the world when it was completed in 1899. Since then it has been overtaken many times by the buildings on this list. Today, the tallest buildings that people live or work in, such as the Sears Tower and Petronas Towers, are more than 3.5 times the size of Park Row.

Building	Year completed	Floors	Height m*
1 Singer Building, New York, USA†	1908	47	186.6
2 Metropolitan Life, New York, USA	1909	50	213.4
3 Woolworth Building, New York, USA	1913	57	241.4
4 The Trump Building (formerly 40 Wall Street), New York, USA	1930	70	282.5
5 Chrysler Building, New York, USA	1930	77	318.8
6 Empire State Building, New York, USA	1931	102	381.0
7 One World Trade Center, New York, USA#	1972	110	417.0
8 Sears Tower, Chicago, USA	1974	108	442.0
9 Petronas Towers, Kuala Lumpur, Malaysia	1998	88	451.9
10 Taipei 101, Taipei, Taiwan	2004	101	509.0

* Excluding masts, etc † Demolished 1970 # Destroyed in terrorist attack of 11 September 2001

The Eiffel Tower

The Eiffel Tower in Paris, France, was built as a temporary structure for the Universal Exhibition held in Paris in 1889. The tower was so popular that it has been there ever since.

- Engineer Gustave Eiffel (1832–1923) also built the framework of the Statue of Liberty. A workforce of 300 steelworkers completed the tower in two years, two months and five days.

- The Eiffel Tower contains 18,038 pieces of steel, weighing a total of 7,175 tonnes. They are connected by 2.5 million rivets.

- The tower's 220,000sq m of surfaces are hand-painted every ten years (last in 2003) with 60 tonnes of paint.

- The tower is 300.5m tall – 320.8m with its antenna – but it can expand or shrink by up to 15cm depending on how hot or cold it is. It was the world's tallest structure until the Chrysler Building in New York overtook it in 1930.

- The tower is lit by 352 1,000-watt projectors and 20,000 lights (installed in 2003). These are switched on after dusk for the first ten minutes of every hour.

- More than 200 million people have visited the tower. Most take the lifts, although there are 1,665 steps for the very energetic. It also attracts publicity-seeking climbers. Birdmen, parachutists and even cyclists have made descents – some of them fatal.

- The Eiffel Tower features in many films, including the James Bond film *A View to a Kill* (1985).

Eiffel Tower, Paris

Tallest structure

The world's tallest free-standing structure is the CN Tower in Toronto, Canada. It measures a mighty 553.33m to the tip of its antenna. There are taller masts, but they are supported with guy wires. The CN Tower also has the world's highest graffiti. It was painted – with permission – in 1976 by 20,000 children before the antenna was lifted into position by helicopter.

The Empire State Building

New York's tallest building is the Empire State Building, which stands on Fifth Avenue, New York, between 33rd Street and 34th Street. It was built on the site of the Waldorf-Astoria Hotel and took 410 days at a rate of 4½ floors a week to complete. The building was opened on 1 May 1931 by remote control, when President Herbert Hoover pressed a button in Washington DC.

The Empire State Building towers 381m above ground – and measures 443.2m to the top of the TV tower. A further 16.7m is below ground. The spire on top was designed as an airship mooring mast, but after a German airship, the *Hindenburg*, burned at its mooring mast in New Jersey in 1937, the mast was never used. For more than 40 years, the Empire State held the record as the world's tallest office or apartment building, until the twin towers of the World Trade Center were completed. Since their destruction in 2001, it is once again New York's tallest. More than 2.5 million tourists a year go up to the observatories on the 86th and 102nd floors. On a clear day you can see 129km from the 102nd floor.

- The workforce – 3,400 at its peak – took a total of seven million man-hours to complete the Empire State Building.
- The cost was $40,948,900 including the land (the building cost only $24,718,000).
- The building's weight is 331,122 tonnes. This includes a 54,431-tonne steel frame, 10 million bricks faced in limestone and 662 tonnes of aluminium and stainless steel.
- The Empire State is served by 73 lifts and contains 3,194,547 light bulbs, 80km of radiator pipes and 113km of water pipes.
- The lightning conductor was struck 68 times in the building's first ten years.
- In 2003 Australian runner Paul Crake broke his own record for racing up the 1575 steps to the 86th floor in 9 minutes 33 seconds.
- On 28 July 1945, a B-25 bomber crashed in fog between the building's 78th and 79th floors, killing the pilot and 13 other people. It happened on a Saturday so most offices were empty, or the casualties would have been higher.
- The building's coloured lights are changed for seasonal celebrations. They are red, white and blue on Independence Day and green on St Patrick's Day. The lights are turned off when birds are migrating to avoid confusing them.
- On St Valentine's Day, couples can marry on the 80th floor.

Empire State Building, New York

→ See also

Cities of the World: pages 118–19

Cities with most skyscrapers

City	Skyscrapers*
1 Hong Kong, China	182
= New York City, USA	182
3 Chicago, USA	83
4 Tokyo, Japan	55
5 Shanghai, China	52

* Completed buildings of more than 152m

Taller and taller

The world's tallest building is the Taipei 101 in Taipei, Taiwan's capital city. It is so-called because it has 101 storeys above ground level. Some experts consider that its spire should not be included in its total height, but international rules count all parts of a skyscraper except masts, antennae and flagpoles. So this building qualifies as the tallest. It also has the highest occupied floor of any building.

The building is based on the design of a traditional Chinese pagoda and has double-decker lifts. Two of these are the fastest lifts ever built, and travel at 1,010m a minute. On Christmas Day 2004 French "Spiderman" Alain Robert climbed up the outside of the building. It took him four hours to reach its 509-m tip.

Famous bridges

Pont du Gard
This Roman bridge in the South of France was built more than 2,000 years ago. It is an aqueduct – a bridge built to carry water or a canal across a valley.

Pont d'Avignon, France
This bridge was built in the 12th century. It was made famous by the song "Sur le Pont d'Avignon" (On Avignon Bridge).

Bridge of Sighs, Venice, Italy
The Bridge of Sighs was designed in 1560. It connects the Doge's Palace with the city jail, and prisoners who had been sentenced to death had to cross the bridge to reach the jail. Its name is said to come from their sighs of despair.

Pont Neuf, Paris, France
Pont Neuf was completed in 1604. The bridge is in two halves and links the Right and Left Banks of the River Seine to Ile de la Cité, the island on which Notre Dame cathedral is built.

Kintai-Kyo Bridge, Iwakuni, Japan
This wooden arch bridge was built across the Nishiki River in 1673. It has been damaged and rebuilt many times.

Iron Bridge, Shropshire
The Iron Bridge was completed in 1781 and was the first bridge built of iron.

Tower Bridge, London
Tower Bridge was completed in 1894. It opens and lifts in the middle to allow tall ships to pass underneath.

Brooklyn Bridge, New York, USA
After many setbacks, Brooklyn Bridge was finally opened in 1883. For a short time it was the world's longest bridge.

Sydney Harbour Bridge, Sydney, Australia (below)
Sydney Harbour Bridge was built in 1932 to carry road and rail traffic across the harbour. It is a famous feature of the Sydney harbour skyline.

Golden Gate Bridge, San Francisco, USA
The Golden Gate bridge was originally designed to take road traffic on the top layer, with trains on a lower deck. It now carries only motor vehicles. It was completed in 1937 and was the world's longest bridge for many years.

 Bridge types

Arch
An arch bridge is a very strong curved structure made of stone, concrete or steel. It is firmly supported on both sides.

Bascule
A bascule bridge has a central section that opens to allow tall ships to pass. London's Tower Bridge is one of the most famous bascule bridges.

Beam
A beam bridge is supported by the shore at both ends. This is the simplest and oldest type of bridge – a log across a stream is a very simple beam bridge. It is not very strong and may need to be strengthened by supports underneath.

Cantilever
This type of bridge has two long arms held in place at the ends by anchors. Some can swing to let large ships through. Cantilever bridges are closest in length to suspension bridges.

Suspension
This bridge is supported by steel cables fixed to high towers on the banks. All the world's longest bridges are suspension bridges because they are very strong.

Swing
A swing bridge can be swung to one side to allow ships through. The Gateshead Millennium Bridge across the Tyne is a unique swing bridge, which rotates upwards to allow boats to pass beneath.

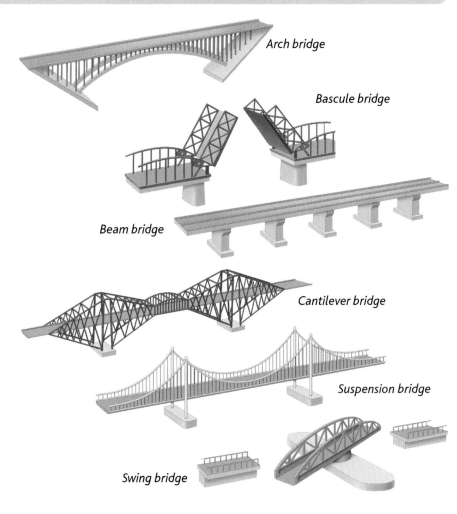

Arch bridge

Bascule bridge

Beam bridge

Cantilever bridge

Suspension bridge

Swing bridge

Longest bridges

All these bridges were the world's longest when they were first built. Today's longest, the Akashi Kaikyo in Japan, is nearly 54 times the length of the Martorell bridge in Spain.

Bridge	Location	Type	Year	span (m)
Martorell	Spain	Stone arch	217 BC	37
Augustus	Narni, Italy	Stone arch	27 BC	43
Trajan†	Danube, Romania	Timber arch/stone piers	AD 104	52
Trezzo†	Adda, Italy	Stone arch	1371	72
Schaffhausen†	Switzerland	Timber	1757	119
Schuylkill Falls†	Philadelphia, USA	Suspension	1816	124
Union/Tweed	Berwick, UK	Iron chain suspension	1820	137
Menai Strait	Anglesey, UK	Chain suspension	1826	177
Fribourg†	Switzerland	Wire-cable suspension	1834	273
Wheeling	West Virginia, USA	Suspension	1849	308
Lewiston-Queenston	Niagara, USA	Suspension	1851	318
Cincinnati-Ohio River	Covington, USA	Suspension	1867	322
Niagara-Clifton†	Niagara, USA/Canada	Suspension	1869	387
Brooklyn	New York	Suspension	1883	486
Firth of Forth Rail	Scotland	Cantilever	1890	521
Quebec Rail	Canada	Cantilever	1917	549
Ambassador	Detroit, USA/Windsor, Canada	Suspension	1929	564
George Washington	New York, USA	Suspension	1931	1,067
Golden Gate	San Francisco, USA	Suspension	1937	1,280
Verazzano Narrows	New York, USA	Suspension	1964	1,298
Humber Estuary	Hull, UK	Suspension	1980	1,410
East Bridge	Denmark	Suspension	1997	1,624
Akashi Kaikyo	Japan	Suspension	1998	1,990

† No longer standing

ONE AND ONLY

The one and only bridge taken from the UK to the USA is London Bridge. The five-arched stone bridge that replaced a medieval wooden bridge was made between 1823 and 1831. In the 20th century, London Bridge needed to be replaced by one better suited to modern traffic. American businessman Robert P. McCulloch bought it for $2,460,000. The bridge was shipped out stone by stone, each of them numbered. It was rebuilt in Lake Havasu City in Arizona and completed in 1971. It is the largest structure ever moved and the largest antique ever sold!

See also

Rail Transport: pages 214-15

Road and rail tunnels

The first tunnel built specially for passenger trains was the 766m Tyler Hill Tunnel in Kent. It opened on 4 May 1830. The first underwater rail tunnel was the Thames Tunnel, Wapping, London, which opened in 1869. Some of the most amazing tunnels are made under the sea. The Seikan tunnel was built to link the Japanese islands of Honshu and Hokkaido. Almost half of it (23.3km) is 100m below the sea bed. The Channel Tunnel is shorter than the Seikan Tunnel, but 38km of it is under the sea. The tunnels listed are all for railways, except the Laerdal in Norway, which is a road tunnel.

Longest tunnels

Tunnel/country	Year completed	Length km
1 AlpTransit Link, Switzerland	2010*	57.07
2 Seikan, Japan	1988	53.85
3 Channel Tunnel, France/England	1994	49.94
4 Lötschberg, Switzerland	2007*	34.58
5 Moscow Metro (Medvedkovo/Belyaevo section), Russia	1979	30.70
6 Guadarrama, Spain	2007*	28.38
7 London Underground (East Finchley/Morden, Northern Line), UK	1939	27.84
8 Hakkouda, Japan	2013*	26.46
9 Iwate, Japan	2013*	25.81
10 Laerdal, Norway	2000	24.51
11 Iiyama, Japan	2013*	22.23
12 Dai-Shimizu, Japan	1982	22.22

* Still being built

Entrance to the Channel Tunnel, Sangatte

The Seven Wonders of the ancient world

Early Greek writers drew up lists of the most important buildings in the world they knew. Of these only the Great Pyramid has survived, but we know about the others from writers' accounts and the work of archaeologists.

The Great Pyramid of Giza
The Great Pyramid of Giza, Egypt, is the oldest, and the only one of the Seven Wonders to survive. It was made as a tomb for King Khufu, who ruled Egypt from about 2551 to 2528 BC, and it is the largest stone structure ever built. Its sides are 230m long and it covers an area the size of 200 tennis courts.

The Hanging Gardens of Babylon
The legendary gardens of King Nebuchadnezzar II may not have existed. Some people believe they were created in about 600 BC in Babylon, 88km south of present-day Baghdad, the capital of Iraq. "Hanging" suggests that they were a series of terraces made of bricks, some glazed and brightly coloured.

The Statue of Zeus at Olympia
This was an enormous statue of the Greek god, carved by the sculptor Phidias. It was inside the Temple of Zeus, built about 466–456 BC. The statue was 13m high and one of the largest indoor sculptures ever made. Today little remains of the temple and nothing of the statue.

The Temple of Artemis
The Temple of Artemis at Ephesus, Turkey, was built to honour the Greek goddess of hunting and nature. The temple was completed in 550 BC. It was the largest of all ancient Greek buildings and measured 114 by 55m. Archaeologists have found the foundations and some columns of this ancient wonder.

The ruins of the Temple of Artemis, Ephesus, Turkey

The Mausoleum at Halicarnassus
This was the tomb of Persian ruler Mausolus, who ruled part of the Persian empire from 377 to 353 BC. Halicarnassus (modern-day Bodrum) in Turkey was his capital. After his death his widow built this magnificent tomb, which measured 105 by 242m and was 43m high. It was damaged by an earthquake and demolished in 1522. The word mausoleum has come to mean any great tomb.

The Colossus of Rhodes
The huge statue of sun god Helios stood in Rhodes harbour, Greece. In 305–304 BC warrior king Demetrius Poliorcetes attacked the city of Rhodes. When he abandoned his siege, the people built the giant statue as an offering to the god Helios. It took 12 years to build and stood 33m high, but in 226 BC it was destroyed by an earthquake.

The Pharos of Alexandria
This was a lighthouse off the coast of the city of Alexandria. Work started on it in about 299 BC and it was completed about 20 years later. It was 124m tall – the tallest lighthouse ever made. It was damaged by earthquakes and in 1375 toppled into the sea. Marine archaeologists have found a few remains.

The Great Wall of China

The Seven Wonders of the medieval world

People have never been able to agree on the Seven Wonders of the medieval world, and this is just one of several lists that have been made. It includes buildings that were built before the medieval era – Stonehenge is even older than any of the ancient wonders – but excludes such buildings as Angkor Wat, Cambodia, the Taj Mahal, India, and Chichen Itza, Mexico, which were unknown to Europeans of the time.

Stonehenge
The famous circle of huge stones was built in stages from about 3000 BC. The origin of the stones, how they were transported (some of them weigh up to 50 tonnes) and the purpose of the site remain a mystery. It was possibly some sort of ancient observatory.

The Great Wall of China
This was a defensive wall designed to protect China from its warlike neighbours to the north. It was built in stages after 220 BC, using a huge labour force of as many as 300,000 workers. The main part is 3,460km long and wide enough for an army to march along it ten abreast.

The Colosseum, Rome, Italy
This amphitheatre was opened in AD 80 with a huge spectacle lasting 100 days. It is oval in shape and measures 48m high, 188m long and 156m wide. It could hold up to 50,000 spectators and could even be flooded for re-enactments of sea battles.

The Catacombs of Alexandria (Kom El Shoqafa), Egypt
These unique Roman tombs beneath the city of Alexandria, Egypt, were discovered in 1900 when a donkey fell into the site. The beautifully preserved and richly carved catacombs had been tunnelled into solid rock during the 2nd century AD.

Hagia Sophia, Istanbul, Turkey
Hagia Sophia (Holy Wisdom), Istanbul, Turkey, was originally built in AD 360 by the Emperor Constantius. It was later rebuilt as one of the world's finest churches, with many mosaics and ornate details. In 1453 the church was converted into an Islamic mosque.

The Leaning Tower of Pisa, Italy
The building of the bell tower of Pisa cathedral began in 1173. Soon afterwards the foundations began to sink into the ground on one side. The design was adjusted, but by the time the tower had reached its full height of 55m it was leaning sharply. The tilt has increased over the centuries and it is amazing that the 14,000-tonne structure is still standing.

The Porcelain Pagoda of Nanking, China
The Porcelain Pagoda was built in about 1412 by Emperor Yung-lo. It was an eight-sided structure covered in glazed tiles, and soared to 79m. It was destroyed during a rebellion in 1853.

→ **See also**

Holy places: page 162

Guggenheim Museum, Bilbao, Spain

Seven modern wonders

There are many candidates for this list and here is one selection.

Hoover Dam, USA
When it was built in 1936, the 221m high Hoover Dam was the largest in the world. A record 3.63 million cubic metres of concrete were used to make the structure, which controls the flooding of the Colorado River.

Deltawerken flood barrier, Netherlands
After a disastrous flood in 1953 engineer Johan van Veen designed the Delta Project, or Deltawerken. This is a series of interconnected dams that forms a movable sea barrier while preserving the habitat and sea life within it.

Kansai International Airport, Japan
This airport was opened in 1994 and stands on a 4 x 1.2km island which is entirely man-made. It was built with 48,000 gigantic blocks, made from earth excavated by flattening three mountains, and designed to withstand earthquakes and typhoon winds. Its terminal building was designed by Italian architect Renzo Piano.

Channel Tunnel, England/France
Work on the second longest underwater rail tunnel in the world began in 1987. It took seven years and 15,000 workers to create the 50km tunnel (38km under sea), which opened in 1994. The tunnel links Folkestone in England to Sangatte, France.

Guggenheim Museum, Bilbao, Spain
The Guggenheim was built in 1997 to the design of Canadian-born architect Frank Gehry. It houses a major collection of modern art in a striking, ultra-modern setting. The structure combines limestone blocks of varied shapes, curved sections covered in panels of titanium (a light, strong metal) and large areas of glass.

The Eden Project, Cornwall, UK
About 1.8 million tonnes of earth were moved to make the foundations for the world's largest greenhouses. These are a series of domes, each devoted to a particular type of climate and housing 100,000 plants. The Eden Project was designed by Nicholas Grimshaw, and opened in 2001. It is now one of the UK's most popular tourist attractions.

EnviroMission Solar Tower, New South Wales, Australia
This has not yet been built, but has been designed by German engineer Jörg Schlaich. It will comprise an area of solar panels, 5km in diameter, that will absorb the Sun's rays. The heat generated from the solar panels will rise through the 1km high tower to drive turbines and produce electricity.

For centuries humans have been developing faster and more efficient ways of moving from place to place. We have journeyed over water, land and through the air in everything from wooden rafts to supersonic planes. In the 21st century people are travelling more than ever before. Is space tourism the next step?

TRANSPORT AND TRAVEL

Biggest ships

All the ships listed here held the record as the biggest ship in the world when they were launched. The first, the *Great Western*, was a giant in its time but was less than 1/100th the size of the current record holder *Queen Mary 2*, which is 345.03m long. The *Great Eastern* measured 211m and the *Titanic* was 269m long. Weights given are the weight of the ship when empty, without cargo, crew, passengers and supplies. Some of these ships are still sailing, but many have been scrapped. The *Titanic* and *Lusitania* both sank with the loss of many lives.

Ship	Launched	Weight (tonnes)
Great Western	1838	1,340
President	1840	2,360
Great Britain	1845	3,448
Great Eastern	1858	18,914
Oceanic	1899	17,274
Baltic	1904	23,884
Lusitania	1907	31,550
Mauretania	1907	31,938
Titanic	1912	46,232
Bismarck/Majestic/Caledonia*	1922	56,621
Normandie/Lafayette*	1935	79,301
Queen Elizabeth	1938	83,673
Voyager of the Seas	1999	137,276
Explorer of the Seas	2000	137,308
Navigator of the Seas	2002	138,279
Queen Mary 2	2003	142,200

* Renamed

The world's largest cruise ship, Queen Mary 2

The world's longest ship

A supertanker called *Jahre Viking* (previously *Happy Giant* and *Seawise Giant*) is the longest ship ever built. It measures 485.45m, which is longer than 20 tennis courts end to end. It is 68.86m wide and can hold 4.1 million barrels of oil.

Famous ships

Some ships, such as the *Titanic*, are famous because they sank, but here are some that are celebrated for a variety of other reasons.

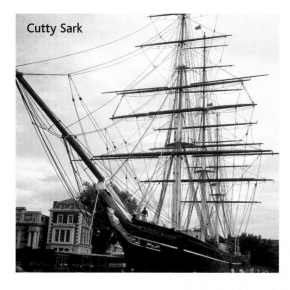

Cutty Sark

Niña, Pinta and Santa Maria
The three ships on Christopher Columbus' voyage of 1492 to America.

Mayflower
The ship that took the settlers known as the Pilgrim Fathers from Plymouth to America in 1620.

Endeavour
Captain James Cook's ship on his exploration of Australia and New Zealand in 1768–71.

Bounty
The crew of this British ship mutinied against Captain William Bligh in 1789.

Victory
Captain Horatio Nelson's flagship at the Battle of Trafalgar, 1805. It is now on display in Portsmouth.

Beagle
The research ship on which British scientist Charles Darwin visited the Galápagos Islands in 1835.

Cutty Sark
A tea clipper (a sailing ship designed to bring tea from China as fast as possible) launched in 1869. The ship is preserved in dry dock at Greenwich, London.

Great Eastern
This ship was designed by Isambard Kingdom Brunel and launched in 1858. It laid the first transatlantic cable in 1866, but was scrapped in 1888.

Marie Celeste
A US ship found abandoned in the Atlantic in 1872. The fate of its crew remains a mystery.

Kon-Tiki
A balsawood raft on which Norwegian anthropologist Thor Heyerdahl sailed from South America across the Pacific to Polynesia in 1947. He made the voyage to prove his theory that Polynesian people came from South America.

Types of ship

Passenger and commercial ships

Barge
This name is used for various types of ship, ranging from a slow canal boat to a small sailing cargo boat or a decorated rowing boat used by royalty.

Catamaran
A boat with two hulls side by side. There are different types of catamaran, including ferries and yachts.

Container ship
A cargo ship designed to carry standard-sized containers, making it easy to load and unload.

Ferry
A ship that takes passengers and vehicles from one port to another.

Galleon
A medieval sailing ship. The word was first used in 1529.

Galley
An ancient warship driven by oars. Biremes have oars on two levels, and triremes on three.

Hydrofoil
A boat with a special device to lift its hull out of the water, so increasing speed.

Junk
A high-sterned (the stern is the aft or back end), flat-bottomed, Chinese or Japanese sailing ship with two or three masts.

Liner or cruise ship
An ocean-going ship once used to take passengers on long journeys, such as across the Atlantic. Cruise ships are luxury liners designed to take people on pleasure cruises.

Oil tanker
A large vessel that carries oil from oil fields to refineries in other countries.

Yacht
A sailing or engine-powered ship used for pleasure cruises or racing.

Warships

Aircraft carrier
A warship from which aircraft can take off and land.

Cruiser
A medium-sized, fast, long-range warship.

Battleship
A large armoured warship.

Destroyer
A small fast warship.

Frigate
A warship that escorted cargo convoys to protect them from attack by submarines, introduced during World War II.

Minesweeper
A naval ship designed to find and destroy mines.

Submarine
Military submarines can travel long distances under water to avoid detection, and can fire torpedoes and missiles. Special civilian submarines are used for undersea research.

Skyscraper?

During the 18th century, a skyscraper was a small triangular flag flown from the tip of a sailing ship's main mast. In the 19th century, the word began to be used to describe a tall horse or even an exceptionally tall person. And when the first very tall buildings were constructed in the 1890s people called them skyscrapers.

Sailors race a catamaran at top speed.

Top speeds

Rowing eight
The Oxford and Cambridge Boat Race is rowed annually on the River Thames, London, and covers 6.8km. The Oxford crew won in 1998 in a record time of 16 minutes 19 seconds, equivalent to a speed of 25km/h.

Aircraft carrier
The US Navy's Nimitz class nuclear-powered aircraft carriers can travel at more than 56km/h.

Submarine (submerged)
Russian Alfa class nuclear submarines could probably travel at 83.4km/h, but these are no longer in use. US Navy Los Angeles class subs are said to achieve 74km/h, but the precise figures are military secrets.

Sailing vessel
During the 19th century clippers could average 36.63km/h. The modern sailing yacht record is held by Simon McKeon and Tim Daddo of Australia. On 26 October 1993 they sailed their yacht *Yellow Pages Endeavour* at 86.21km/hr.

Car ferry
The Spanish-built Australian catamaran *Luciano Federico L* can carry 52 cars and 450 passengers at a top speed of 107km/h.

Hovercraft
On 25 January 1980 a US Navy Bell SES-1008 experimental vehicle achieved a speed of 170km/h.

Hydroplane
These super-fast racing motor boats are capable of remarkable speeds: Dave Villwock set a new record average speed of 343.5km/h in *Miss Budweiser* at Oroville, California, USA, on 13 March 2004.

Ocean liners
Steam ships began carrying passengers across the Atlantic between Europe and the USA from 1838 onwards. In the early years, the journey (about 4,828km) could take 18 days or longer. Shipping companies competed with each other and the fastest ship carried a blue flag, or Blue Riband. There were separate Blue Ribands for westbound and eastbound crossings, and after 1934 an award, the Hales Trophy, was presented to the ship with the fastest average speed. In 1952 the newly launched liner *SS United States* won both the westbound and eastbound Blue Riband with a time of 3 days 10 hours 40 minutes, and the Hales Trophy with an average speed of 65.9km/h. *Cat-Link V*, a Danish catamaran ferry, is the current Blue Riband and Hales Trophy holder. It set a new transatlantic record of just 2 days 20 hours 9 minutes and an average speed of 76.5km/h.

See also

The World's Oceans: pages 40–41

Car timeline

1883	First experimental petrol-driven car (France)
1886	Karl Benz and Gottlieb Daimler (Germany) build first cars
1892	First US car built by Charles and Frank Duryea
1893	Rudolf Diesel patents engine
1894	First cars in UK
1895	First car race, Paris-Bordeaux-Paris, France, 1,178km
1895	Michelin (France) make first pneumatic car tyres for cars
1895	First car show in UK
1896	First speeding fine (UK)
1896	First car theft (France)
1896	First motoring death (UK)
1897	First woman driver in UK, Minnie Palmer
1898	First woman driver in USA, Genevra Mudge
1899	Jacob German arrested for speeding in New York (12mph)
1900	8,000 vehicles on the road in USA
1903	First driving licences issued, Paris, France
1903	Registration plates introduced in UK
1903	30,204 vehicles made in France, 11,235 USA, 9,437 UK
1903	National speed limit in UK 20mph (32km/h)
1904	28,842 vehicles in UK
1907	First Rolls-Royce made, the Silver Ghost (UK)
1908	First Model T Ford made (USA)
1909	143,000 vehicles in UK
1910	468,500 vehicles in USA
1912	First petrol station built (USA)
1915	Headlamp dipping and stoplights introduced (USA)
1919	Mechanical windscreen wipers developed (USA)
1921	First autobahn (high speed road or motorway) built in Germany
1930	First traffic lights installed in New York
1933	First drive-in cinema built (USA)
1935	First parking meters installed in Oklahoma City, USA
1935	Driving tests introduced in UK
1939	3,148,000 vehicles in UK
1940	32,453,200 vehicles in USA
1955	Highway Code issued in UK
1958	First motorway built in UK (Preston by-pass)
1960	8,512,000 vehicles in UK
1960	73,868,600 vehicles in USA
1962	200 millionth car produced in USA
1969	Czechoslovakia becomes first country to make seat belts compulsory
1970	Unleaded fuel introduced in USA
1978	Bosch (Germany) patents first satellite navigation
1980	19,199,000 vehicles in UK
1980	155,796,000 vehicles in USA
1983	Seat belts made compulsory in UK
1985	Seat belts made compulsory in New York
1999	Peak year for vehicle manufacture in USA (13,024,978 made)

Amazing vehicles

Biggest dumper trucks
The General Motors Terex Titan 33-19 mine truck, first made in 1974, can carry 317.5 tonnes. An average truck carries about 5 tonnes.

Biggest tyres
The largest road vehicle tyres are 3.82m in diameter. They are made by the Bridgestone Corporation, Tokyo, Japan, for giant dumper trucks. Normal car tyres are 60cm in diameter.

Biggest fire engines
Fire trucks made by the Oshkosh Truck Corporation of Wisconsin, USA for airports have eight wheels, 860-horsepower engines and weigh 60 tonnes.

Longest limos
The current record-holder, built by Jay Ohrberg of California, measures 30.5m and has 26 wheels. It is so long that it has to be hinged in the middle to enable it to turn corners.

Biggest bus
The articulated Super City Train Buses used in the Democratic Republic of Congo are 32.2m long. They can carry 110 seated passengers and 140 standing in the first part, and 60 seated and 40 standing in the second, a total of 350 people.

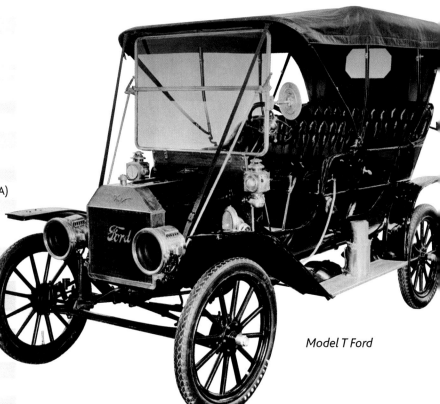

Model T Ford

Driving on the left

Drivers in most countries drive on the right. But in more than 70 countries and territories people drive on the left. These include the UK, Japan, Australia, India, South Africa, Thailand, Indonesia, Malaysia, New Zealand, Ireland and Pakistan. The different explanations for the tradition of keeping to the left side of a road date back to the time when most road users were on horseback. One is that it is usual to mount a horse from the left, and it is then easiest to stay on the left. Another is that as most people are right-handed, riding on the left allowed them to use a sword to defend themselves against approaching riders.

Two-wheel timeline

1817 The Draisienne, or hobby horse, invented by Baron Karl von Drais. The body was set on two wheels but there were no pedals. The rider sat on the saddle with his feet on the ground and pushed himself along.

1839 Crank-driven cycle built by Kirkpatrick Macmillan (Scotland)

1861 The vélocipède (fast foot), also called a boneshaker, driven by pedals attached to the front wheel hub, built by Pierre Michaux (France)

1869 First metal spoked wheels and solid rubber tyres; word "bicycle" first used

1870 Ariel Ordinary, or "Penny-farthing", patented by James Starley and William Hillman (UK)

1885 Motorcycle patented by Wilhelm Maybach and Gottlieb Daimler (Germany)

Man riding a penny-farthing

1888 First pneumatic tyres made by John Boyd Dunlop (Scotland)

1894 First motorcycle, the Motorrad, sold in Germany

1899 Charles "Mile-a-Minute" Murphy (USA) set bicycle speed record of one mile (1.6km) in 57.75 seconds

1903 First Tour de France cycle race

1946 Vespa motor scooter launched in Italy

1972 Bicycles first outsell cars in the US (13 million bikes to 11 million cars)

1983 BMX bikes made by Raleigh (UK)

1995 50-year-old Fred Rompelberg (Netherlands) sets new bicycle speed record of 268.831 km/h

Top vehicle-owning countries

There are so many cars today that there is one car for every 10.6 people in the world. In the USA there are 2.2 people per car and in the UK 2.1, but in some countries the ratio is amazingly high. In Myanmar, for example, there are 6,780 people for every car!

Country	Cars	Commercial vehicles	Total
1 USA	128,714,022	87,968,915	216,682,937
2 Japan	53,300,000	19,985,000	73,285,000
3 Germany	44,383,323	3,592,054	47,975,377
4 Italy	33,239,029	3,755,552	36,994,581
5 France	28,700,000	5,897,000	34,597,000
6 UK	27,790,025	3,412,086	31,202,111
World total	561,686,927	202,218,380	767,905,307

Fastest car

Thrust SSC is the most powerful car ever built. It uses two Rolls-Royce engines from Phantom fighter aircraft. In 1997, driven by Royal Air Force fighter pilot Andy Green, *Thrust* set a new land speed record of 1,227.986km/h. It was also the first road vehicle to break the sound barrier.

Famous cars

Mercedes
The German luxury car which has been made since 1901 took its name from Mercédès, the daughter of Daimler car company director Emil Jellinek.

Rolls-Royce
British car enthusiasts Henry Royce and Charles Rolls joined forces to form Rolls-Royce in 1906 and set new standards for a luxury vehicle. The company's engines are also used in many of the world's aircraft.

Model T Ford
The first Model T Ford, nicknamed the Tin Lizzie, was made in the USA in 1908 by the Ford Motor Company. The company was founded in 1903 by Henry Ford. By 1927, when production finished, a total of 16,536,075 had been built. During its peak years, more than half the new cars in the world were Model Ts.

Aston Martin
This luxury sports car has been made in the UK since the 1920s. It became one of the most featured and gadget-laden cars in the James Bond films.

Bugatti Royale
Only six Bugatti Royales (1926) were ever made. The Royale was designed by Italian Ettore Bugatti and was one of the largest vehicles of all time. It was 6.7m long with a 12.7 litre engine originally designed for aircraft. In 1980 one of these rare vehicles set a new world record price when it was sold for $15 million (£9.1 million).

Bugatti Royale

Volkswagen Beetle
The Volkswagen Beetle was designed by Ferdinand Porsche and first manufactured in Germany in 1937. When production ended in 2003 a total of 21,529,464 Beetles had been made, the last of them in Brazil and Mexico. A new version of the Beetle was introduced in 1998.

Mini
The Mini was launched in the UK in August 1959, when it cost just under £500. More than 5.3 million Minis had been made by 2000. It was designed by Alec Issigonis (1906–88) and was the first British car to sell more than a million. A new Mini was launched in 2001.

Famous trains

Orient Express
The Orient Express began trips from Paris, France, to Bulgaria on 5 October 1883 and from 1889 went as far as Constantinople (now Istanbul), Turkey. It was the first trans-European train and travelled a total of 2,736km across six countries in great style. It stopped running in 1977, but was re-launched five years later.

20th Century Limited
The luxurious 20th Century Limited ran between New York and Chicago from 1902 to 1967.

Trans-Siberian Express
The Trans-Siberian Express travels 9,297km between Moscow and Vladivostok. The line opened in 1914 and is the world's longest continuous rail line.

Flying Scotsman
The Flying Scotsman provided a luxurious non-stop journey from King's Cross, London to Edinburgh, Scotland. It ran for 40 years, from 1923 until 1963.

Golden Arrow
From 1929 to 1971, the Golden Arrow ran from Victoria, London to Dover. From there passengers could sail across the Channel and then take the French Flèche d'Or to Paris.

Blue Train
This is one of the world's most luxurious trains and it has operated between Cape Town and Pretoria, South Africa since 1939. The train, carriages and decor are mainly blue – hence the name.

Bullet Train
Japanese bullet trains (shinkansen) are the world's fastest scheduled rail services. They were introduced in 1964 to coincide with the Tokyo Olympic Games.

TGV
The French TGV (Train à Grande Vitesse, or high speed train) was launched in 1981 and is an electric train service between Paris and Lyon. A specially modified TGV, the Atlantique, set a world speed record of 515.3km/h on 18 May 1990.

Eurostar
The Eurostar service was launched on 14 November 1994 to carry passengers between London, Paris and Brussels through the Channel Tunnel. It can reach speeds of 300km/h. In its first ten years it carried a total of 59 million passengers.

Ghan
The Ghan is the first rail service from Adelaide to Darwin on the north-south route across Australia. It was named after the camel trains that were once the only way to cross the desert. The first train ran in 2004. It had 43 carriages, measured more than 1km in length, and carried 330 passengers.

Longest rail networks

These countries all have more than 10,000km of railway lines. At the other end of the scale, Nicaragua, Nauru, Lesotho and Monaco have less than 10km each – and some countries have none at all.

Country	Railways (km)	Country	Railways (km)
USA	194,731	Japan	23,168
Russia	87,157	Ukraine	22,473
China	71,600	South Africa	22,298
India	63,518	Mexico	19,510
Canada	49,422	Italy	19,493
Germany	45,514	UK	16,893
Australia	41,588	Spain	14,189
Argentina	34,463	Kazakhstan	13,601
France	32,682	Sweden	11,481
Brazil	31,543	Romania	11,385
Poland	23,420	**World total**	**1,122,650**

The Ghan on its first journey

ONE AND ONLY
The only time a train has been powered by fish was during a coal shortage in Turkestan in 1919. Dried fish, caught in the Aral Sea, were used as fuel. A total of almost 9,000 tonnes were used to stoke the train's boilers.

Maglev train in Shanghai

Types of train

Not all trains are the same: these are just some of the variations around the world.

Monorail
A monorail train runs on a single rail, instead of on a track or two rails. It is either suspended from the rail or straddles it. The Tokyo Monorail in Japan carries 100 million passengers a year. There are also monorails in Malaysia, Australia and the USA. Several American airports have monorails, as does Disney World in Florida.

Maglev
The name maglev comes from the words magnetic and levitation. These trains do not run on a track, but float above it by means of magnetic repulsion. The lack of contact means there is no friction, so the trains can travel very smoothly at high speeds – up to 650km/h – and use little energy. Germany and Japan are trying out maglev trains, and a maglev railway from Shanghai to Pu Dong International Airport, China, was opened in 2002.

Rubber-tyred metro
These electric trains run along a tracked roadway on rubber tyres. They are quiet, and can accelerate quickly and tackle slopes. They first ran in Paris in the 1950s and have been introduced in other French cities as well as in Santiago, Chile, Mexico City and Montreal, Canada.

Funicular
Funiculars (from the Latin *funiculus*, a thin rope) are designed to go up and down steep hills or mountains. Cars are drawn up by cables and descend by gravity. Funiculars are used in mountain and other resorts, and in hilly parts of cities, such Montmartre in Paris, and Montjuic in Barcelona. The steepest passenger funicular is the Katoomba Scenic Railway in New South Wales, Australia.

Cog railway
Cog or rack-and-pinion railways are mountain railways. The train has a rotating cog wheel that meshes with a rack rail, enabling the train to climb steep slopes safely. Mount Pilatus near Lucerne, Switzerland, has the world's steepest. The Snowdon Mountain Railway in Wales is the only one of this type in the UK.

Taking the train

How often people travel by train depends on many things, such as how reliable and affordable the rail system is and what alternatives there are. This list shows the world's most used rail systems. The figures are the number of passengers multiplied by the distance travelled.

Country	Passenger/km	Country	Passenger/km
China	405,000,000,000	France	67,000,000,000
India	404,000,000,000	Ukraine	48,000,000,000
Japan	241,000,000,000	USA	42,000,000,000
Russia	141,000,000,000	Italy	41,000,000,000
Germany	73,000,000,000	South Korea	30,000,000,000
Egypt	68,000,000,000	UK	29,000,000,000

Underground railways

An underground railway is an urban train line that runs mostly, or completely, underground. The world's first underground system was the London Metropolitan Line, opened between Bishop's Road, Paddington, and Farringdon Street, in 1863. Steam trains were used on this and London's Circle Line, completed in 1884. They had to be fitted with a device to absorb smoke so that passengers were not suffocated in their gas-lit carriages. During the 1890s, several inventions made deep tunnelling, electric motors, electric lights and lifts or escalators possible. After that, underground railways in London and other countries were all electrified.

First underground railways

City	Opened
London, UK	10 January 1863
Budapest, Hungary	2 May 1896
Glasgow, UK	14 December 1896
Boston, USA	1 September 1897
Paris, France	19 July 1900

Longest underground rail networks

City	Stations	Total track length (km)
London, UK	267	392
New York, USA	468	371
Moscow, Russia	160	262
Tokyo, Japan*	241	256
Paris, France#	297	202

* Includes Toei, Eidan lines   # Metro and RER

Busiest underground systems

City	Annual passengers (billion)
Moscow	3.2
Tokyo	2.7
Seoul	1.6
Mexico City	1.3
New York City	1.3
Paris	1.2

(London: 886 million)

Aviation pioneers

John Alcock (UK, 1892–1919) and **Arthur Whitten Brown** (UK, 1886–1948) On 14–15 June 1919, they completed the first ever non-stop flight across the Atlantic from Newfoundland to Ireland.

Louis Blériot (France, 1872–1936) On 25 July 1909 Blériot became the first person to fly across the English Channel.

Samuel F. Cody (USA, c 1861–1913) The first person to fly in England, 16 October 1908.

Glenn Curtiss (USA, 1878–1930) Rival to the Wright Brothers, Curtiss made the first public flight in the USA on 4 July 1908. He set up the first aeroplane manufacturing company in the USA.

Amelia Earhart (USA, 1898–1937) The first woman to fly the Atlantic. She went on to establish many flying records but disappeared during an attempt to fly round the world.

Amy Johnson (UK, 1903–41) She made the first solo flight from England to Australia in 1930.

Charles Lindbergh (USA, 1902–74) The first pilot to fly solo across the Atlantic, from New York to Paris, 20–21 May 1927, in his aircraft, *The Spirit of St Louis.*

Harriet Quimby (USA, 1875–1912) America's first female pilot. On 16 April 1912 she was the first woman to fly the English Channel – but on the day the sinking of the *Titanic* was reported, so her triumph was barely noticed!

Wilbur Wright (USA, 1867–1912) and **Orville Wright** (USA, 1871–1948) The Wright brothers, two bicycle mechanics from Dayton, Ohio, made the first ever powered flights on 17 December 1903.

Concorde

Concorde fact file

Concorde, the only passenger aircraft ever to fly faster than the speed of sound, was first named in a speech by General de Gaulle on 13 January 1963. The Anglo-French project began the following year.

- The first prototype Concorde was shown at the Toulouse Air Show on 11 December 1967.
- The first French flight took place on 2 March 1969.
- The first British flight took place on 9 April 1969.
- The first landing at London Heathrow was on 13 September 1970.
- The first Concorde landing in the USA was at Dallas-Fort Worth on 20 September 1973.
- The only Concorde crash was near Paris, 25 July 2000, when 109 passengers and crew and four people on the ground died.
- Concorde's last flight took place on 24 October 2004. All surviving BA and Air France Concordes are on public display in museums and airports in the USA, UK, France, Germany and Barbados.

The Wright brothers demonstrate their Wright Model A plane.

The Wright brothers

Orville Wright was the first person to fly a powered aircraft. He also became the first to fly a plane for more than one hour, on 9 September 1908 at Fort Meyer, Virginia, USA. His brother Wilbur became the first to fly for more than two hours on 31 December 1908 at Auvours, France. On 20 May 1909 French pilot Paul Tissandier became the first person other than the Wright Brothers to fly for more than one hour.

✈ First manned balloon flights

The first balloons worked on the principle that when air is heated, it rises. They were filled with hot air by burning things under them, such as paper, straw and wool – and even old shoes and rotten meat! But the balloons often caught fire and once the air cooled, they quickly came down. Soon after the first hot-air flights, people realized that the gas hydrogen could be used instead. Hydrogen is the lightest of all elements – almost 15 times lighter than air. Gas balloons can also be filled with helium, which is not as light as hydrogen but does not catch fire so easily. Most balloons today use hot air made by burning propane gas. This can be carried in cylinders, so is comparatively safe.

Breaking the sound barrier

Charles "Chuck" Yeager became the first person to break the sound barrier on 14 October 1947. His Bell X-1 rocket plane was dropped from a carrier aircraft above Muroc Dry Lake, California. At 12,800m he reached a speed of 1,078km/h. He did not break the air speed record because only aircraft that take off and land under their own power are eligible.

The speed of sound is not fixed and varies according to height and air conditions. In dry air at sea level the speed of sound is 1,229km/h, but at high altitudes, where air density is less, it is lower.

First hot air balloon flight

The first hot-air balloon flight

The Montgolfier brothers, Joseph and Etienne, tested their first unmanned hot-air balloon in the French town of Annonay on 5 June 1783. On 21 November 1783, François Laurent, Marquis d'Arlandes and Jean-François Pilâtre de Rozier took off from the Bois de Boulogne, Paris, in a Montgolfier hot-air balloon. During this first ever manned flight they travelled about 9km in 23 minutes.

First hydrogen balloon flight

On 1 December 1783, Jacques Alexandre César Charles and Nicholas-Louis Robert made the first flight in a hydrogen balloon. They took off from the Tuileries, Paris, watched by a crowd of 400,000, and travelled 43km north to Nesle in about two hours. Charles then took off again alone, so becoming the first ever solo pilot.

First British flight

On 27 August 1784 James Tytler, a doctor and newspaper editor, took off in a home-made balloon from Comely Gardens, Edinburgh. He reached an altitude of 107m in a 0.8km hop.

First Channel crossing

On 7 January 1785 Jean-Pierre Blanchard made the first Channel crossing in a balloon with Dr John Jeffries (the first American to fly). They also carried the first airmail letter. As they lost height, they had to reduce weight, so they threw almost everything overboard – including their clothes!

First flight in the USA

On 9 January 1793 in Philadelphia, Blanchard made the first balloon flight in America. He took a small black dog with him as a passenger. The flight was watched by George Washington, who gave Blanchard a passport permitting his flight, which was the first pilot's licence and America's first airmail document.

First non-stop solo

US millionaire and adventurer Steve Fossett made the first non-stop solo and fastest round-the-world balloon flight, 19 June–3 July 2002.

ONE AND ONLY

A Soviet plane, the Tupolev Tu-144, nicknamed "Concordski" for its similarity to Concorde, first flew on 31 December 1968. On 3 June 1973 a prototype at the Paris Air Show fell apart and crashed in a Paris suburb. Airline Aeroflot's first Tu-144 flight – for freight and mail, but not passengers – took place on 1 November 1977, but the aircraft was withdrawn on 1 June 1978 and never flew again.

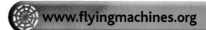
www.flyingmachines.org

Shipwrecks

Shipping disasters as a result of collisions, storms, fires, explosions or military action are among the most famous of human tragedies. Some wrecks were carrying treasure that has since been recovered by divers.

The Mary Rose, *which sank in 1545*

Mary Rose
This Tudor galleon sank in 1545 as Henry VIII watched from the shore. She was found in 1968, raised in 1982, and is exhibited in Portsmouth.

Spanish Armada
Between August and October 1588 military action and storms combined to destroy the Spanish fleet off the British coast. About half the 130 ships that set out were wrecked, killing about 4,000 men.

St George, Defence and Hero
On 4 December 1811 these three British warships were stranded off the Jutland coast. More than 2,000 people died.

Tek Sing
This Chinese junk carrying 2,000 passengers and 350,000 pieces of porcelain sank in 1822. It was found in 1999 and its treasures sold for high prices.

Sultana
On 27 April 1865, the *Sultana*, a steamboat on the Mississippi River near Memphis, USA, was destroyed by a boiler explosion. This was the USA's worst ever marine accident and a total of 1,547 people died.

Princess Alice
On 3 September 1878 the pleasure steamer *Princess Alice* was taking people on a holiday trip down the Thames in London. She collided with the *Bywell Castle* and 786 people lost their lives.

Titanic
On the night of 14 April 1912, the "unsinkable" *Titanic* struck an iceberg on its maiden voyage and sank the next day, killing 1,517. The wreck was discovered and explored by Robert Ballard in 1986.

Lusitania
The British liner was torpedoed off the Irish coast by a German U-boat on 7 May 1915, with the loss of 1,198 lives.

Wilhelm Gustloff
The German liner, laden with refugees, was torpedoed off Gdansk, Poland, on 30 January 1945 by a Soviet submarine, *S-13*. Between 5,348 and 7,800 people died, making this the worst ever marine disaster.

Dona Paz
The *Donna Paz* sank off the Philippines on 20 December 1987, killing up to 3,000 people. This was the world's worst passenger ferry disaster.

Kursk
This Russian nuclear submarine sank in the Barents Sea on 12 August 2000, with the loss of all 118 crew.

Rail disasters

Rail travel is one of the safest ways of journeying from place to place, taking into account the large numbers of passengers carried and distances travelled. But there have been accidents. One of the earliest rail disasters was at Versailles, France. It happened on 8 May 1842, when the Versailles to Paris train crashed.

World's worst
On 6 June 1981 a train plunged off a bridge crossing the Bagmati River, India. The driver may have had to brake sharply to avoid hitting a sacred cow. The train was overcrowded and more than 800 people may have died.

UK
On 22 May 1915 a troop train crashed head-on into another at Quintinshill near Gretna Green, Scotland. The wreckage was then struck by an express. The crashes and fire that followed left 227 dead and 246 injured.

USA
Two USA accidents both resulted in 101 deaths. On 10 August 1887 a bridge at Chatsworth, Illinois caught fire and collapsed as a train was passing over. In the crash, 81 people were killed immediately and a further 20 died later. As many as 372 were injured. The second accident happened on 9 July 1918 at Nashville, Tennessee, when two trains collided head-on.

Underground
On 28 October 1995, at Baku, Azerbaijan, an underground train caught fire one Saturday evening. The accident killed more than 300 people.

British underground
Britain's worst tube disaster took place on 8 March 1943 at Bethnal Green, London. About 173 people who were trying to enter the underground station during an air raid were killed in the crush.

American underground
America's worst subway accident was on 1 November 1918 at Brooklyn, New York. A train was derailed in the Malbone Street tunnel, leaving 97 dead.

The Tay Bridge Disaster

Britain's worst rail disaster during the 19th century took place on 28 December 1879. The Tay Bridge in Scotland collapsed as a train crossed, killing all 75 passengers and the crew of five. The train itself was later recovered from the river. The bridge – the longest in the world at that time – had only been opened on 31 May the previous year. Queen Victoria had crossed it in a train soon afterwards.

The locomotive that fell from the Tay Bridge

Road disasters

Many people are killed and injured on the roads – more than 40,000 a year in the USA – but accidents involving more than a few drivers or pedestrians are rare.

Worst road disaster
On 3 November 1982 a petrol tanker collided with a Soviet army truck and exploded in the 2.7km Salang Tunnel in Afghanistan. At least 2,000, and perhaps as many as 3,000, people died as a result of the explosion, fire and fumes.

US road disaster
The worst US road disaster took place on 15 December 1967. The Silver Bridge across the Ohio River from Kanauga, Ohio, to Point Pleasant, West Virginia, collapsed during heavy pre-Christmas rush hour traffic. About 60 vehicles plunged into the river.

British road accident
On 27 May 1975 a coach crashed near Grassington, North Yorkshire, killing 33.

Air disasters

Worst ever
The two terrorist attacks on the twin towers of the World Trade Center, New York, on 11 September 2001, killed all the passengers and crew on both hijacked planes (92 on one and 65 on the other). More than 2,000 people also died in the buildings.

On the ground
On 27 March 1977, two Boeing 747s collided and caught fire on the runway of Los Rodeos airport in Tenerife in the Canary Islands. The aircraft were carrying 614 passengers and 30 crew between them. A total of 61 people managed to escape.

Single-aircraft disaster
On 12 August 1985 a JAL Boeing 747 on an internal flight from Tokyo to Osaka crashed, killing 520. Four passengers survived.

Mid-air collision
At Charkhi Dadri, India, on 12 November 1996, a Saudi Airways Boeing 747 collided with a Kazakh Airlines Ilyushin IL-76 cargo aircraft. A total of 349 people died.

Planes crash into the World Trade Center, New York

The Hindenburg disaster

The *Hindenburg* was the world's biggest airship at 245m long. The airship made several successful transatlantic crossings, then flew from Frankfurt, Germany, to Lakehurst, New Jersey, USA. She arrived on 6 May 1937 after a three-day trip. As the airship was moored, she caught fire and turned into an inferno.

See also
Hydrogen:
page 79

Mardi Gras parade in New Orleans, USA

History of tourism

People have been travelling from place to place since ancient times. Nomadic people moved about to graze their livestock. Later people travelled to trade, or to seek their fortunes in gold rushes, and millions emigrated to other countries to escape persecution or to seek better lives. Apart from a few historical examples, tourism – travelling for pleasure – is a relatively modern idea. Today, people spend nearly $500 billion a year on tourism.

Taking the waters
The Romans placed great value on bathing. They settled in many places with natural springs and developed cities as spas (the name comes from Spa in Belgium). In the 18th century, it became fashionable to visit these spas to "take the waters" – drinking and bathing as cures for various illnesses. Bath in England is a well-known Roman spa.

The Grand Tour
From the 18th century onwards, taking a Grand Tour of historic European cities was part of the education of wealthy young men. The idea of sightseeing holidays – visiting great buildings and art treasures in museums and galleries, battlefields and other historical sites – is a modern version of this.

Package tours
On 5 July 1841, British travel pioneer Thomas Cook took 570 members of the Temperance Society (an organization opposed to drinking alcohol) on the newly-opened railway from Leicester to Loughborough. This journey was the first package tour, and the beginning of what was to become the world's best-known travel company. When the Paris Exhibition opened in 1851, Cook took "excursionists" abroad for the first time. By the time Thomas Cook died in 1892, he had made travel possible for the masses.

Exhibitions
During the 19th and 20th centuries, major exhibitions in Europe and the USA brought millions of people to the big cities of the world. Many had never travelled before. The Great Exhibition in London in 1851 had more than 6 million visitors. A century later, the 1951 Festival of Britain attracted 8.5 million. The Paris Exposition of 1889, for which the Eiffel Tower was built, had 28 million visitors, and more than 51 million visited the New York World's Fair of 1964–65.

Festivals
The world's major arts and music festivals receive large numbers of visitors. The annual Texas State Fair in the USA can attract as many as three million, and many other North American fairs receive one million or more. Festivals such as the carnival held in Rio De Janeiro, Brazil, and Mardi Gras in New Orleans, USA, are attended by large crowds.

Sport tourism
Winter sports such as skiing, water sports (sailing, surfing, diving) and adventure sports such as white-water rafting have become very popular. When the Olympic Games is held, the host country can expect a huge boost to its tourist industry.

Amusement parks
The world's most-visited amusement park is Disney World, Florida, USA, which attracts more than 14 million visitors a year. The total number of visitors at all Disney attractions around the world approaches 100 million a year. Britain's leading amusement park is Blackpool Pleasure Beach, with more than 6 million visitors a year, while Alton Towers has 2.5 million visitors.

Space tourism
This is not yet developed as a type of tourism but may be in the future. The first space tourist was wealthy American Denis Tito. In 2001 he paid $20 million to spend eight days as a guest of the Russian space programme. In July 2004 test pilot Mike Melvill took his own privately built craft, *SpaceShipOne*, into space. He travelled to an altitude of more than 100km.

Top tourist attractions

The world's most popular tourist attractions range from major cities offering a variety of buildings, museums and entertainments, to unspoiled landscapes and wildlife reserves. These are the top five attractions in the UK.

Attraction/location	Visitors (2004)
1 Blackpool Pleasure Beach, Blackpool	6,200,000
2 National Gallery, London	4,959,946
3 British Museum, London	4,868,176
4 Tate Modern, London	4,441,225
5 British Airways London Eye	3,700,000

Top tourist countries

In 2003, one in every nine people in the world travelled as tourists to another country – a total of 740 million. Of these, about half visited the top ten destinations below. By the year 2020 the number of international tourists is likely to more than double to 1.5 billion.

Country	Visitors*	% of world total
1 France	75,000,000	10.1
2 Spain	52,500,000	7.1
3 USA	40,500,000	5.5
4 Italy	39,600,000	5.4
5 China	33,000,000	5.2
6 UK	24,800,000	4.5
7 Austria	19,100,000	2.6
8 Mexico	18,700,000	2.5
9 Germany	18,400,000	2.5
10 Canada	17,500,000	2.4

* In 2003; international tourist arrivals, excluding day visitors

Venice is one of Italy's most visited cities.

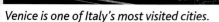

See also
Countries of the World: pages 116–17

National parks

National parks are established by governments to preserve areas of land and the plants and animals they contain. Yellowstone National Park in the USA, set up in 1872, was the first. There are now more than 1,200 national parks in 100 or more countries. These are a few examples of the different types.

Everglades
(park founded 1934; 5,929sq km)
The Everglades in the USA is the only subtropical park in North America. Many different types of creatures live in its swamps, including alligators.

Great Barrier Reef
(park founded 1979; 343,800sq km)
Australia's Great Barrier Reef, off the coast of Queensland, is the world's largest coral reef system, supporting many rare marine animals and plants.

Galápagos Islands
(park founded 1986; 6,937sq km)
These volcanic islands off the coast of Ecuador are home to birds, seals and unique creatures including giant turtles and marine iguanas.

Lake District
(park founded 1951; 2,292sq km)
The largest and most visited of Britain's national parks. The parks receive a total of 100 million visitors a year.

Serengeti
(founded 1951; 14,763sq km)
Wildebeest, gazelle and zebra) graze in this vast park in Tanzania, along with lions, elephants, giraffe and other animals. It is one of Africa's most popular tourist attractions.

Wood Buffalo
(park founded 1922; 44,807sq km)
This area of Canada contains forests, plains and many lakes. It has the largest herd of wild buffalo anywhere on Earth as well as many rare species such as the whooping crane.

Wrangell-St Elias
(founded 1980; 33,820sq km)
This national park in Alaska is the largest in the USA. It contains the most glaciers and peaks higher than 4,880m in North America, as well as many wild animals, including bears, wolves and moose.

Yellowstone
(founded 1872; 8,991sq km)
This area of the Rocky Mountains in the USA is famed for its hot springs and geysers. Most famous is the Old Faithful geyser which sprays steam and water up to 56m high.

Xingu
(founded 1961; 22,000sq km)
This large area of Brazilian rainforest is teeming with tropical wildlife. It is also inhabited by tribes of indigenous peoples who have little contact with outsiders.

A diver exploring the Great Barrier Reef

Being able to speak is one of the things that makes humans different from all other animals. There are at least 5,000 languages spoken around the world. Language can also be written down so we can share information through books, newspapers and magazines, as well as letters, e-mails and texts.

LANGUAGE
AND
LITERATURE

Most spoken languages

Chinese (Mandarin)
Approximate number of speakers: 874,000,000
Chinese has many dialects, but about two-thirds of the people speak Mandarin, which is considered the standard. Wu is the next most common dialect, with approximately 77 million speakers. Very few people who are not of Chinese origin speak Chinese.

Hindustani
Approximate number of speakers: 426,000,000
Hindustani includes Hindi and Urdu, which are almost the same language. Hindustani is the official language of Pakistan, where it is written in modified Arabic script and called Urdu. It is also the official language of India, but there it is written in the Devanagari script and called Hindi.

Spanish
Approximate number of speakers: 358,000,000
Spanish is one of the most widely used of all languages. It is spoken not only in Spain but also in South America, the west coast of Africa and the USA.

English
Approximate number of speakers: 341,000,000
Far fewer people have English as their main language than Chinese, but millions more know at least some English and it is spoken in every corner of the globe.

The USA dominates cinema, television, pop music, technology (Internet) and business and this has increased the importance of the English language. At least 800 million people use the Internet and about 35 per cent of them communicate in English. There are probably more than one billion people worldwide learning English.

The English language is a particularly rich one: native English speakers use around 200,000 words. Most French speakers use only about 100,000 words.

Bengali
Approximate number of speakers: 207,000,000
Bengali is spoken in Bengal, a region in both Bangladesh, where there are over 100 million speakers, and India, which has more than 70 million, as well as in Nepal.

Arabic
Approximate number of speakers: 206,000,000
Arabic is the official language of 17 countries and it is also the language of the Muslim religion. As a result, many millions of Muslims in other countries have some knowledge of the language.

Other major languages

Portuguese
Approximate number of speakers: 176,000,000

Russian
Approximate number of speakers: 167,000,000

Japanese
Approximate number of speakers: 125,000,000

German (standard)
Approximate number of speakers: 100,000,000

Korean
Approximate number of speakers: 78,000,000

French
Approximate number of speakers: 77,000,000

A stop sign in English and Inuktituk (the language of the Inuit people)

The languages spoken in most countries

English:	57 countries	**Spanish:**	21 countries
French:	33 countries	**Portuguese:**	7 countries
Arabic:	23 countries		

Letters of the alphabet

Chinese	40–50,000	English	26
Japanese	18,000	French	26
Khmer/Cambodian	74	Roman	23
Sanskrit	48	Greek	24
Cyrillic	33	Hebrew	27
Persian	32	Early Latin	21
Turkish	29	Italian	21
Spanish	29	Hawaiian	12
Arabic	28	Rotokas (Solomon Islands)	11
German	27		

Disappearing languages
There are about 6,500 living languages that we know about. At least 1,820 of these languages are now spoken by fewer than 1,000 people.

Alphabets

An alphabet is the basis of a system of writing, using letters or characters to represent sounds or words. These are some of the oldest and most important alphabets.

Greek
The Greek alphabet is the oldest surviving European alphabet. The early Greek alphabet was written from right to left, but by about 500 BC it was written from left to right. The Greeks introduced an upper case (capital letters) and a lower case (small letters). The two cases are very different for some letters.

Cyrillic
The Cyrillic alphabet was invented in the 9th century by two Greek missionaries, St Cyril and his brother St Methodius. It is used for Slavonic languages such as Russian, Bulgarian and Ukrainian. The Russian Cyrillic alphabet originally had 43 letters, but the number was reduced to 33 after the Russian Revolution of 1917. Like the Greek alphabet, Cyrillic also has upper case and lower case versions of the alphabet.

Hebrew
Hebrew is written horizontally from left to right. It does not have its own numerals but uses standard Western numbers.

Arabic
Arabic evolved from Aramaic in the 4th century, and is written from left to right. It consists of 28 consonants. Vowels are shown by marks placed above or below the consonants but are not always used. Arabic letters are written differently depending upon where they appear in a word. The positions of characters are known as final (end), medial (middle), initial (beginning) and isolated (on its own).

Chinese and Japanese
These are logographic writing systems. This means that each symbol represents a word, or part of a word, instead of a sound. The Chinese system has 40–50,000 characters and the Japanese system has 18,000, but you need to know only about 2,000 and 1,850 respectively to get by in these languages. In 1966 the Chinese language changed quite dramatically, when books and newspapers were printed with the characters running horizontally from left to right rather than vertically from right to left. There is now a phonetic alphabet known as pin-yin, made up of 25 letters taken from the Roman alphabet.

Most Chinese characters are made up of eight basic strokes. These are all in the character for eternity (right). Words in a Chinese dictionary are in order of the number of strokes they contain.

Chinese verbs and adjectives usually contain only one character or syllable, but nouns often consist of two characters or more. The examples below show how some compound words are made up.

eternity

tree   *woodland*   *forest*
            (2 trees)   (3 trees)

Braille

Braille is a system of raised dots that allows blind people to read by touch. It was invented in the 19th century by a blind Frenchman named Louis Braille. The dots are embossed on to paper, either by hand or using a machine. They are read by moving the fingers across the top of the dots. The reader uses both hands – the right works out the message while the left feels ahead for the beginning of the next line. A skilled Braille reader can understand up to 150 words a minute, which is about half the speed of a sighted person reading ordinary text. The basic unit of Braille is called a cell. It is made up of six dots, which allows for 63 possible combinations to represent letters, numbers and punctuation marks.

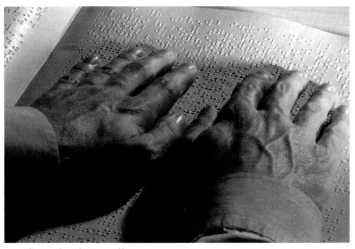
Reading a book in Braille

Phonetic alphabet

You may have heard pilots and soldiers on television and in films using the phonetic alphabet in radio messages. The alphabet is used to spell out parts of a message that might be difficult to recognize in unclear radio transmissions. The version generally used was developed in the 1950s. It is known as the NATO (North Atlantic Treaty Organization) Phonetic Alphabet and was designed to be understood and easily pronounced by all NATO members. They chose words that were used in lots of different languages and could not be confused with other common words or those used for another letter. Aircraft and ship crews also use the phonetic alphabet.

For example, in the phonetic alphabet "over and out" becomes Oscar Victor Echo Romeo Alpha November Delta Oscar Uniform Tango.

A	Alpha	J	Juliet	S	Sierra	W	Whiskey
B	Bravo	K	Kilo	T	Tango	X	X-ray
C	Charlie	L	Lima	U	Uniform	Y	Yankee
D	Delta	M	Mike	V	Victor	Z	Zulu
E	Echo	N	November				
F	Foxtrot	O	Oscar				
G	Golf	P	Papa				
H	Hotel	Q	Quebec				
I	India	R	Romeo				

→ See also

Brainchildren: young inventors: page 81

Keeping in touch

From cave paintings onwards, there have always been ways of conveying information and ideas to other people. Pictographs are pictures or symbols that represent words. Egyptian hieroglyphics are pictographs. They eventually developed into alphabets so that languages could be written down. People have also used signs and flags to communicate with each other and found ways of turning language into codes to send messages quickly. Until inventions such as Morse code, the fastest anyone could send information from place to place was at the speed of a horse. Now electronic messages can be sent around the world instantaneously via e-mail.

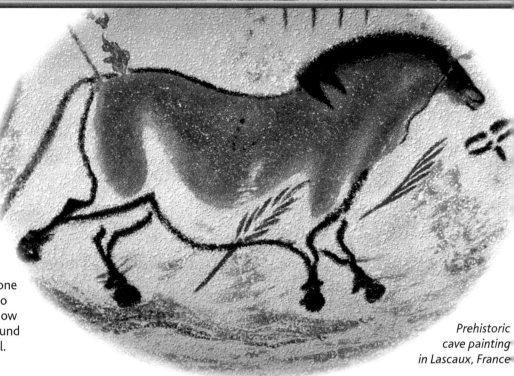

Prehistoric cave painting in Lascaux, France

Ancient Egyptian hieroglyphics on a tomb in the Valley of the Kings

Hieroglyphics

The simplest of all writing systems use pictures. These are called pictograms and look like the things they describe – just like many road signs and computer icons today. Writing or carving pictograms is very slow and a lot of work, so people began to use simpler versions of images, such as hieroglyphics. Ancient Egyptian hieroglyphics were used on obelisks, wall paintings, tombs and papyri (documents on a type of paper made from reeds). They are symbols that represent an object, a sound or an idea. They are not a code: you cannot simply convert an Egyptian hieroglyph into a letter and read it as we read words in a book.

People stopped using hieroglyphics in the 1st century AD. From then on, no one could understand them until 1822 when French scholar Jean François Champollion worked out how to translate the text of the Rosetta Stone in the British Museum.

Morse code

By using Morse code you can send a signal in a series of dots and dashes. The signal can be sent by sound or by flashing lights – a dash is three times as long a dot. There are five parts to the code: a dot (·), a dash (-), a short gap or pause (between letters), a medium gap (between words) and a long gap (between sentences).

Morse was created by and named after American artist and inventor Samuel Finley Breese Morse (1791–1872). He sent the first Morse code message over a wire from Washington DC, to Baltimore, Maryland, on 24 May 1844. It read "What hath God wrought!" An international version of Morse code became widely used to send telegrams by wire from place to place. Once people could send messages by radio transmissions they still used Morse code to keep in touch in situations such as warfare, when clear voice signals were not always possible.

The Morse code alphabet

A	·-	K	-·-	U	··-	0	-----
B	-···	L	·-··	V	···-	1	·----
C	-·-·	M	--	W	·--	2	··---
D	-··	N	-·	X	-··-	3	···--
E	·	O	---	Y	-·--	4	····-
F	··-·	P	·--·	Z	--··	5	·····
G	--·	Q	--·-			6	-····
H	····	R	·-·			7	--···
I	··	S	···			8	---··
J	·---	T	-			9	----·

Post firsts

First air letter, England to France, by balloon	1785
First mail carried by rail, UK	1830
First postage stamps in regular use, Penny Blacks, UK	1840
First Christmas cards, invented by Henry Cole, UK	1843
First US stamps	1847
First perforated stamps, Penny Reds, UK	1847
First letter boxes in UK (St Helier, Jersey)	1852
London postal districts first used	1858
First postcard sent, USA	1861
First picture postcard, Switzerland	1872
First commemorative stamps, Germany	1887
First Christmas stamp, Canada	1898
First airmail service, India	1911
First transatlantic airmail service	1939
First postcodes, Germany	1942
First zip (Zone Improvement Plan) codes, USA	1963
First self-adhesive stamps, Sierra Leone	1964

Most valuable stamp

The world's most valuable single stamp is a Swedish Treskilling Yellow. It was issued in 1855 and used in 1857 to mail a letter. The stamp was printed with the wrong colour ink (yellow instead of green), so it is unique. It was sold for £1.4 million ($2.3 million) at an auction in Switzerland in 1996, making it the world's most valuable object by weight. The stamp is now part of a private stamp collection in Denmark.

Sign language

Everyone makes hand gestures to show certain feelings: you might rub your stomach to show you are hungry, raise your fist as a threat or hold your thumb up to show approval.

The most important means of "speaking" by hand gestures is between deaf people. Sign languages for the deaf were first used in 17th-century Europe. In the 18th century schools were set up where national systems of sign language developed. As a result, a number of versions are used around the world with different ways of signing words.

Signers use the different finger positions, a variety of hand movements – upward, downward and so on – and make the signs against certain parts of the body such as the neck, arm and wrist. Both hands are used in the British system, but only one is used in American Sign Language.

Deaf children learning sign language with their teacher

Semaphore

In 1791 French inventor Claude Chappe (1763–1805) and his brothers developed a way of signalling called semaphore. They used two wooden arms which could both be set to seven positions. This made a total of 196 combinations, each representing a letter or other symbol. The signalling device was mounted on a high building. It could be seen from a distance by an operator viewing it through a telescope from the next semaphore station. From this, a system of signalling using human arms and flags was developed and used at sea to send information from ship to ship. This system was kept up to the 1960s, even after radio was commonly used to send messages at sea.

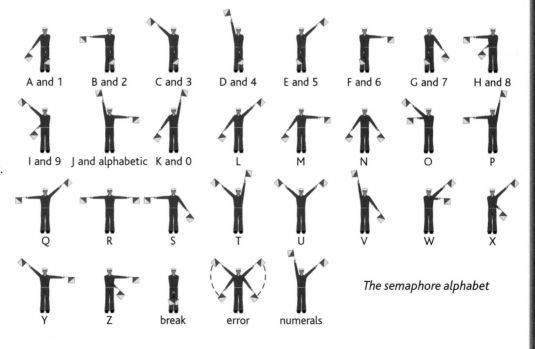

A and 1   B and 2   C and 3   D and 4   E and 5   F and 6   G and 7   H and 8

I and 9   J and alphabetic   K and 0   L   M   N   O   P

Q   R   S   T   U   V   W   X

Y   Z   break   error   numerals

The semaphore alphabet

Largest libraries

A library is a collection of books and other printed material. The word library can also be used to describe the building where a collection of books is kept. Below are some of the world's largest libraries. The figure for the Library of Congress is for printed books only, but the library also contains more than 100 million catalogued items, including manuscripts, maps and photographs.

Library	Location	Founded	Books
Library of Congress	Washington DC, USA	1800	29,000,000
National Library of China	Beijing, China	1909	22,000,000
Library of the Russian Academy of Sciences	St Petersburg, Russia	1714	20,000,000
National Library of Canada	Ottawa, Canada	1953	18,800,000
Deutsche Bibliothek*	Frankfurt, Germany	1990	18,557,445
British Library†	London, UK	1753	16,000,000

* Formed in 1990 when the Deutsche Bibliothek, Frankfurt joined the Deutsche Bucherei, Leipzig

† Founded as part of the British Museum, 1753; became independent in 1973

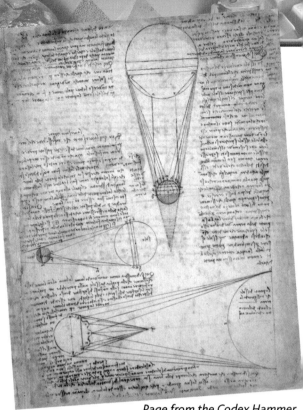

Page from the Codex Hammer

Valuable books and manuscripts

- The Codex Hammer (previously called the Codex Leicester) was sold in New York, USA, in 1994 for $28,800,000 (£18,643,190). It was bought by Bill Gates, the billionaire founder of Microsoft. The Codex is one of Leonardo da Vinci's notebooks and includes many of his scientific drawings and diagrams.

- John James Audubon's *The Birds of America* (1827–38) was sold in New York, USA in 2000 for $8,000,000 (£5,187,731), making it the most expensive printed book. Its giant pages feature more than 400 hand-coloured engravings of birds.

- One of the first-ever printed books was Geoffrey Chaucer's *The Canterbury Tales* (c 1477). A copy was sold in London in 1998 for £4,621,500 ($7,570,941).

- A "first folio" (early edition) of the works of William Shakespeare dating from 1623 was sold in London in 2001 for £4,156,947 ($6,166,000).

- A rare copy of the Gutenberg Bible, one of the first books ever printed, was sold in New York, USA, in 1987 for $5,390,000 (£3,264,688).

Unusual libraries

Around the world, there are some unusual ways of carrying books to readers. In Kenya, there is a camel-drawn library: one camel carries 500 books, another carries a tent which is set up as a mobile library, and there is a third camel as a spare. Other mobile libraries use donkeys, boats, bikes and trains to carry books.

The main reading room at the Library of Congress in Washington DC

Book firsts and records

First printed books
Books were printed in China in the 8th century using woodblocks, and in 14th-century China and Korea using movable type.

First book printed in Europe
The Gutenberg Bible was printed in 1455 by Johann Gutenberg and Johann Fust.

First books printed in English
William Caxton printed his first books in Bruges, Flanders. In about 1474 he printed the first book in English there, *Recuyell of the Historyes of Troye*, followed by *The Game and Playe of the Chesse*. He moved to Westminster in London, where his *Propositio ad Carolum ducem Burgundiae* (1476) was the first book to be printed in England. Chaucer's *Canterbury Tales* was probably the first book in English to be printed in England, in about 1477.

First books printed in America
Massachusetts Bay Colony: The Oath of a Free-Man (1638) and *An Almanack for the Year of Our Lord* (1639) are the first two books known to have been printed in the new American colonies.

Longest novel
A science-fiction novel by French writer Georges-Jean Arnaud, *La Compagne des Glaces* (1980–92), runs to 62 volumes and has about 11,000 pages.

First sequel
Daniel Defoe wrote *The Farther Adventures of Robinson Crusoe* in 1719, after the success of *Robinson Crusoe* earlier that year.

First American novel
The Power of Sympathy (1789) was the first novel published in America. It was published anonymously, but is believed to have been written by William Hill Brown.

First detective story
Murders in the Rue Morgue, by American author Edgar Allan Poe, was first published in *Grahame's Magazine* in 1841.

Smallest book
This was produced by a German typographer Josua Reichert and called *The World's Smallest Book*. It measures 2.4 x 2.9mm – the size of a match head.

Largest book
The largest ever book was published in 2003. It is a collection of photographs called *Bhutan: A Visual Odyssey Across the Kingdom*. When opened out it measures 2.1 x 1.5m – almost the size of a table-tennis table! It costs $10,000 a copy.

The largest book ever published

Types of book

Almanac
This is an annual calendar of dates and events. It originally contained astronomical facts and figures, but now includes useful statistics and other information. Almanac is sometimes spelled almanack.

Anthology
A collection of writings by one author or on a theme, such as an anthology of animal poems.

Atlas
A book of maps.

Autobiography
An account of a person's life written by himself or herself. Sometimes a "ghost" writer may help someone write an autobiography.

Bibliography
A list of books or sources on a particular subject.

Biography
A book about someone's life written by another person.

Chronology
A dictionary of dated events.

Dictionary
An alphabetical list of words and their meanings. There are also dictionaries on a single subject, for example *Dictionary of Art*.

Dictionary of quotations
A listing of interesting remarks or extracts from the writings of famous people.

Directory
An alphabetical list of names and addresses of people or organizations.

Encyclopedia
A book of articles on many subjects, arranged alphabetically. Encyclopedias are often published in many volumes or, today, on CD-ROM or on the Internet.

Gazetteer
A book that lists and describes places (countries, cities, etc).

Glossary
A list of words and phrases used in a particular subject area, for instance *A Glossary of Computer Terms*.

Language dictionary
A dictionary that gives translations of words and phrases to and from other languages, for example a *French-English/English-French Dictionary*.

Monograph
A book on a specialized subject, such as the work of a particular artist.

Novel
A work of fiction, usually involving imaginary people. A historical novel may be about real historical characters.

Novella
A short work of fiction.

Phrasebook
A book for travellers, with translations of words and phrases into and from a foreign language.

Pop-up book
A book, usually for children, made so that pictures stand up or move when the pages are opened.

Thesaurus
A book organized to show words with similar meanings.

Travel guide
A book of information about a particular country or area.

Who's who or biographical dictionary
Alphabetical summaries of the lives of famous people, living or dead, sometimes by their subjects (such as a *Dictionary of Scientists*).

Yearbook
An annual reference book with information about the events of the previous year. Yearbooks containing statistical information about a country are often called *Abstracts*.

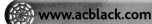 www.acblack.com

Famous diaries

People have kept personal diaries for more than 500 years. Most were written as personal records about the times the writers lived through or events that happened to them, but they are often fascinating for other people to read.

Samuel Pepys (1633–1703)
Pepys kept a diary for nearly ten years from 1660. He lived in London and wrote about events such as the Great Plague and Great Fire of London. He wrote in a special code, which was not translated until the 19th century. Pepys' original diaries are kept in the library of Magdalene College, Cambridge.

John Evelyn (1620–1706)
Evelyn was an English writer and gardener who lived at about the same time as Pepys. In his diaries he described the events of the Civil War and many aspects of 17th and 18th-century daily life. The original manuscript of Evelyn's diary is in the British Library.

Anne Frank (1929–1945)
Anne Frank was forced to hide with her family in Amsterdam, Netherlands, during World War II. This was at a time when Jewish people were being persecuted by the Nazis. Anne kept her diary while she was in hiding, but left it behind when she and her family were discovered. She was deported and died in a German concentration camp. Her father survived and edited her diary, which was published after the war. *The Diary of Anne Frank* became a bestselling book and was translated into more than 55 languages. It has also been made into an award-winning play and a film. The house in which the Frank family hid is now a museum.

 ## Bestsellers

These are some of the bestselling books ever. But the Bible has outsold them all. It is believed to have sold more than six billion copies in hundreds of versions and translations.

- One of the bestselling books of all time is a collection of quotations by Chinese leader Mao Zedong, known as his *Little Red Book*. Between 1966 to 1971 every Chinese adult had to own a copy and 900 million were printed.

- J.R.R. Tolkien's *The Lord of the Rings* trilogy was first published in 1954–55. It has sold well over 100 million and its sales received a further boost when the films based on the books were released between 2001 and 2003.

- *The American Spelling Book* by Noah Webster (1783) was used in American schools for generations. It has sold nearly 100 million copies.

- *The Common Sense Book of Baby and Child Care* by American doctor Benjamin Spock came out in 1946. Since then more than 50 million copies have been sold.

- British crime writer Agatha Christie has sold at least one billion copies of her novels in English and another billion in 45 foreign languages. In 1935 her novel *The Mysterious Affair at Styles* was one of the first Penguin paperbacks ever published.

- American author Margaret Mitchell's only book, *Gone With the Wind* (1936), has sold around 30 million copies. It is one of the bestselling novels ever.

 ## Translations

These are the ten most translated authors in the world, according to UNESCO's *Index Translationum* (1979–96).

- Walt Disney Productions
- Agatha Christie
- (The Bible)
- Lenin
- Jules Verne
- Barbara Cartland
- Enid Blyton
- William Shakespeare
- Hans Christian Andersen
- The Brothers Grimm

The following are the top languages into which books are translated.

German	153,367
Spanish	111,701
French	79,889
English	69,728
Russian	50,936
Japanese	49,327
Dutch	48,544
Portuguese	35,110
Other languages	**305,842**

The following are the top languages from which books are translated.

English	446,724
French	101,154
German	81,935
Russian	80,176
Italian	26,354
Spanish	18,073
Swedish	16,256
Other languages	**133,772**

 Imaginary lands

Writers usually invent the characters in their books, but some have also created imaginary lands in which the action of the book takes place. These are some of the best known fictional worlds, and the books in which they first appeared. Some featured again in later books by their authors.

Writer	Book	Land
Thomas Moore	*Utopia* (1516)	Utopia
Jonathan Swift	*Gulliver's Travels* (1726)	Lilliput
Voltaire	*Candide* (1759)	Eldorado
Lewis Carroll	*Alice's Adventures in Wonderland* (1865)	Wonderland
Samuel Butler	*Erewhon* (1872)	Erewhon*
Anthony Hope	*The Prisoner of Zenda* (1894)	Ruritania
L. Frank Baum	*The Wonderful Wizard of Oz* (1900)	Oz
J.M. Barrie	*Peter and Wendy* (1911)	Neverland
James Hilton	*Lost Horizon* (1933)	Shangri-La
J.R.R. Tolkien	*The Hobbit* (1937)	Middle Earth
C.S. Lewis	*The Lion, The Witch and The Wardrobe* (1950)	Narnia
Terry Pratchett	*The Colour of Magic* (1983)	Discworld

* An anagram for nowhere

Gulliver in Lilliput

 Nobel Prize for Literature

Nobel prizes have been given every year since 1901 for achievements in different fields, including literature. Nobel Prize winners for literature include poets, playwrights and authors from all over the world. Below are some of the best known winners.

2004 Elfriede Jelinek (Austria, 1946–)
2003 J.M. Coetzee (South Africa, 1940–)
2001 V.S. Naipaul (UK, 1932–)
2000 Gao Xingjian (China, 1940–) first win by a Chinese writer
1999 Günter Grass (Germany, 1927–)
1995 Seamus Heaney (Ireland, 1939–)
1993 Toni Morrison (USA, 1931–)
1991 Nadine Gordimer (South Africa, 1923–)
1983 William Golding (UK, 1911–93) author of *The Lord of the Flies*
1973 Patrick White (Australia, 1912–90)
1970 Alexander Solzhenitsyn (Russia, 1918–)
1962 John Steinbeck (USA, 1902–68) author of *The Grapes of Wrath*
1958 Boris Pasternak (Russia, 1890–1960) author of *Doctor Zhivago*
1954 Ernest Hemingway (USA, 1899–1961)
1953 Winston Churchill (UK, 1874–1965) British Prime Minister and writer
1948 T.S. Eliot (US-born, UK, 1888–1965) author of the book that inspired the musical *Cats*
1938 Pearl Buck (USA, 1892–1973)
1932 John Galsworthy (UK, 1867–1933) author of *The Forsyte Saga*
1925 George Bernard Shaw (UK, 1856–1950)
1923 William Butler Yeats (Ireland, 1865–1939)
1911 Maurice Maeterlinck (Belgium, 1862–1949)
1907 Rudyard Kipling (UK, 1865–1936) author of *The Jungle Book*
1901 Sully Prudhomme (France, 1839–1907) the first winner

Judy Garland in the film version of The Wonderful Wizard of Oz

Children's firsts

First children's book
The first English children's book for entertainment (not a school book) was a collection of rhymes called *A Booke in Englyssh Metre, of the Great Merchante Man called Dives Pragmaticus, very preaty for Children to reade*. It was printed in London in 1563.

First children's book printed in the USA
John Cotton's *Milk for Babies* was printed in Cambridge, Massachusetts, America, in 1641–45.

First children's encyclopedia
Pera Librorum Juvenilium (Collection of Juvenile Books) was compiled in Germany by Johann Christoph Wagenseil in 1695.

First story for children
The History of Little Goody Two-Shoes was published by John Newbery in London in 1765. Some experts believe it was written by the famous British poet and playwright Oliver Goldsmith.

First nursery rhyme book
Tommy Thumb's Pretty Song Book was published in London in 1744. It contained well-known rhymes such as "London Bridge is Falling Down", "Hickory, dickory dock" and "Sing a song of sixpence".

First children's library
The Bingham Library for Youth was set up in Salisbury, Connecticut, USA, in January 1803 when Caleb Bingham, who came from the town, donated 150 books.

Fairy tale authors

Fairy tales are fantastic stories for children that do not always involve fairies. They are traditional tales that were retold from generation to generation. The writers below collected the stories and wrote or re-wrote them in books that became hugely popular all over the world. Many fairy tales have been made into films – especially animated films by Disney.

Charles Perrault
French writer Charles Perrault (1628–1703) put together a collection of stories with the help of his son Pierre (1678–1700). Their collection contained *Cinderella, Little Red Riding-Hood, Sleeping Beauty* and *Puss in Boots*. The stories were translated into English in 1729. Later editions had the French title, *Contes de ma mère l'Oye*, or *Mother Goose's Tales*.

Brothers Grimm
German brothers Jacob Ludwig Carl Grimm (1785–1863) and Wilhelm Carl Grimm (1786–1859) were the authors of *Grimm's Fairy Tales*, which were first published for Christmas 1812. This was a collection of traditional stories, re-written for a young audience. It included many famous fairy tales, such as *Hansel and Gretel, Rumpelstiltskin* and *Snow White and the Seven Dwarfs*. They were translated into English in 1823 and became a worldwide bestseller.

Hans Christian Andersen
Danish author Andersen (1805–75) wrote 156 fairy tales, including *The Little Mermaid, The Emperor's New Clothes* and *The Ugly Duckling*. His stories first appeared in English in 1846.

Young author

At the age of six Dennis Vollmer (USA) wrote and illustrated his book *Joshua Disobeys*, which was published in 1988.

© Hergé/Moulinsart 2005

Tintin by Hergé

Famous illustrators

Below are some of the artists who have produced the best-loved illustrations for children's books. Some, such as Beatrix Potter, also wrote the books they illustrated.

Illustrator	Well-known books
Mabel Lucie Attwell (British, 1879–1964)	*The Boo Boos*
Alfred Bestall (British, 1892–1986)	*Rupert* stories
Quentin Blake (British, 1932–)	Illustrated Roald Dahl's books and others
Raymond Briggs (British, 1934–)	*The Snowman, Father Christmas*
Jean de Brunhoff (French, 1899–1937)	*Babar the Elephant* series
Walter Crane (British, 1845–1915)	*The Baby's Opera* and others
Hergé (Belgian, 1907–83)	*Tintin* books
Tove Jansson (Finnish, 1914–2001)	*Moomin* series
Henriette Willebeek Le Mair (Dutch, 1889–1966)	*Our Old Nursery Rhymes*
Beatrix Potter (British, 1866–1943)	*Peter Rabbit* books and others
Arthur Rackham (British, 1867–1939)	Illustrated classics
William Heath Robinson (British, 1872–1944)	Illustrated classics
Maurice Sendak (American, 1928–)	*Where the Wild Things Are* and others
Ernest Shepard (British, 1879–1976)	*The Wind in the Willows*
Jessie Willcox Smith (American, 1863–1935)	*The Water Babies*
Albert Uderzo (French, 1927–)	*Astérix* books

ONE AND ONLY

British writer Philip Pullman won the Whitbread Children's Book of the Year Award in 2001 for *The Amber Spyglass*, the final book in the trilogy *His Dark Materials*. *The Amber Spyglass* also won the Whitbread Book of the Year Award. This was the first time a children's book had won this prize.

Did Cinderella really wear glass slippers?

In Perrault's re-telling of the story of Cinderella, he used the French phrase *pantoufle de verre*, which means glass slipper. It may be, though, that he mistook *verre*, glass, for *vair*, an old French word for fur, and what Cinderella was actually wearing were furry slippers!

Mark Twain

Mark Twain was not the real name of the American author of *The Adventures of Tom Sawyer* and other books. It was a name he adopted for his work as a writer and comes from his time as a riverboat pilot on the Mississippi river. "Mark twain" means two fathoms or 3.7 metres. It was what boatmen shouted to tell the captain the water was deep enough for the boat to go ahead.

The Cat in the Hat, a character from one of Dr Seuss' most popular books

Multi-million sellers

All these children's authors wrote books that have sold millions of copies.

René Goscinny (France, 1926–77) and Albert Uderzo (France, 1927–)

René Goscinny and Albert Uderzo created the comic-strip character Astérix the Gaul in 1959. They have produced 31 books with total worldwide sales of more than 300 million copies.

J.K. Rowling (UK, 1965–)

By the end of 2003, the five *Harry Potter* books then in print had sold more than 250 million copies worldwide.

R.L. Stine (USA, 1943–)

R.L. Stine has written 80 titles in his *Goosebumps* series. They have sold a total of 220 million copies worldwide.

The first Harry Potter *book*

Hergé (Belgium, 1907–83)

Georges Rémi was the author-illustrator who wrote under the pen-name Hergé. He created the comic-strip character Tintin in 1929. The boy detective's adventures have appeared in book form since 1948 onwards and have been translated into about 45 languages and dialects. Total sales are probably at least 160 million.

Enid Blyton (UK, 1897–1968)

Enid Blyton wrote more than 700 children's books. Total sales of her works are more than 100 million. She was the bestselling English-language author until the arrival of J.K. Rowling.

Dr Seuss (USA, 1904–91)

Green Eggs and Ham, one of Dr Seuss' most popular books, has sold more than 8 million in the USA alone. Worldwide, he has sold more than 100 million copies of his books.

Beatrix Potter (UK, 1866–1943)

The Tale of Peter Rabbit (1901) has sold more than nine million copies in the USA. Altogether, at least 50 million copies of her books have been sold.

Lewis Carroll (UK, 1832–98)

There are no world figures for sales of Lewis Carroll's two classic children's books, *Alice in Wonderland* and *Alice Through the Looking Glass*, but these two books have never been out of print. They have appeared in hundreds of editions and in many languages.

Rev W. Awdry (UK, 1911–97)

Rev Awdry began writing his *Thomas the Tank Engine* books in 1946. The books have sold more than 50 million copies.

Mark Twain (USA, 1835–1910)

Book sales in the USA were not accurately recorded before 1895. *The Adventures of Tom Sawyer* and *The Adventures of Huckleberry Finn* have probably each sold more than 20 million copies worldwide since they were published in 1876 and 1884.

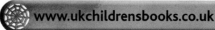 www.ukchildrensbooks.co.uk

Ancient poems

Before stories and poems were written down they were passed from generation to generation orally. Some of the most famous long narrative, or story, poems were passed on this way for hundreds of years before being written down by the poet who is now known as the author.

The Iliad – Homer
This Greek poem dates from 850 BC and tells the story of the final year of the war between the Greeks and the Trojans. It describes the great battle and the story of how beautiful Helen left her husband Menelaus for the Trojan prince Paris. It also tells us about the interference of the gods and their quarrels about the action on the battlefield below them.

The Odyssey – Homer
This describes Odysseus' journey home from the Trojan war. Odysseus features briefly in the *Iliad*. Again, human characters work side by side with the gods, who are given human characteristics. Although they are so powerful, the gods bear grudges, seek revenge and are very proud. The word odyssey has now come to mean any long, hard journey. The poem has strongly influenced other works of literature – most famously the novel *Ulysses* by the Irish writer James Joyce.

Rubáiyat of Omar Khayyám – Omar Khayyám
Omar Khayyám was a Persian writer, astronomer and mathematician who lived in the 11th and early 12th centuries. His *Rubáiyat* was introduced to the rest of the world in 1859, when it was translated by Edward Fitzgerald. It consists of a series of quatrains (four-line verses) rhymed a-a-b-a. Each verse contains a complete thought.

Beowulf
Beowulf is an epic poem of almost 3,200 lines written in Old English (or Anglo-Saxon). This is an early form of the English language that modern readers find hard to understand. The main theme is the struggle of the hero Beowulf with the water monster Grendel. Details of the poem's exact date and author are not known, but it may have been written in the 8th century by more than one person.

Sir Gawain and the Green Knight
This poem was written by a monk from the northwest of England during the second half of the 14th century. Its 2,530 lines describe events in King Arthur's court and the testing of Sir Gawain, a model knight. There are many opportunities for the character to fail, but he does not.

Haiku
This is a traditional Japanese form of poetry which has 17 syllables. For example:

> *Clouds appear*
> *and bring to men a chance to rest*
> *from looking at the moon.*

Matsuo Basho

Epic poem
An epic is an extended narrative poem, written in a grand style about the life of a heroic or mythological person. The *Mahabharata*, a famous Indian epic, is about four times longer than the Bible and seven times longer than Homer's great epics, the *Odyssey* and the *Iliad*.

Beowulf, hero of the 8th-century epic poem

www.poetrysociety.org.uk

Famous poets and poems

Most poets write many poems. Below are some of the most famous poets and their best-known works.

Charles Baudelaire (1821–67), France	*Les Fleurs du Mal*
William Blake (1757–1827), England	*The Tyger; London*
Matsuo Basho (1644–94), Japan	Numerous haiku
Elizabeth Barrett Browning (1806–61), England	*How Do I Love Thee?*
Robert Burns (1759–96), Scotland	*Tam o' Shanter*
Lord Byron (1788–1824), England	*Don Juan*
Geoffrey Chaucer (c 1343–1400), England	*The Canterbury Tales*
Samuel Taylor Coleridge (1772–1834), England	*Kubla Khan; The Rime of the Ancient Mariner*
Dante Alighieri (1265–1321), Italy	*The Divine Comedy*
Emily Dickinson (1830–86), USA	*Because I Could Not Stop for Death*
T.S. Eliot (1888–1965), USA/England	*The Waste Land*
Robert Frost (1874–1963), USA	*Stopping by Woods on a Snowy Evening; The Road Not Taken*
Seamus Heaney (1939–), Ireland	*Death of a Naturalist*
Homer (c 8th century BC), Greece	*The Iliad; The Odyssey*
John Keats (1795–1821), England	*Ode to a Nightingale; La Belle Dame Sans Merci; To Autumn*
Rudyard Kipling (1865–1936), England	*If*
Mikhail Lermontov (1814–41), Russia	*The Novice*
Li Po (701–762), China	*Drinking Alone Under the Moon*
John Milton (1608–74), England	*Paradise Lost; Paradise Regained*
Pablo Neruda (1904–71), Chile	*Canto General*
Nezami (1140–c 1217), Iran	*Khamseh* (or *The Quinary*)
Ovid (43 BC–AD 17), Ancient Rome	*Metamorphoses*
Sylvia Plath (1932–63), USA	*Ariel*
Arthur Rimbaud (1854–91), France	*Une Saison en Enfer* (or *A Season in Hell*)
Christina Rossetti (1830–94), England	*Remember*
William Shakespeare (1564–1616), England	*Sonnet 18* (or *Shall I Compare Thee to a Summer's Day*)
Percy Bysshe Shelley (1792–1822), England	*Ozymandias*
Edmund Spenser (1552–99), England	*The Faerie Queene*
Alfred Tennyson (1809–92), England	*In Memoriam; The Lady of Shalott*
Dylan Thomas (1914–53), Wales	*Fern Hill*
Virgil (70–19 BC), Ancient Rome	*The Aeneid*
Walt Whitman (1819–92), USA	*Song of Myself*
William Wordsworth (1770–1850), England	*The Prelude; Daffodils*
William Butler Yeats (1865–1939), Ireland	*Sailing to Byzantium; The Lake Isle of Innisfree*

Elizabeth Barrett Browning

Sylvia Plath

Poets laureate

The word laureate means crowned with laurel. The expression dates back to Ancient Rome, where a successful person was traditionally crowned with a wreath of laurel leaves.

In Britain, the position of poet laureate was created as a royal office in 1668 with the appointment of John Dryden by King Charles II. The position was traditionally held for life, but is now restricted to ten years. When it becomes vacant the prime minister has a list of names drawn up and the monarch chooses a new laureate. The poet laureate's main task is to write odes to celebrate royal birthdays, marriages and important state occasions. Poets laureate receive a salary of £70 per annum – the same as in the 17th century! Some famous poets laureate in the UK include William Wordsworth, Alfred Tennyson, Sir John Betjeman and Ted Hughes. The present laureate is Andrew Motion.

In the United States the first poet laureate (Joseph Auslander) was appointed in 1937. A new laureate is appointed every year. He or she serves from October to May and is paid $35,000.

Sir John Betjeman, British poet laureate from 1972 to 1984

All about comics

Comic strips

A comic strip is a story told in a series of pictures published in a newspaper. The New York *Daily Graphic* was the first newspaper to feature a comic strip. It started on 11 September 1875 with *Professor Tigwissel's Burglar Alarm*. The first regular strip was *The Yellow Kid*, which began in a supplement of the *New York World* on 5 May 1895. The first comic strip in the UK was *Adventures of Teddy Tail*, which ran in the *Daily Mail* from 5 April 1915 to 25 October 1960. A syndicated comic strip is one that appears in more than one newspaper. Some appear in hundreds of papers all over the world.

Comics

These are usually weekly collections of cartoon strips, humorous text and jokes. The first comic was the British *Ally Sloper's Half Holiday*, which appeared in 1884. British comics were most popular in the 1950s when some sold more than a million copies a week. Among these were *Eagle* (1950–69), *Rainbow* (1914–56) and *School Friend* (1950–65). *Dandy* appeared on 4 December 1937 and *Beano* on 30 July 1938. Both are still published.

 First appearances

Some comic strip and comic book characters are older than you might think. Below are the publications in which some of the most famous comic characters first appeared.

Character	Publication/country	Date
Rupert Bear	*Daily Express* strip (UK)	8 Nov 1920
Tintin	*Le Vingtième Siècle* (Belgium)	10 Jan 1929
Popeye	*Thimble Theatre* strip (USA)	17 Jan 1929
Dick Tracy	*Chicago Tribune* strip (USA)	4 Oct 1931
Flash Gordon	Syndicated strip (USA)	7 Jan 1934
Desperate Dan	*Dandy* (UK)	4 Dec 1937
Superman	*Action Comics* No 1 (USA)	June 1938
Batman	*Detective Comics* No 27 (USA)	May 1939
Captain Marvel	*Whiz Comics* No 1 (USA)	Feb 1940
The Green Lantern	*All American Comics* No 16 (USA)	July 1940
The Flash	*Flash Comics* No 1 (USA)	Jan 1940
Robin (Batman's assistant)	*Detective Comics* No 38 (USA)	Apr 1940
Wonder Woman	*All-Star Comics* No 8 (USA)	Dec 1941
Captain America	*Captain America Comics* No 1 (USA)	Mar 1941
Dan Dare	*Eagle* (UK)	14 Apr 1950
Peanuts	Syndicated strip (USA)	2 Oct 1950
Dennis the Menace (USA)	Syndicated strip (USA)	12 Mar 1951
Dennis the Menace (UK)	*Beano* (UK)	17 Mar 1951
Astérix the Gaul	*Pilote* (France)	29 Oct 1959
Supergirl	*Action Comics* No 252 (USA)	May 1959
Spiderman	*Amazing Fantasy* No 15 (USA)	Aug 1962
The Incredible Hulk*	*Hulk* (USA)	Mar 1962
X-Men	*The X-Men* (USA)	Sep 1963
Daredevil	*Daredevil* (USA)	June 1964

* The Hulk had grey skin in March 1962, but became The Incredible Hulk, with green skin, in the May issue two months later.

 Comic books

The first American comic book was called *Funnies on Parade* and came out in 1933. The first to be published regularly was *Famous Funnies* in 1934. Many comic books were about the adventures of a single superhero, such as Batman or Superman, who used special powers to fight crime and defeat evil villains.

Captain America

Most valuable comics

Copies of old American comic books first featuring superheroes Superman and Batman are the most valuable. Perfect copies of *Action Comics* No 1, with the first appearance of Superman, are valued at $440,000 (£230,000). *Detective Comics* No 27, the first to feature Batman, is valued at $375,000 (£183,000).

Newspaper fact file

First newspapers

From 59 BC onwards Roman emperor Julius Caesar had handwritten reports on news posted in public places in Rome. China had newspapers from about AD 713. The first European printed newspapers appeared in Germany in 1609. The first daily newspaper, *Einkommende Zeitungen*, also started in Germany, in 1650. Britain's first daily paper was the *Perfect Diurnall*, published in London in 1660. America's first successful newspaper was the *Boston News-Letter*, which appeared in 1704.

Largest

The edition of the Belgian newspaper *Het Volk* published on 14 June 1993 had pages measuring 142 x 99.5cm, which is more than six times the area of an ordinary broadsheet (large page size) newspaper.

Heaviest

The Sunday edition of the *New York Times* for 14 September 1987 contained 1,612 pages and weighed 5.4kg. At one time 127 hectares of forest containing almost 63,000 trees had to be chopped down to make the paper for one edition of *The New York Sunday Times*. Nowadays, much of the paper used for newspapers is recycled.

Smallest

Newspaper publishers sometimes produce miniature editions for publicity purposes. The smallest regular publication was the *Daily Banner*, published in 1876 in Oregon, USA. It measured just 9.5 x 7.6cm.

Top selling

The *Yomiuri Shimbun* (Japan) sells more than 14 million copies a day. *Bild-Zeitung* (Germany) is the highest-circulation newspaper outside Japan, selling more than 4 million copies a day. *The Sun* (UK) sells 3.5 million copies, more than any other English-language newspaper in the world. The USA's biggest-selling newspaper is *USA Today*, which sells 2.5 million a day.

Top newspaper-reading countries

	Country	Daily copies per 1,000 people
1	Norway	719.7
2	Japan	668.7
3	Finland	545.2
4	Sweden	541.1
	UK	408.5
	USA	263.6

Most mistakes

The Times (UK) of 22 August 1978 contained 97 misprints in one story about the Pope. He was called "the Pop" throughout the article.

See also

Book firsts and records: page 229

Magazine fact file

First-ever popular magazine
Mercure Galant, a gossip magazine, was first published in Paris in March 1672.

First women's magazine
The Ladies' Mercury was first published in London on 27 June 1693.

First American magazine
The American Magazine, published in Philadelphia, probably began on 13 February 1741.

First children's magazine
The *Lilliputian Magazine* appeared in the UK in June 1751 and ran for just over a year. The first in the USA was the *Children's Magazine*, published in January 1789.

First fashion magazine
The Paris magazine *Le Cabinet des Modes* was first published in 1785.

Oldest British weekly
The Lancet, a British journal for doctors, has been published every week since 5 October 1823.

Longest-running US magazine
Scientific American was launched on 28 August 1845 and is the longest continuously published magazine in the USA. At first, it was a four-page newspaper and included features on science and technology as well as topics such as religion and poetry. Later it began to focus on science and is now the world's most popular scientific journal.

First photograph in a magazine
Each copy of the June 1846 issue of the *Art Union* (UK) contained a photograph by Henry Fox Talbot, one of the inventors of photography.

First advertising magazine
Exchange & Mart was launched in the UK in 1868.

Do you know where the world's first university was? And which was the first ever museum? Can you guess which is the most expensive painting ever sold and what King Louis XIV collected? This section contains the answers to these and many other fascinating questions about education and the arts.

EDUCATION
AND THE ARTS

Education timeline

3000 BC	The Sumerians pioneer the idea of teaching. Education available only to those who could afford to pay a teacher for each lesson
590 BC	The city of Athens becomes the first to offer public education to all men for a small fee. Free education available to the sons of war veterans
597	King's School in Canterbury opens – the first school in the UK
859	The world's first university still in existence is founded in Fez, Morocco
1064	The first European university is founded in Parma, Italy
1160	Oxford University becomes the first university in England
1538	The first university of the New World opens in Santo Domingo (now the Dominican Republic)
1635	The first publicly funded high school in the USA opens in Boston
1636	Harvard University becomes the first university in the USA
1760	The first school for deaf children opens in Paris. Pupils are taught an early version of sign language
1781	The first nursery school is opened in Scotland for parents who have to go to work
1783	Poland becomes the first country to ban corporal punishment in schools
1784	The first school for blind children is started in Paris
1841	Oberlin College becomes the first university in the USA to award degrees to women
1871	A school in New York introduces the first distance-learning courses for young people who live too far away from schools to travel to them
1878	London University becomes the first UK university to award degrees to women
1987	Corporal punishment is banned in all state schools in the UK
1999	Corporal punishment is banned in all independent schools in the UK

UK public schools

In Great Britain a public school is a fee-paying school that's independent of the state. The term public was invented by the famous public school Eton College to emphasize the fact that anyone (provided they could pay) could attend. In other English-speaking countries, a public school is one paid for and governed by the state. In Britain the schools which other countries call public schools are called state schools.

Students in further education

The figures give the percentage of school leavers enrolled in further education. These countries have the highest number of students, but information is not available for all countries.

Country	%	Country	%	Country	%
Finland	85	Belarus	62	Belgium	58
South Korea	82	Greece	61	Poland	58
USA	81	Slovenia	61	Ukraine	58
Sweden	76	Estonia	60	Netherlands	55
New Zealand	72	Canada	59	France	54
Norway	70	Denmark	59	Italy	50
Russia	70	Lithuania	59	Portugal	50
Australia	65	Spain	59	Germany	48
Latvia	64	UK	59		

USA grade system

American children have 12 years of schooling. They start at five and the first year at school is called kindergarten. The grade system begins in the second year with first grade (six year olds) and continues to twelfth grade (18 year olds). In high schools, years have names instead of numbers: ninth grade is known as the freshman year, tenth as the sophomore year, eleventh as the junior year and twelfth as the senior year.

Harvard University, USA

Children at a Chinese boarding school doing their morning exercises

Schooling around the world

Time spent at school

- Schoolchildren in China spend more time at school than children in any other country. They have 251 schooldays a year – 59 days more than British children, and 71 more than American children.
- In the United Kingdom, the United States, France, Canada, Germany, Belgium, the Netherlands, Australia and New Zealand children have 10, 11 or 12 years of education. In most African countries and parts of South America children spend just five or six years at school. Only two African countries, Gabon and Tunisia, have ten years of compulsory schooling.
- In Italy and China, children can legally finish school at the age of 14. In Myanmar, Angola and Pakistan, children are allowed to finish at the age of nine, after only four or five years at school. In several European countries, including Croatia, Denmark, Sweden and Switzerland, parents don't have to send their children to school until they are seven years old – two years later than in many other countries.

Largest school

The largest school in the world is the City Montessori school in Lucknow, northern India; it has more than 27,000 pupils.

Most remote school

The world's most remote school is Kiwirrkurra Remote Community School in Australia. It is a 25-hour road journey from the nearest major town. The 100 pupils and seven teachers at another school in the region, Oombulgurri Remote Community School, can only get to school by light aircraft or by barge. The aircraft takes just 35 minutes, but the barge can take up to 12 hours.

One solution to the problem of teaching children in isolated parts of Australia is the School of the Air. This began transmitting lessons by high-frequency radio in the Alice Springs area in 1951. This is still used, but lessons are also delivered by e-mail, the Internet, video and telephone. There are now 12 Schools of the Air in Australia, serving more than 1,000 pupils spread over vast areas of outback.

Countries with the most...

Primary school pupils

The country with the most primary school pupils is China, which has the world's biggest population. In China, there are 125,756,891 children in primary school (2004). In India there are 113,826,978 primary school children (2004).

Secondary school pupils

China has the most secondary pupils – 90,722,796 – although not all children go on from primary to secondary school. In India there are 71,030,516 secondary school children.

University students

In China and India numbers of students go down dramatically at each stage of education. The United States tops the table at university level, with 15,927,987 students, followed by China (12,143,723), India (9,834,046) and Russia (8,030,034).

Pupils per teacher at primary school

Primary school pupils in the African nation of Chad are in classes of about 70, and in Cameroon and Mozambique there are more than 60 pupils for each teacher. At the other end of the scale, some teachers in Bermuda teach classes of just nine pupils. In Denmark, Hungary and the Netherlands, there are about ten pupils in a class.

Pupils per teacher at secondary school

In secondary schools in Eritrea there are as many as 50 pupils for each teacher. The Philippines has the second-largest class sizes at secondary level, with 38 pupils for each teacher. In Bermuda and Lebanon, secondary school pupils share their teacher with just six other pupils, and in Armenia and Israel, classes contain only eight students.

 See also

Largest countries: page 116

Famous painters

Artist	Dates	Nationality	Famous work
Fra Angelico	c 1400–55	Florentine	Deposition of Christ
Sandro Botticelli	1445–1510	Florentine	Birth of Venus
Hieronymus Bosch	c 1450–1516	Flemish	Garden of Earthly Delights
Leonardo da Vinci	1452–1519	Italian	Mona Lisa
Albrecht Dürer	1471–1528	German	Four Apostles
Michelangelo	1475–1564	Italian	Sistine chapel ceiling
Raphael	1483–1520	Italian	Madonna
Hans Holbein	1497–1543	German	Sir Thomas More
El Greco	1541–1614	Greek	Burial of Count Orgaz
Sir Peter Paul Rubens	1577–1640	Flemish	Descent from the Cross
Rembrandt Van Rijn	1606–69	Dutch	The Night Watch
Jan Vermeer	1632–75	Dutch	Girl with a Pearl Earring
Antonio Canaletto	1697–1768	Venetian	The Grand Canal and the Church of the Salute, Venice
Sir Joshua Reynolds	1723–92	English	The Family of the Duke of Marlborough
Thomas Gainsborough	1727–88	English	Blue Boy
Francisco Goya	1746–1828	Spanish	Maja Nude/Clothed
J.M.W. Turner	1775–1851	British	Rain, Steam, and Speed
John Constable	1776–1837	British	The Haywain
Dante Gabriel Rossetti	1828–82	British	Proserpine
Sir John Everett Millais	1829–96	British	Ophelia
Sir Edward Burne-Jones	1833–98	British	The Golden Stairs
Edgar Degas	1834–1917	French	The Rehearsal
James McNeill Whistler	1834–1903	American	Symphony in White
Paul Cézanne	1839–1906	French	Large Bathers
Claude Monet	1840–1926	French	Waterlilies
Berthe Morisot	1841–95	French	The Cradle
Pierre Renoir	1841–1919	French	Luncheon of the Boating Party
Mary Cassatt	1844–1926	American	The Bath
Paul Gauguin	1848–1903	French	Nevermore
Vincent van Gogh	1853–90	Dutch	Sunflowers
Georges Seurat	1859–91	French	Sunday Afternoon on the Island of La Grand Jatte
Henri de Toulouse-Lautrec	1864–1901	French	Aristide Bruant (poster)
Henri Matisse	1869–1954	French	The Dance
Piet Mondrian	1872–1944	Dutch	Broadway Boogie Woogie
Pablo Picasso	1881–1973	Spanish	Guernica
Salvador Dali	1904–89	Spanish	The Persistence of Memory
Francis Bacon	1909–92	British	Study after Velazquez's Portrait of Pope Innocent X
Jackson Pollock	1912–56	American	Number One 1948
Lucien Freud	1922–	British	Girl with Roses
Roy Lichtenstein	1923–97	American	Whaam!
Jasper Johns	1930–	American	Flag
Andy Warhol	1930–89	American	Marilyn Monroe
David Hockney	1937–	British	A Bigger Splash
Damien Hirst	1965–	British	The Physical Impossibility of Death in the Mind of Someone Living (shark)

Art terms

acrylic
Quick-drying plastic-based paint

cartoon
A preliminary sketch for a painting

chiaroscuro
Light and shade in painting

collage
A work made from pieces of paper and other materials stuck on to a background

composition
The arrangement of the elements and colour within a work

fresco
A painting on a freshly plastered wall

gouache
Water-based paint

icon
A portrait of a religious subject, such as a saint

impasto
Thickly applied paint

landscape
A painting of the natural world

medium
The material used to create a work of art

montage
Cut-out objects mounted on a surface

palette
The surface used by an artist for mixing paints, but also used to refer to the selection of colours

pastel
Coloured pigments in stick form used for drawing

still-life
A painting of an object or a group of objects

tempera
Pigments mixed with egg yolk and oil or water

trompe l'oeil
A painting that plays tricks on the eye to look as if it is three-dimensional

watercolour
Coloured pigments mixed with water

Girl with a Pearl Earring *(1665–66) by Jan Vermeer*

Western art styles

Medieval
Paintings, mosaics and miniatures in manuscripts, mostly of religious subjects.

Renaissance
The word means rebirth – the Renaissance art of the 15th and 16th centuries replaced medieval styles and revived the art of the Greek and Roman period.

Mannerism
A style of 16th-century Italian art, which uses bright colours and distorts scale and perspective.

Baroque/rococo
An ornate style that was popular in Italy during the 17th and 18th centuries.

Neoclassicism
A style of the 18th century modelled on classical (Greek and Roman) art.

Romanticism
This late 18th/early 19th-century style explores emotion and shows nature in its untamed state.

Realism/naturalism
19th-century style that showed real life, including its unpleasant side such as poverty.

Pre-Raphaelitism
This short-lived but important style was invented in 1848, and was inspired by medieval history and myths. The aim was to go back to the simplicity of painting before Raphael.

Impressionism
This style of painting developed in France and was named in 1874. The aim was to convey an impression of what the eye sees rather than what the mind knows is there. It was unpopular at first, but is now a much-loved style.

Symbolism
An attempt by late 19th-century artists to link the real and the spiritual worlds in their work.

Art nouveau-style vase by Louis Comfort Tiffany

Post-Impressionism
A development from Impressionism, which includes the Pointillism (dot painting) of Seurat and others. In Pointillism, small dots of colour are applied to the canvas. These appear to fuse when seen from a distance.

Art nouveau
A flowing ornamental style of the late 19th/early 20th centuries, which influenced architects and furniture makers as well as painters.

Expressionism/abstract expressionism
Early 20th-century styles in which the emotions of the painter are powerfully expressed.

Cubism
An abstract style – art that is not a direct representation of a subject – which is mostly about shape and colour.

Art deco
An angular, decorative style popular in the 1920s and 1930s.

Surrealism
A style that emerged between the World Wars, in which artists explore dreams and fantasy.

Abstract art
Non-naturalistic art in which shapes, lines and colour are more important than the objects they represent.

Pop art
A style that began in the 1950s, using images from popular culture such as films, comics and advertising.

Performance art
An art form that combines visual art with dramatic performance.

Environmental art
Art in which the landscape is decorated or altered. The artist uses natural objects such as stones to create his work.

Britart
Modern art by a group of young British artists. The movement began in 1988.

Upside-down masterpiece

On 4 December 1961, someone realized that Henri Matisse's painting, *Le Bateau* (*The Boat*), was hanging upside down in the Museum of Modern Art (MOMA), New York. It had been there for 47 days since it was first hung on 18 October and none of the museum's 116,000 visitors had noticed.

Portrait of Dr Gachet (1890), by Vincent van Gogh

Most expensive paintings

Only few people in the world are rich enough to buy these paintings for their private collections. Most prefer to bid anonymously and keep their identities secret for as long as possible for security reasons.

- Pablo Picasso, *Garcon à la pipe* (*Boy with a Pipe*), £58 million, May 2004
- Peter Paul Rubens, *Massacre of the Innocents*, £45 million, July 2002
- Vincent van Gogh, *Portrait of Dr Gachet*, £44 million, May 1990
- Pierre Auguste Renoir, *Au Moulin de la Galette*, £42 million, May 1990
- Vincent Van Gogh, *Portrait de l'artiste sans barbe* (*Portrait of the Artist without a Beard*), £39 million, November 1998

Record price for a photo

One of the first photographs ever taken in Greece was sold for £500,000 at a London auction in 2003. This was a record price for a single print. The photograph was of the Temple of Jupiter in Athens and it was taken in 1842 by French photographer Joseph Philibert Girault de Prangey (1804–92).

Museum fact file

First museum open to the public
Uffizi Gallery, Florence, Italy, 1591.

First museum in England
The Ashmolean Museum, Oxford, opened in 1683 to display the collection of natural history exhibits, coins, weapons and other items belonging to the collector and antiquary Elias Ashmole (1617–92).

The first national museum
The British Museum, London, opened to the public in 1759.

First public museum in the USA
Charleston Museum, Charleston, South Carolina, opened 1773.

First open-air museum
Skansen, Stockholm, Sweden, opened in 1891.

First children's museum
Brooklyn, New York, USA, opened 1899 and was the first of more than 300 children's museums worldwide.

First interactive museum
The Exploratorium, San Francisco, California, USA, opened in 1969 and has hundreds of hands-on exhibits.

Largest museum complex
The Smithsonian Institution, Washington DC, USA, consists of 16 museums with a total of more than 140 million items in their collections.

The Unisphere, made for the New York World's Fair, 1964–65

Art exhibitions and world fairs

Major art exhibitions and world fairs have been held for more than 200 years. Art exhibitions focus on a particular artist or style. World fairs promote the trade or image of a country and display new inventions. These are some of the most important.

Great Exhibition, London, 1851
This was a showpiece of the arts and industries of the world and the first exhibition of its kind in the UK. It was seen by 6,039,195 visitors.

First Impressionist Exhibition, Paris, France, 1874
Many Impressionist painters, including Claude Monet, first showed their work at this exhibition, which was shocking to many people.

Philadelphia Centennial Exposition, Philadelphia, USA, 1876
This first major show in the USA was held to celebrate the 100th anniversary of the Declaration of Independence. It was seen by 9,910,966 people. Inventor Alexander Graham Bell first demonstrated the telephone at the Exposition.

Exposition Universelle, Paris, 1889
The Eiffel Tower was built as a temporary exhibit for this show, which commemorated 100 years since the French Revolution. It attracted 28,121,975 visitors.

World's Columbian Exposition, Chicago, USA, 1893
This show celebrated the 400th anniversary of Christopher Columbus' discovery of America and had more than 27.3 million visitors. Many Americans saw electricity and hand-held cameras for the first time here.

Louisiana Purchase Exposition, St Louis, USA, 1904
The ice cream cone was invented at this fair, which attracted 19,694,855 visitors.

Armory Show, New York, 1913
This was the first exhibition of modern art in the United States and included the work of Picasso. It influenced American artists, collectors and museums.

Exposition Internationale des Arts Décoratifs et Industriels Modernes, Paris, 1925
This exhibition of art marked the beginning of Art Deco style and attracted 5,852,783 visitors.

World's Fair, Flushing Meadow Park, Queens, New York, 1939–40
The fair had 44,932,978 visitors and first introduced television to the public.

Festival of Britain, London, 1951
This was a celebration of post-war life, held 100 years after the Great Exhibition. It attracted 8.5 million visitors.

Exposition Universelle, Brussels, Belgium, 1958
The Exposition had 41.1 million visitors. Its Atomium structure, a giant model of a molecule, still stands.

New York World's Fair, 1964–65
A record 51,607,307 visitors attended this fair. The Unisphere, a large globe, is still on the site of the fair and so is the Shea Stadium, used for baseball and football.

Treasures of Tutankhamen, British Museum, London, 1972–73
This was one of the most popular exhibitions of all time and attracted an amazing 1,694,117 visitors. The show was repeated in New York in 1978–79, where it was seen by 1,226,467 people.

Expo 2000, Hanover, Germany, 2000
More than 180 nations took part in this show, which 40 million people visited.

Antony Gormley's Angel of the North *sculpture in Gateshead*

 # Unusual museums

Cockroach Hall of Fame, Plano, Texas, USA
Record-breaking cockroaches, and insects dressed as famous people.

Colman's Mustard Museum, Norwich, Norfolk, UK
Tells the fascinating history of mustard.

The Museum of Dog Collars, Leeds Castle, Maidstone, Kent, UK
A collection of dog collars, most of them dating from the Middle Ages.

Gallery of Also-Rans, Norton, Kansas, USA
A collection celebrating people who came second or lost political campaigns and other contests.

The Lawnmower Museum, Trerice, Cornwall, UK
Mechanical lawnmowers through the ages.

The Medieval Crime Museum, Rothenburg, Germany
Medieval crime, punishment and torture implements.

National Wool Museum, Geelong, Australia
The only museum devoted to wool, opened in 1988.

Nut Museum, Old Lyme, Connecticut, USA
Nut carvings, 2.4-m long nutcrackers and other nut-related exhibits.

Philips Mushroom Museum, Kennett Square, Pennsylvania, USA
A museum focusing on all types of mushrooms and other fungi.

The Piggy Bank Museum, Amsterdam, Netherlands
Displays 12,000 piggy banks from all periods.

Porter Thermometer Museum, Onset, Massachusetts, USA
More than 3,000 devices for taking temperatures.

Giant statues

There are many larger-than-life statues and monuments around the world. Here are some of the largest and most famous.

Chief Crazy Horse, South Dakota, USA
This is the world's biggest monument. It is carved into Thunderhead Mountain and is 172m high and 195m long. Work on the carving started in 1948 and continues to this day.

Ushiku Daibutsu (Buddha), Tokyo, Japan
This was unveiled in 1993. It weighs 1,000 tonnes and is 120m tall.

Motherland, Volgograd, Russia
This 82m concrete statue of a woman with a raised sword commemorates the Soviet victory at the Battle of Stalingrad (1942–43). It was completed in 1967.

Leshan Giant Buddha, China
Work on this huge statue began in AD 713 and was completed 90 years later. It is 71m high, with shoulders 28m across. Its feet measure 8.5m and the head is 15m high, with ears 7m long.

Statue of Liberty, New York, USA
This famous statue was presented to the USA by the people of France. It was shipped in sections and unveiled in 1886. The statue is made of sheets of copper on an iron frame, and weighs 229 tonnes. The height of the statue is 46m from the base to the top of the torch. It stands on a massive pedestal which more than doubles the overall height to 93m from the base to the torch. The hands are 5m long, the eyes are 0.76m across and the nose measures 1.48m. The statue was originally called Liberty Enlightening the World.

Christ the Redeemer, Rio de Janeiro, Brazil
This statue stands high above the city and is reached by a mountain railway. The figure of Christ is 38m tall and weighs 1,163 tonnes. It was unveiled in 1931 by the radio pioneer Guglielmo Marconi, who had designed its lighting. He unveiled it by sending a radio signal from his yacht in Genoa, Italy.

Colossi of Memnon, Karnak, Egypt
These two seated sandstone figures of Pharaoh Amenhotep III stand 21m tall.

Abu Simbel, Egypt
The four huge statues, each standing 20m high, used to guard a temple. They were moved in 1966 when the Aswan High Dam was built and the area flooded.

Sphinx, Giza, Egypt
This statue was carved in about 2500 BC. It is about 20m high and 73m long, and has the huge body of a lion, with the head of a pharaoh.

Angel of the North, Gateshead, UK
The Angel stands 19.8m high, has a wingspan of 53.3m and weighs 200 tonnes. It was designed by Antony Gormley and erected in 1998.

Mount Rushmore, South Dakota, USA
This is a massive sculpture of the heads of US presidents George Washington, Thomas Jefferson, Theodore Roosevelt and Abraham Lincoln. Each one is about 18.3m high. It was carved out of a cliff face between 1927 and 1939 and is one of America's most popular tourist attractions.

 See also

Tourism: pages 220–21
World History: page 101

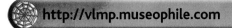 http://vlmp.museophile.com

Amazing collectors

Louis XIV
The French king owned a collection of 413 ornate beds. He kept them in different places all over France, so wherever he travelled, he could sleep in his own bed.

The Schlumpf brothers
French factory owners Hans and Fritz Schlumpf built up one of the world's largest car collections. They had 427 vehicles, including 120 rare Bugattis. These are now on public display at the National Auto Museum of France in Mulhouse.

Sir Thomas Phillips
Eccentric English book collector Sir Thomas Phillips (1792–1872) wanted to own a copy of every book ever printed – and he almost succeeded. He acquired more than 50,000 books and 100,000 manuscripts. His collection plunged his family into debt, but he rescued many priceless treasures from destruction. Sales from his collection have continued almost every year since his death.

Robert Opie
Robert Opie began his collection in 1963 with the wrapper from a packet of sweets. He now owns the world's largest collection of British packaging and advertising material, a total of more than 500,000 items.

Henry Holt
Lancashire collector Henry Holt built up the world's largest collection of bricks. When he died in 1996 he left 7,000 of them to the local museum, stacked up in various locations. The museum has been puzzling over what to do with them ever since.

Some of Elvis Presley's stage outfits, sold at auction in 1999

Unusual auction items

- In 1888 a cemetery containing 300,000 mummified cats was found in Egypt. Almost 20 tonnes of the mummies were shipped to Liverpool, UK, and sold at auction for £4 per ton. They were ground up and used for fertilizer.

- The skull of the Swedish philosopher Emanuel Swedenborg was sold at Sotheby's, London in 1978 for £1,500. Stockholm Royal Academy of Science bought the skull and reunited it with the rest of his body, which was buried in Uppsala Cathedral.

- A pair of Napoleon's socks was sold at Sotheby's, London, in 1996 for £2,990.

- A burnt loaf from the Great Fire of London, 1666, was sold at Sotheby's, London, in 1996 for £322.

- A pair of Queen Victoria's underpants were sold at Sotheby's, London, in 1996 for £253. A pair of Victorian rollerblades dating from c 1860 was sold at the same sale for £575.

- A dish containing a sample of penicillium mould prepared by penicillin inventor Alexander Fleming in 1935 was sold by Christie's, London, in 1997 for £14,950. At the same sale a box of 300 glass eyes was sold for £2,760.

- More than 2,000 items that had belonged to the singer Elvis Presley were sold at an auction in Las Vegas in 1999. These included clothing as well as letters, one of Elvis's school report cards and 29 dry-cleaning bills made out to Elvis.

- Britney Spears' used chewing gum is often auctioned on eBay, fetching prices as high as $14,000.

Young enthusiasts sorting a collection of baseball cards

Who collects what?

As soon as someone starts to collect something a word is invented to describe the collector. Most end in -ist, which means a person who does something (as a motorist is someone who drives a car or a violinist someone who plays a violin). Another ending is -phile or -philist, which means a lover of something.

Collectable	Collector
airmail stamps	aerophilatelist
autographs	philographist
badges and patches	scutelliphilist
banknotes	notaphilist
beer bottle labels	labeorphilist
beer mats	tegestologist or tegetologist
books	bibliophile or bibliophilist
butterflies and moths	lepidopterist
cameos	cameist
cheese labels	laclabphilist
cigar bands	brandophilist or cigrinophilist
cigarette cards	cartophilist
coins, money, medals	numismatist
corkscrews	helixophile
dolls	plangonologist
eggs	oologist (illegal in many countries)
egg-cups	pocillovist
flags and banners	vexillologist
gramophone records	discophilist
keyrings	copoclephilist
keys	cagophilist
match books	phillumenist
matchboxes	cumyxaphilist
money boxes	argyrothecologist
postcards	deltiologist
prints and book illustrations	iconophilist
shells	conchologist
stamps	philatelist
sugar packets	sucrologist
teddy bears	arctophilist
telephone cards	fusilatelist

Stamp collection themes

Many philatelists (stamp collectors) follow topical philately, which means they collect stamps by theme. They may acquire stamps from many different countries and periods. Here are some of the hundreds of popular themes.

aircraft	dinosaurs	mountains
animals	dogs	mushrooms
art and artists	dolls	music
authors	exploration	Nobel Prize
bicycles	famous people	Olympic Games
birds	fish	police
butterflies	flags	railways
cars	flowers	religion
castles	food	scouting
cats	heraldry	seashells
chess	horses	ships
children	insects	space
Christmas	lighthouses	sports
cinema	literature	stamps
costumes	maps	theatre
dance	medicine	uniforms

Postage stamps from around the world

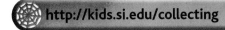
http://kids.si.edu/collecting

Music is the arrangement of a sequence of sounds in a rhythmic pattern. There are many kinds of music, from pop and folk to opera and classical, and every culture has music in some form. Music also plays an important role in performance arts such as theatre and the many different types of dance.

MUSIC
AND
PERFORMANCE

Musical instrument records

Double bass
A double bass 4.26m long and weighing 590kg was built by Arthur K. Ferris of Ironia, New Jersey, USA, in 1924.

Drum
The University of Texas Longhorn Band has a drum nicknamed Big Bertha which is 7.6m in circumference.

Guitar
A giant version of a Gibson guitar 11.63m long was made in 1991 by students at Shakamak High School, Jasonville, Indiana, USA. Large stringed instruments that are bigger than the span of human hands are difficult or even impossible to play.

Organs
The world's loudest instrument is the Auditorium Organ in Atlantic City, USA. It was built in 1930 at a cost of $500,000, has more than 32,000 pipes and is powered by a 365 horsepower blower.

The second-largest organ is the pipe organ built in 1911 in the Wanamaker Department Store (now Lord & Taylor's), Philadelphia, USA.

The world's largest cathedral organ was built in St Stephen's Cathedral, Passau, Germany in 1928. It has 17,774 pipes.

Pianos
In 1935 in London Charles H. Challen built a piano which is probably the largest in the world. It weighs 1.25 tonnes and is 3.55m long.

One of the lightest pianos ever made was a baby grand weighing just 180kg. It was made mostly of aluminium covered in yellow pigskin. It was constructed by the Blüthner company of Germany for the airship *Hindenburg*, and was destroyed when the airship exploded in 1937.

Tuba
In 1896 John Philip Sousa, who is the American inventor of the sousaphone, played a 2.28m tuba on a world tour. This is the largest brass instrument ever made and had 11.8m of tubing.

Famous songs

Auld Lang Syne
The words of this song come from verses written by Scottish poet Robert Burns in 1788. The music is based on an old ballad. "Auld Lang Syne" (meaning old long since) is traditionally sung at midnight on New Year's Eve, except in Taiwan where it is a graduation song.

Happy Birthday to You
In 1893 two American sisters, who were teachers, wrote this song to sing in school assemblies. Mildred J. and Patty Smith Hill originally called the song "Good Morning to You". After the words were changed in 1924, it became known the world over. The song will be in copyright until 2030, but only for commercial purposes. Singing it at a birthday party does not infringe copyright!

Waltzing Matilda
"Waltzing Matilda" has been described as Australia's unofficial national anthem. The song was written in Australia in 1895 by Andrew Barton "Banjo" Paterson. He was inspired by events during a sheep-shearers' strike the previous year. The music is by Christina Macpherson and is based on a traditional Scottish song.

The world's largest church organ is in St Stephen's Cathedral, Passau, Germany.

Largest orchestras

- In 1872 Austrian composer Johann Strauss conducted an orchestra of 987 (including 400 first violinists) and a choir of 20,000. The performance was in Boston, USA.

- In 1958, the Norwegian National Meeting of School Bands assembled 12,600 players at Trondheim, Norway.

- A total of 6,452 musicians from the Vancouver Symphony Orchestra and Canadian music students played together in Vancouver, Canada, on 15 May 2000.

- An ensemble of 1,013 cellists played on 29 November 1998 in Kobe, Japan.

- On 14 July 1999 Piers Adams conducted 710 recorder players performing "Roaring Rag" by Beverley Wragg at Cressing Temple Barn, Essex, UK.

Musical terms

Many musical terms are derived from Italian words. Here are the meanings of some common ones.

Term	Meaning
Agitato	Agitated or excited
Brillante	Sparkling, brilliant
Brio	Spirit or vigour
Crescendo	Gradual increase in volume
Dolce	Sweet, soft and gentle
Dolente	Sad
Forte	Loud or strong
Fortissimo	Very loud
Grave	Slow and serious
Lento	Slow
Molto	Much or very
Pianissimo	Very soft
Piano	Soft
Ritenuto	Slowing in tempo
Scherzo	Lively
Sotto voce	Quiet and subdued
Tutti	All the players

Musical tempos

Tempo	Meaning
Larghissimo	As slow as possible
Largo	Very slow and solemn
Largementa	Slow, broad
Larghetto	Slightly less slow
Lento	Slow
Adagissimo	Very slow
Adagio	Slow (from the Italian for at ease)
Adagietto	Slightly faster
Andante	Moderately slow (from the Italian for walk)
Andantino	Slightly slower than andante
Moderato	At a brisk walking pace
Allegretto	Fairly lively
Allegramente	Lightly
Allegro	Lively, fast (from the Italian for cheerful)
Vivace	Fast
Vivacissimo	Very quick
Presto	Very fast
Prestissimo	Extremely fast

See also

Inventions: pages 80–81

Thomas Edison (1847–1931) with his first phonograph

Recording timeline

1877	Thomas Alva Edison first recorded a human voice (singing "Mary Had a Little Lamb") on a tinfoil cylinder phonograph
1878	Edison is granted phonograph patent
1885	"Graphophone" with wax cylinders is invented by Alexander Graham Bell and Charles Tainter
1888	"Gramophone", with 7-inch flat disk, is patented by Emile Berliner
1895	First spring-driven phonograph is sold by Edison
1896	Improved gramophone produced by Eldridge Johnson
1897	Shellac discs introduced
1898	First magnetic recorder, with steel wire, patented by Valdemar Poulsen
1904	First mass-produced, double-sided discs are sold in Germany
1925	First electrically-recorded discs make it possible to record entire orchestral works
	Sound recordings for films are introduced
1927	First coin-operated juke box is produced
1931	Stereo recording introduced
1934	First hi-fi (high-fidelity sound) records are made
1935	"Magnetophone" (tape recorder) is demonstrated in Berlin
1948	First 12-inch $33\frac{1}{3}$ rpm, micro-groove LP vinylite record is produced, with 23-minute capacity per side
1949	First 7-inch, 45 rpm, micro-groove EP (Extended Play) vinylite record and player is introduced
1958	First stereo LPs are sold
1963	First compact audio cassette is produced
1969	Dolby Noise Reduction is introduced
1979	First Sony Walkman portable audio cassette players are sold
1980	First camcorders are sold
1982	First CDs are sold
1987	DAT (Digital Audio Tape) players are launched
1988	More CDs are sold than vinyl discs
1992	Mini-discs are introduced
1997	MP3 format is launched
1999	DVD-Audio format is introduced
2001	Apple Computer's iPod is launched
2005	More than 15 million iPods sold worldwide by March 2005

🎵 Instruments of the orchestra

The range and number of instruments in a modern orchestra varies enormously. There may be as many as 100 or more, and less familiar instruments are brought in for special performances. These are the most common instruments.

STRINGS

Violin

Viola

Cello

Double bass

Harp

The violin has a hollow wooden body which resonates when the violinist pulls a bow over the four strings. There may be 30 or more violins in a modern orchestra.

The viola is larger and deeper-voiced than the violin, and is played in the same way.

The cello's full name is the violoncello. It is the third-largest member of the violin family and is played sitting down.

The largest and deepest stringed instrument in an orchestra is the double bass. Double bass players usually stand to play, pulling a bow across the strings, or plucking them.

The orchestral harp has 48 strings of different lengths, attached to the top and side, and seven pedals at the base.

WOODWIND

Flute

Piccolo

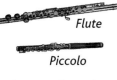

Oboe

Clarinet

Bass clarinet

Bassoon

Cor anglais

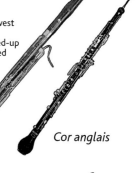

The concert flute is played through a blow hole at one end. Alto and bass flutes are larger versions which play lower notes. The piccolo is half the size of the concert flute and plays the highest notes in the orchestra.

Oboe players blow through a double reed made from two small slices of cane tied together and inserted into the mouthpiece of the instrument.

The clarinet is also played through a reed. There are several different types of clarinet. B flat and A are played most often.

The bassoon plays the lowest notes of the woodwind instruments. It is a doubled-up wooden tube with a curved metal crook at one end, which holds the reed.

BRASS

French horn

Trumpet

Trombone

Tuba

Flugelhorn

Euphonium

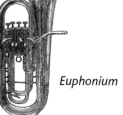

French horn players make different notes by changing the shape of their lips as they blow into the mouthpiece of this coiled metal tube.

A trumpet is a tightly-coiled metal tube with a cone called the bell at one end. Trumpets have three small buttons called valves which make different notes when pressed.

The trombone is also made from coiled metal and has a section called the slide, which players move in and out to create different notes. The trombone plays lower notes than the trumpet.

There is usually just one tuba in an orchestra. It plays the lowest notes of all the brass instruments.

PERCUSSION

Timpani/Kettledrums

Triangle

Bass drum

Cymbals

Side drum

Orchestras usually have three or four timpani or kettledrums. They are made of copper with a plastic skin stretched over the top.

Various other instruments are sometimes played in orchestras, including keyboards (piano, organ, celesta, etc), bells, castanets, glockenspiels, gongs, marimbas, rattles, tambourines, wind machines, wood blocks, xylophones, guitars, mandolins and saxophones.

🎵 Singing parts

Name	Female voices
Soprano	The highest female voice
Mezzo soprano	Between a soprano and a contralto
Contralto	The lowest female voice

Name	Male voices
Alto	The highest male voice, traditionally sung by choirboys
Tenor	A high male voice. A countertenor voice is very high
Baritone	A voice higher than a bass, but lower than a tenor
Bass	The lowest male voice. Basso profundo is the lowest possible voice
Falsetto	An unnaturally high voice sung by tenors and basses

Scene from The Magic Flute, *an opera by Mozart*

Dame Nellie Melba

The real name of Australian opera singer Dame Nellie Melba (1881–1931) was Helen Mitchell. She adopted the name Melba from Melbourne, the city near her birthplace. The dessert known as Peach Melba was named in her honour by celebrated chef Escoffier, and Melba toast was named after the toast served to her at the Savoy Hotel, London.

Opera terms

aria
A song for a single voice

comic opera
Opera with a comic plot

finale
The ending, when the whole cast often sing together

libretto
The text of an opera, from the Italian for little book

operetta
A light (rather than serious) opera, usually with an amusing story

prima donna
First lady (from the Italian) – the main female singer, or diva

recitative
A part in an opera that is spoken rather than sung

 ## Opera facts

Most-performed operas
Puccini's *La Bohème* is the most-performed opera in London and New York. It has been staged 545 times since 1897 at London's Royal Opera House, and 1,140 times at the Metropolitan Opera House in New York. *Aïda* and *Carmen* are the closest runners-up in both places.

Longest operas
Richard Wagner's *Gotterdämmerung* is the longest regularly-performed opera. The opera can last up to six hours, including intervals.

Largest opera venues
The two largest opera houses where operas are regularly performed are in Italy and America. They are the Arena di Verona in Verona, which holds 16,663 people, and the Municipal Opera Theatre in St Louis, USA, which holds 11,745. The Teatro alla Scala, Milan, Italy, which has 3,600 seats, is one of the world's largest indoor opera theatres, although several US opera houses come close in size.

Grandest grand opera
The opera *Aïda* has often been performed on a grand scale, with a huge cast including elephants and other animals. It has been staged at the pyramids, Egypt, and in the year 2000 was performed in a football stadium in Shanghai, China, with a cast of 3,000 and an audience of 45,000.

Singer Whitney Houston at the World Music Awards, 2004

♫ Top singles of all time

The numbers of singles sold outside the USA and some European countries have only been recorded fairly recently, so world sales here are estimates. "White Christmas" was the world's bestselling single for more than 50 years until it was overtaken by Elton John's tribute to Princes Diana in 1997.

Artist/single/year	Estimated sales (millions)	
	USA	World total
Elton John, Candle in the Wind (1997)/Something about the Way You Look Tonight (1997)	11	37
Bing Crosby, White Christmas (1945)	n/a	30
Bill Haley and His Comets, Rock Around the Clock (1954)	n/a	up to 25
The Beatles, I Want to Hold Your Hand (1963)	0.5	12
The Beatles, Hey Jude (1968)	4.0	10
Whitney Houston, I Will Always Love You (1992)	4.0	10
Elvis Presley, It's Now or Never (1960)	1.0	10
Paul Anka, Diana (1957)	n/a	9
Elvis Presley, Hound Dog/Don't Be Cruel (1956)	4.0	9
Bryan Adams, (Everything I Do) I Do it for You (1991)	3.0	8
The Monkees, I'm a Believer (1966)	0.5	8

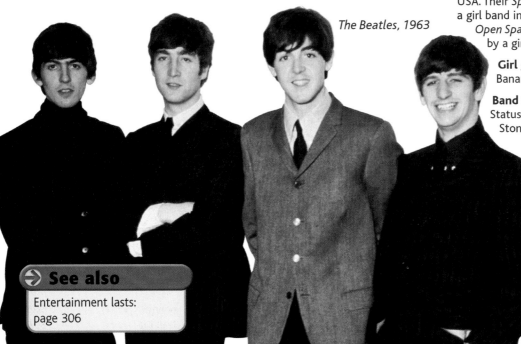

The Beatles, 1963

♫ Rock and pop facts

First CD single by a band
Dire Straits, *Brothers in Arms*, 1985

Loudest rock band
During the 1960s and 70s, British group The Who played at 140 decibels – as loud as a jet at takeoff. Members of the band suffered hearing loss.

Biggest-selling album in the UK
The Beatles' *Sgt Pepper's Lonely Hearts Club Band* (1967) sold 250,000 in the UK in its first week and 500,000 within the month. It stayed at No 1 for 27 weeks and total UK sales now exceed 4.5 million.

Biggest-selling album by a teenage solo singer
Britney Spears holds the record for her album *Baby One More Time* (1999). She is also the biggest-selling teenage artist – she'd sold more than 37 million records worldwide before her 20th birthday on 2 December 2001.

Most successive No 1 albums (UK)
Robbie Williams had a string of five No 1 albums in the UK between 1997 and 2002. He has also won 14 BRIT awards, more than any other artist.

Biggest-selling group in the world ever
The Beatles' total sales of singles and albums on vinyl, tape and CD are well over one billion.

Albums longest in the charts
Pink Floyd's *The Dark Side of The Moon* (1973) stayed in the UK charts for 741 weeks (14 years) and on the US Top 200 for 591 weeks. Fleetwood Mac's *Rumours* (1977) stayed in the UK charts for 477 weeks. It was also No 1 in the US for 31 weeks, 19 of them consecutive, both a record for any group.

Bestselling single ever by a group in the UK
Queen, "Bohemian Rhapsody" (1975)

Bestsellers by a girl band
"Wannabe" (1996) by the Spice Girls is the bestselling single by a girl band in both the UK and USA. Their *Spice* (1996) is the bestselling album by a girl band in the UK, but the Dixie Chicks' *Wide Open Spaces* (1998) is the bestselling album by a girl band in the USA.

Girl group with most UK chart hits
Bananarama – 26

Band with most UK chart hits
Status Quo – 58, followed by The Rolling Stones – 51

ONE AND ONLY

Group to have all top 5 positions in the USA singles chart was The Beatles, on 4 April 1964, with:

1 Can't Buy Me Love
2 Twist and Shout
3 She Loves You
4 I Want to Hold Your Hand
5 Please Please Me

➜ **See also**

Entertainment lasts: page 306

Major rock events

The following are the best-attended rock events ever. The *Live Aid* concerts in Philadelphia and London on 13 July 1985 had smaller audiences – 90,000 and 75,000 at each venue – but were reckoned to have the greatest TV audience of all time. About 1.5 billion people, or a quarter of the world's population, watched the concerts on television.

Event/date	Estimated audience
Rod Stewart, Copacabana Beach, Rio de Janeiro, Brazil, 31 December 1994	3,500,000
Golden Jubilee Concert, Buckingham Palace, London, 3 June 2002	over 1,000,000
Garth Brooks in Central Park, New York, USA, 7 August 1997	750,000
US Festival, San Bernardino, California, 28–30 May 1982	725,000
Summer Jam, Watkins Glen, New York, 28 July 1973	600,132
Third Isle of Wight Festival, UK, 30 August 1970	up to 600,000
Simon and Garfunkel in Central Park, New York, USA, 19 September 1981	500,000
Rolling Stones Free Concert, Hyde Park, London, 5 July 1969	up to 500,000
Molson Canadian Rocks for Toronto, Toronto, Canada, 30 July 2003	489,176
Woodstock Festival, Bethel, New York, USA, 15–17 August 1969	over 400,000
Blockbuster RockFest 1997, Fort Worth, Texas, USA, 21 June 1997	385,000
Altamont, California, USA, 6 December 1969	300,000
Woodstock 94, Saugerties, New York, USA, 12–14 August 1994	300,000

Jimi Hendrix playing at Woodstock Festival, New York, 1969

Treasures of rock

Fans of rock music often like to buy items that belonged to their favourite singers and bands. The more successful the artist, the higher the price.

1965 Rolls-Royce Phantom V touring limousine, painted in psychedelic colours, owned by John Lennon of The Beatles. Sold at auction in New York, USA, on 29 June 1985 for £1,768,462 ($2,299,000).

Steinway Model Z upright piano owned by John Lennon. Sold in an online auction on 17 October 2000 for £1,450,000 ($2,098,860).

"Tiger" guitar owned by Jerry Garcia of Grateful Dead. Sold in New York, USA, on 9 May 2002 for £657,850 ($957,500).

"Blackie" Fender Stratocaster guitar owned by Eric Clapton. Sold in New York, USA, on 25 June 2004 for £528,068 ($959,500).

Bernie Taupin's handwritten lyrics for the re-written "Candle in the Wind", sung by Sir Elton John in Westminster Abbey at the funeral of Diana, Princess of Wales. Sold in Los Angeles, USA, on 11 February 1998 for £278,512 ($400,000).

John Lennon's Rolls-Royce

Top albums of all time worldwide

The USA has always led the world in album sales. About 100 albums have sold more than 10 million copies each in the US. Total worldwide sales are less easy to find, but using the best estimates available these albums can claim to be world-beaters.

Artist/album/year	USA	World total
Michael Jackson, *Thriller* (1982)	26	47
Pink Floyd, *Dark Side of The Moon* (1973)	23	up to 35
Eagles, *Their Greatest Hits 1971–1975* (1976)	28	31
Saturday Night Fever (Soundtrack) (1977)	15	30
Shania Twain, *Come On Over* (1997)	19	30
Alanis Morissette, *Jagged Little Pill* (1995)	16	29
Fleetwood Mac, *Rumours* (1977)	19	26
Led Zeppelin, *Led Zeppelin IV* (1971)	22	26
Meat Loaf, *Bat Out of Hell* (1977)	14	24

These are the leading singers and groups in the USA based on the total sales of all their albums.

Artist	Total US sales (millions)	Artist	Total US sales (millions)
The Beatles	166.5	AC/DC	63.0
Elvis Presley	117.5	Bruce Springsteen	61.5
Led Zeppelin	106.0	Madonna	60.0
Garth Brooks	105.0	Michael Jackson	58.5
Eagles	88.0	Mariah Carey	57.0
Billy Joel	78.5	Metallica	57.0
Pink Floyd	73.5	George Strait	54.5
Barbra Streisand	71.5	Whitney Houston	54.0
Elton John	67.5	Van Halen	50.5
Aerosmith	64.0	Kenny Rogers	50.5
The Rolling Stones	63.5	Neil Diamond	50.0

Theatre records

First actor
Thespis was the first performer ever recorded. He was an actor in Greece in 534 BC. At this time, Greek actors used masks, and Thespis was the first to use stage make-up.

World's oldest theatres
The oldest indoor theatre in the world is the Teatro Olimpico, Vicenza, Italy, which opened on 3 March 1585.

London's oldest theatre is the Theatre Royal, Drury Lane, which opened on 7 May 1663. It was burnt down in 1672, rebuilt by Sir Christopher Wren, and restored again in 1812. In 1800 it became the world's first theatre to have safety curtains.

The oldest surviving theatre in the USA is the Walnut Street Theatre in Philadelphia, Pennsylvania. It opened in 1809 and was originally built as a circus. It was the first theatre with gas footlights and the first to have air conditioning.

World's biggest theatres
The National People's Congress Building Theatre, Beijing, China was built in 1959 and can hold audiences of 10,000. The Perth Entertainment Centre, Australia (1976) has up to 8,500 seats, the Chaplin (originally Blanquetta), Havana, Cuba (1949) has 6,500 and Radio City Music Hall, New York, USA, has 6,200. The 3,483-seater Hammersmith Odeon is the largest theatre in Britain, but the Royal Albert Hall in London can hold up to 7,000, depending on the event and how the seating is organized.

Worst disasters at a theatre
Fires, in which people were burned to death or trampled in the panic to escape, have caused the worst disasters at theatres. The worst ever was at Canton (now Guangzhou), China, in 1845 when 1,670 died. Europe's worst was at the Ring Theatre, Vienna, Austria, in 1881, which killed at least 620 people. The worst in the USA was at the Iroquois Theatre, Chicago, in 1903, which left 602 dead. These are the worst single-building (rather than city or forest) fires in history.

Longest play
Neil Oram's *The Warp* was first performed at the ICA (Institute of Contemporary Art) in London from 18–20 January 1979. It lasted 18 hours and 5 minutes.

Famous playwrights

Playwright	Nationality/dates	Famous play
Aeschylus	Greek, c 525–546 BC	Oresteia
J.M. Barrie	Scottish, 1860–1937	Peter Pan
Samuel Beckett	Irish, 1906–89	Waiting for Godot
Anton Chekhov	Russian, 1860–1904	The Cherry Orchard
Noël Coward	English, 1899–1973	Private Lives
Euripides	Greek, c 484–406 BC	The Trojan Women
Federico García Lorca	Spanish, 1898–1936	Blood Wedding
Oliver Goldsmith	English 1728–74	She Stoops to Conquer
David Hare	English, 1947–	Plenty
Henrik Ibsen	Norwegian, 1828–1906	Hedda Gabler
Ben Jonson	English, 1572–1637	The Alchemist
Christopher Marlowe	English, 1564–93	Doctor Faustus
Arthur Miller	American, 1915–2005	The Crucible
Molière	French, 1622–73	Tartuffe
John Osborne	English, 1929–94	Look Back in Anger
Harold Pinter	English, 1930–	The Birthday Party
Peter Shaffer	English, 1926–	Amadeus
William Shakespeare	English, 1564–1616	Hamlet
George Bernard Shaw	Irish, 1856–1950	Pygmalion
Richard Brinsley Sheridan	English, 1751–1816	The Rivals
Neil Simon	American, 1927–	Plaza Suite
Sophocles	Greek, c 496–405 BC	Antigone
Tom Stoppard	Czech, 1937–	Rosencrantz and Guildenstern are Dead
J.M. Synge	Irish, 1871–1909	The Playboy of the Western World
John Webster	English, 1580–1625	The Duchess of Malfi
Oscar Wilde	Irish, 1854–1900	The Importance of Being Earnest
Tennessee Williams	American, 1911–83	A Streetcar Named Desire

ONE AND ONLY
There is only one reference to America in all Shakespeare's works. It is in *The Comedy of Errors*, Act III Scene ii.

Punch and Judy
British diarist Samuel Pepys was the first person to describe a Punch and Judy puppet show after seeing one in London on 9 May 1662. Traditionally, the show features scenes between the aggressive Mr Punch and other characters, including his wife Judy, Toby (a live dog), a baby and a crocodile. Since the 19th century, travelling Punch and Judy men have presented the show from inside a folding booth of striped cloth.

Punch and the policeman in a Punch and Judy puppet show

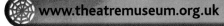
www.theatremuseum.org.uk

Scene from the Singapore production of Les Misérables

🎵 Longest-running shows

Show	Performances
The Golden Horseshoe Revue (Disneyland, California, 1955–86)	47,250
The Mousetrap (London, 1952–)	*21,713
The Fantasticks (New York, 1960–2002)	17,162
La Cantatrice Chauve (The Bald Soprano) (Paris, 1957–)	*14,863
Shear Madness (Boston, 1980–)	*10,367
The Drunkard (Los Angeles, 1933–59)	9,477
The Mousetrap (Toronto, 1977–2004)	over 9,000
Cats (London, 1981–2002)	8,949
Les Misérables (London, 1985–2004)	7,602
Cats (New York, 1982–2000)	7,485
Starlight Express (London, 1984–2002)	7,406
Perfect Crime (New York, 1987–)	*7,265
Shear Madness (Chicago, 1983–99)	7,232
The Phantom of the Opera (London, 1986–)	*7,162
The Phantom of the Opera (New York, 1988–)	*7,141
Shear Madness (Washington, 1987–)	6,857
Les Misérables (New York, 1987–2003)	6,680
Tubes (New York, 1991–)	*6,637
A Chorus Line (New York, 1975–90)	6,137

* Still running in 2005

🎵 Short runs

A play is expensive to stage, so everyone involved hopes that it will run for long enough to earn back the money spent on it. Shows that run for years earn back their initial investment many times over, but some fail on their first night, or even earlier!

- On 18 December 1816 the one and only performance of J.R. Ronden's *The Play Without an A* took place at the Paris Théâtre des Variétés. It was written with words without the letter "a", which made it very hard to perform and understand. The audience rioted and did not allow the play to finish.

- In 1888, at London's Shaftesbury Theatre, *The Lady of Lyons* failed to make its first night when the safety curtain jammed.

- The *Intimate Revue* opened and closed at the Duchess Theatre, London, on 11 March 1930. It was a disaster from start to finish. The scenery changes took so long that seven scenes were abandoned to allow the long-suffering audience to go home before midnight.

- *Little Johnny Jones*, a musical starring Donny Osmond, opened and closed at the Alvin Theater, New York, on 21 March 1982.

- *Carrie* closed in New York on 17 May 1988 after struggling through five performances. It is said to have cost the Royal Shakespeare Company, who performed it, $7 million.

Oberammergau

Oberammergau is a town in Bavaria, Germany, where a Passion play (a play dealing with the crucifixion of Christ) is performed. The first play was put on in 1634 after an outbreak of plague in the town. The people vowed to repeat the play every ten years from then on. More than 2,000 people take part in the play, nearly all of them from Oberammergau, and the performance lasts six hours.

Actors rehearsing the Oberammergau Passion play in May 2000

John Travolta in Saturday Night Fever, *1977*

🎵 Dance marathons

Dance marathons began in New York in 1923, when Alma Cummings won a contest by dancing for 27 hours with six different partners. Marathons were popular during the Depression years of the 1930s, when unemployed people danced non-stop for many days to win money. The last couple standing won. Dancers were allowed only very short breaks and partners pinched and kicked each other to stay awake or tied themselves together to prevent one from falling down. Dance marathons were banned in many places because they were so dangerous for people's health.

Mike Ritof and Edith Boudreaux danced from 29 August 1930 to 1 April 1931 at the Merry Garden Ballroom, Chicago, USA, to win a prize of $2,000. They danced for a total of 5,154 hours 28 minutes 30 seconds (215 days) with only short rest breaks.

🎵 Highest-earning dance films

The most successful dance film of all time is *Saturday Night Fever*. It starred John Travolta as a talented disco dancer and has earned nearly $300 million around the world. *Dirty Dancing* (1987), starring Patrick Swayze and Jennifer Grey, made more than $200 million and won an Oscar for best song, "(I've had) the Time of My Life". The British film *Billy Elliot* (2000) starred Jamie Bell as a young boy who wanted to be a ballet dancer. It was a worldwide hit and won BAFTA Awards for best actor and best British film. *Shall We Dance* (2004), with Richard Gere as a lawyer who takes up ballroom dancing, is the highest-earning dance film of the 21st century.

	Film	Year
1	Saturday Night Fever	1977
2	The Full Monty	1997
3	Dirty Dancing	1987
4	Shall We Dance	2004
5	Save the Last Dance	2001
6	Staying Alive	1983
7	Coyote Ugly	2000
8	Billy Elliot	2000
9	Flashdance	1983
10	Footloose	1984

Famous film dancers

Fred Astaire and Ginger Rogers were one of the greatest film dance partnerships. They made ten films together, including *Flying Down to Rio* (1933) and *Top Hat* (1935). Another favourite film dancer was Gene Kelly, who appeared in musicals with spectacular dance numbers. The most famous of Gene Kelly's films was *Singin' in the Rain* (1952), which won a Golden Globe award for best picture.

Fred Astaire and Ginger Rogers in Swing Time *(1936)*

Flamenco dancers at a festival in Seville, Spain

Popular dances

arn dances
hese developed from traditional Scottish ancing. They were popular in the USA in the 890s when they were held to celebrate the uilding of a barn on a farm. Barn dances are till held today in country areas.

elly dance
he popular name of a style of dance that riginated in the Middle East, especially gypt. It was originally danced only by omen and men were not permitted to atch. An Essex woman named Eileen oucher set a belly dance record. She danced or 106 hours, from 30 July to 3 August 1984.

reakdancing
reakdancing began in New York in the te 1970s and early 1980s. Some of its ovements came from martial arts such kung fu and from gymnastics. It became feature of hip-hop culture.

he Charleston
he Charleston was named after the city South Carolina, USA and was one of e most popular dances of the 1920s.

he conga
eople dance the conga in a line, each ancer holding on to the person in front. he conga began in Latin American carnivals nd spread to the USA in the 1930s. The iami Super Conga was held on 13 March 988. The conga line was made up of 19,986 people – only 14 short of 120,000.

Flamenco dancing
Flamenco is popular in Andalusia, Spain, and comes from Moorish and gypsy dancing. It is lively and exciting; the dancers usually play castanets and are accompanied by guitars, clapping and drumming.

The hula
The hip-swaying hula is danced by Polynesian islanders who settled in Hawaii. It was banned by Christian missionaries for a while, but became popular again in the late 19th century. In 1958, a craze for hula hoops swept the world. Both adults and children swung plastic hoops round their hips to a hula dance movement.

The limbo
This competitive dance comes from Trinidad. Dancers lean back to pass under a bar, which is placed lower and lower. The winner is the dancer who passes under the lowest bar. On 2 March 1991 Dennis Walston, known as King Limbo (USA) limboed under a bar 15.25cm high.

Lindy Hop
The Lindy Hop was a version of the Charleston and another dance called the Breakaway. It started at the Savoy Ballroom, New York, and was named after US aviator Charles Lindbergh (nicknamed Lindy). In 1927 he became the first person to fly solo across the Atlantic.

Morris dancing
This is a traditional English folk dance. Dancers wear special costumes with bells, and hold sticks, handkerchiefs and swords.

The polka
The polka was originally a Czech peasant dance which developed in Bohemia in the 1830s. It became popular in Paris in the 1840s and eventually spread worldwide.

The twist
The twist started when Hank Ballard recorded the song of this name in 1959. It became popular when Chubby Checker performed his cover version on US television on 22 October 1961. A woman called Ra Denny holds the twist record. She twisted for 100 hours at Christchurch, New Zealand, in March 1962.

The waltz
The waltz began in Austria in the late 18th century. Its name comes from a German word meaning to revolve. Many people were shocked by the dance when it first came to England in 1812 because it involved men and women dancing close to each other.

→ **See also**

Film winners: pages 268–69

Sleeping Beauty *by the Royal Ballet*

 ## Best-known ballets

Ballet	Composer	Choreographer	First performed
La Bayadère	Minkus	Petipa	1877
Cinderella	Prokofiev	Ashton	1948
Coppélia	Delibes	Saint-Léon	1870
The Firebird	Stravinsky	Fokine	1910
Giselle	Adam	Perrot/Coralli	1841
The Nutcracker	Tchaikovsky	Ivanov	1892
Romeo and Juliet	Prokofiev	Lavrovsky	1940
The Sleeping Beauty	Tchaikovsky	Petipa	1890
Swan Lake	Tchaikovsky	Petipa	1895
La Sylphide	Schneitzhoeffer	F. Taglioni	1832
Les Sylphides	Chopin	Fokine	1909

Best-known ballet companies

Company	Home	Founded
Alvin Ailey American Dance Theater	New York, USA	1958
American Ballet Theater	New York, USA	1940
Australian Ballet	Melbourne, Australia	1962
Ballet Rambert	London, UK	1926
Ballets Russes*	Moscow, Russia	1909
Bolshoi Ballet	Moscow, Russia	1776
Dance Theater of Harlem	New York, USA	1961
English National Ballet	London, UK	1950
Kirov/Marlinsky Ballet	St Petersburg, Russia	1935
Martha Graham Dance Company	New York, USA	1927
Merce Cunningham Dance Company	New York, USA	1953
New York City Ballet	New York, USA	1948
Paris Opéra Company	Paris, France	1669
Royal Ballet	London, UK	1936
Royal Danish Ballet	Copenhagen, Denmark	1748

* not in existence today

Ballet terms

arabesque
Position in which the dancer stands on one leg, with arms extended, the body bent forwards and the other leg stretched back

ballerina
A female ballet dancer

barre
The bar dancers hold on to while they practise, to help them balance

choreographer
The person who works out the steps and movements in a ballet

corps de ballet
Chorus of dancers (not those dancing solo)

entrechat
Rapid crossing and uncrossing of the feet during a jump

fouetté
A turn in which one leg is whipped round

glissade
A gliding movement

jeté
A jump from one foot to the other

pas
A dance step

pas de deux
A dance for two (usually the principal male and female dancers in the company)

pas seule
A solo dance

pirouette
A complete turn on one leg

plié
A knee-bending movement

pointes
On the tips of the toes. Dancers wear special point shoes with blocks in the toes to help them stand on their toes

positions
A range of five positions that are the basis of ballet dancing

prima ballerina
The leading ballerina in a company

tutu
The stiff skirt worn by ballerinas performing classical ballet

Famous ballet dancers

Carlos Acosta (Cuban, 1973–)
Trained in Cuba and became a principal dancer with the Royal Ballet in London. He has also staged his own show.

Mikhail Baryshnikov (Russian, 1948–)
One of the greatest male dancers. He began with the Kirov in Russia but later joined the American Ballet Theatre.

Matthew Bourne (British, 1960–)
Began as a dancer and became a famous choreographer and director. He is best known for his production of *Swan Lake*, in which all the swans are played by male dancers.

Darcey Bussell (British, 1969–)
Became a principal dancer with the Royal Ballet at the age of 20. She is one of their most popular soloists, and in 1995 she was awarded an OBE for her work in dance.

Michael Clark (British, 1962–)
Danced with the Royal Ballet and Merce Cunningham companies before becoming a choreographer and starting his own company. He's best known for his very original shows and for using music such as punk in his work.

Sir Anton Dolin (British, 1904–83)
Originally danced with Diaghilev's Ballets Russes. He founded the London Festival Ballet (now English National Ballet).

Sir Anthony Dowell (British, 1943–)
He was principal dancer with the Royal Ballet for many years and was Director of the Royal Ballet for 15 years from 1986.

Dame Margot Fonteyn (British, 1919–91)
Royal Ballet prima ballerina, she is most famous for her long-term partnership with Rudolf Nureyev.

Dame Beryl Grey (British, 1927–)
Prima ballerina at the Sadler's Wells Ballet, London and the first English ballerina to perform with the Bolshoi.

Sylvie Guillem (French, 1965–)
Principal guest artist with the Royal Ballet, she is a versatile and athletic dancer, famous for her extraordinarily high leg extensions.

Dame Alicia Markova (British, 1910–2004)
She danced with Anton Dolin and they are most famous for their *Giselle*. Dolin and Markova formed a ballet company.

Vaslav Nijinsky (Russian, 1890–1950)
One of most famous of all male dancers. He was a leading dancer with the Ballets Russes and best known for his performance in Stravinsky's *Rite of Spring*.

Rudolf Nureyev (Russian, 1938–93)
Former Kirov star who defected to the West and became the most popular male dancer of his generation.

Anna Pavlova (Russian, 1881–1931)
Became the most famous ballerina of her generation through her world tours.

Dame Marie Rambert (Polish/British, 1888–1982)
Dancer and teacher whose dance company promoted many new works.

Maria Taglioni (Swedish/Italian, 1804–84)
One of the first ballet stars, famous for her role in *La Sylphide*.

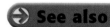
See also

Famous last words:
page 304

Darcey Bussell dancing with Igor Zelensky

Ballet firsts and records

First ballet
In the late 16th century, performances that included dancing, music and acting were given at the French court of Henri II and Catherine de Médici. The *Ballet Comique de La Reine* (1581) was the first recorded.

First professional ballerina
On 21 January 1681 Mademoiselle de La Fontaine appeared in Jean Baptiste Lully's *The Triumph of Love* at the Paris Opéra.

First ballet in the USA
On 7 February 1827 Francisquy Hutin performed a ballet in the play *The Deserter* at the Bowery Theatre, New York. The women in the audience were so shocked by it that they fled from the theatre.

First tutu/first on points
Ballerina Maria Taglioni (1804–84) wore a muslin dress known as a tutu when she danced in *La Sylphide* at the Paris Opéra on 12 March 1832. The dress allowed more freedom of movement so became popular in classical ballet. In the same ballet she danced on points without support – the first time any dancer had done so.

Most curtain calls for a ballet performance
In October 1964 Margot Fonteyn and Rudolf Nureyev received 89 curtain calls after their performance in *Swan Lake* at the Staatsoper, in Vienna, Austria.

Most pirouettes
Delia Gray (15) performed 166 consecutive turns at The Playhouse, Harlow, Essex, UK, on 2 June 1991.

www.ballet.co.uk

Which are the highest-earning films of all time? What was Mickey Mouse's first film? Which country has the most cinema screens? And when were the first radio and TV broadcasts? Find the answers to these and many other questions in the following pages.

FILMS
RADIO AND TV

Who does what in a film?

Person	What they do
Director	The director controls everything, gives orders to the cast and crew and makes sure that the script is followed.
Producer(s)	There can be more than one producer, who is responsible for raising the money to make the film and for other important activities, such as casting and controlling the costs.
Screenplay writer	The person who writes the script. This gives the actors and actresses their lines and explains how the action takes place.
Cast	The actors and actresses who appear in the film.
Extras	The people who appear in crowd scenes but do not have speaking parts.
Animatronic engineer	The technician responsible for making the robotic creatures used in science-fiction and fantasy films.
Art director	The art director coordinates the costumes, sets and make-up to set the overall style of the film.
Best boy	The deputy electrician, assistant to the gaffer.
Casting director	The person who chooses the actors for each role in the film.
Caterer	The caterer supplies meals so that the cast and crew can work all day.
Cinematographer	The person who directs the lighting and films the action, originally called the cameraman.
Clapper loader	Details of each scene are written on a special board called a clapper board. The clapper loader snaps it shut in front of the camera as filming begins to record what is being filmed.
Composer	The composer writes the music or adapts an existing score as a backing track to the film.
Costume designer	The costume designer is responsible for designing and supplying the special clothing worn by the cast.
Editor	The editor cuts and connects the best versions of each section of film to create the final version.
Gaffer	The chief electrician, who is responsible for lighting the set. The word may come from slang for grandfather – a senior person respected by everyone. Gaffer tape is the heavy-duty tape used on sets to secure cables and almost anything else.
Key grip	A grip is responsible for moving the sets and for laying the tracks on which the camera runs. The key grip is in charge of all the other grips.
Make-up artist	He or she applies the cosmetics which alter or improve an actor's looks under the studio lights.
Sound engineer	This engineer makes sure that the actors' dialogue and all the other sounds heard on the film are properly recorded and synchronized with the action.
Special-effects coordinator	This person is responsible for creating spectacular scenes through a mixture of photographic, mechanical and computer methods.
Stunt man/woman	Specialists who perform the actions that are too difficult or dangerous for an actor. Stunt doubles are stunt men or women made up to look like the actors so it looks as though the actors have performed a feat themselves.
Wardrobe mistress	The wardrobe mistress (or master) is in charge of the costumes, making sure they fit, are in good condition and available when they are needed for a scene.

Crowd scene from the film Gandhi

Casts of thousands

About 200,000 of the extras in *Gandhi* were volunteers, but another 94,560 were paid a small fee. They appeared in the scene showing Gandhi's funeral, which lasted just two minutes and five seconds after editing. In *Around the World in 80 Days* (1956), there were animal extras as well as people – 3,800 sheep, 2,448 buffalos, 950 donkeys, 800 horses, 512 monkeys, 17 bulls, 15 elephants, 6 skunks and 4 ostriches. In recent films, such as the *Lord of the Rings* trilogy, scenes featuring thousands of people were computer-generated, so the days of films with casts of thousands may be over.

Film/country/year	Extras
Gandhi, UK, 1982	294,560
Kolberg, Germany, 1945	187,000
Monster Wangmagwi, South Korea, 1967	157,000
War and Peace, USSR, 1968	120,000
Ilya Muromets (*The Sword and the Dragon*), USSR, 1956	106,000
Dun-Huang (*Ton ko*), Japan, 1988	100,000
Razboiul Independentei (*The War of Independence*), Romania, 1912	80,000
Around the World in 80 Days, USA, 1956	68,894
Intolerance, USA, 1916	60,000
Dny Zrady (*Days of Betrayal*), Czechoslovakia, 1973	60,000

Top feature film-producing countries

Country	Feature films produced (2003)
India	1,100
USA	593
Japan	287
France	212
UK	175
China	140
Italy	117
Spain	110
World total	*4,087*

www.imdb.com

Countries spending most at the cinema

Country	$US per head (2003)
1 Iceland	49.11
2 USA	33.44
3 Ireland	28.84
4 Australia	27.97
5 Norway	25.39
6 Switzerland	24.72
7 New Zealand	22.20
8 Canada	20.94
9 Denmark	20.52
10 Singapore	20.45
11 UK	20.15
12 Luxembourg	19.89

Most screens

Country	Estimated number of cinema screens (2003)
1 China	42,000
2 USA	35,786
3 India	11,000
4 France	5,295
5 Germany	4,868
6 Spain	4,253
7 Italy	3,628
8 UK	3,433
9 Mexico	3,197
10 Canada	2,822
11 Japan	2,681
12 Australia	1,907

Top cinema-goers

Country	Number of cinema visits per person (2003)
1 USA	5.53
2 Singapore	4.75
3 Ireland	4.56
4 New Zealand	4.49
5 Australia	4.45
6 Canada	3.83
7 Spain	3.43
8 India	3.15
9 Luxembourg	2.98
10 France	2.93
11 UK	2.78
12 Norway	2.73
World average	*1.14*

La Géode cinema stands in the Parc de la Villette, Paris. Inside the enormous dome is a giant screen measuring 1,000sq m.

Film budgets

The production budgets of a film include the salaries paid to the director, writer(s), stars and crew, the designing and building of sets, costumes, the transport and location costs (filming away from the studio) and the cost of making and editing the film. Other costs include P & A (Prints and Advertising) – making thousands of copies of the film, distributing them to cinemas and advertising the film in the press, on television and on the Internet.

An average Hollywood feature film takes eight weeks to film. It may cost $5 million or more a week, depending on how lavish the production is and how expensive the stars are. *Titanic* took 163 days to make. During this time 240 hours 45 minutes of film were made. These were edited down to 3 hours 14 minutes. The production budget for *Titanic* was an all-time record $200 million.

The costs and income of a typical big-budget Hollywood film, *My Best Friend's Wedding* (1997)

COSTS	Estimated cost ($US million)
Actors	
Julia Roberts	20
Rupert Everett	1
Cameron Diaz	2
Dermot Mulroney	1
All other actors	1
Director (P.J. Hogan)	3
Writer (Ronald Bass)	2
Producers	1
Labour, materials, post-production	20
Prints and advertising (P & A)	22
Total budget	**73**
Income	
US box office	127.1
World box office	172.2
Home video/DVD sales and rentals	58.5
TV broadcast rights	15.0
Total gross	**372.8**
Profit	**299.8**

Highest-earning films

These are the films that have made the most money at the box office worldwide.

Film	Year	World total ($US million)
Titanic	1997	1,845.0
The Lord of the Rings: The Return of the King	2003	1,118.8
Harry Potter and the Sorcerer's Stone	2001	985.8
Star Wars: Episode I – The Phantom Menace	1999	926.3
The Lord of the Rings: The Two Towers	2002	925.6
Shrek 2*	2004	918.5
Jurassic Park	1993	914.7
Harry Potter and the Chamber of Secrets	2002	876.7
The Lord of the Rings: The Fellowship of the Ring	2001	871.4
Finding Nemo*	2003	864.6
Spider-Man	2002	821.7
Independence Day	1996	817.0
E.T. the Extra-Terrestrial	1982	792.9
Harry Potter and the Prisoner of Azkaban	2004	789.8
Spider-Man 2	2004	784.0
The Lion King*	1994	783.8
Star Wars: Episode IV – A New Hope	1977	775.4
The Matrix Reloaded	2003	738.6
Forrest Gump	1994	677.4
The Sixth Sense	1999	672.8
Pirates of the Caribbean: The Curse of the Black Pearl	2003	653.9
Star Wars: Episode II – Attack of the Clones	2002	649.5
The Incredibles*	2004	631.1
The Passion of the Christ	2004	623.5
The Lost World: Jurassic Park	1997	618.6
Men in Black	1997	589.4
Star Wars: Episode VI – Return of the Jedi	1983	573.0
Armageddon	1998	553.7
Mission: Impossible II	2000	545.9
The Day After Tomorrow	2004	542.5
Star Wars: Episode V – The Empire Strikes Back	1980	538.4
Home Alone	1990	533.8
Monsters, Inc.*	2001	529.0
Terminator 2: Judgment Day	1991	519.8
Ghost	1990	505.7

* animated film

R2D2 and C3PO, robots from the film Star Wars

Top documentary films

Documentary films present true factual situations and real people, instead of stories acted out by film stars. These include the exploration of the world and space, and actual events filmed as they happen. Some of the most successful documentaries are IMAX (large format) films that have earned steadily over several years, unlike feature films, which have more limited runs.

Film	Subject	Year	World total ($US million)
Fahrenheit 9/11	War on terrorism	2004	222.4
The Dream is Alive*	Space shuttle	1985	150.0
Everest	Exploration	1998	128.0
Grand Canyon: The Hidden Secrets*	Exploration	1984	116.7
To Fly*	History of flying	1976	115.7
Jackass: The Movie	Comedy stunts	2002	79.5
Space Station 3-D*	International space station	2002	77.8
Blue Planet*	Earth from space	1990	71.9
Mysteries of Egypt*	Historical	1998	70.8
Antarctica	Exploration/nature	1991	65.0
Into the Deep	Underwater exploration	2002	65.0
In Search of Noah's Ark	Exploration	1977	55.7
Eddie Murphy Raw	Comedy performance	1987	51.7

*IMAX film

Computer games and films

Computer games are big business and a number of recent blockbuster films have been based on some of the most popular games. These include *Lara Croft: Tomb Raider* (game 1996, film 2001), *Mortal Kombat* (game 1992, film 1995) and *Super Mario Bros* (game 1985, film 1993). The link between films and games also works the other way, with games based on live-action and animated films – for example, *The Incredibles* (film and game 2004) and *The Lord of the Rings: Battle for Middle Earth* (2004) – a game based on *The Lord of the Rings* trilogy (2001–2003).

www.worldwideboxoffice.com

James Bond films

Ian Fleming's 12 James Bond books have been made into 20 official and two unofficial films. The unofficial ones were *Casino Royale*, a comedy featuring 56-year-old David Niven as the retired spy Sir James Bond, and *Never Say Never Again* (1983), which was a remake of *Thunderball*.

Film	Bond actor	Year	World total ($US million)
Die Another Day	Pierce Brosnan	2002	432.0
The World is Not Enough	Pierce Brosnan	1999	361.8
Tomorrow Never Dies	Pierce Brosnan	1997	348.9
GoldenEye	Pierce Brosnan	1995	353.4
Licence to Kill	Timothy Dalton	1990	156.2
The Living Daylights	Timothy Dalton	1987	191.2
A View to a Kill	Roger Moore	1985	152.4
Octopussy	Roger Moore	1983	183.7
For Your Eyes Only	Roger Moore	1981	187.4
Moonraker	Roger Moore	1979	210.3
The Spy Who Loved Me	Roger Moore	1977	185.4
The Man with the Golden Gun	Roger Moore	1974	98.6
Live and Let Die	Roger Moore	1973	126.4
Diamonds Are Forever	Sean Connery	1971	116.0
On Her Majesty's Secret Service	George Lazenby	1969	64.6
You Only Live Twice	Sean Connery	1967	111.6
Thunderball	Sean Connery	1965	141.2
Goldfinger	Sean Connery	1964	124.9
From Russia with Love	Sean Connery	1963	78.9
Dr No	Sean Connery	1962	59.6

Unofficial

Never Say Never Again	Sean Connery	1983	55.4
Casino Royale	David Niven	1967	22.7

Sean Connery as James Bond

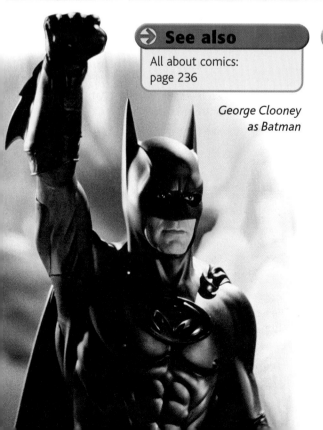

See also

All about comics: page 236

George Clooney as Batman

Top films based on comic books

Comic book characters have been popular subjects for film makers ever since the 1930s. The characters are already familiar, so are immediately appealing to audiences. The exploits of superheroes such as Superman and Batman are perfect for exciting action films, many of which have been hugely successful.

	Film	Comic first published	Film released	World total ($US million)
1	Spider-Man	1962	2002	821.7
2	Spider-Man 2	1962	2004	784.0
3	Men in Black	1960	1997	589.4
4	Men in Black II	1960	2002	441.8
5	Batman	1939	1989	413.4
6	X2: X-Men United	1963	2003	406.4
7	The Mask	1991	1994	351.4
8	Batman Forever	1939	1995	336.5
9	Superman	1938	1978	300.2
10	X-Men	1963	2000	296.0
11	Casper	1945	1995	287.9
12	Batman Returns	1939	1992	282.8

The American Film Institute's top films

The American Film Institute has listed greatest films in a number of categories, based on the views of a panel of 1,500 film experts.

Greatest films

1 Citizen Kane (1941)
2 Casablanca (1942)
3 The Godfather (1972)
4 Gone with the Wind (1939)
5 Lawrence of Arabia (1962)
6 The Wizard of Oz (1939)
7 The Graduate (1967)
8 On the Waterfront (1954)
9 Schindler's List (1993)
10 Singin' in the Rain (1952)

Funniest films

1 Some Like It Hot (1959)
2 Tootsie (1982)
3 Dr Strangelove, or: How I Learned to Stop Worrying and Love the Bomb (1964)
4 Annie Hall (1977)
5 Duck Soup (1933)
6 Blazing Saddles (1974)
7 M*A*S*H (1970)
8 It Happened One Night (1934)
9 The Graduate (1967)
10 Airplane! (1980)

Love stories

1 Casablanca (1942)
2 Gone With the Wind (1939)
3 West Side Story (1961)
4 Roman Holiday (1953)
5 An Affair to Remember (1957)
6 The Way We Were (1973)
7 Doctor Zhivago (1965)
8 It's a Wonderful Life (1946)
9 Love Story (1970)
10 City Lights (1931)

Thrillers

1 Psycho (1960)
2 Jaws (1975)
3 The Exorcist (1973)
4 North by Northwest (1959)
5 The Silence of the Lambs (1991)
6 Alien (1979)
7 The Birds (1963)
8 The French Connection (1971)
9 Rosemary's Baby (1968)
10 Raiders of the Lost Ark (1981)

Orson Welles in Citizen Kane

Film songs

	Song	Film
1	Over the Rainbow	The Wizard of Oz (1939)
2	As Time Goes By	Casablanca (1942)
3	Singin' in the Rain	Singin' in the Rain (1952)
4	Moon River	Breakfast at Tiffany's (1961)
5	White Christmas	Holiday Inn (1942)
6	Mrs Robinson	The Graduate (1967)
7	When You Wish Upon a Star	Pinocchio (1940)
8	The Way We Were	The Way We Were (1973)
9	Stayin' Alive	Saturday Night Fever (1977)
10	The Sound of Music	The Sound Of Music (1965)

Julie Andrews in The Sound of Music

The Oscars

What is an Oscar?
The Academy Awards or Oscars are the most famous of all film awards. They have been presented since 1929. The awards are voted for by the US Academy of Motion Picture Arts & Science, which has more than 5,500 members, including previous nominees and winners. They make a shortlist of five nominees in each of 24 categories (apart from special, honorary and technical awards) then select the winners.

The award is a gold-plated statuette, which stands 34.3cm high and weighs 3.8kg. According to legend, academy librarian Margaret Herrick named the statuette Oscar because she thought it looked like her Uncle Oscar! Main categories include Best Picture, Best Director, Best Actor, Best Actress, Best Supporting Actor and Best Supporting Actress, as well as awards for screenplay, cinematography, soundtrack, documentary, foreign film and so on.

Most wins
These three films have each won 11 Oscars, including Best Picture: *Ben-Hur* (1959), *Titanic* (1997) and *The Lord of the Rings: The Return of the King* (2003).

A no-win situation
The Turning Point (1977) and *The Color Purple* (1985) had 11 nominations each but didn't win a single Oscar. *Gangs of New York* (2002) received 10 nominations without a win. *Cabaret* (1972) is the only film to win eight Oscars without winning Best Picture.

Long and short
Gone with the Wind (1939) was the longest film (238 minutes) and the first colour film to win Best Picture. *Marty* (1955) was the shortest Best Picture winner at 91 minutes.

Black and white
Marty was also one of the last black and white films to win Best Picture. *The Apartment* (1960) and *Schindler's List* (1993) are the only black and white films to have won since then.

ONE AND ONLY

Wings (1927) was the first ever winner of a Best Picture Oscar – and the only silent film ever to win. It received the award at the first Academy Awards ceremony in 1929, almost two years after it had been released. The second Best Picture winner was *The Broadway Melody*. By this time sound films, or talkies, had replaced silent films.

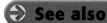 **See also**

Awards: page 154

Oscar winners

These are the Best Picture, Best Actor and Best Actress winners since 1980. The date given is the date of release. Oscars are awarded the following year.

Year	Best Picture	Best Actor	Best Actress
2004	Million Dollar Baby	Jamie Foxx	Hilary Swank
2003	The Lord of the Rings: The Return of the King	Sean Penn	Charlize Theron
2002	Chicago	Adrien Brody	Nicole Kidman
2001	A Beautiful Mind	Denzel Washington	Halle Berry
2000	Gladiator	Russell Crowe	Julia Roberts
1999	American Beauty	Kevin Spacey	Hilary Swank
1998	Shakespeare in Love	Roberto Benigni	Gwyneth Paltrow
1997	Titanic	Jack Nicholson	Helen Hunt
1996	The English Patient	Geoffrey Rush	Frances McDormand
1995	Braveheart	Nicholas Cage	Susan Sarandon
1994	Forrest Gump	Tom Hanks	Jessica Lange
1993	Schindler's List	Tom Hanks	Holly Hunter
1992	Unforgiven	Al Pacino	Emma Thompson
1991	The Silence of the Lambs	Anthony Hopkins	Jodie Foster
1990	Dances With Wolves	Jeremy Irons	Kathy Bates
1989	Driving Miss Daisy	Daniel Day-Lewis	Jessica Tandy
1988	Rain Man	Dustin Hoffman	Jodie Foster
1987	The Last Emperor	Michael Douglas	Cher
1986	Platoon	Paul Newman	Marlee Martin
1985	Out of Africa	William Hurt	Geraldine Page
1984	Amadeus	F. Murray Abraham	Sally Field
1983	Terms of Endearment	Robert Duvall	Shirley MacLaine
1982	Gandhi	Ben Kingsley	Meryl Streep
1981	Chariots of Fire	Henry Fonda	Katharine Hepburn
1980	Ordinary People	Robert De Niro	Sissy Spacek

Julia Roberts and Russell Crowe, Best Actor and Best Actress in 2001

Walt Disney's first animated features

Walt Disney (1901–66) produced short animated films, including Mickey Mouse cartoons, before making main features. *Snow White* was Hollywood's first full-length animated feature film and earned Disney an honorary Oscar. The film made $188 million in the USA alone.

Film	First released in cinemas
1 Snow White and the Seven Dwarfs	21 December 1937
2 Pinocchio	7 February 1940
3 Fantasia	12 November 1940
4 Dumbo	23 October 1941
5 Bambi	9 August 1942

First appearances

These are the films in which some of the most famous animated characters made their first appearances.

Mickey Mouse *Plane Crazy* (1928)
Plane Crazy was Walt Disney's first Mickey Mouse cartoon and was silent. Two months later Mickey appeared in Disney's *Steamboat Willie,* the first Mickey Mouse cartoon with sound. Mickey starred in *Fantasia* (1940), and his *Lend a Paw* won an Oscar in 1941.

Popeye *Popeye the Sailor with Betty Boop* (1933)
Popeye was born in 1929 as a newspaper comic strip by Elzie Crisler Segar. Animator Max Fleischer adapted it for the screen. Popeye cartoons were made for cinema and TV until the 1980s, and the live-action *Popeye* film was released in 1980.

Donald Duck *The Wise Little Hen* (1934)
Clarence Nash was the voice of Donald Duck for 50 years. The Donald Duck anti-Hitler film *Der Fuehrer's Face* (1942) won an Oscar.

Bugs Bunny *Porky's Hare Hunt* (1938)
A Wild Hare (1940) was the first cartoon in which Bugs Bunny said "Eh, what's up, Doc?" but he was not named until *Elmer's Pet Rabbit* (1941). *Knighty-Knight Bugs* (1958) won an Oscar.

Tom and Jerry *Puss Gets The Boot* (1940)
The very first Tom and Jerry cartoon was nominated for an Oscar. The characters also appeared in the 1992 film *Tom and Jerry: The Movie*. This full-length film is the only one in which they speak.

Casper the Ghost *The Friendly Ghost* (1945)
Casper starred in more than 50 cartoons and in a part live action/part computer animated feature film in 1995, which earned nearly $300 million around the world.

The Flintstones *The Flintstone Flyer* (1960)
This was the first episode of *The Flintstones* to be broadcast on TV. It went on to become the longest-running cartoon series until it was overtaken by *The Simpsons*. The live-action film *The Flintstones* (1994) was one of the top-earning films of the year.

Simpsons *Simpsons Roasting on an Open Fire* (1989)
Matt Groening's hugely successful animated series began in 1987 as short episodes screened on the Tracey Ullman Show. It was developed into longer weekly episodes and has become the longest-running and most successful cartoon series ever.

Walt Disney in his studio

Most expensive animated films

Making animated films has become more and more expensive. In 1937 *Snow White and the Seven Dwarfs* cost $1.49 million – a record-breaking sum at the time. *Tarzan* (1999) and *The Polar Express* (2004) are the costliest animated films ever made and were more than 100 times as expensive as *Snow White*!

Film	Year	Budget ($US million)
The Polar Express	2004	150
Tarzan	1999	150
Treasure Planet	2002	140
Final Fantasy: The Spirits Within	2001	137
Dinosaur	2000	128
Monsters, Inc.	2001	115
The Emperor's New Groove	2000	100
Home on the Range	2004	110

Highest-earning animated films of all time

Film	Year	World total ($US million)
Shrek 2	2004	918.5
Finding Nemo	2003	864.6
The Lion King	1994	783.8
The Incredibles	2004	628.4
Monsters, Inc.	2001	529.0
Aladdin	1992	504.0
Toy Story 2	1999	485.0
Shrek	2001	484.4
Tarzan	1999	449.4
Ice Age	2002	382.7
Beauty and the Beast	1991	378.4
A Bug's Life	1998	363.4
Toy Story	1995	362.0
Dinosaur	2000	355.1
Pocahontas	1995	347.2
Shark Tale	2004	334.4
The Hunchback of Notre Dame	1996	325.7

Shark Tale (2004), a CGI film

Types of animation

The word animation comes from the Latin *animatus*, meaning filled with life. Even before the invention of cinema, people realized that if the human eye sees a series of images that change at a rate of at least 24 frames a second, the brain can be tricked into thinking it is seeing a live moving image. Nineteenth-century optical toys such as zoetropes worked on this principle.

A zoetrope – when the viewer spins the zoetrope and looks through a slit, the pictures inside appear to be moving.

That's all folks

Mel Blanc was the voice of many famous cartoon characters, from Bugs Bunny to the Flintstones' Barney Rubble. The headstone on his grave in the Hollywood Forever Cemetery has the sign-off line used at the end of Looney Tunes cartoons: "That's All Folks".

Traditional animation
Individual frames of a story are hand drawn on cels – transparent sheets of plastic. They are then photographed as a sequence against painted backgrounds.

Cut-out
In this type of animation, two-dimensional drawings are placed on a fixed background. These are moved and photographed to create the impression of movement.

Stop motion
This type of animation is created by moving three-dimensional figures and other objects a tiny distance between shots. This method was used to create the dinosaurs in the silent film *The Lost World* as early as 1925. The best-known examples of this technique are the Wallace and Gromit films by Aardman Animation, which use clay figures. These are *A Grand Day Out* (1989), *The Wrong Trousers* (1993) and *A Close Shave* (1995).

CGI
CGI (Computer Generated Imagery) has been used since the 1970s, originally for short films. The 1989 film *The Abyss* used some CGI visual effects, but the hugely successful *Toy Story* (1995), from the Disney and Pixar Animation Studio, was the first CGI feature film. Another development known as 3D motion capture has been used in films such as *The Polar Express* (2004). In this film, which stars Tom Hanks, the motions of live actors are converted into computer images.

CGI films	
1995	Toy Story
1998	Antz
	A Bug's Life
1999	Toy Story 2
2001	Monsters, Inc.
	Jimmy Neutron: Boy Genius
	Shrek
	Final Fantasy: The Spirits Within
2003	Finding Nemo
2004	Shrek 2
	Shark Tale
	The Incredibles
2005	Robots
	Curse of the Wererabbit
	Delgo
	The Barnyard
2006	Cars

Top 10 screen legends

This is the Top 10 of the American Film Institute's list of the greatest American screen legends.

James Cagney

Actor		Actress
1	Humphrey Bogart	Katharine Hepburn
2	Cary Grant	Bette Davis
3	James Stewart	Audrey Hepburn
4	Marlon Brando	Ingrid Bergman
5	Fred Astaire	Greta Garbo
6	Henry Fonda	Marilyn Monroe
7	Clark Gable	Elizabeth Taylor
8	James Cagney	Judy Garland
9	Spencer Tracy	Marlene Dietrich
10	Charlie Chaplin	Joan Crawford

Marlene Dietrich

Stage names

Actors and actresses choose stage names for a variety of reasons. Their real names may be the same as or similar to those of other people, or they may be difficult to spell or pronounce. Here are some famous performers who decided to change their names.

Film name	Real name
Woody Allen	Allan Stewart Konigsberg
Jennifer Aniston	Jennifer Linn Anastassakis
Nicolas Cage	Nicholas Kim Coppola
Michael Caine	Maurice Joseph Micklewhite
Jackie Chan	Chan Kong-sang
Tom Cruise	Thomas Cruise Mapother IV
Kirk Douglas	Issur Danielovitch Demsky
Whoopi Goldberg	Caryn Elaine Johnson
Richard E. Grant	Richard Grant Esterhuysen
Goldie Hawn	Goldie Jean Studlendegehawn
Hulk Hogan	Terry Gene Bollea
Angelina Jolie	Angelina Jolie Voight
Ben Kingsley	Krishna Bhanji
Queen Latifah	Dana Elaine Owens
Jet Li	Li Lian Jie
Demi Moore	Demetria Gene Guynes
Natalie Portman	Natalie Hershlag
Winona Ryder	Winona Horowitz
Susan Sarandon	Susan Abigail Tomalin
Christian Slater	Christian Michael Leonard Hawkins
Sigourney Weaver	Susan Weaver

→ See also

Blockbusters: pages 266–67

Nicole Kidman

Stars of the most $100 million-plus films

These are the stars who have appeared (or supplied voices) in the greatest number of films that have made more than $100 million at the US box office. Tom Hanks leads the list, having appeared in 14 of these top-earning films.

Star	$100m+ films
Tom Hanks	14
Tom Cruise	13
Harrison Ford	11
Mel Gibson	11
Eddie Murphy	11
Samuel L. Jackson	10
Julia Roberts	10
Jim Carrey	9
Cameron Diaz	9

Top stars

Since the 1920s, Cinemas across the USA have nominated the top stars of the year according to the number of people who pay to watch the films in which they appear. John Wayne holds the record with 25 appearances in the annual lists, followed by Clint Eastwood with 21. These are the top stars of 2003.

1. Jim Carrey
2. Nicole Kidman
3. Jack Nicholson
4. Tom Cruise
5. Julia Roberts
6. Johnny Depp
7. Russell Crowe
8. Tom Hanks
9. Will Ferrell
10. Renee Zellweger

Monsters in the movies

Ever since cinema began, film-makers have played on everyone's fear of monsters. These are some of the most popular monster films.

Aliens
Hundreds of films have been made about alien monsters attacking Earth. The most successful of these was *Independence Day* (1996).

Dinosaurs
One of the first ever cartoons was *Gertie* (1914). It featured a drawing of a friendly brontosaurus which comes to life. Dinosaur films *Jurassic Park* (1993) and its two sequels, *The Lost World: Jurassic Park* (1997) and *Jurassic Park III* (2001), are among the biggest blockbusters of all time. The dinosaur-like creature *Godzilla* (1998) was also a monster success.

Egyptian mummies
The Mummy (1932) featured an Egyptian mummy that comes to life and attacks people. *The Mummy* was remade in 1999 and its sequel, the comedy-adventure *The Mummy Returns* (2001), has made more than $433 million.

Frankenstein's monster
Frankenstein is the name of the creator of the monster, not the monster itself. The original story was written in 1816 by English writer Mary Shelley, when she and her friends competed to write the scariest story. It was first made into a silent film in 1910 by the inventor Thomas Edison and has been remade many times since. *Mary Shelley's Frankenstein* (1994) is the highest-earning of all the versions.

Funny monsters
Some of the most successful cartoon monsters are those in *Monsters, Inc.* (2001). The monsters are led by Sulley, whose secret is that the monsters are actually scared of children!

Killer creatures
Giant ape King Kong is one of the most famous animal monsters and the star of the 1933 film *King Kong*.

Giant spiders are the subject of many people's worst fears and have featured in films such as *Arachnophobia* (1990) and *Eight Legged Freaks* (2002). Harry Potter also meets an army of huge spiders in *Harry Potter and the Chamber of Secrets* (2002). Other famous killer creatures include sharks (*Jaws*, 1977), alligators (*Lake Placid*, 1999) and snakes (*Anaconda*, 1997 and *Anacondas: The Hunt for the Blood Orchid*, 2004).

Vampires
Irish writer Bram Stoker's vampire novel *Dracula* was first published in 1897. Since then it has been made into countless films. The version starring Bela Lugosi (1931) is one of the most famous. *Bram Stoker's Dracula* (1992) and *Van Helsing* (2004) have been the most successful at the box office.

Zombies
Zombies are the "undead" – bodies that come out of their graves and terrorize the living. They have been the subject of many films, including *Night of the Living Dead* (1968) and the comedy *Shaun of the Dead* (2004). This was billed as the first "Rom-Com-Zom" (Romantic Comedy Zombie film).

www.afi.com

Actors who have played Superman

Kirk Alyn (1910–99)
The Adventures of Superman (1948) and *Atom Man vs Superman* (1950), both made as cinema serials

George Reeves (1914–59)
Superman and the Mole Men (1951) and the *Superman* TV series (1953–57)

Christopher Reeve (1952–2004)
Superman (1978), *Superman II* (1980), *Superman III* (1983) and *Superman IV: The Quest for Peace* (1987)

Brandon Routh (1979–)
Superman Returns (2006)

Dean Cain (1966–)
Lois & Clark: The New Adventures of Superman (TV series, 1993-97)

Tom Welling (1977–)
Smallville: Superman the Early Years TV series (2001–) about Superman as a teenager

...and Supergirl
Helen Slater (1963–)
Supergirl (1984)

George Reeves

 **See also**
All about comics: page 236

TV milestones

1922
18 October, BBC (British Broadcasting Company) founded

1929
First transmissions of Scottish inventor John Logie Baird's experimental mechanical television system and, in the USA, Philo T. Farnsworth's electronic TV system

1936
22 November, BBC opens the world's first regular high-definition television service, from Alexandra Palace, London

1937
21 June, Wimbledon Tennis Championships first broadcast

1938
30 April, television coverage of the FA Cup Final

31 May, first BBC TV panel game, *Spelling Bee*

21 September, first current affairs programme in the UK, *News Map*

1939
1 September, BBC television service is suspended throughout World War II

1939
Franklin D. Roosevelt is the first president to appear on TV, opening the World's Fair in New York on 30 April

1939
The first king and queen on TV in the USA are King George VI and Queen Elizabeth, seen visiting the World's Fair on 10 June

1941
1 July, the first ever TV commercial, for a Bulova clock, is broadcast by WNBT New York, during a game between the Brooklyn Dodgers and the Philadelphia Phillies

1946
1 June, first TV licences are issued in the UK (cost £2)

7 June, BBC television broadcasts resume

7 July, first British children's TV programme, *For the Children* is broadcast

1947
21 February, America's first regular daytime serial, or soap opera, *A Woman to Remember*, begins its run

1948
29 July, London Olympic Games is televised

1951
24 December, in the USA *Amahl* and *The Night Visitors* becomes the world's first commercial colour broadcast

1953
2 June, the coronation of Queen Elizabeth II is watched live by about 20 million people in Britain and as many as 200 million worldwide

11 November, current affairs programme *Panorama* is launched; goes on to become the longest-running programme on British TV

1954
1 January, the *Tournament of Roses* parade at Pasadena, California, USA, becomes the first programme ever broadcast coast-to-coast

11 January, first TV weather forecast in the UK, by George Cowling

9 April, Britain's first TV soap opera, *The Grove Family*

1955
22 September, first TV advert in the UK, for Gibbs SR toothpaste

1957
13 May, first schools programmes broadcast in the UK

25 December, the Queen's first annual TV Christmas message broadcast

1958
16 October, *Blue Peter* starts, the longest-running children's programme

1969
21 July, first live broadcasts from the Moon (Apollo XI)

15 November, BBC1 and ITV start broadcasting in colour

Philo T. Farnsworth in 1928 with parts of his new television apparatus.

1981
1 August, MTV launched; The Buggles' *Video Killed the Radio Star* the first music video to be broadcast

1989
5 February, Sky begins satellite broadcasting in the UK

1994
19 November, National Lottery first broadcast in the UK

1997
9 November, BBC1 begins broadcasting 24 hours a day, seven days a week (previously, TV closed down at night)

2000
18 July, the UK launch of the first series of *Big Brother* starts a fashion for reality TV

TV, telly or television?

The word television was invented before television even existed. In 1907 scientists talking about the possibility of broadcasting images used the word, which comes from the Greek *tele*, meaning far, and the Latin *visio*, meaning sight. The word telly was used by 1940, but TV was not used until about 1948. Slang words such as box and goggle box began in the 1950s.

First countries to have television*

The BBC's first broadcasts used Baird's mechanical television system. In this, spinning disks were used to scan images. This was later dropped in favour of US inventor Philo Taylor Farnsworth's electronic system. Electronic television did not rely on moving parts, was more reliable and gave a better picture.

Country	Year
UK	1936
USA	1939
USSR	1939
France	1948
Brazil	1950

* High-definition regular public broadcasting service

Why soap opera?

Radio (and later TV) serials about everyday life in the USA have been sponsored by soap manufacturers since the 1930s. They advertised their products during the shows. The name of these serials has been shortened to soaps since 1943.

TV-owning countries

Country	TVs per 1,000 people in 2000	Country	TVs per 1,000 people in 2000
Qatar	869	Canada	715
USA	854	Finland	692
Denmark	807	Norway	669
Latvia	789	UK	653
Australia	738	Germany	580
Japan	725	*World average*	*270*

TV viewing

- In the average US home, the TV is switched on for 7 hours 40 minutes a day.

- US children aged 2 to 17 watch an average of 19 hours 40 minutes' TV every week. That is 1,023 hours a year compared with 900 hours a year in school.

- In the UK children aged 8 to 15 spend an average of 2 hours 13 minutes a day watching TV and adults over 16 spend an average of 2 hours 23 minutes.

Video and DVD fact file

- The terms video recording and videotape were first used in the early 1950s, but only among TV professionals.

- The abbreviation VCR (video cassette recorder) was first used in the UK and USA in 1971.

- The first domestic video cassette recorders were sold in 1974, but both machines and tapes were very expensive and few people bought them.

- The VHS (video home system) was launched in 1976 in the US and 1978 in Europe.

- By 1980, about 7,687,000 homes had video recorders; by 1996 the global figure was put at 400,976,000.

- DVD (digital video disc or digital versatile disc) players and discs were launched in Japan and the USA in 1997.

- Worldwide, sales of DVDs overtook video sales in 2002.

- In 2003 consumers in the USA spent $22.5 billion on DVDs and videos, compared with $9.2 billion at the cinema.

- By 2003 almost one in three UK households had a DVD player; the figure is predicted to rise to 83 per cent by 2007.

www.bbc.co.uk

Radio milestones

1896
2 June, Italian inventor Guglielmo Marconi applies for first British "wireless" patent

1906
24 December, first radio programme (music and speech) broadcast by Professor Reginald Fessenden from the US coast and received by ships. The first radios were crystal sets, operated by adjusting metal wires known as cat's whiskers.

1920
15 June, Marconi broadcasts a concert by opera singer Dame Nellie Melba

1920
6 September, first sports broadcast in USA featuring the Jack Dempsey v Billy Miske boxing match

Guglielmo Marconi

1922
18 October, BBC (British Broadcasting Company) founded

14 November, first BBC broadcast made – the six o'clock news read by Arthur Burrows

5 December, first children's programme, *Children's Corner*, broadcast by BBC

24 December, first play written for radio, *The Truth about Father Christmas*, broadcast by BBC

1923
26 April, first daily weather forecast by the BBC

1926
24 January, launch of *The Week's Good Cause*, the BBC's longest-running programme

1933
28 August, first BBC woman announcer, Sheila Borrett

1939–45
During World War II the BBC provides information and stirring speeches from Winston Churchill and other wartime leaders

1951
1 January, launch of *The Archers*, longest-running BBC radio serial

1964
Pirate radio stations broadcast from ships to UK, encouraging the BBC to launch a pop music station (Radio 1, 30 September 1967)

1970
24 February, National Public Radio launched in the USA

1993
First Internet radio broadcasts

1995
First experimental DAB (digital audio broadcasting) in UK

2004
Sales of DAB (digital audio broadcasting) digital radios top 1 million

Sport is an important part of modern life for everyone, from children kicking a ball in the park, to world-famous sportsmen and women earning thousands of pounds a week. Major competitions, such as the Olympics, bring many countries together as the world's best athletes and players compete, watched by millions.

SPORTS

Teams and competitors

Team sizes

These are the number of players allowed on a pitch at any one time. The full team can also include some substitutes. In American football, for example, there are 45 full-time team members. Different players come on the pitch for defensive and offensive moves.

Sport	Team on pitch
Australian Rules football	18
Gaelic football, hurling, Rugby Union	15
Rugby League	13
Canadian football, korfball, women's lacrosse	12
American football, bandy, cricket, field hockey, soccer, speedball	11
Men's lacrosse, slow-pitch softball	10
Baseball, rounders, fast-pitch softball	9
Tug-of-war	8
Team handball, netball, water polo	7
Ice hockey, volleyball	6
Basketball, roller hockey	5
Polo	4

Most competitors

- The Boston Marathon centenary race in 1996 attracted a record 38,706 competitors, the most ever for a marathon.
- The Athens Olympic Games (2004) had 11,099 competitors, the most of any Olympics.
- The world's biggest road race is the 12km Bay to Breakers race in San Francisco, USA. It has been held every year since 1912. The 1988 race had a record 78,769 official entries, but the total number of people taking part was probably about 110,000, many of them in fancy dress.
- In 1929 the Grand National horse race had a record 66 runners, but only nine of these reached the finish line.

Sporting sizes

Dimensions and distances	
Blade of an ice skate (width)	33mm
Tenpin height	38cm
Parallel bars in gymnastics (distance between)	42cm
Dartboard diameter	45cm
Tennis net height (at centre)	91cm
Hurdles height (men's 400m)	91.4cm
Cricket bat (maximum)	96.52 x 10.8cm
Water polo pool depth (minimum)	1m
Women's javelin length (minimum)	2.2m
Soccer goal height	2.44m
Men's javelin length (minimum)	2.6m
Table tennis table	2.74 x 1.52m
Rugby goal crossbar height	3.05m
Snooker table (full size)	3.66 x 1.86m
Boxing ring	6.1 x 6.1m
Soccer goal width	7.32m
Marathon distance	42.195km
Australian Rules football pitch (oval)	135–185 x 110–155m
Polo pitch	275 x 183m
Formula One Grand Prix (Brazilian Grand Prix circuit)	306km
Isle of Man TT motorcycle race (longest, 1957)	485.8km
Longest hole in open golf (6th at Troon)	527m
Iditarod dog sled race, Alaska	
north route (even-numbered years)	1,757km
south route (odd-numbered years)	1,773km
Le Mans 24 Hour race (greatest distance covered in the time, 1971)	5,333.7km
Tour de France cycle race (record longest, 1926)	5,745km
Tour d'Afrique, Cairo to Cape Town (longest cycle race)	10,500km
Around alone (solo round-the-world yacht race)	46,276.7km

Marathon sprint!

If an athlete could run a marathon at the same rate as a 100m sprint, he would finish in 43 minutes. In reality, no one has ever run a marathon in under two hours.

Sport origins

When did basketball start?
The inspiration for basketball may have been the Aztec game *ollamalitzli* and other ball and hoop games played by South American peoples. The modern game was invented in 1891 by Canadian physical education teacher Dr James A. Naismith at the International YMCA College at Springfield, Massachusetts. He wanted to find a game that could be played indoors during the winter. Peach baskets were originally used as goals – players had to climb a ladder to fetch the ball after scoring. Then someone hit on the idea of removing the bottom! The baskets were soon replaced by metal rings with netting.

Who invented baseball?
Baseball is a much older game than you might think. Medieval manuscripts show ball games with bats, while a game called "base-ball" appears in a picture published in London in 1744. Baseball is also mentioned in Jane Austen's novel *Northanger Abbey*, which she began writing in 1798. The game of rounders was first described 30 years later, and this or a similar game was known among British settlers in America. Abner Doubleday is sometimes said to have invented baseball in 1839, but Alexander Joy Cartwright Jr drew up the game's rules in 1845. He founded the first team, the Knickerbocker Base Ball Club of New York.

Sport top speeds

Sport	km/h
Competition rifle bullet	3,787
Longbow arrow	547
Drag racer (0.4km from standing start)	535
Free-fall skydiver	531
Pelota (jai-alai) ball	302
Indy 500 racing car (record, 1990)	299
Golf ball (leaving tee)	273
Downhill skier (record)	248
Squash ball (record, 1988)	243
Tennis serve (record, 2004)	241
Racing car (Formula One)	238
Water skiing (record, 1983)	230
Snowboarding (record)	202
Isle of Man TT race (record, 2002)	201
Ice hockey puck	190
Ski-bob (record, 1999)	185
Table tennis ball	170
Baseball (pitched)	162
Cricket bowl (record, 2002)	161
Luge	137
Frisbee	119
Cyclist (record)	105
Skateboard (record, 1998)	101
4-man bobsleigh	90
Racehorse	72
Greyhound	67
100-m sprinter	59
Boxing punch	56
Karate chop	51

Famous US basketball player Michael Jordan about to score

Longest events

- In Formula One motor racing the 16-race season is spread over nine months.

- The Tour d'Afrique cycle race includes 100 days of cycling and 20 days of rest.

- The Tour de France lasts 22 days (with rest days).

- The Iditarod dog sled race, held in Alaska, lasts nine days.

- The longest-ever cricket match was between England and South Africa at Durban in 1939. They played for 43 hours 16 minutes over ten days, ending when England had to catch their ship home.

- The longest boxing match with gloves was a 100-round bout between Andy Bowen and Jack Burke (both USA). It started at 9.15 pm on Thursday, 6 April 1893 and finished at 4.34 am on Friday, 7 April – a total of 7 hours 19 minutes.

Most-watched sporting event
The 2000 Olympic Games in Sydney was the most-watched sporting event ever on television, with 3.7 billion viewers worldwide. And 1,159,249 tickets for watching the events live were sold.

Oldest sporting events

Doggett's Coat and Badge Race is the world's oldest continuous sporting event. It is a rowing contest held on the River Thames in England and has been held every year since 1715. The Newmarket Town Plate horse race is even older, but the race was discontinued for a while.

Event	First held
Newmarket Town Plate horse race	1665
Doggett's Coat and Badge Race (rowing)	1715
Real Tennis Championship	1740
St Leger horse race	1776
Epsom Derby horse race	1780
County Cricket Championship	1827
Oxford and Cambridge Boat Race	1829
Grand National steeplechase	1836
Henley Regatta	1839
British Open golf championship	1860
Melbourne Cup horse race	1861
America's Cup yachting series	1870
Football Association Challenge Cup	1872
Kentucky Derby horse race	1875
Test Match cricket	1877
Wimbledon Lawn Tennis Championships	1877
Football League championship (England)	1888
Stanley Cup ice hockey competition	1893
US Open golf championship	1895
Davis Cup tennis tournament	1900
Baseball World Series	1903
Tour de France cycle race	1903
Ryder Cup golf tournament	1927
FIFA Soccer World Cup	1930
Formula One World Championship	1950
Super Bowl (US football championship)	1967
Cricket World Cup	1975
Athletics World Cup	1977
World Athletics Championships	1983
Breeders' Cup horse race series	1984
Rugby Union World Cup	1987

Grand National steeplechase (19th century)

Bare-knuckle boxing match (1820)

Sports timeline

Experts argue about the exact origins of many sports. The dates here are generally agreed to be when these sports were first played or contested on an organized basis.

Athletics	3800 BC
Horse racing	AD 1540
Boxing	1681
Rowing	1715
Ice skating	1742
Cricket	1744
Golf	1744
Swimming	1791
Baseball	1839
Rugby Union	1839
Soccer	1848
Tenpin bowling	1850
Show jumping	1864
Cycling	1867
Badminton	1873
Lawn tennis	1873
American football	1874
Hockey (field)	1875
Hockey (ice)	1887
Motor racing	1887
Basketball	1891
Rugby League	1895
Darts	1896
Motor cycling	1896
Speedway	1902

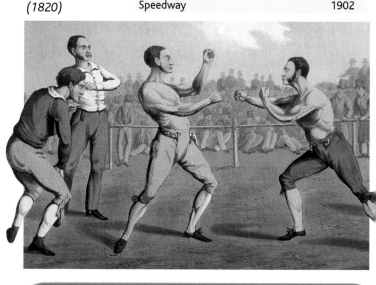

Strange sport

A world championship in mobile phone throwing has been held in Finland every year since 2000. Competitors take part in individual or team events. There is also an under-12 category. The current world record was set in 2002 when the winning contestant threw his Nokia 5110 phone a distance of 66.72m.

Huge crowds cheer on competitors in the 2003 Tour de France.

Biggest crowds

In the past, more than 100,000 people at a time crammed into American football's Rose Bowl, the old Wembley Stadium and other venues across Europe to watch sport. Today, there are laws which limit the number of people allowed in a sports stadium. Outdoor events such as the New York City Marathon and the Tour de France now draw the biggest crowds. They are held over open roads and people don't have to pay to watch them.

- About 2.5 million people watch the New York Marathon – the biggest crowd for a single day at a sporting event. As many as 15 million people turn out to see the Tour de France during its three weeks.

- The record crowd for a golf tournament was set at the 1996 Phoenix Open when 156,875 people saw the final round. The total for the tournament week was 421,095.

- The biggest-ever crowd for a soccer match was at the final of the 1950 World Cup. The match between Brazil and Uruguay at the Maracana Stadium in Brazil on 16 July 1950 was watched by 199,854 people. The biggest crowd for a soccer match in Britain was at Hampden Park, Glasgow, on 17 April 1937. Scotland was playing England and 149,547 people paid to watch, though another 10,000 may have got in without paying!

- In horse racing, more than 60,000 watch the Grand National and about 120,000 go to the Epsom Derby every year.

- Cricket attracts big crowds. Nearly a million people watched the 1936–37 series between Australia and England over its three months. More than 400,000 people watched the India v Pakistan Test match in Calcutta in 1998–99.

- Some of the biggest crowds at US sporting events are for Indy car races. About 350,000 fans attend the Indianapolis 500 every year and as many as 140,000 people go to Formula One Grand Prix races.

Top sporting events

These are the leading events in the world's most popular sports, in addition to the Olympics.

American football	Super Bowl
Athletics	IAAF (International Association of Athletics Federations) Grand Prix
Auto racing (US)	Indianapolis 500
Baseball	World Series
Basketball	NBA (National Basketball Association) Final
Cycling	Tour de France
Golf	British Open, US Open, Ryder Cup (every two years)
Horse racing	Epsom Derby, Grand National, Breeders' Cup, Kentucky Derby
Ice hockey	Stanley Cup
Motor racing	World Formula One Championship
Rallying	Paris-Dakar Rally
Rugby League	Challenge Cup, Super League
Rugby Union	Six Nations Tournament, World Cup (every four years)
Soccer	UEFA Champions League, FIFA World Cup (every four years)
Tennis	Wimbledon Championships, US Open

Sport on TV

TV audiences for many sporting events were larger 30 years ago than they are today. Fewer people had televisions, but there were not as many channels and no video recorders, so more people watched events live.

UK Event	Audience*
World Cup Final, England v West Germany, 1966	32,500,000
World Cup, Brazil v England, 1970	32,500,000
FA Cup Final replay, Chelsea v Leeds United, 1970	32,000,000
World Heavyweight boxing match, Muhammad Ali v Joe Frazier, 1970	27,000,000

USA Event	Audience*
Super Bowl XXXVIII, New England Patriots v Carolina Panthers, 2004	143,600,000
Super Bowl XXXVII, Tampa Bay Buccaneers v Oakland Raiders, 2003	138,900,000
Super Bowl XXX, Dallas Cowboys v Pittsburgh Steelers, 1996	138,488,000
Super Bowl XXVIII, Dallas Cowboys v Buffalo Bills, 1994	134,800,000
Super Bowl XXVII, Dallas Cowboys v Buffalo Bills, 1993	133,400,000
Super Bowl XXXII, Denver Broncos v Green Bay Packers, 1998	133,400,000

* Number of people who watched at least part of broadcast

See also

Major rock events: page 255

Summer Olympics

The modern Olympic Games have been held every four years since 1896, except during World Wars I and II. Over this time the numbers of competitors, events and nations taking part have all increased dramatically. In 1906 an extra event, known as the Intercalated Games, was held to celebrate the tenth anniversary of the founding of the modern Olympics.

Poster for the 1936 Berlin Olympic Games

Year	City/country	Competitors	No of nations	Events	Most golds	Most medals
1896	Athens, Greece	245	14	43	USA 11	Greece 47
1900	Paris, France	1,225	26	95	France 26	France 95
1904	St Louis, USA	687	13	91	USA 79	USA 245
1906	Athens, Greece	884	20	76	France 15	France 40
1908	London, UK	2,035	22	110	UK 54	UK 138
1912	Stockholm, Sweden	2,547	28	102	USA 25	Sweden 64
1920	Antwerp, Belgium	2,669	29	154	USA 41	USA 95
1924	Paris, France	3,092	44	126	USA 45	USA 99
1928	Amsterdam, Netherlands	3,014	46	109	USA 22	USA 56
1932	Los Angeles, USA	1,408	37	117	USA 41	USA 103
1936	Berlin, Germany	4,066	49	129	Germany 33	Germany 89
1948	London, UK	4,099	59	136	USA 38	USA 84
1952	Helsinki, Finland	4,925	69	149	USA 40	USA 76
1956*	Melbourne, Australia	3,342	72	145	USSR 37	USSR 98
1960	Rome, Italy	5,348	83	150	USSR 43	USSR 103
1964	Tokyo, Japan	5,140	93	163	USA 36	USA 90
1968	Mexico City, Mexico	5,531	112	172	USA 45	USA 107
1972	Munich, West Germany	7,123	121	195	USSR 50	USSR 99
1976	Montreal, Canada	6,028	92	198	USSR 49	USSR 125
1980	Moscow, USSR	5,217	80	203	USSR 80	USSR 195
1984	Los Angeles, USA	6,797	140	221	USA 83	USA 174
1988	Seoul, South Korea	8,465	159	237	USSR 55	USSR 132
1992	Barcelona, Spain	9,367	169	257	EUN† 45	EUN 112
1996	Atlanta, USA	10,744	197	271	USA 44	USA 101
2000	Sydney, Australia	10,651	199	300	USA 39	USA 97
2004	Athens, Greece	11,099	202	301	USA 35	USA 103

* The equestrian events in 1956 were held in Stockholm, Sweden, from 10–17 June, because of quarantine restrictions in Australia at the time.

† The Unified Team (EUN) was made up of the former Soviet republics of Russia, Ukraine, Kazakhstan and Uzbekistan.

Olympic firsts

1896 First modern Olympics. Doves released to symbolize peace

1896 First American gold medal winner, James Connolly (triple jump)

1896 First British gold medal winner, Launceston Elliot (weightlifting)

1900 First women competitors. First woman to win a gold medal, Charlotte Cooper from Great Britain for tennis

1908 First parade of athletes with national flags

1908 First athlete to win ten gold medals (in four Olympics, 1900, 1904, 1906 and 1908), Ray Ewry (USA)

1912 Electronic timing and photo-finish equipment first used

1920 Olympic oath, "We swear that we will take part in the Olympic Games in a spirit of chivalry, for the honour of our country and for the glory of sport", first taken by Belgian fencer Victor Boin

1920 Olympic flag first raised. The flag had been adopted by the International Olympic Committee (IOC) in 1914

1924 First Olympics with more than 100 women competitors (there were 136 women and 2,956 men)

1924 First live radio transmissions of events

1928 First Olympic flame, large results display board first used

1928 First women competitors in track and field events

1932 First Olympic logo, three-tier victory stand, national anthem played and flag raised for winner

1936 Introduction of Olympic torch relay (from Olympia, Greece, to Berlin, Germany)

1936 Games televised for the first time

1956 Athletes enter closing ceremony together to symbolize unity

1956 First games in the southern hemisphere (Melbourne, Australia)

1960 Worldwide TV coverage for the first time

1968 Norma Enriqueta Basilio (Mexico) became first woman to light Olympic flame

1984 Professionals allowed to compete for the first time

The Olympic flag

The five-ring Olympic flag was first raised at the 1920 Antwerp Olympics. The rings on the flag represent the five major regions of the world: the Americas, Europe, Asia, Africa and Australasia. At least one of the colours on the flag (blue, yellow, black, green and red) can be found on the flags of every nation in the world.

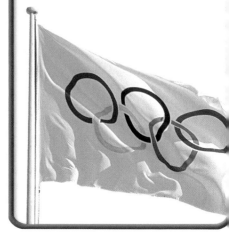

Top medal winners

hese athletes have won the most medals in the history f the Summer Olympics from 1896–2004.

Athlete/Country	Sport	Years	Gold	Silver	Bronze	Total
Larissa Latynina, USSR	Gymnastics	1956–64	9	5	4	18
Nikolai Andrianov, USSR	Gymnastics	1972–80	7	5	3	15
Boris Shakhlin, USSR	Gymnastics	1956–64	7	4	2	13
Edoardo Mangiarotti, Italy	Fencing	1936–60	6	5	2	13
Takashi Ono, Japan	Gymnastics	1952–64	5	4	4	13
Paavo Nurmi, Finland	Athletics	1920–28	9	3	0	12
Sawao Kato, Japan	Gymnastics	1968–76	8	3	1	12
Alexei Nemov, Russia	Gymnastics	1996–2000	4	2	6	12

Athlete Ray Ewry (USA) won only ten medals but they were all gold! He still holds the record for the most individual gold medals. Ewry won his medals between 1900 and 1908 in the standing jump events: high jump, long jump and triple jump. Amazingly, Ewry had suffered polio as a child, but overcame his illness to become one of the greatest athletes ever.

Olympic history

The Ancient Olympic Games were dedicated to the Olympian gods and held at Olympia, on the border between Greece and Macedonia. They began in 776 BC and were held every four years. There were fewer events than now, and only Greeks could take part. The 293rd and last Olympiad was held in AD 392. After this, they were banned by the Emperor Theodosius. The games were revived in 1896 when the first modern Olympic Games were held in Athens.

Olympic gold medal from the 2000 games

The big five

Only five sports have been contested at every Summer Olympics since the first Modern Olympics in 1896. These are cycling, fencing, gymnastics, swimming and track and field. Rowing would have been on this list, but the events in 1896 were cancelled due to bad weather.

Medal-winning nations

The following are the number of medals won by the top ten countries from all the Summer Olympics (1896 to 2004).

Country	Gold	Silver	Bronze	Total
USA	907	697	615	2,119
Russia*	525	436	409	1,370
Germany#	228	258	298	784
Great Britain	189	242	237	668
France	199	202	230	631
Italy	189	154	168	511
Sweden	140	157	179	476
Hungary	158	141	161	460
East Germany	159	150	136	445
Australia	119	126	154	399

* Includes USSR (1952–88) and Unified Team (1992)
# Includes West Germany (1968–88)

ONE AND ONLY

Softball is the only sport that women contest at the Olympics but men do not. The sport has been played at three Olympics (1996, 2000, 2004) and the USA has won gold each time.

Out of the Olympics

Various sports have been dropped from the Olympic Games over the years. These include croquet, underwater swimming, duelling pistol shooting, stone-throwing, lacrosse, archery with live birds, tug-of-war, club-swinging and rope climbing.

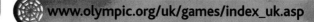

www.olympic.org/uk/games/index_uk.asp

Decathlon and heptathlon

The decathlon is a two-day event for men which first featured in the Olympic Games in 1912. The seven-event heptathlon is for women only. It was introduced in 1984, when it replaced the five-event pentathlon. Competitors score points for each event and the person with the highest total wins.

Decathlon events
Day 1:
- 100 metres
- Long jump
- Shot put
- High jump
- 400 metres

Day 2:
- 110 metres hurdles
- Discus • Pole vault
- Javelin • 1500 metres

Heptathlon events
Day 1:
- 100 metre hurdles • High jump
- Shot put • 200 metres

Day 2:
- Long jump • Javelin • 800 metres

Cuban high jumper Javier Sotomayor

The world's fastest

The world's fastest man is Asafa Powell (Jamaica). He ran the 100 metres in 9.77 seconds in Athens on 14 June 2005, equivalent to a speed of 36.80km/h. The world's fastest woman was Florence Griffith-Joyner (USA), who died in 1998. She ran 100 metres in 10.49 seconds (34.32km/h) in Indianapolis on 16 July 1988. The fastest living woman is Marion Jones (USA). She ran the 100 metres in 10.65 seconds (33.80km/h) in Johannesburg in 1998.

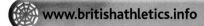

Competitors in the London Marathon

www.britishathletics.info

The marathon

The race takes its name from a place called Marathon in Greece, which was the scene of a battle between Athenian and Persian troops in 490 BC. When the Athenians won, a messenger named Phidippides was sent from Marathon to Athens, a distance of about 25 miles, to spread the news. It is said that Phidippides dropped dead after delivering his message! The current marathon distance of 26 miles 385 yards (42.195km) was first used at the 1908 Olympics in Britain. It was worked out so that the race from Windsor would finish in front of the Royal Box at the White City Stadium. This distance has been the standard for all marathons since 1924.

Marathon fact file

Hundreds of marathon races are held all over the world every year. There is an Antarctica Marathon, a Sahara Marathon and even a night-time marathon, run in Marburg, Germany. The following are some of the biggest and most popular events.

Boston Marathon
This race has been held since 1897 and is run on Patriots' Day every April. It is the oldest marathon in the United States and one of the world's most important road races. Clarence DeMar won it a record seven times between 1911 and 1930.

New York City Marathon
First held in 1970, the race goes through all five boroughs of New York and finishes in Central Park. It is usually held on the first Sunday in November. Norway's Greta Waitz won the women's race an amazing nine times in the 11 years between 1978 and 1988.

Chicago Marathon
The Chicago Marathon began in 1977. It was originally called the Mayor Daley Marathon after Chicago mayor Richard J. Daley, who died in office in 1976. Khalid Khannouchi of Morocco won the men's race a record four times between 1997 and 2002.

London Marathon
The London Marathon was first run in 1981. Since then it has become the world's most famous road race. Dionicio Ceron (Mexico) has won the men's race a record three times between 1994 and 1996. Norway's Ingrid Kristiansen won the women's race four times between 1984 and 1988.

Marathon record holders
The current male record holder is Puul Tergat (Kenya), who ran the Berlin Marathon on 28 September 2003 in 2 hours 4 minutes 55 seconds. The female record is held by Paula Radcliffe (GB), who ran the London Marathon on 13 April 2003 in 2 hours 15 minutes 25 seconds.

Track and field records

These are the current world records for major track and field events as at 13 March 2005.

Event	Men Time (min:sec)		Date	Women Time (min:sec)		Date
100 metres	9.77	Asafa Powell (Jamaica)	2005	10.49	Florence Griffith-Joyner (USA)	1988
200 metres	19.32	Michael Johnson (USA)	1996	21.34	Florence Griffith-Joyner (USA)	1988
400 metres	43.18	Michael Johnson (USA)	1999	47.60	Marita Koch (GDR)	1985
800 metres	1:41.11	Wilson Kipketer (Den)	1997	1:53.28	Jarmila Kratochvílová (Cze)	1983
1500 metres	3:26.00	Hicham El Guerrouj (Mar)	1998	3:50.46	Qu Yunxia (Chn)	1993
1 mile	3:43.13	Hicham El Guerrouj (Mar)	1999	4:12.56	Svetlana Masterkova (Rus)	1996
5,000 metres	12:37.35	Kenenisa Bekele (Eth)	2004	14:24.68	Elvan Abeylegesse (Tur)	2004
10,000 metres	26:20.31	Kenenisa Bekele (Eth)	2004	29:31.78	Wang Junxia (Chn)	1993
3,000 metres Steeplechase	7:53.63	Saaeed Shaheen (Qat)	2004	9:01.59	Gulnara Samitiva (Rus)	2004
110m Hurdles	12.91	Colin Jackson (GBR)/Xiang Lu (Chn)	1993/2004	–		
100m Hurdles	–			12.21	Yordanka Donkova (Bul)	1988
400m Hurdles	46.78	Kevin Young (USA)	1992	52.34	Yuliya Pechonkina (Rus)	2003
4 x 100m Relay	37.40	USA	1992/1993	41.37	GDR	1985
4 x 400m Relay	2:54.20	USA	1998	3:15.17	USSR	1988

	Height/distance (m)			Height/distance (m)		
High jump	2.45	Javier Sotomayor (Cub)	1993	2.09	Stefka Kostadinova (Bul)	1987
Pole vault	6.14	Sergey Bubka (Ukr)	1994	4.92	Yelena Isinbayeva (Rus)	2004
Long jump	8.95	Mike Powell (USA)	1991	7.52	Galina Chistyakova (USSR)	1988
Triple jump	18.29	Jonathan Edwards (GBR)	1995	15.50	Inessa Kravets (Ukr)	1995
Shot	23.12	Randy Barnes (USA)	1990	22.63	Natalya Lisovskaya (USSR)	1987
Discus	74.08	Jürgen Schult (GDR)	1986	76.80	Gabriele Reinsch (GDR)	1988
Hammer	86.74	Yuriy Sedykh (USSR)	1986	76.07	Mihaela Melinte (Rom)	1999
Javelin	98.48	Jan Zelezny (Cze)	1996	71.54	Osleidys Menéndez (Cub)	2001

	Points			Points		
Decathlon	9,026	Roman Sebrle (Cze)	2001	8,150	Marie Collonvillé (Fr)	2004
Heptathlon	–			7,291	Jackie Joyner-Kersee (USA)	1988

Florence Griffith-Joyner

Running a mile

For decades, athletes struggled to run a mile in less than four minutes. At 6.07pm on 6 May 1954, British runner Roger Bannister eventually broke the record. He ran a mile in 3 minutes 59.4 seconds at the Iffley Road track in Oxford. Since that historic day, Bannister's record has been beaten many times as this list shows. The current record speed for running a mile is 3 minutes 43.13 seconds.

Athlete	Place	Date	Min:sec
Roger Bannister, UK	Oxford, England	6 May 1954	3:59.40
John Landy, Australia	Turku, Finland	21 June 1954	3:58.00
Derek Ibbotson, UK	London, England	19 July 1957	3:57.20
Herb Elliott, Australia	Dublin, Ireland	6 August 1958	3:54.50
Peter Snell, New Zealand	Wanganui, New Zealand	27 January 1962	3:54.40
Peter Snell, New Zealand	Auckland, New Zealand	17 November 1964	3:54.10
Michel Jazy, France	Rennes, France	9 June 1965	3:53.60
Jim Ryun, USA	Berkeley, USA	17 July 1966	3:51.30
Jim Ryun, USA	Bakersfield, USA	23 June 1967	3:51.10
Filbert Bayi, Tanzania	Kingston, Jamaica	17 May 1975	3:51.00
John Walker, New Zealand	Gothenburg, Sweden	12 August 1975	3:49.40
Sebastian Coe, UK	Oslo, Norway	17 July 1979	3:48.85
Steve Ovett, UK	Oslo, Norway	1 July 1980	3:48.80
Sebastian Coe, UK	Zurich, Switzerland	19 August 1981	3:48.53
Steve Ovett, UK	Koblenz, Germany	26 August 1981	3:48.40
Sebastian Coe, UK	Brussels, Belgium	28 August 1981	3:47.33
Steve Cram, UK	Oslo, Norway	27 July 1985	3:46.32
Noureddine Morceli, Algeria	Rieti, Italy	5 September 1993	3:44.39
Hicham El Guerrouj, Morocco	Rome, Italy	7 July 1999	3:43.13

See also

Ancient Greece:
page 106

Soccer timeline

500 BC	Football (tsu chu, meaning to kick a ball) played in China.
1314	First reference to football in England when Edward II prohibited the game because "too many people were bustling over footballs on London streets".
1848	The first rules of football drawn up at Cambridge University
1852	First inter-school football match, Westminster v Harrow.
1855	Sheffield football club, the oldest still in existence, formed.
1862	Notts County, the oldest current League club, formed.
1863	Football Association (FA) formed.
1870	First international match, England v Scotland, played at Kennington Oval.
1871	FA Cup launched.
1872	Corner kick introduced.
1873	Scottish FA formed; Scottish Cup started.
1874	Shin pads first worn.
1875	The crossbar replaced a tape across the top of the goals.
1876	Welsh FA formed.
1878	Irish (now Northern Ireland) FA formed.
1878	Referee's whistle first used.
1885	Professional football legalized.
1888	Football League formed.
1889	The term "soccer" first used. May be an abbreviation of association football – the Football Association was formed to standardize the rules of the game.
1890	Scottish League formed.
1891	Goal nets first used.
1891	Linesmen (now assistant referees) replace umpires.
1891	Penalty kick adopted by the FA.
1904	FIFA formed in Paris; first international match outside Britain – Belgium v France played near Brussels.
1907	Professional Footballers' Association (PFA) formed (as the Football Players and Trainers Union).
1921	FA of Ireland (Republic of Ireland) formed.
1923	First Wembley Cup Final (Bolton v West Ham).
1928	Players' numbers introduced.
1930	First World Cup in Uruguay.
1932	Substitutes formally agreed by FIFA.
1950	England's first World Cup (lost 1–0 to USA).
1954	Union of European Football Associations (UEFA) formed.
1955	European Cup started.
1960	Football League Cup started.
1965	Football League agrees use of substitutes.
1968	Red cards introduced (at the Mexico Olympic Games).
1975	Scottish Premier Division (now Premier League) formed.
1976	Goal difference replaces goal average.
1981	Football League changed the number of points for a win from two to three.
1982	Professional foul rule introduced.
1992	FA Premier League formed.
1993	Champions' League replaces the European Cup.

Football firsts

The first FA Cup Final was played in front of just 2,000 spectators at Kennington Oval, London on 16 March 1872. Wanderers beat Royal Engineers 1–0 with Morton Peto Betts scoring the only goal of the game after 15 minutes.

Brazil, winners of the 2002 World Cup

The World Cup

The first soccer World Cup was played in 1930 in Uruguay. Thirteen teams took part and the hosts beat Argentina 4–2 in the final in Montevideo. They won the Jules Rimet trophy, named after the man who was president of FIFA (Fédération Internationale de Football Association) when the competition began. Brazil were allowed to keep the trophy after winning it for the third time in 1970 and it was replaced by the FIFA World Cup trophy. The World Cup final takes place every four years.

Winning country	Year	Winning country	Year
Uruguay	1930	Argentina	1978
Italy	1934	Italy	1982
Italy	1938	Argentina	1986
Not held	1942	West Germany	1990
Not held	1946	Brazil	1994
Uruguay	1950	France	1998
West Germany	1954	Brazil	2002
Brazil	1958		
Brazil	1962	**Most World Cup wins**	
England	1966	Brazil	5
Brazil	1970	Italy, West Germany	3
West Germany	1974	Uruguay, Argentina	2

World Cup facts

- The first World Cup goal was scored by Lucien Laurent of France. The goal came 19 minutes into the first World Cup game on 13 July 1930.

- The first player to score four goals in a World Cup match was Ireland's Paddy Moore in a qualifying match against Belgium in 1934. It was the Republic's first ever World Cup match.

- Brazil is the only country to have competed in the final stages of every World Cup competition.

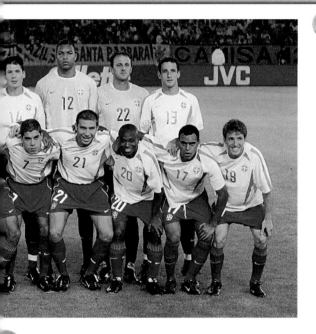

International caps

On 10 May 1886 the English Football Association decided: "That all players taking part for England in future international matches be presented with a white silk cap with red rose embroidered on the front. These to be termed International Caps." This tradition has spread throughout world football. The number of caps show how many times players have represented their countries. The following footballers are the most-capped players in their countries.

Player	Country	Years	Caps*
Claudio Suárez	Mexico	1992–2004	172
Cobi Jones	USA	1992–2004	164
Lothar Matthäus	Germany	1980–2000	150
Cafu†	Brazil	1990–2005	130
Paolo Maldini	Italy	1988–2002	126
Andoni Zubizarreta	Spain	1985-1998	126
Peter Shilton	England	1970–1990	125
Pat Jennings	Northern Ireland	1964–1986	119
Marcel Desailly	France	1993–2004	116
Diego Pablo Simeone	Argentina	1988–2002	106
Steve Staunton	Republic of Ireland	1989–2002	102
Kenny Dalglish	Scotland	1972–1987	102
Neville Southall	Wales	1982–1998	92

* As at 16 March 2005   † Real name Marcos Evangelista de Morais

First to 100 caps

The first player to win 100 caps was England's Billy Wright, who played his 100th game against Scotland at Wembley Stadium on 11 April 1959.

American football

American Football, or Gridiron, is the number one sport in the USA. The National Football League (NFL) is split into two conferences, the American Football Conference (AFC) and National Football Conference (NFC). Each conference is split into four divisions – North, South, East and West – and each division has four teams. Each team plays 16 matches and the top teams go through to conference play-offs. The two conference winners then meet in a final called the Super Bowl, played in late January every year. The winning team receives the coveted Vince Lombardi Trophy.

No.	Year	Winners	No.	Year	Winners
I	1967	Green Bay Packers	XXI	1987	New York Giants
II	1968	Green Bay Packers	XXII	1988	Washington Redskins
III	1969	New York Jets	XXIII	1989	San Francisco 49ers
IV	1970	Kansas City Chiefs	XXIV	1990	San Francisco 49ers
V	1971	Baltimore Colts	XXV	1991	New York Giants
VI	1972	Dallas Cowboys	XXVI	1992	Washington Redskins
VII	1973	Miami Dolphins	XXVII	1993	Dallas Cowboys
VIII	1974	Miami Dolphins	XXVIII	1994	Dallas Cowboys
IX	1975	Pittsburgh Steelers	XXIX	1995	San Francisco 49ers
X	1976	Pittsburgh Steelers	XXX	1996	Dallas Cowboys
XI	1977	Oakland Raiders	XXXI	1997	Green Bay Packers
XII	1978	Dallas Cowboys	XXXII	1998	Denver Broncos
XIII	1979	Pittsburgh Steelers	XXXIII	1999	Denver Broncos
XIV	1980	Pittsburgh Steelers	XXXIV	2000	St Louis Rams
XV	1981	Oakland Raiders	XXXV	2001	Baltimore Ravens
XVI	1982	San Francisco 49ers	XXXVI	2002	New England Patriots
XVII	1983	Washington Redskins	XXXVII	2003	Tampa Bay Buccaneers
XVIII	1984	Los Angeles Raiders	XXXVIII	2004	New England Patriots
XIX	1985	San Francisco 49ers	XXXIX	2005	New England Patriots
XX	1986	Chicago Bears			

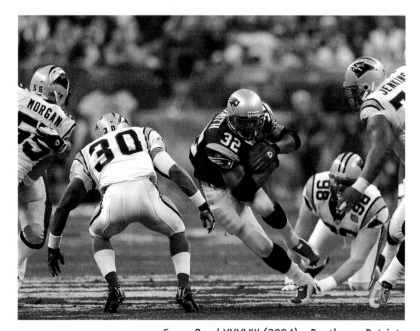

Super Bowl XXXVIII (2004) – Panthers v Patriots

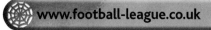
www.football-league.co.uk

Basketball

Basketball is hugely popular in the US and is now played in other parts of the world, as well as at the Olympics. The game is played by two teams of five players each, usually on an indoor court. Players score points by shooting the ball through the basket. The National Basketball Association (NBA) in the USA was formed in 1949. It contains 29 teams divided into two conferences, Eastern and Western. At the end of the season the two conference winners meet in a best-of-seven series for the NBA Championship.

Record breakers

Outstanding player Kareem Abdul-Jabbar (Milwaukee Bucks and Los Angeles Lakers) scored a record 38,387 points during his career.

Teams with most wins

Boston Celtics	16
Minnesota/Los Angeles Lakers	14
Chicago Bulls	6

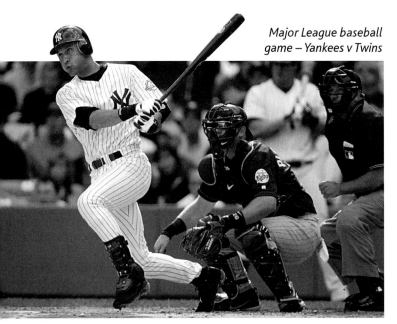

Major League baseball game – Yankees v Twins

Baseball

Baseball is one of the most popular sports in the USA and is also played in Japan, Mexico, Cuba and a number of South American countries. It is played by two teams of nine players each. The major event in the sport is the World Series – a best-of-seven series of games between the winners of the two major leagues in the US. These are the National League and the American League. The competition began in 1903 when the Boston Red Sox from the American League beat the Pittsburgh Pirates 5–3.

Teams with most wins

New York Yankees	26
Philadelphia/Kansas City/Oakland Athletics	9
St Louis Cardinals	9
Brooklyn/Los Angeles Dodgers	6

Australian Rules football

This is a tough, fast-moving game, in which players can kick, bounce, catch or punch the ball. It has been played in Australia since the Melbourne Football Club was formed in 1858. The Australian Football League (known as the Victorian Football Association up to 1990) started in 1877. The season-long series of matches ends in the Grand Final at the Melbourne Cricket Ground, one of the great sporting occasions in Australia.

There are 18 players in an Australian Rules team. This is more than any other team sport. The game is played on one of the biggest pitches. The oval-shaped area measures 135–185m x 110–155m. A professional soccer pitch measure 90–120m x 45–90m wide.

Golf majors

The four big competitions in golf are known as the majors. They are the US Masters, British Open, US Open and US PGA Championship, and are played in that order every year. The Masters, founded in 1934, is the only one of the four played on the same course each year, at Augusta National in Georgia, USA. The oldest of the majors is the British Open, which was first held in 1860. It is also the only one played outside the USA. The US Open was first played in 1895 and the US PGA in 1916.

Players with most professional major wins

Jack Nicklaus (USA) 18: 3 British Open, 4 US Open, 5 US PGA, 6 Masters
Walter Hagen (USA) 11: 4 British Open, 2 US Open, 5 US PGA
Ben Hogan (USA) 9: 1 British Open, 4 US Open, 2 US PGA, 2 Masters
Gary Player (S Africa) 9: 3 British Open, 1 US Open, 2 US PGA, 3 Masters
Tom Watson (USA) 8: 5 British Open, 1 US Open, 2 US Masters
Tiger Woods (USA) 8: 1 British Open, 2 US Open, 2 US PGA, 3 Masters

Tiger Woods

Tiger Woods

At just 21 years, three months and 14 days, Tiger Woods was the youngest-ever Masters champion. In 2001 Tiger won his second US Masters and became the first player to hold all four professional major championships at the same time.

Rugby Union

The game of rugby probably started in 1823 at Rugby School in England, when William Webb Ellis picked up a football and ran with it. However, various football games played in medieval Britain and Europe allowed handling of the ball, while a type of football similar to today's Australian Rules was played at Rugby almost 100 years before Webb Ellis. The first rules were drawn up in 1848 and the Rugby Football Union (RFU) was formed by Edwin Ash in 1871.

Today's game is played between two teams of 15 players. The two biggest events in the sport are the International Championship and the World Cup. The International Championship began in 1884 and was originally played by four teams: England, Ireland, Scotland and Wales. France joined in 1910 and Italy in 2000, making it a six-nation tournament.

The Rugby World Cup was launched in 1987 and has been held every four years since then. In 2003, 20 teams took part and nearly two million people attended the 48 matches.

Rugby World Cup winners
1987 New Zealand
1991 Australia
1995 South Africa
1999 Australia
2003 England

2003 Rugby Union World Cup final – England v Australia

Rugby League

Rugby League dates from 29 August 1895, when 21 major clubs in the north of England formed a league outside the Rugby Football Union. They were protesting against the RFU's refusal to pay players who had to take time off work. To make Rugby League less like Rugby Union they changed various rules, including reducing the team size from 15 to 13. Rugby League is now played in Australia, New Zealand, France, Russia and some Pacific nations, as well as in Britain.

One of the major events in Rugby League is the Challenge Cup. This is a knockout competition for all British clubs, now also open to French and Russian teams. The first Challenge Cup final was held at Headingley, Leeds, in 1897, with Batley the first winners. There is also a Rugby League World Cup, first played in 1954 and currently held every five years.

Test cricket

Cricket is a bat and ball game played between two teams of 11 players. The aim is to score more runs than the opposing team. Among the major competitions are the Test matches, which are normally played over five days.

They are called Test matches because they were started as a test of the relative skills of the two sides.

Test matches are played between teams representing their countries. There are currently ten countries that play Test cricket.

Test match cricket – West Indies v Australia

Countries taking part	Year first played	Countries taking part	Year first played
Australia	1877	India	1932
England	1877	Pakistan	1952
South Africa	1889	Sri Lanka	1982
West Indies	1928	Zimbabwe	1992
New Zealand	1930	Bangladesh	2000

The Ashes

Cricket's most famous trophy is the Ashes. England and Australia were the first two Test teams. When England lost to Australia at home in 1882, the *Sporting Times* joked that English cricket was dead and that its body would be cremated and the ashes taken to Australia. When the England team next visited Australia, it was presented with a tiny urn, containing the burnt bails from the wicket used in the Third Test. Since then, whichever team wins an England-Australia Test series is said to have won the Ashes. The trophy is kept permanently at Lord's Cricket Ground in London.

Women's cricket

Cricket between village women's teams was played in Sussex and Surrey in England during the mid 18th century. The first recorded match was at Gosden Common, Surrey, in 1745 between teams representing Bramley and Hambleton. The first Test match between Australia and England was held in Brisbane, Australia, in 1934, when England won. The women's World Cup started in 1973, two years before the men's version, and raised the profile of women's cricket. One of the best-known woman cricketers is Rachael Heyhoe Flint. She was captain of England from 1966 until 1977, during which time her team was never defeated.

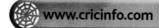

www.cricinfo.com

Badminton

Badminton probably came from an old children's game called battledore and shuttlecock. The battledore is a small wooden bat which the player uses to hit the shuttlecock. The game was popular in India and other Asian countries, and the aim was to keep the shuttlecock in the air as long as possible. British army officers played the game in India in the 1860s and they added a net to hit the shuttlecock over. They called the game *poona*.

When the officers returned to England they continued enjoying *poona*. The game was renamed badminton at a garden party at the home of Duke of Beaufort in 1873. His home was called Badminton House.

By 1877 the first official rules of the game were drawn up and in 1893 the first governing body, The Badminton Association of England, was set up. The Badminton Club of New York began in 1878, although the game did not become popular until the 1930s.

Badminton's greatest player

Rudy Hartono from Indonesia won the world's oldest badminton tournament, the All-England Championships, a record eight times between 1968 and 1976. He was also the 1980 world champion at the age of 32, and unbeaten in six Thomas Cup ties.

New rules for table tennis

Traditionally, the winner of a table tennis game was the first player to score 21 points, but in 2001 the International Table Tennis Federation (ITTF) announced changes in the rules. These included a new scoring system in which the first player to score 11 points wins the game. In major tournaments, matches were normally the best-of-three games or best-of-five under the "first to 21 points" rule. Under the new rules a match is now the best-of-five games or the best-of-seven.

Last amateur winners

The last amateur Wimbledon singles champions were John Newcombe (Australia) and Billie Jean King (USA) in 1967.

Serena Williams winning Wimbledon 2002

 ## Pelota

Pelota is the name given to a variety of sports that are played by hitting a ball with the hand, a racquet, or a basket attached to the hand. Pelota and its variations were first played during the 13th century in the Basque region of Spain.

There are variations of the game depending upon the equipment used.

- Played with the hand it is called *pelota mano*, or just pelota.
- Played with a racquet, it is called *frontenis*.
- Played with a hand basket, it is called *jai-alai*.

The game is similar to squash – players hit the ball against the end wall of a three-sided court, if possible, out of reach of their opponent. Pelota is popular in Spain, Mexico, South America, Cuba, Italy and many US states, including Florida.

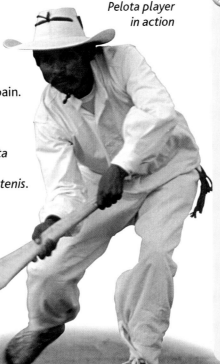

Pelota player in action

Squash champions

Jahangir Khan

Jahangir Khan is the greatest male squash player of all time. He has won six World Open titles, three World Amateur titles, four World Masters and ten consecutive British Open titles. Khan was born in Karachi in 1963. His father Roshan was a British champion, as were Roshan's cousins Hashan and Azam. At one point in his career, Jahangir competed for an amazing five years and eight months without defeat, playing more than 800 matches. He was voted Pakistan's Sportsman of the Millennium and elected President of the World Squash Federation in 2002.

Heather McKay

Heather McKay (born Blundell) dominated ladies' squash during the 1960s and 1970s. She was born in New South Wales, Australia in 1942, the eighth of 11 children. Between 1962 and 1977 she won 16 consecutive British Open titles and remained undefeated for 17 years before her retirement. She lost just two games in her career. In 1999 Heather McKay became a founder member of the WISPA Hall of Fame, and was awarded the Australian Sports Medal in 2000.

Lawn tennis Grand Slam events

The Grand Slam consists of the Australian, French, Wimbledon and US Championships. A player is said to have completed the Grand Slam if he or she holds all four titles simultaneously, although not necessarily in the same year. These events were originally for amateur players but are now open to all, including professionals.

Wimbledon Championships
First held in 1877, Wimbledon is the world's most famous tennis championship. From 1877 to 1921 it was a challenge event with the defending champion qualifying for the next year's final. Women first took part in 1884. Since 1968 Wimbledon has been an open event. This means it is open to all players, including professionals.

US Open
This was first held in 1881. Until 1911, the US tournament operated as a challenge system, with the defending champion automatically going through to the following year's final. Women first competed in 1887. Two championships were held in 1968 and 1969, one for amateurs and an open championship. It became completely open in 1970.

French Open
The French Open was first held in 1891 and until 1925 it was only for French nationals. It became the French Open in 1968 and has been played at the Stade Roland Garros (named after a famous French aviator) since 1928. Women have competed since 1897.

Australian Open
This competition was first held in 1905 as the Australasian Tennis Championship. Women first competed in 1922. The competition became the Australian Championship in 1927, and since 1969 has been the Australian Open. It is played at Melbourne every January.

Most titles in Grand Slams
Australian Roy Emerson won 28 titles in Grand Slam events between 1961 and 1967. He is the only male tennis player in history to win singles and doubles titles at all four Grand Slam events. Margaret Court (born Margaret Smith), also from Australia, won a record 62 Grand Slam titles, between 1960 and 1973.

Lawn tennis timeline

1877	First Wimbledon Championship.
1881	First US Championship.
1891	First French Championship – until 1925 for French nationals.
1896	Tennis played at the first Modern Olympics in Athens.
1900	Davis Cup began after Dwight F. Davis donated his trophy.
1905	First Australian Open.
1913	International Lawn Tennis Federation (now the ITF) founded in Paris with 12 member countries.
1922	Seeding (method of ranking players) first used, at the US National Championships.
1923	Women's tennis became international with the launch of the Wightman Cup (named after US team captain Hazel Wightman).
1938	Donald Budge (USA) became the first player to complete the Grand Slam.
1950	Louise Brough (USA) became the first woman to complete the Grand Slam.
1963	The Federation Cup, the women's equivalent of the Davis Cup, began.
1968	Tennis tournaments were opened to professional players, effectively ending the amateur game.
1971	The tie-break was introduced by the British LTA as an experiment.
1972	Davis Cup changed from being run on a challenge basis to a knockout tournament involving all competing nations.
1973	Introduction of official world rankings by the ATP and LTA.
1978	US Open moved to Flushing Meadows.
1988	Tennis revived as an Olympic sport after 64 years.

Tennis scoring

No one knows exactly how the tennis scoring system came about, but it may have started in France in medieval times. People think the system may be based on the movement of the hand of a clock located at one end of the court: on winning a point, the hand would be moved 15 minutes, or a quarter round the clock. Next comes 30, half the clock, and so on. As a player had to win four points to win the game, the first round the clock face won. The score 40 may be used instead of 45 because in French *quarante* (40) is easier to say than *quarante-cinq* (45).

When both sides reach 40 the score is deuce. This comes from the French *quarante à deux*, or 40 to both, or simply from *deux*, two, as players must gain two points to win.

"Love", the zero score, may come from the French word *l'oeuf*, meaning egg, as the symbol for zero is egg-shaped.

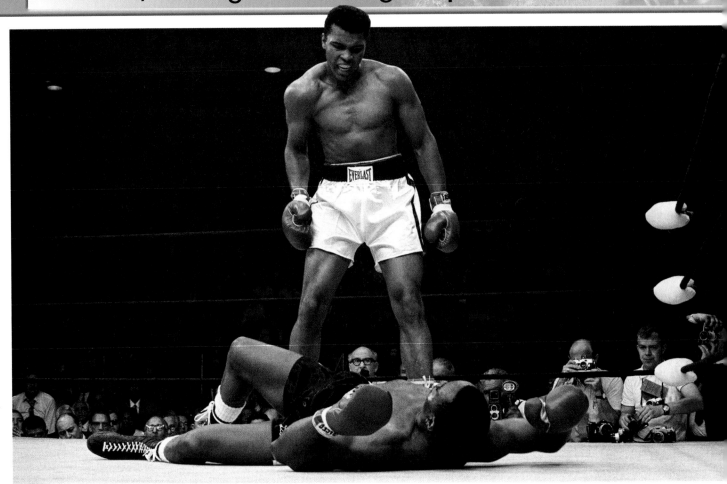

Muhammad Ali defeating Sonny Liston, 1965

Boxing weights

Boxing matches are held between two contestants of similar weight. The weight classes were first used in the 19th century and more were added during the 20th century.

Weight class	Max (kg)
Strawweight/Mini flyweight	48
Junior flyweight/Light flyweight	49
Flyweight	51
Junior bantam/Super flyweight	52
Bantamweight	54
Junior featherweight/Super bantamweight	55
Featherweight	57
Junior lightweight/Super featherweight	59
Lightweight	61
Junior welterweight/Super lightweight	65
Welterweight	67
Junior middleweight/Super welterweight	70
Middleweight	73
Super middleweight	76
Light heavyweight	79
Cruiserweight	91
Heavyweight	91+

Boxing's greatest champions

- "Sugar" Ray Robinson was one of the best boxers in any weight division. His first world title was at welterweight in 1946. Moving up a division, he beat Jake La Motta in 1951 to capture the middleweight title. He even had a crack at the light heavyweight title, but failed after a 14th-round knockout. Robinson was born in Detroit in 1920 and turned professional in 1940. He went on to have 201 fights and won 174 of them, 109 with knockouts.

- "Sugar" Ray Leonard was born in Wilmington, Carolina in 1956. He began boxing at 14 and in 1976 won the Olympic light welterweight title. He turned professional in 1977. Two years later he won the first of many world titles when he beat Wilfred Benitez to become welterweight champion. Leonard went on to become the first man to win world titles at five different weights, all within ten years. He held welterweight, light middleweight, middleweight, light heavyweight and super middleweight titles.

- Oscar de la Hoya from Los Angeles first became famous at the 1992 Barcelona Olympics – he won the USA's only boxing gold that year. La Hoya turned professional after the Olympics. He went on to become only the third man to capture world titles at five different weights, from junior lightweight to junior middleweight. His greatest win was beating his idol Julio Cesar Chavez in four rounds at Caesar's Palace, Las Vegas, in 1996.

- Muhammad Ali was born Cassius Clay in Louisville, Kentucky in 1942. He burst on to the boxing scene at the 1960 Rome Olympics where he took the light heavyweight gold medal. In 1964, aged 22, he won his first world heavyweight title by beating Sonny Liston. He beat George Foreman ten years later to become only the second man to regain his title. In 1978, at the age of 36, he beat Leon Spinks to become the first man to win the title a third time. He lost his last world title fight to Larry Holmes in 1980.

Wrestling

The World Wrestling Federation was started in the 1960s as the WorldWide Wrestling Federation (WWWF) by Vince McMahon. In the early 1980s Vince's son, Vince McMahon Jr, renamed it WWF. The sport changed and became widely popular. Characters such as Hulk Hogan became household names, attracting huge crowds to live matches and millions of followers via TV. The WWF is now known as WWE®, World Wrestling Entertainment, Inc.

The two biggest events in the WWE calendar are Wrestle Mania, which decides the world champions, and the Royal Rumble. The first WWF Wrestle Mania was at Madison Square Garden on 31 March 1985.

Top wrestlers

- Texan Shawn Michaels is one of the most popular of all wrestlers. He weighs in at about 116kg. Michaels has won the WWE title, WWE World Heavyweight title, the WWE World Tag Team title and twice won the Royal Rumble, among many other top honours and titles.

- The Rock (real name Dwayne Johnson) is probably the best known fighter in the sport today. He is 1.94m tall and weighs 118kg. He has been the WWE Champion, the WWE World Tag Team Champion and was the winner of Royal Rumble 2000. He took to the sport after a brief professional football career, and has also appeared in several films, including *The Mummy Returns* (2001), *The Scorpion King* (2002) and *Be Cool* (2005).

- Triple H made his WWE debut in 1995 as Hunter Hearst Helmsley, but now is known as Triple H, or "The Game". He weighs in at around 118kg. He has been WWE Champion, WWE World Heavyweight Champion, WWE World Tag Team Champion, King of the Ring and Royal Rumble. He is the only man to win the Grand Slam, King of the Ring and Royal Rumble.

- Hulk Hogan's real name is Terry Bollea. He is 2.03m tall and weighs a massive 122kg. Hogan helped to make the sport more popular in the early WWF days. His first ring name was Sterling Golden and then he became Terry Boulder before settling with Hulk Hogan. He played the wrestling villain Thunderlips in *Rocky III* in 1982, and has appeared in other films, including *Spy Hard* (1996) and *Muppets from Space* (1999).

Weightlifting records

In an Olympic weightlifting competition contestants perform two types of lifts, the snatch and the clean and jerk. They have three attempts at each. The score is the total of the best of each type of lift.

In the snatch the contestant lifts the bar from the floor directly above the head and holds it for two seconds. In the clean and jerk, the contestant first takes the bar from the floor to the shoulders and then above the head.

- The men's record is 472.5kg set by Hossein Rezazadeh (Iran) at the Sydney Olympics in September 2000. This is heavier than a cow!

- A new women's record was also set at the 2000 Sydney Olympics when Meiyuan Ding of China successfully lifted 300kg.

Iranian weightlifter Hossein Rezazadeh

Snooker and pool

Snooker was first played by British army officers in India and later became popular in Britain, while pool began in America. Both are becoming more popular on opposite sides of the Atlantic. One of pool's top events is the Mosconi Cup, named after the great American pool player and 14 times world champion Willie Mosconi. It is now an annual contest in the UK and pitches the best pool players from Europe against those from the USA. The European team has contained some of the most popular snooker players, including Ronnie O'Sullivan, Jimmy White, Steve Davis and Alex Higgins. Steve Davis is the only person to have played in all ten Mosconi Cups since its launch in 1994.

Pool champion

Earl Strickland from Greensboro, North Carolina turned professional in 1980 and has won three world titles (1990, 1991, 2002). He has also been the US Open champion five times. Nicknamed "The Pearl", he has appeared in eight Mosconi Cups, winning 24 of his 36 matches, and has twice captained the winning team.

Snooker champions

The greatest players of the modern game still playing are Steve Davis and Stephen Hendry. Between them they have won the Embassy World Professional Snooker title 13 times, and both have won all the other major trophies in the game. Davis turned professional in 1978 and three years later won the first of six world titles when he beat Doug Mountjoy 18–12 at The Crucible, Sheffield. He won his last world title in 1989. Scottish-born Hendry turned professional in 1985. He won his first world titles in 1990 and went on to win a record seven, including five consecutive titles between 1992 and 1996.

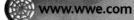 www.wwe.com

Olympic water sports

Sailing
The first Modern Olympics in 1896 should have included sailing, but the races could not be held because of bad weather. Sailing was included for the first time four years later in Paris and has been a full Olympic sport since 1908. Boardsailing made its debut in 1988. Men and women have competed together in sailing events over the years, but in 1988 women had events of their own. Until the 2000 Olympics, sailing was known as yachting.

Top gold-medal winning nations (1900–2004)
Great Britain	24
Norway	17
USA	17

Canoeing
Canoeing was first included as a demonstration sport in 1924, and did not become a full Olympic sport until 1936. Women took part for the first time in 1948.

The top gold-medal winning nations (1936–2004)
USSR/Unified Team	30
Germany/West Germany	28
East Germany	14
Hungary	17
Sweden	15

Racers in an Olympic canoeing competition

Rowing
Rowing was to have been part of the 1896 Olympics, but the events were cancelled. It was first included in Paris four years later, and has appeared at every Olympics since. Women first competed in 1976.

The top gold-medal winning nations (1900–2004)
East Germany	33
USA	30
Germany/West Germany	27
Great Britain	22

Olympic swimming

These are the top medal-winning Olympic swimmers. Totals include medals won in relays.

Swimmer	Gold	Silver	Bronze	Total
Men				
Mark Spitz (USA)	9	1	1	11
Matt Biondi (USA)	7	2	1	10
Aleksandr Popov (Russia)	4	5	0	9
Zoltán Halmay (Hungary)	3	5	1	9
Women				
Jenny Thompson (USA)	8	1	1	10
Dara Torres (USA)	4	1	4	9
Dawn Fraser (Australia)	4	4	0	8
Kornelia Ender (GDR)	4	4	0	8
Shirley Babashoff (USA)	2	6	0	8

The following are the top medal-winning nations in swimming events at all Olympics up to and including the 2004 Athens Games. Medals for water polo and discontinued events are included.

Men		Women	
Country	Golds	Country	Golds
USA	150	USA	110
Australia	33	East Germany	33
Hungary	21	Australia	21
USSR/Unified Team/Russia	21	China	15

Swimmer in the women's 100m breaststroke semi-final in the 2000 Olympics

Mark Spitz

When swimmer Mark Spitz took part in the 1968 Mexico Olympics he was already a record holder – he set a total 26 world records during his career. He predicted he would win six gold medals at the Olympics, but he won just two, both in relay events. But in 1972, in Munich, Spitz became the first and only person to win seven gold medals at one Summer Olympics. He also set new world records with all his medals.

Mark Spitz's gold medals at the 1972 Olympics

Date	Event	Time (min:sec)
28 August	200 metres butterfly	2:00.70
28 August	4 x 100 metres freestyle	3:26.42
29 August	200 metres freestyle	1:52.78
31 August	100 metres butterfly	0:54.27
31 August	4 x 200 metres freestyle	7:35.78
3 September	100 metres freestyle	0:51.22
4 September	4 x 100 metres medley	3:48.16

 # Swimming strokes

Breaststroke
The breaststroke was the first stroke used in competitive and recreational swimming. It is also the stroke that most people learn when they first take up swimming. The first reference to the breaststroke was in a French book in 1696. The sidestroke, with a scissor leg action, developed from breaststroke. Top swimmers can swim the breaststroke at 1.37m a second.

Backstroke
The backstroke is the only stroke in which the swimmers start in the water, rather than diving in. The stroke, in which swimmers lie on their backs and use their arms in a windmill style, was first made popular in the USA by Harry Hebner in 1912. An earlier form of the backstroke was first seen at the 1900 Olympics. For this fast stroke, top speed is about 1.52m a second.

Butterfly
In this stroke, both arms enter and leave the water at the same time, while the legs perform a dolphin kick. It was developed in the 1930s and evolved from the breaststroke. Swimming coach David Armbruster developed the arm movement of the stroke at the University of Iowa in 1934 and the following year one of his swimmers, Jack Sieg, developed the foot and leg movements. The two combined produced the butterfly. The stroke was not officially approved until 1953 and became an Olympic event in 1956. Maximum speed is 1.67m a second.

Front crawl/freestyle
In 1844 two native Americans competing in a swimming regatta in London introduced their new revolutionary overarm stroke. Flying Gull beat Tobacco to take the winner's medal. The stroke was later developed by Englishman John Trudgen, and then by Australian Richard Cavill, who realized the importance of kicking the feet at the same time as moving the arms. Front crawl is the fastest swimming stroke and has a maximum speed of 1.71m a second.

Competitors in the America's Cup, 2003

The America's Cup

The America's Cup is the top sailing trophy and one of the best known trophies in the sporting world. It began in 1851 when the English Royal Yacht Squadron organized a 6-mile regatta of 17 boats around the Isle of Wight. The 101-ft American schooner *America* entered and won the trophy, then called the One Hundred Guinea Cup. The trophy was re-named the America's Cup after their win, and given to the New York Yacht Club. There it remained unless won by a challenger. Over the next 132 years the New York Yacht Club successfully defended the trophy against 25 challengers, until in 1983 it was won by Australia. In 2003 the trophy returned to Europe when Russell Coutts in *Alinghi* won for Switzerland – a landlocked country!

Recent winners

Yacht	Country	Skipper	Year
Alinghi	Switzerland	Russell Coutts	2003
Black Magic	New Zealand	Russell Coutts	2000
Black Magic	New Zealand	Russell Coutts	1995
America 3	USA	Bill Koch	1992
Stars and Stripes	USA	Dennis Conner	1988
Stars and Stripes	USA	Dennis Conner	1987
Australia II	Australia	John Bertrand	1983
Freedom	USA	Dennis Conner	1980

Oympic Tarzans

Johnny Weissmuller won the 100 metres freestyle at the 1924 Paris and 1928 Amsterdam Olympics. He went on to win a total of five golds and one bronze medal during his Olympic career. While training for the 1932 Olympics, he was offered a $500-a-week contract to advertise swimwear. This meant the end of his Olympic career, but a Hollywood executive saw the adverts and offered Weissmuller the role of Tarzan. In 1932 he made his debut in the film *Tarzan the Ape Man*. He played the character in 11 more films over the next 16 years and was the first of four Olympic medallists to play the film role. The others were Buster Crabbe (freestyle swimmer), Herman Brix (shot put) and Glenn Morris (decathlon).

Tour de France

The oldest and best-known of the world's great cycling tours is the Tour de France. The others are the Vuelta – Tour of Spain, and Giro – Tour of Italy.

- The Tour de France was first staged in 1903 when the course was made up of six stages over 2,428km. Now contestants race 5,000km or more and the course takes in more than 20 stages, often going out of France into neighbouring countries.

- The famous yellow jersey (*maillot jaune*) is worn by the current overall time leader in a race. It was first worn in 1919.

- Lance Armstrong (USA) has won the Tour de France a record six times, one more than Jacques Anquetil (France), Eddie Merckx (Belgium), Bernard Hinault (France) and Miguel Indurain (Spain).

- The longest race was in 1926 when Lucien Buysse of Belgium won after a gruelling 5,745km.

- Around 15 million people every year line the streets to watch the Tour de France over its three weeks.

- The first US winner of the Tour de France was Greg LeMond who won it in 1986, and again in 1989 and 1990. He was also the first English-speaking winner of the race.

- Eddie Merckx has won more of the big three tours than any other man. He has won the Tour de France five times, the Giro five times and the Vuelta once.

Mountain biking

Mountain biking, or off-road biking, was started in 1974 by a group of Californian enthusiasts, who modified their bikes. By 1977, there was so much interest in the sport that manufacturers started to produce mountain bikes, and in 1983 the National Off-Road Bicycle Association (NORBA) was formed. There are two types of mountain bike competitions – downhill riding and cross-country – and the first world championships were held in 1990. Cross-country mountain biking was first held at the Olympics in 1996. Competitors ride over a hilly, sometimes mountainous, natural course. Men race 40 to 50km, and women 30 to 40km.

The top riders, male and female, are both French. François Gachet won the men's downhill world titles six times between 1994 and 1999. Anne C. Chausson has won 12 world titles. She won the downhill every year from 1996 to 2003 and was the dual solo and 4-cross champion in both 2002 and 2003.

Olympic Keirin race, in which teams chase a moped around a velodrome track.

Olympic cycling

Cycling was included in the first Modern Olympics in 1896. Léon Flameng (France) won the first cycling gold in the 100km race. Only two men competed – Flameng and Georgios Kolettis of Greece – and they had to race around a 333.3m track 300 times! During the race, Kolettis's bicycle needed repairing, so Flameng waited for him while the repairs were carried out. Cycling has been included in every Olympics since then. These are the current Olympic events.

Men
Track	Sprint (1,000 metres)
	Time trial (1,000 metres)
	Individual pursuit (4,000 metres)
	Team pursuit (4,000 metres)
	Points race (40 kilometres)
	Madison (60 kilometres)
	Keirin (2,000 metres)
Road	Road race (individual)
	Time trial (individual)
Mountain bike	Cross-country

Women
Track	Sprint (1,000 metres)
	Time trial (500 metres)
	Individual pursuit (3,000 metres)
	Points race (25 kilometres)
Road	Road race (individual)
	Time trial (individual)
Mountain bike	Cross-country

Olympic women's mountain bike race

Formula One

The Formula One World Championship normally lasts from March until October. In 2004 there were 18 races. The winner in each race receives ten points and runners-up get eight to one points. The driver with the most points at the end of the season is the champion. There is also a manufacturers' championship.

Michael Schumacher in a Ferrari at the US Grand Prix.

World champion

German Michael Schumacher is the world's most successful Formula One driver. He has won a record seven world titles (1994, 1995, 2000, 2001, 2002, 2003, 2004) and also has the most race wins in a season – 13 in 2004.

Driver	Country	Wins
Michael Schumacher	Germany	83
Alain Prost	France	51
Ayrton Senna	Brazil	41
Nigel Mansell	UK	31
Jackie Stewart	UK	27
Jim Clark	UK	25
Niki Lauda	Austria	25

Constructor	Wins
Ferrari	184
McLaren	138
Williams	113
Lotus	79
Brabham	35
Benetton	27

Motor cycle racing

Grand Prix bikes used to come in engine sizes 50cc, 90cc, 125cc, 250cc, 350cc and 500cc. Now there are Grand Prix championships only in 125cc, 250cc and Moto GP (which replaced the old 500cc event). Grand Prix bikes are made in small numbers just for racing. Superbikes are made in larger quantities and can be used on the road.

Top manufacturers

- An Aprilia machine first won at 250cc in 1987, and the make is now dominant in both the 125 and 250cc classes. They enjoyed their first Superbike success in 2000.

- Ducati have been in Grand Prix racing since the 1950s. They are now by far the most successful manufacturer in Superbike history.

- Kawasaki bikes won their first world title (125cc) in 1969. They have now won nine world titles in three classes as well as producing the 1993 Superbike world champion.

- Honda are the most successful manufacturer in motor cycle racing. They have now won 43 Grand Prix world titles in six classes and had 570 race wins. They are now also making a name for themselves in Superbike racing.

- Suzuki began life as clothing makers before starting to make motor cycles. They won their first Grand Prix in 1962 and in the same year won the first ever 50cc title.

- The Yamaha company started in 1887 as musical instrument manufacturers and made their first motor cycle in 1955. They first entered a bike in the 1961 French Grand Prix, but did not compete regularly until 1964, when they won the world 250cc title.

Young winners

The youngest ever Formula One race winners are Fernando Alonso (Spain), Troy Ruttman (USA) and Bruce McLaren (New Zealand). Alonso won the Hungarian Grand Prix in 2003 at the age of 22 years, 1 month. In 1952 Ruttman won the Indianapolis 500 (at that time part of the Formula One World Championship) at 22 years, 3 months. McLaren was the same age when he won the US Grand Prix in 1959.

The youngest Formula One world champions are Emerson Fittipaldi (Brazil) who was 25 years, 9 months when he won in 1972; Michael Schumacher (Germany) who won in 1994 at the age of 25 years 10 months; Jacques Villeneuve (Canada), champion in 1997 aged 26 years, 5 months; and Niki Lauda (Austria), 1975 champion at 26 years 6 months.

Indianapolis 500

The biggest event in American motor racing is the Indianapolis 500, which is not just a race but a day-long carnival. The auto race is part of the Memorial Day celebrations at the end of May and crowds of 250,000 flock to the Indianapolis raceway from all over the USA. The course, which opened in 1909, is known as The Brickyard because the original circuit was made out of thousands of bricks. The first Indy 500 was held in 1911 and was won by Ray Harroun in his Marmon Wasp. Contestants race over 200 laps of the 4km oval circuit.

ONE AND ONLY

One of the great Indy 500 drivers was A.J. Foyt, the first of only three men to win the race four times. He had his first success in 1961 and followed it up with wins in 1964, 1967 and 1977. He drove a record 11,785 miles in 34 Indy 500 races. Foyt started racing in 1953. He is the only man to win the Indy 500, the Daytona 500 and the Le Mans 24 Hour races.

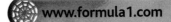

www.formula1.com

Ice hockey

Ice hockey probably developed from a game called bandy that was played on ice-covered pitches. The modern game is played over three 20-minute periods between two teams. Each team has six players on the ice at any one time. The object is to move the puck (a hard rubber disc) across the ice with a stick (maximum length 160cm) and put it into the opponent's goal.

The National Hockey League (NHL) was formed in 1917. Today the NHL is made up of 30 teams split into two conferences. The Eastern Conference has 15 teams divided into three divisions: Atlantic, North-East and South-East. The Western Conference is also divided into three divisions: Central, North-West and Pacific. At the end of season the leading teams in each conference play each other. The winner of each plays for the Stanley Cup which was donated by the Governor-General of Canada, Lord Stanley of Preston, in 1893.

The Stanley Cup

Every player on the winning team takes the Stanley Cup home for 24 hours to show off to family and friends. New York Islander Clark Gillies used it in 1980 to feed his dog, and in 1996 Colorado Avalanche defenceman Sylvain Lefebvre had his daughter baptized in it.

Top teams Stanley Cup wins	
Montreal Canadiens	24
Toronto Maple Leafs	13
Detroit Red Wings	10
Boston Bruins	5
Edmonton Oilers	5

NHL's top goalscorers	
Player	**Goals**
Wayne Gretzky	894
Gordie Howe	801
Brett Hull	741
Marcel Dionne	731
Phil Esposito	717
Mike Gartner	708

NHL ice hockey 2004 – New York Rangers v New Jersey Devils

Ski-jumping

The world ski-jumping record of 225m, set by Austrian Andreas Goldberger in 2000, was broken in 2003 by Finland's Matti Hautamaeki. Matti, who is known as The Flying Finn, broke the record three times on successive days. During the last World Cup event of the season at Planica, Slovenia, he jumped 227.5m, 228.5m and then a remarkable 231m. During his third record-breaking jump Matti was airborne for eight seconds.

Ice skating

Famous skaters
- Ulrich Salchow, born in Sweden in 1877, was the greatest men's figure skater of all time. He won the first Olympic skating title at the 1908 London Olympics and between 1901 and 1911 he was the world champion on ten occasions.

- Norway's Sonja Henie won Olympic golds in 1928, 1932 and 1936. She also won ten world titles. At her peak she was so popular that police had to control the crowds that gathered around her. She won nearly 1,500 cups and medals during her career. After leaving the sport in 1936 she became a film star and appeared in 11 films.

Fastest speed skaters
- **Men:** Gerard van Velde of Holland skated 1,000 metres in 1 minute 7.18 seconds at the Salt Lake City Winter Olympics in 2002, a speed of 53.6km/h.

- **Women:** Chris Witt of the USA set the women's record at the same games when she covered the 1,000 metres in 1 minute 13.83 seconds – 48.8km/h.

Olympic skater leans into a curve on the way to winning gold in the men's speed skating event at the 2002 Winter Games.

Winter Olympics

The Winter Games (officially the International Winter Sports Week, but later recognized as the first Winter Olympics) was first held in 1924. It included five events: Nordic skiing, figure skating, speed skating, bobsledding and ice hockey. Winter Olympics were held in the same years as the Summer Olympics until 1992, but since 1994 they have taken place every four years between the Summer Games. The Winter Olympics now include the following events.

- Alpine skiing
- Biathlon cross-country (skiing and rifle-shooting)
- Bobsleigh
- Cross-country skiing
- Curling
- Figure skating
- Freestyle skiing
- Ice hockey
- Luge
- Nordic combined
- Short-track speed skating
- Skeleton (similar to the luge but competitors travel on their stomachs, head first)
- Ski-jumping
- Snowboarding
- Speed skating

Young star

The first athlete aged under 14 to win a Winter Olympic gold was Kim Yoon-mi of South Korea. She was in the winning 3,000m speed skating relay team at Lillehammer, Norway in 1994.

Top medal-winning nations at the Winter Olympics (1924–2002)

Country	Gold	Silver	Bronze	Total
USSR/Unified Team/Russia	113	82	78	273
Norway	94	93	73	260
USA	70	70	51	191
Germany/West Germany	68	67	52	187
Austria	41	57	65	163

Top medal winners at the Winter Olympics (1924–2002)

Athlete/country – Men	Sport	Gold	Silver	Bronze	Total
Bjorn Dählie, Norway	Cross-country	8	4	0	12
Sixten Jernberg, Sweden	Cross-country	4	3	2	9
Peter Angerer, Germany/West Germany	Biathlon	3	2	2	7
Ivar Ballangrud, Norway	Speed skating	4	2	1	7
Veikko Hakulinen, Finland	Cross-country	3	3	1	7
Eero Mäntyranta, Finland	Cross-country	3	2	2	7
Bogdan Musiol, Germany/East Germany	Bobsled	1	5	1	7
Clas Thunberg, Finland	Speed skating	5	1	1	7

Athlete/country – Women	Sport	Gold	Silver	Bronze	Total
Raisa Smetanina, USSR/Unified Team	Cross-country	4	5	1	10
Stefania Belmondo, Italy	Cross-country	2	3	4	9
Lyubov Egorova, Unified Team/Russia	Cross-country	6	3	0	9
Larissa Lazutina, Unified Team/Russia	Cross-country	5	3	1	9

Winter Olympic facts and figures

Medal totals from all the Winter Olympics from 1924 to 2002

Year	City/country	Competitors	Nations	Most golds		Most medals	
1924	Chamonix, France	294	16	Norway	4	Norway	17
				Finland	4		
1928	St Moritz, Switzerland	495	25	Norway	6	Norway	15
1932	Lake Placid, USA	306	17	USA	6	USA	12
1936	Garmisch-Partenkirchen, Germany	755	28	Norway	7	Norway	15
1948	St Moritz, Switzerland	713	28	Norway	4	Norway	10
				Sweden	4	Sweden	10
						Switzerland	10
1952	Oslo, Norway	732	30	Norway	7	Norway	16
1956	Cortina D'Ampezzo, Italy	818	32	USSR	7	USSR	16
1960	Squaw Valley, USA	665	30	USSR	7	USSR	21
1964	Innsbruck, Austria	1,186	36	USSR	11	USSR	25
1968	Grenoble, France	1,293	37	Norway	6	Norway	14
1972	Sapporo, Japan	1,232	35	USSR	8	USSR	16
1976	Innsbruck, Austria	1,128	37	USSR	13	USSR	27
1980	Lake Placid, USA	1,067	37	USSR	10	USSR	22
1984	Sarajevo, Yugoslavia	1,278	49	East Germany	9	USSR	25
1988	Calgary, Canada	1,423	57	USSR	11	USSR	29
1992	Albertville, France	1,801	63	Germany	10	Germany	26
1994	Lillehammer, Norway	1,739	67	Russia	11	Norway	26
1998	Nagano, Japan	2,302	72	Germany	12	Germany	29
2002	Salt Lake City, USA	2,399	78	Germany	12	Germany	35

www.torino2006.org

Greyhound racing

Dog racing has been popular since ancient times, when dogs were used for hunting. Modern greyhound racing takes place on an oval-shaped track over distances from 210m up to 1,097m. An electric "hare" goes round the track on rails, and the dogs are released from traps to chase it. In the UK most greyhound races are run with six dogs, but in the USA they are run with eight. There is a draw before the race to decide which trap each dog starts from. Each dog wears a coloured jacket which matches its starting trap.

Harness racing

In harness racing the horses pull the drivers who sit in a two-wheeled cart called a sulky. There are two forms of harness racing – pacing and trotting.

The difference between pacing and trotting is in the way the horse moves. A pacing horse moves its right front and back legs together, then its left front and back legs. A trotter moves its left front leg and right back leg at the same time, followed by its right front leg and left back leg.

Hambletonian harness race

Main races
The leading race for trotters is the Hambletonian. This race was first held at Syracuse, New York, in 1926 and is now run every year at The Meadowlands, East Rutherford, New Jersey. It is named after a trotter called Hambletonian. The leading race for pacers is The Little Brown Jug, named after a 19th-century horse. It has been held at Delaware, Ohio, every year since 1946.

Top drivers
Hervé Filion, born in Quebec, Canada, is the most famous driver in harness-racing history. He set many records in his 35-year career and had almost 15,000 wins. In 1968 he became the first driver to win 400 races in a season. He went on to achieve 400 or more wins per season in 14 other years. When he retired in 1995 Filion's final tally of wins was 14,783, and he had been Driver of the Year a record ten times.

John Campbell, from Ontario, Canada, is the top money-winning jockey in the sport. He started driving in 1972 at the age of 17 and was the first man to pass the $100 million and $200 million milestones in career earnings. He won the Hambletonian five times.

Top horse
Moni Maker was the first horse to pass the $5-million mark. Remarkably, she achieved this during a four-year career between 1997–2000. She won 60 of her 91 trotting races and won the Horse of the Year Award in 1998 and 1999. A horse named Varenne from Italy became the top prize winner in 2003.

World's most successful jockey
Laffit Pincay Jr was the first man to win more than 9,500 races. He won the US Breeders' Cup seven times, but the Kentucky Derby only once. When he retired in March 2003 his prize winnings totalled more than $225 million.

Rodeo

Professional rodeo developed from the early days of ranching, when bull riding and calf roping were common activities. The first known rodeo with prize money was held at Deer Trail, Colorado, in 1869. The All-Round Cowboy World Champion is decided each year – the champion is the cowboy who wins the most money over a series of events. Top cowboys win more than $250,000 a year.

 # Record horse jumps

- The highest officially recognized horse jump is 2.47m. The jump was made by Captain Alberto Larraguibel Morales (Chile) on Huasó on 5 February 1949 at Santiago, Chile. Richard "Dick" Donnelly (USA) claimed to have cleared 2.515m on a horse named Heatherbloom in Richmond, Virginia, USA, in 1902, but this is an unofficial record.

- The world record height jumped by a horse in a puissance event (a showjumping competition in which horses jump a limited number of walls and high obstacles) was set on 9 June 1991. German rider Franke Sloothaak on Obtibeurs Leonardo cleared 2.4m during an event in Chaudfontaine, Switzerland.

- The longest horse jump over water is 8.4m. The jump was made by André Ferreira (South Africa) in Johannesburg, South Africa, on 25 April 1975 on a horse named Something.

The Breeders' Cup

The Breeders' Cup Limited was started in 1982 to encourage thoroughbred racing throughout the United States. The first Breeders' Cup day was held on 10 November 1984 at Hollywood Park, Inglewood, California. It is now one of the most important race days anywhere and entries come from all over the world.

There are eight races on Breeders' Cup Day, which is held at a different course each year in October or November. The total prize money is more than $13 million. The winner of the Breeders' Cup Classic, which is run over a distance of one mile two furlongs, takes the biggest individual prize of more than $2 million.

Breeders' Cup records

Most wins (jockey)	14 (Jerry Bailey)
Most prize money (jockey)	$22,730,000 (Pat Day)
Most wins (trainer)	17 (D. Wayne Lukas)
Most prize money (trainer)	$18,608,400 (D. Wayne Lukas)
Most used track	Churchill Downs, Kentucky, used in 1988, 1991, 1994, 1998, 2000

Breeders' Cup firsts

The 2003 Breeders' Cup produced two firsts. Julie Krone, who rode Halfbridled to victory in the Juvenile Fillies race, was the first woman to ride a winner at the event. One race ended in a dead heat – the first in Breeders' Cup history.

Top horse races

England

- The Epsom Derby was first held in 1780 and is now run over one-and-a-half miles at Epsom Downs each June. The first winner was a horse named Diomed. Jockey Lester Piggott won the Derby a record nine times.

- The Grand National is the world's best-known steeplechase, a horse race over a course with obstacles to be jumped. It was first run as the Grand Liverpool Steeplechase in 1839. The race now takes place every spring over four-and-a-half miles at Aintree in England and the winning horse has to clear 30 challenging fences. The famous horse Red Rum won the race a record three times between 1972–76.

France

- The Prix de L'Arc de Triomphe was first run in 1920. It takes place on the first Sunday in October every year and covers 2,400m over the Longchamps race course, Paris. Alleged, ridden by Lester Piggott, won the race in 1977 and 1978 and was the last horse to win two years in a row.

Australia

- The most important horse race in Australia is the Melbourne Cup which dates from 1861. It is run on the first Tuesday in November at the Flemington Park race track in Victoria. Trainer Bart Cummings won the race a record 11 times between 1965 and 1999.

United States

- The Kentucky Derby was first held in 1875. It is run over one mile two furlongs at Churchill Downs, Kentucky, on the first Saturday in May and is the most famous of all US horse races. Eddie Arcaro and Bill Hartack have been the most successful jockeys with five wins each.

- Breeders' Cup (see right)

Winner of the Breeders' Cup Classic 2002

All good things have to come to an end, even this book, so this final section is a collection of "lasts". Do you know when Concorde last flew or what Anna Pavlova's last words were? And when did the Beatles play their last concert? Find the answers to these and many more questions in the following pages.

LAST LISTS

Joan of Arc, 15th-century French heroine who was burned at the stake at 19 years old

 ## Forever young

The following are some of the most famous people who died early and so remain forever young in our minds.

Name/cause/year	Age at death
King Edward V of England, murdered, 1483	12
Saint Agnes, martyred, c 304	13
King Edward VI of England, natural causes, 1553	15
Anne Frank, German diarist, in concentration camp, 1945	15
Lady Jane Grey, Queen of England, executed, 1554	16
Thomas Chatterton, English poet, took poison, 1770	17
Anastasia, Grand Duchess of Russia, assassinated, 1918	17
Ritchie Valens, American rock singer, plane crash, 1959	17
King Tutankhamen, Egyptian pharaoh, c 1340 BC	18
Heliogabalus, Roman Emperor, assassinated, 222	18
Joan of Arc, French heroine, burned at the stake, 1431	19
Catherine Howard, Queen of Henry VIII, beheaded, 1542	20
Billy the Kid (William H. Bonney), American outlaw, shot, 1881	21
Eddie Cochran, American rock singer, car accident, 1960	21
Pocahontas, Native American Indian princess, smallpox, 1617	22
Buddy Holly, American rock singer, plane crash, 1959	22
Aaliyah (Aaliyah Haughton), singer, plane crash, 2001	22
River Phoenix, actor, drug overdose, 1993	23
Clyde Barrow, US outlaw, shot by Texas Rangers, 1934	24
James Dean, American film actor, car crash, 1955	24
Lee Harvey Oswald, assassin of John F. Kennedy, murdered, 1963	24
John Keats, English poet, tuberculosis, 1821	25
"Red Baron" Manfred von Richthofen, German flying ace, shot down, 1918	25
Jean Harlow, film actress, illness, 1937	26
Brian Jones, Rolling Stones guitarist, drowned, 1969	26
Jimi Hendrix, rock guitarist, drugs, 1970	27
Kurt Cobain, Nirvana lead singer, shooting suicide, 1994	27
Anne Brontë, British writer, tuberculosis, 1849	29

 ## Famous last words

Marie Antoinette, 1893
French queen, who accidentally trod on her executioner's foot as she went to the guillotine: "Pardonnez-moi, monsieur" (Pardon me, sir).

Billy the Kid (aka William Bonney, Henry McCarty), 1881
American outlaw, before being shot by Sheriff Pat Garrett: "Who is it?"

Julius Caesar, 44 BC
Roman emperor, who was assassinated by conspirators, including Brutus, a man he thought was his friend. According to legend and Shakespeare, Caesar said: "Et tu Brute?" (You as well, Brutus?)

Caligula, AD 41
Roman emperor who was assassinated: "I am still alive!"

Catherine de Medici, 1589
Queen of France: "Ah, my God, I am dead!"

Douglas Fairbanks Sr, 1939
American film actor: "I've never felt better."

Joseph Henry Green, 1863
British doctor, after checking his own pulse: "Stopped."

Heinrich Himmler, 1945
Nazi leader, as he committed suicide by taking poison: "I am Heinrich Himmler!"

Captain Lawrence Oates, 1912
Oates was a member of Scott's expedition to the South Pole. He was terribly injured from frostbite and went to his death rather than hold up his companions. When he left the tent he said, "I am going outside and may be some time."

Viscount Palmerston 1865
British Prime Minister: "Die, my dear doctor? That's the last thing I shall do."

Anna Pavlova, 1931
Ballerina: "Get my swan costume ready!"

John Sedgwick, 1864
American Civil War general shot by a sniper: "They couldn't hit an elephant at this distance."

Lytton Strachey, 1932
English writer: "If this is dying, then I don't think much of it."

Queen Victoria, 1901
British queen: "Oh, that peace may come." (a reference to the war at the time in South Africa). "Bertie!" (her husband, Prince Albert).

H.G. Wells, 1946
English novelist, author of *The Time Machine*: "I'm all right."

Oscar Wilde, 1900
Opinions differ about the Irish writer's last words. Some people claim he said: "Either these curtains go/that wallpaper goes, or I do." Others believe he said: "I am dying, as I have lived – beyond my means."

Anna Pavlova as The Dying Swan

Unusual deaths

Aeschylus
Aeschylus was a famous Greek dramatist who died in 456 BC. A prediction that he would be killed by a blow from heaven came true when an eagle carrying a tortoise dropped it on his head.

King Alexander of Greece
He died after being bitten by his pet monkey in 1920.

Francis Bacon
This Elizabethan philosopher caught a chill while trying to deep-freeze a chicken by stuffing it with snow. He died in 1626.

Hilaire Belloc
Although born in France, Hilaire Belloc was an English writer and Member of Parliament. He died in 1953 after a burning coal fell out of his fire and set him ablaze.

Madéleine-Sophie Blanchard
Madame Blanchard was the widow of pioneer balloonist Jean-Pierre Blanchard. She was killed in Paris in 1819, when fireworks set fire to her balloon.

Jerome Cardan
Cardan was an Italian physician, mathematician and astrologer. He starved himself to death in 1576 to make sure that his own prediction of his death would come true.

Howard Carter
Carter was a British archaeologist who discovered Tutankhamen's tomb. He died after being bitten by a mosquito in 1939 and this began the legend of the Curse of Tutankhamen.

Isadora Duncan
This American dancer was strangled in 1927 by her scarf. It became caught in the wheel of a Bugatti sports car in which she was a passenger.

Anton Dvořák
The Czech composer died in 1904 of a chill which he caught while train-spotting.

Frederick, Prince of Wales
Frederick was the son of George II and heir to the British throne. He died in 1751 after being hit by a cricket ball.

Harry Houdini (Erich Weiss)
Houdini was a famous escapologist who claimed he could withstand being punched in the stomach. He died in 1926 – after being punched in the stomach.

William Huskisson
Huskisson was a British Member of Parliament. He was run down by a train during the opening of the first railway in 1830.

Jean-Baptiste Lully
This Italian-French composer died in 1687 after accidentally stabbing his foot with a stick while beating time. The short conductor's baton came into use soon afterwards.

Thomas Midgley
Midgley was an American inventor who was strangled in 1944 by a machine he had invented to help him move after contracting polio. He invented three products that have since been found to be environmentally harmful: lead in petrol, CFCs in fridges and aerosols, and the insecticide DDT.

Prince Philippe
Prince Philippe, heir to the French throne, was killed when his horse tripped over a pig in the streets of Paris in 1131.

Poster for Houdini show

Pliny the Elder
Roman writer Pliny was choked by the fumes of the erupting volcano Vesuvius in AD 79.

Sir Thomas Urquhart
Urquhart was the Scottish author of books with extraordinary titles such as *Logopandecteision*. He died laughing when told of the Restoration of Charles II in 1660.

William III
This British king died in 1701 after a fall when his horse stumbled over a molehill. His opponents drank a toast to the mole, calling it "The little gentleman in black velvet".

See also

Volcanic eruptions: page 46

www.findagrave.com

Crime and punishment lasts

Last executions for witchcraft in America
On 22 September 1692 seven women and one man were hanged for witchcraft at Salem and other places in New England.

Last beheading in the UK
On 9 April 1747, 80-year-old Simon Fraser, Lord Lovat, was beheaded for treason at Tower Hill, London.

Last person to be burned at the stake in England
Catherine Murphy belonged to a gang of coiners (coin forgers). She was strangled and then burnt at the stake at Newgate, London on 18 March 1789.

Last duel in the UK
The last duel in the UK in which a person was killed was fought by two Frenchmen at Egham in Surrey. Emile (or Emanuel) Barthelemy shot Frédéric Cournet on 19 October 1852. Barthelemy was found not guilty, but two years later he was hanged for murdering another man.

Last public hanging in the UK
Michael Barrett was hanged outside Newgate Prison, London on 26 May 1868 for the murder of Sarah Ann Hodgkinson. She was one of several victims who died from a bomb he had planted.

Last witness to the assassination of Abraham Lincoln
Samuel James Seymour, who died on 13 April 1956, was the last surviving witness to the assassination of the American president. Seymour was only five years old when he saw John Wilkes Booth shoot Abraham Lincoln at Ford's Theatre, Washington DC, on 14 April 1865.

Last person executed by guillotine
The last person to be executed in public was the murderer Eugene Weidmann who had his head cut off at Versailles, France, on 17 June 1939. The last official use of the guillotine in France was on 10 September 1977, when Hamida Djandoubi was executed for murder at Baumetes Prison, Marseilles.

Entertainment lasts

Shakespeare's last play
Most people agree that *The Tempest*, 1611, is the last play Shakespeare wrote, although some think he may have written a later play that has been lost. Shakespeare died in 1616, and *The Tempest* was first published in 1623.

Beethoven's last symphony
Ludwig van Beethoven's Ninth Symphony was the last he composed before his death in 1827. He promised the London Philharmonic Society that he would write his Tenth Symphony for them, but died before he could begin work on it.

Charles Dickens' last story
The Mystery of Edwin Drood was Charles Dickens' last novel. It was published in monthly episodes, but ended, unfinished, when Dickens died in 1870.

The last silent film
The Four Feathers (1929) was the last silent film released by a major studio. The 1976 film *Silent Movie* does contain one word, "Non!" (French for no), which is spoken by Marcel Marceau, a mime artist.

The last Beatles concert
The Beatles last played together in public at Candlestick Park, San Francisco, on 29 August 1966. Their last publicly performed song was "Long Tall Sally".

The last episode of Friends
Friends finished its ten-year run when the last episode was shown on 6 May 2004. The advertising spots were sold for $1.25 million.

Last men on the Moon

US Apollo 17 astronauts Eugene A. Cernan and Harrison H. Schmitt spent three days on the Moon, blasting off to return to Earth on 14 December 1972. This was the last day on which any human walked on the surface of the Moon.

Last of the Seven Wonders

The last of the Seven Wonders of the world to be built was the 124m Pharos (lighthouse) of Alexandria, Egypt, which was completed in 279 BC. It was partly knocked down by invaders and later destroyed by an earthquake. The only one of the Seven Wonders that survives today is the Great Pyramid at Giza in Egypt.

The Pyramids at Giza

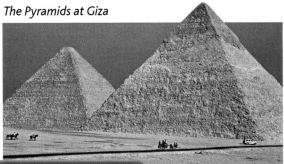

Pharos of Alexandria

See also

The Seven Wonders of the ancient world: page 206

Montezuma II, last Aztec emperor

Transport lasts

The last stagecoach
Horse-drawn stagecoaches carried passengers and mail in Britain from the 17th century until the 19th century, when they were gradually replaced by trains. The Royal Mail between Inverness and Thurso, Scotland last operated in October 1874.

The last horse-drawn London bus
The last horse-drawn bus ran in London on 25 October 1911.

The last voyage of the Titanic
The last voyage of the *Titanic* was also its first. It sank on 15 April 1912 after striking an iceberg, killing 1,517 people.

The last Model T Ford
The Model T, first produced in 1908, was one of the most popular cars of all time. Model T number 15,007,033 rolled off the US production line on Thursday 26 May 1927. Others were built in Canada and the UK, bringing the world total to 16,536,075 vehicles.

The first and last flight of the Spruce Goose
The biggest aircraft ever built was an eight-engined plane built by millionaire aviator Howard Hughes. The plane, called the *Spruce Goose*, flew just once, on 2 November 1947. Hughes was the pilot.

Last flight of Concorde
Concorde was the world's only supersonic airliner. It was in service for 34 years until it made its last commercial flight, from New York to London, on 24 October 2003.

Royal lasts

The last Egyptian pharaoh
Cleopatra VII ruled from 69 BC, when she was 17 years old, until 30 BC, when Egypt became a province of the Roman empire.

The last Roman emperor
Romulus Augustulus was about 14 when he was removed from power in AD 476. The Roman empire split into western and eastern divisions.

The last British king killed in battle
Richard III was killed at the battle of Bosworth on 22 August 1485.

The last Aztec emperor
Montezuma II was removed from power by Spanish invaders and killed in June 1520.

The last British king born abroad
George II was born in Hanover, Germany, on 10 November 1683.

The last king of France
Louis-Philippe (1773–1850) reigned from 1830 until 24 February 1848, when he gave up his throne. Disguised as "Mr Smith", he travelled to England where he lived until his death.

The last Emperor of China
Hsüan T'ung gave up his throne on 12 February 1912 and later took the name Henry Pu-yi. The film *The Last Emperor* is about his life.

The last Tsar of Russia
Nicholas II was removed from power by the Russian Revolution of 1917, and murdered with his family at Ekaterinburg in July 1918. Their remains were reburied in St Petersburg in July 1998.

Prow of the wreck of the Titanic

See also

Shipwrecks: page 218

Author's acknowledgements

The author would like to thank the following people, organizations and publications for kindly supplying information for this book.

Whitaker's Almanack

Academy of Motion Picture Arts and Sciences (AMPAS)*

Piers Adams

American Film Institute

American Forests

Amnesty International

Association of Leading Visitor Attractions

Alexander Ash

Caroline Ash

Nicholas Ash

BP Statistical Review of World Energy 2004

Richard Braddish

Thomas Brinkoff

British Broadcasting Corporation (BBC)

The British Council

British Greyhound Racing Board

British Library

British Museum

British Phonographic Industry (BPI)

Central Intelligence Agency (CIA)

Richard Chapman

Christian Research

Christie's

Kaylee Coxall

De Beers

Department for Environment, Food and Rural Affairs (DEFRA)

The Economist

Ethnologue

Euromonitor

Food and Agriculture Organization of the United Nations (FAO)

Gold Fields Mineral Services

Nathalie Golden

Monica Grady

Greyhound Racing Association of America

Wendy Hamilton

Home Accident Surveillance System (HASS)

Home Office

Andreas Hörstemeier

Imperial War Museum

International Centre for Prison Studies

International Olympic Committee (IOC)

International Telecommunication Union (ITU)

International Union for the Conservation of Nature (IUCN)

Inter-Parliamentary Union

Irish Greyhound Board

Emma Johns

Todd M. Johnson

London Zoo

Dr Benjamin Lucas

Mattel, Inc

Chris McNamara

Chris Mead

The Military Balance

National Aeronautics and Space Administration, USA (NASA)

National Basketball Association, USA (NBA)

National Football League, USA (NFL)

National Phobics Society

National Statistics

Natural History Museum

Niagara Falls Museum

The Nobel Foundation

Official UK Charts Company

Organisation for Economic Co-operation and Development (OECD)

Organisation Internationale des Constructeurs d'Automobiles (OICA)

The Overstreet Comic Book Price Guide

Parker Brothers

Patent Office

Tony Pattison

Recording Industry Association of America (RIAA)

Dafydd Rees

Royal Astronomical Society

Royal Observatory, Greenwich

Screen Digest

Robert Senior

Sidney S. Culbert

Sotheby's

Time magazine

Tree Register of the British Isles

United Nations (UN)

United Nations Children's Fund (UNICEF)

United Nations Educational, Scientific and Cultural Organization (UNESCO)

United Nations Population Division (UNPD)

US Census Bureau

Variety

Lucy T. Verma

Ward's Motor Vehicle Facts & Figures

WebElements

Edward O. Wilson

World Association of Newspapers

World Bank

World Christian Database

World Gold Council

World Health Organization (WHO)

World of Learning

World Tourism Organization (WTO)

* The terms "Academy Award(s)"® and "Oscar(s)"® are registered trademarks and service marks of the Academy of Motion Picture Arts and Sciences. This book is neither endorsed by nor affiliated to the Academy of Motion Picture Arts and Sciences.

Publisher's acknowledgements

A&C Black would like to thank Jill Williams for proof-reading and Amanda Crook for compiling the index

Country names
The following abbreviations are used for country names on page 285

BUL: Bulgaria

CHN: China

CUB: Cuba

CZE: Czech Republic

DEN: Denmark

ETH: Ethiopia

FRA: France

GBR: Great Britain

GDR: German Democratic Republic (1955–90)

MAR: Morocco (Maroc)

QAT: Qatar

ROM: Romania

RUS: Russian Federation

UKR: Ukraine

USA: United States of America

USSR: Union of Soviet Socialist Republics (1922–91)

Picture acknowledgements

l = left, r = right, c = centre, t = top, b = bottom

page **5r** George B Diebold/Corbis; **6r** Archivo Iconografico/Corbis; **7r** Matt A Brown/Newsport/Corbis; **9l** Staffan Widstrand/Corbis, **ct** John Conrad/Corbis, **cc** Reuters/Corbis, **cb** Pichon P/Corbis Sygma, **tr** Chase Swift/Corbis, **br** Michael Kim/Corbis; **10** Joe McDonald/Corbis; **12** Jeremy Horner/Corbis; **14l** Araido de Luca/Corbis, **r** Eileen Tweedy/The Art Archive; **15l** Mario Beauregard/Corbis, **tr** Jan Butchofsky-Houser/Corbis, **br** Joe McDonald/Corbis; **16** Charles & Josette Lenars/Corbis;**17** REGIS MADEC/Thaiworldview.com; **19 & 21l** NASA, **r** Roger Ressmeyer/Corbis; **22tr** NASA; **23tl** & **tr** NASA, **br** Roger Ressmeyer/Corbis; **25t** Gianni Dagli Orti/Corbis; **26** Roger Ressmeyer/Corbis; **27** Bettmann/Corbis; **28r** Roger Ressmeyer/Corbis; **29** NASA; **30t** Corbis; **31** NASA; **34-35** Charles & Josette Lenars/Corbis; **35b** Paul Thompson; Eye Ubiquitous/Corbis; **36l** Jose Fuste Raga/Corbis, **r** Galen Rowell/Corbis; **37** Digital Image/Corbis; **38** Free Agents Ltd/Corbis; **39t** Planetary Visions Ltd/Science Photo Library; **40t** Bill Ross/Corbis, **b** Rick Doyle/Corbis; **41b** Tom Stewart/Corbis; **46t** Roger Ressmeyer/Corbis, **b** Gary Braasch/Corbis; **47** Roger Ressmeyer/Corbis; **50t** Robert Essel NYC/Corbis, **b** Michael Nicholson/Corbis; **51r** Thomas Wiewandt; Visions of America/Corbis; **52** Richard Nowitz/Corbis; **53b** Michael & Patricia Fogden/Corbis; **54b** Staffan Widstrand/Corbis; **55t** John Conrad/Corbis, **b** Chase Swift/Corbis; **56** Amos Nachoum/Corbis; **57t** Amos Nachoum/Corbis, **c** Hal Beral/Corbis; **58t** Tim Davis/Corbis, **b** Lynda Richardson/Corbis; **59** Eric & David Hosking/Corbis; **60** Gary W Carter/Corbis; **61tl** David A Northcott/Corbis, **tr** Scott T Smith/Corbis; **62b** David A Northcott/Corbis; **63l** Daniel Heuclin/NHPA; **64l** David Scharf/Science Photo Library, **r** John Van Hasselt/Corbis; **65** Wolfgang Kaehler/Corbis; **66l** Roger Wood/Corbis; **67t** Lew Long/Corbis, **b** Penny Tweedie/Corbis; **69b** Alamy; **70tr** Hekimian Julien/Corbis Sygma, **br** Vince Streano/Corbis; **71t** Wayne Lawler; Ecoscene/Corbis; **73b** Jose Fuste Raga/Corbis; **76** Patrick Ward/Corbis; **77tr** Clayton J Price/Corbis, **b** A & J Verkalk/Corbis; **78br** Michael Freeman/Corbis; **79** Bettmann/Corbis; **80b** Strauss/Curtis/Corbis; **81 tl** Corbis, **bl** Bettmann/Corbis; **82** Nik Wheeler/Corbis; **84** William Whitehurst/Corbis; **85tl** Hulton-Deutsch Collection/Corbis, **br** Handout/Reuters/Corbis; **86t** Bettman/Corbis; **86** background Bettmann/Corbis; **87r** Ed Kashi/Corbis; **89t** Bettmann/Corbis; **91** Clouds Hill Imaging Ltd/Corbis; **92l** George B Diebold/Corbis, **r** Susumu Nishinaga/Science Photo Library; **94** Bettmann/Corbis, **r** Wellcome Library, London; **95t** Bettmann/Corbis, **b** Corbis; **96** David Stoecklein/Corbis; **97** Bettmann/Corbis; **98bl** Jim Cornfield/Corbid, **tr** Mary Evans Picture Library, **br** James Noble/Corbis; **99t** O Alamany & E Vicens/Corbis; **102** Geray Sweeney/Corbis; **104** Gianni Dagli Orti/Corbis; **105t** Bettmann/Corbis, **b** Reuters/Corbis; **107t** The Art Archive, **b** Owaki-Kulla/Corbis; **108** Wally McNamee/Corbis; **109t** Arte & Immagini SRL/Corbis, **b** Palazzo Barberini, Rome/Dagli Orti/The Art Archive; **110t** Underwood & Underwood/Corbis, **b** James P Blair/Corbis; **111tl** Wally McNamee/Corbis, **r** Clive Newton; The Military Picture Library/Corbis; **116t** Sandro Vannini/Corbis, **b** Tom Bean/Corbis; **116-117** Bob Krist/Corbis; **117b** Sergio Pitamitz/Corbis; **118** James Sparshatt/Corbis; **119r** Reuters/Corbis; **120t** Paul A Souders/Corbis, **b** MacDuff Everton/Corbis; **121** James Sparshatt/Corbis; **122** Neil Rabinowitz/Corbis; **123t** Diego Lezama Orezzoli/Corbis, **b** Enrique Marcarian/Reuters/Corbis; **124t** Hans Strand/Corbis, **124b** & **125** Richard Clune/Corbis; **126** Patrick Ward/Corbis; **127l** Herwig Prammer/Reuters/Corbis, **r** Chris Lisle/Corbis; **128t** Barry Lewis/Corbis, **b** Torleif Svensson/Corbis; **129** Dave Bartruff/Corbis; **130t** Robert Van Der Hilst/Corbis; **131** Nik Wheeler/Corbis; **132** Penny Tweedie/Corbis; **133t** Paul Almasy/Corbis, **b** Kennan Ward/Corbis; **134t** Jim Zuckerman/Corbis, **b** Torleif Svensson/Corbis; **135** Gallo Images/Corbis; **136t** Jose Fuste Raga/Corbis, **b** Benjamin Rondel/Corbis; **137** Massimo Listri/Corbis; **138t** Ludovic Maisant/Corbis, **b** Rafiqur Rahman/Reuters/Corbis; **139** David Ball/Corbis; **140t** Roger Ressmeyer/Corbis, **b** Owen Franken/Corbis; **141t** Christine Osborne/Corbis, **b** Stuart Westmorland/Corbis; **142t** Theo Allofs/Corbis, **b** Hans Strand/Corbis; **143** Anders Ryman/Corbis; **145** Mousis Francois/Corbis Sygma; **147t** Manuel Blondeau/Corbis, **b** Reuters/Corbis; **148l** Ariel Skelley/Corbis, **r** Nik Wheeler/Corbis; **150t** Historical Picture Archive/Corbis, **c** & **b** Bettmann/Corbis; **151l** Joseph Sohm; Chromosohm Inc/Corbis, **r** Reuters/Corbis; **152** Ann Hawthorne/Corbis; **153tl** Bettmann/Corbis, **bl** Hulton Deutsch Collection/Corbis, **r** Joel W Rogers/Corbis; **154tl** Lisa O'Connor/Zuma/Corbis, **bl** Henry Diltz/Corbis, **r** Bettmann/Corbis; **155l** Reuters/Corbis, **r** Hulton Deutsch Collection/Corbis; **156** Alison Wright/Corbis; **157tl** Clive Newton; The Military Picture Library/Corbis; **bl** Julio Donoso/Corbis Sygma, **r** Bettmann/Corbis; **160** Christine Osborne/Corbis; **161l** Richard A Cooke/Corbis, **r** Eileen Tweedy/The Art Archive; **162** Bennett Dean; Eye Ubiquitous/Corbis; **163t** Liu Liqun/Corbis, **b** Ted Streshinsky/Corbis; **164t** Corbis, **b** Ted Spiegel/Corbis; **165** Elio Clol/Corbis; **166** Hulton Deutsch Collection/Corbis; **167** National Gallery Collection; by kind permission of the Trustees of The National Gallery, London/Corbis; **168** Earl & Nazima Kowall/Corbis; **169t** Reuters/Corbis, **b** Ajay Verma/Reuters/Corbis; **170l** Sunset Boulevard/Corbis Sygma; **172** Taxi/Getty Images; **173l** Lauren Shear/Science Photo Library; **175t** Gideon Mendel/Corbis, **b** Jason Hawkes/Corbis; **177** Bettmann/Corbis; **178** background Bettmann/Corbis; **179l** China Features/Corbis Sygma, **tr** Reuters/Corbis, **br** Hulton Deutsch Collection/Corbis; **180** Bettmann/Corbis; **181l** Archivo Iconografico/Corbis, **r** Fine Art Photographic Library/Corbis; **182t** Michael Nicholson/Corbis, **b** Jose Luis Palaez,Inc./Corbis; **183b** Tim Wright/Corbis; **184l** Bettmann/Corbis; **184-185** Gerald French/Corbis; **185tr** Ed Bock/Corbis, **b** Vernier Jean Bernar/Corbis Sygma; **187** Larry Lee Photography/Corbis; **188l** Sandro Vannini/Corbis, **tr** The Advertising Archive, **br** Thom Lang/Corbis; **189** Hulton Deutsch Collection/Corbis; **190l** Christie's Images/Corbis, **r** Neema Frederic/Corbis Sygma; **191b** Private Collection/Dagli Orti/ The Art Archive; **191r** Leigh Simpson; **192l** Phil Schermeister/Corbis, **r** Tim Graham/Corbis; **193l** Michael Freeman/Corbis, **r** Archivo Iconografico,SA/Corbis; **194** Mark E Gibson/Corbis; **198l** Charles O'Rear/Corbis, **r** Adam Woolfitt/Corbis; **199l** David Muench/Corbis, **c** Andrea Jemolo/Corbis, **r** Paul Hardy/Corbis; **200l** Roger Antrobus/Corbis, **201tr** Jim Zuckerman/Corbis, **br** Franken Owen/Corbis; **203l** Ralph Pitchford, **r** Bill Ross/Corbis; **204** Tibor Bognar/Corbis; **205** Roininen Juha/Corbis Sygma; **206t** Dave Bartruff/Corbis, **b** Liu Liqun/Corbis; **207r** Jose Fuste Raga/Corbis; **210t** Courtesy Cunard, **bl** Michael Nicholson/Corbis; **211l** Tony Arruza/Corbis, **r** Joel W Rogers/Corbis; **212t** Lester Lefkowitz/Corbis, **b** Bettmann/Corbis; **213t** Sean Sexton Collection/Corbis, **b** Bob Masters Photography; **214** Tim Wimborne/Reuters/Corbis; **215tl** Claro Cortes IV/Reuters/Corbis, **r** Royalty-Free/Corbis; **216t** Bettmann/Corbis, **b** Underwood & Underwood/Corbis; **217** Bettmann/Corbis;

Images on section openers